SECOND EDITION

MACROECONOMICS

WILLIAM H. BRANSON / JAMES M. LITVACK

Princeton University

1817

HARPER & ROW, PUBLISHERS, New York

Cambridge, Hagerstown, Philadelphia, San Francisco,

London, Mexico City, São Paulo, Sydney

Sponsoring Editor: John Greenman
Project Editor: Rhonda Roth
Designer: Gayle Jaeger
Production Manager: Willie Lane
Compositor: Bi-Comp, Inc.
Printer and Binder: Halliday Lithograph Corporation
Art Studio: J & R Technical Services Inc.

MACROECONOMICS, Second Edition

Library of Congress Cataloging in Publication Data
Branson, William H.
  Macroeconomics.

  Includes bibliographies and index.
  1. Macroeconomics.   I. Litvack, James M., 1941–
II. Title.
HB172.5.B74   1981   339   81-1436
ISBN 0-06-040937-1   AACR2

CONTENTS

PREFACE

In teaching the introductory and the nonmathematical intermediate courses in macroeconomics at Princeton, we had great difficulty finding a text that was both nonmathematical and sufficiently analytical in the logical development of basic material. This led to our first edition. Our objective, as we have revised this text, has continued to be to present basic macroeconomics in a manner that is sufficiently rigorous to deal with the difficult questions of policy and sufficiently broad to indicate to students the impact of differing ideas among economists.

The revisions consist of more than simply updating the statistical tables and the reading lists. Particular attention has been paid to rewriting the chapters on the supply side of the economy to reflect both developments in macroeconomic theory and in the real macroeconomy since the first edition. In Chapter 6, we have recast the supply of labor as a function of the real wage rate as perceived by labor. The supply-side model of Chapter 6 includes the classical real-wage model, the "new classical" rational expectations model, and the ultra-Keynesian money-wage model as particular cases. Chapter 7 includes a discussion of demand-and-supply equilibrium in the economy under each of these cases. The review of monetary and fiscal policy in Chapter 14 has been revised, with a discussion of demand-side distinctions between monetarists and Keynesian, and supply-side differences between neo-Keynesian and the new classical theorists. Chapters 7 and 9 include a careful analysis of the effects of supply disturbances, an important new element in the real world and in theory since the first edition of this text. We have incorporated both the Phillips curve and inflation discussions into a single chapter, Chapter 15. These were treated separately in the first edition. In general, we have attempted to provide proper recognition of new schools of thought that have developed around the supply side of the economy and which may provide some insight as to the difficulties that modern, industrial economies have had in dealing with both inflation and unemployment. Most of the chapters have been rewritten so as to incorporate helpful criticism that we have received and to keep them current with economic research. In addition, each chapter now includes a series of questions for review and discussion through which we hope students can assure themselves that they have assimilated what they have read. A manual has been prepared by Guninder Gill and Laura Tuck to assist instructors.

A good intermediate macro text should begin with the microeconomic foundations of macroeconomics, and give the students an understanding of general equilibrium in the macroeconomy. We feel strongly that this is best achieved by first introducing the skeletal structure of the entire system before examining each sector in detail. The student should have a good intuitive grasp of how the entire system works before he or she is faced with specifics about consumption, investment, and so forth. A good text should also provide an up-to-date and clear review of the empirical facts, once the structure is in place. It is important for students to gain a sense of the empirical magnitudes involved, and the text should lead them through the more important empirical literature, evaluating it as it progresses. Finally, the text should provide optional extensions of the basic material that may be assigned according to the instructor's preferences. Generally, these should either expand the theoretical structure or present applications to current problems.

This book tries to meet these three objectives concerning substance (*what* material is presented) while adhering to three principles concerning methodology (*how* the material is presented). Our first substantive objective is to display to the reader the skeleton of the macroeconomy, showing how its parts interact, before discussing controversies concerning the precise measurement of those parts. After the three brief introductory chapters in Part I that deal with the national income accounts and basic multiplier models covered in the principles course, this basic theoretical overview is presented in Part II.

Our second substantive objective is to provide a fairly thorough review of the empirical work that has been done to date concerning various sections of the economy that were presented in skeletal form in Part II. Part III provides this basic empirical review, which is meant to acquaint the student with typical quantitative relationships in the U.S. economy. It examines the development of alternative theories of consumer behavior, investment demand, and so forth; empirical estimates that have been made on the basis of these theories; and lastly, modifications of the basic structure that these estimates require.

Part IV of the text reflects our third objective concerning content. It extends the basic structure built in Parts II and III and relates it to the

international economy, problems of economic growth, as well as to inflation and the unemployment problems of the 1970s. The three chapters in
Part IV may be assigned independently. Chapter 15 analyzes the
inflation-recession problems of the 1960s and 1970s, using the structure of
Parts II and III. Chapters 16 and 17—on the foreign sector and on
growth—provide connections to other areas and courses in macroeconomics. We think the analysis in Chapter 15 is particularly important, because the "new economics" so highly praised in the 1960s was
considered obsolete by many in the 1970s. Even Nobel laureates suggested
that economic theory was no longer adequate to explain or suggest policy
remedies for the problems facing us. We feel strongly that this is not the
case and that basic theory does provide a useful framework within which
to analyze current problems. What has been lacking—and is omitted in
many texts—is proper attention to the supply side. Macroeconomists have
been guilty of overemphasizing demand theory. Therefore, we pay particular attention in this text to developing the aggregate supply curve,
which, in concert with the aggregate demand curve, can provide a proper
explanation of current problems. We cannot forecast what shieks will do,
but we can analyze the results of their actions.

Concerning methodology, our first principle is to present a general
equilibrium view of the macroeconomy within which to analyze supply
and demand in several aggregate markets, impose the equilibrium condition that supply equals demand at the equilibrium price, and study the
interrelationships between sectors as government monetary and fiscal policy variables change. We use this approach in Part II, where the macroeconomy is developed from the single-market model of the Keynesian
multiplier, in which only the product market for goods and services is
considered, to a multisector model that includes product, money, and
labor markets.

Our second methodological principle is to develop the aggregate macroeconomic functions from basic microeconomic principles. For example,
in Chapter 10 the aggregate consumption function is built up from the
microeconomic theory of consumer behavior. We use this principle in
order to give the reader an intuitive feeling for the relation of the macroeconomic functions to observed individual behavior, and also to help
erase the imaginary boundary between micro- and macroeconomics that
develops in many economics curricula.

Finally, our third methodological principle is to present consistently
the logic of an argument in expository form and then to show a graphical
example of it. We try throughout the book to give the student a clear
explanation of a theoretical point and a clear picture of how it works, side
by side.

The book focuses on policy questions and the current "state of the art"
in macroeconomics, bringing in doctrinal controversies only where they
are relevant to current problems. We have not footnoted references in the

text; however, whenever theories or results associated with particular individuals are discussed, appropriate references are included in lists of selected readings at the ends of chapters.

All authors incur many debts in the course of developing a manuscript; specifically, we have received many welcome suggestions and comments from our colleagues and students at Princeton. R. S. Hanna, Thomas Havrilesky, J. H. McClure, Michael K. Salemi, and Charles E. Webster provided valuable reviews of the manuscript. We also received helpful written comments from Bao-Toa Chang, James A. M. Elliott, Arvind Panagariya, Michael Schmid, and Kao Chung-Wang.

We are grateful to Dorothy Gronet and Isobel Abelson for typing the manuscript and keeping things organized. The editors at Harper & Row have been cooperative and expert.

Our special debt, though, is to the students at Princeton—undergraduate and graduate—who ask questions, catch mistakes, and press for clarification of difficult points. They have been enormously helpful in the development of this material. Among the graduate students, we particularly thank Guninder Gill, Janet Luck, Uday Mehta, Julio Rotenberg and Laura Tuck. They, and the rest of the economics students at Princeton, deserve a special mention.

William H. Branson
James M. Litvack

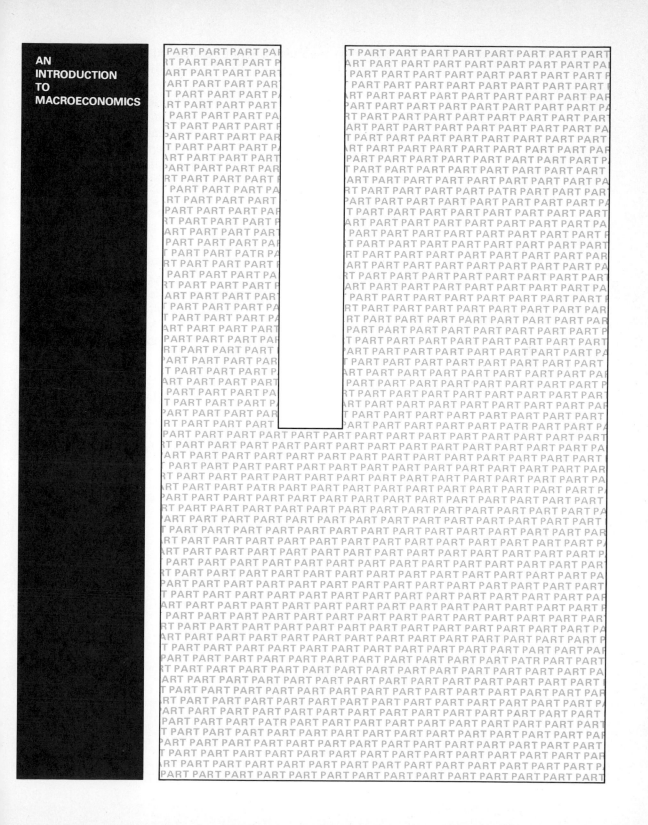

AN
INTRODUCTION
TO
MACROECONOMICS

ACTUAL AND POTENTIAL GNP: FLUCTUATIONS AND GROWTH

In *micro*economic theory, full employment of resources is generally assumed, so that the focus of the analysis is on the determination of relative prices and the allocation of scarce resources among alternative uses. On the other hand, in its now traditional form, *macro*economics focuses on the level of utilization of resources—especially the level of employment—and the general level of prices. In addition, macroeconomics is turning more toward the question of what determines the rate of growth of resources—the growth of potential output—as well as the determinants of their level of utilization at any one time.

The focus of classical microeconomics on the allocation of scarce resources to their best uses implicitly assumed that full employment—scarcity of resources—is the normal state of the economy. If the economy is operating at substantially less than full employment, resources are, at least temporarily, really not scarce, and the opportunity cost of additional output of almost any kind is about zero—more total output can be produced by simply reducing unemployment. Because the U.S. economy, to take just one example, suffered major recessions or depressions with high unemployment in the years 1907–1908, 1920–1921, and 1930–1939, the relevance of classical microeconomics was bound to be questioned by more than just the hard-core skeptics.

THE DEVELOPMENT OF MACROECONOMICS

Partly as a reaction to the "Great" Depression—that's what the historians call it, even though one suspects the people living then didn't think it was so great—of the 1930s, and with the publication of Keynes' *The General Theory of Employment, Interest and Money* in 1936, modern mac-

3

roeconomics has developed as an analytical framework for understanding what causes large, and sometimes prolonged, fluctuations in the level of employment.

From 1950 to the early 1970s post-Keynesian macroeconomic analysis focused almost exclusively on those fluctuations in employment that had their origins in fluctuations in aggregate demand. Implicit in this demand-oriented analysis, and soon made explicit, was the explanation of how to prevent such fluctuations, that is, how to keep the economy operating near full employment. Once this became understood, in the period from World War II to 1972, the economy was kept operating reasonably close to its full-employment level, with exceptions in 1949, 1954, 1958, 1961, and 1970. These recessions were mild, with unemployment reaching at most 7 percent, compared with the unemployment rates of 15–25 percent in the 1930s.

In 1974 a deep recession developed that had its origins in a shift in aggregate supply, a possibility largely ignored by previous macroeconomic analysis. By 1975 the unemployment rate reached 9 percent. The shift in the source of fluctuations has moved macroeconomics on to the study of supply-side fluctuations completing the earlier story begun on the demand side. This work is included at several points in this book to integrate both demand and supply disturbances into the analysis of fluctuations in employment.

One important consequence of the development of modern macroeconomics, which has taught us reasonably well how to maintain full employment, is that it restores the importance of classical microeconomics, as suggested by Samuelson's term *the neoclassical synthesis*. If we can keep the economy operating near full employment, the theory of the optimum allocation of scarce resources is once again valid and crucially important. Increases in output under these conditions do have opportunity costs—for example, a $25 billion increase in defense spending from mid-1965 to mid-1967, once the economy had reached roughly full employment in 1965, had to come from reduced output *somewhere*. In that case, it came mainly from reduced output of housing and consumer durables, at a time when family formation was soaring.

ACTUAL AND POTENTIAL OUTPUT

Macroeconomic theory in its current stage of development focuses on two main questions:

1. What determines the level of actual output relative to potential at any given time? This is the question of income determination.
2. What determines the path—level and rate of growth—of full employment or potential output? This is the question of growth theory.

The first question is the main object of this book. The second is a more advanced topic in macroeconomics, fairly near the frontier of research. A brief discussion of growth topics is presented in Part IV.

A third question concerning the behavior of the price level—the rate of inflation—could be added to the second of these two central questions, and it too will occupy a good deal of space here.

Theory and policy

Implicit in these questions, and inextricably bound up with them, are questions of policy. If we know, for example, that the level of actual output depends, at least in part, on the level of the money supply, then we also know, at least in part, how to change the level of output if it is unsatisfactorily low. Thus, it is almost impossible to talk about theory without implying possibilities for policy, and the best way to approach policy is probably by studying theory and its empirical applications.

In this book we deal with the two main questions in inverse order, mostly because, as was suggested earlier, much more is known about stabilization theory and, especially, policy than about growth theory and its applications. For this reason, the traditional macroeconomics course focuses on the problem of income determination and its implications for stabilization policy. Before we go on to a brief preview of the methods we use in Parts II–IV of the book, it should be useful to review the movement of actual and potential GNP, unemployment, and prices in the U.S. economy since 1960. This is to give the reader a feeling for the relationships between these variables and also for the context in which this book is set.

The record: 1960–1980

Movements of actual and potential output—or *real* GNP—are shown in Figure 1.1(a) for the period 1960–1979. The movement of the unemployment rate—the fraction of the labor force that is unemployed—is shown in Figure 1.1(b). Finally, in Figure 1.1(c), we show the rate of increase of the implicit GNP price index, or GNP deflator (GNPD).

The potential real GNP line in Figure 1.1(a) shows the real GNP that would be produced with an unemployment rate just under 5 percent. This is the Council on Economic Advisers' rough estimate of the unemployment rate consistent with full employment, given the fact that full employment is literally impossible. The potential GNP line has a slope that reflects the rate of growth of potential output. The current rate of 2.5 percent may be derived by taking the average growth rate in labor supply, 1.8 percent during the last decade, and subtracting the annual 0.3 percent decline in the work week. Adding to this a 1.0 percent growth rate in labor productivity gives a rate of 2.5 percent for growth of potential output.

The actual GNP line in Figure 1.1(a) is just that—the *real* GNP actually produced. The difference between potential and actual GNP is the GNP *gap*—the amount of output lost when actual output falls short of potential and unemployment rises above 4.9 percent.

Figure 1.1(b) plots the unemployment rate corresponding to the gap in Figure 1.1(a). In general, the larger the GNP gap is, the greater the unemployment rate will be. A rule of thumb characterizing this relationship was developed by Arthur Okun. Roughly, *Okun's law* states that a 3 percent increase in real GNP will yield a 1 percentage-point decrease in the unemployment rate. Figure 1.1(c) shows the percentage (annual) rate of change of the GNPD—the rate of inflation—corresponding to the GNP gap

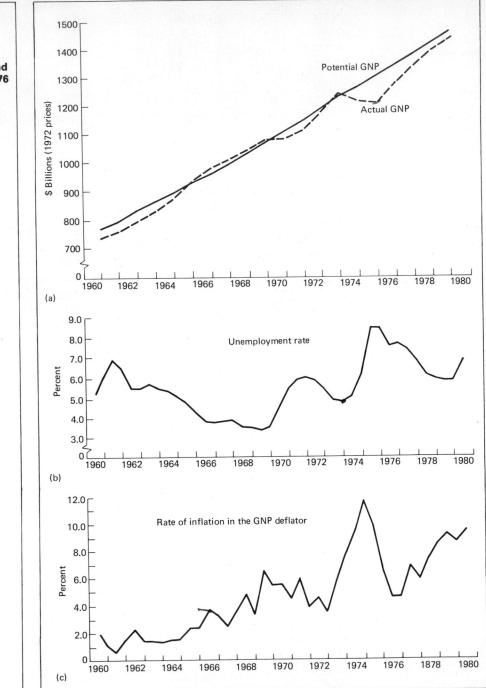

FIGURE 1.1

The GNP gap, unemployment, and inflation, 1960–1976 (a) actual and potential GNP; (b) unemployment rate; (C) rate of inflation

and unemployment-rate series. Comparison of Figures 1.1(b) and 1.1(c) shows that, in general, as the unemployment rate is reduced, the rate of inflation rises. This is the *Phillips curve* relationship between unemployment and the rate of inflation that is discussed in Chapter 15. It is also interesting that from 1961 to early 1965, as the unemployment rate gradually came down, there was no perceptible increase in the rate of inflation. But the further drop in unemployment from early 1965 to 1966 brought a sharp increase in the rate of inflation, and the maintenance of a level of demand pressure that kept unemployment below 4 percent from 1966 through 1969 generated a continuing inflation that only showed faint signs of slowing by mid-1970.

The 1960s opened with unemployment at a cyclical peak of 6.7 percent in the second quarter of 1961 (1961 II), and, correspondingly, actual real GNP at a cyclical trough with a GNP gap of $35 billion in 1972 dollars. The price level was very stable as a result of the maintenance of slack demand conditions since 1958. The unemployment rate peaked at 7.1 percent in 1958 II and fell only to 4.9 percent in 1959 II before flattening out and then rising to 6.7 in 1961 II.

The gradual closing of the GNP gap and reduction of unemployment from 1962 to mid-1965 was due to increased demand for output stimulated by a series of expansionary fiscal policy actions combined with a mildly expansionary growth of the money supply that averaged 3.1 percent per year from 1961 I to 1965 I. In 1961 the administration increased federal government expenditures to stimulate the economy, and in 1962 revisions of the investment tax laws to liberalize depreciation allowances and provide a tax credit on purchases of new equipment stimulated investment demand.

When in late 1962 the rate of growth and the unemployment rate flattened out, the administration proposed a tax cut in January 1963 to give the economy a further boost. The tax cut was passed in March 1964, adding to consumer demand. This stimulus, along with a continued expansion of the money supply, took the economy almost up to full employment by mid-1965, as can be seen in Figure 1.1(a).

At this point, in mid-1965, the story of stabilization policy in the 1960s was a success story. Fiscal and monetary policy had reduced the GNP gap from $35 billion in 1961 to zero by 1965, unemployment was close to 4 percent, and the rate of inflation, while beginning to rise, was still under 2 percent. To be sure, the stabilization problem in 1961 was fairly easy, or seems so ,with the advantage of hindsight. With stable prices, a large GNP gap, and high unemployment, the right direction for policy was obvious: Expand! The expansion was carried out in a gradual, noninflationary way; the only real difference of opinion that appeared was whether the fiscal stimulus proposed in 1963 should come from a tax cut, boosting consumer spending, or from an increase in public spending on housing, health, and other programs. The decision came down on the side of a tax cut, partially for political expediency. Considering the difficulty that the administration later had in first deciding to propose, and then getting Congress to pass a tax increase when excess demand appeared, it seems clear to these authors that the increased-spending route would have been preferable, but the record is hard to fault in terms of stabilization policy, per se.

In mid-1965 the expansion of the Vietnam War began an extremely rapid expansion of federal purchases of goods and services in the defense sector. In 1965 III, these expenditures stood at $50 billion; by 1966 III they had risen to $63 billion, and by 1967 III they stood at $73 billion—an increase of nearly $25 billion, or 50 percent, in two years. This huge stimulus to demand was not balanced by the tax increase needed to reduce private-sector demand, and money supply growth continued from mid-1965 to mid-1966 at 5.5 percent. So with no offset to the large and unexpected (from the point of view of economic policy makers) increase in demand from the federal budget, unemployment fell below 4 percent in 1966, and the rate of inflation rose to nearly 4 percent, as shown in Figure 1.1(c).

Then in the middle of 1966 the Federal Reserve halted the rate of growth of the money supply—from June 1966 to January 1967 it grew not at all—and the investment tax credit (ITC) was suspended. Credit tightness reduced housing demand substantially by restricting mortgage credit, and business investment fell off in late 1967 due to both credit tightness and suspension of the ITC. These steps reduced the growth of demand and actual output, and the reduction in demand pressure brought the unemployment rate up slightly in late 1967. The rate of inflation also flattened as a result of eased demand pressure.

With the economy slowing in late 1966, the Federal Reserve permitted the money supply to resume its growth at an annual rate of 7 percent from January to June 1967, and the investment tax credit was restored in March 1967. To balance these expansionary moves, in January 1967 the administration requested a temporary income tax increase, to become effective in July 1967, to slow down the growth in consumer demand. However, the tax increase was not passed until July 1968, and by then the combination of continued money supply growth of 6.4 percent from June 1967 to June 1968 and the further increase in federal government purchases of $5.8 billion in defense and $3.7 billion in nondefense areas from 1967 III to 1968 III had pushed the unemployment rate back down to 3.6 percent and raised the rate of inflation to 5.1 percent. Passage of the explicitly temporary income tax increase of about 2 percent in July 1968 did little to dampen demand, while money supply growth continued into early 1969.

In late 1968 and early 1969 the growth of government purchases slowed: there was almost no increase in purchases from 1968 III into 1970. At the same time the growth of the money supply was again slowed in early 1969 and held to 1 percent in the last half of 1970. Even with the expiration of the income tax increase—half in January 1970 and half in

July 1970—this shift to a restrictive monetary and fiscal policy slowed the growth of demand in late 1969, and by the end of 1970 a GNP gap of $29.5 billion had reappeared. The unemployment rate was up to 6 percent at the end of 1970, and the first signs of a slowdown in the rate of inflation were appearing.

Thus, in early 1971, it appeared that the economy, in a way, was coming back to a position similar to its starting point in 1960, but with a smaller GNP gap relative to potential GNP, and an unemployment rate around 6 to 6.5 percent instead of the 6.5 to 7 percent of 1961. The reduction in demand seemed to be slowing the rate of inflation, so that in 1971 the economy might begin another gradual expansion with stable prices and slowly falling unemployment.

However, this pleasant scenario, written in early 1971, did not describe the actual developments that followed. The inflation and recession of the 1970s are analyzed in detail in Chapter 15; here we conclude this narrative with a short summary.

In mid-1971 the unemployment rate peaked at 6.1 percent. The rate of inflation on the GNPD (Figure 1.1(c)) was falling from 5.3 percent in the first quarter of 1971 to 4.2 percent in the second quarter and 2.5 percent in the third. This steady fall in the inflation rate was not apparent at the time, however, and in August 1971 the administration began the first phase of wage and price controls, which continued into 1974.

With the controls in place, the administration provided a substantial stimulus to demand in 1972 (an election year). Federal purchases, which had been in the $97–99 billion range from 1968 through 1971, jumped to $105 billion in 1972. The money supply grew 8.8 percent from the end of 1971 to the end of 1972. The result, with a lag, was a drop in the unemployment rate from its 6.1 peak to 5.1 percent at the end of 1972 and eventually to 4.6 percent in mid-1973.

This rapid expansion put upward pressure on the rate of inflation again, and the shortfall of agricultural output in 1972 and the oil price increases of 1973 and 1974 resulted in a sudden jump in the inflation rate. Monetary and fiscal policy shifted to neutrality in 1973 and were drastically tightened in 1974 in reaction to the jump in inflation. In real terms government purchases *fell* by 8 percent from 1972 to 1974, and the rate of growth of the money stock was held to just over 5 percent in 1974, in the face of an inflation rate rising to 13 percent by the end of the year.

The effect of the monetary and fiscal squeeze in 1974 was apparent in the unemployment rate, which rose to 9 percent, and in the rate of inflation, which was about 7 percent in mid-1975. At that point, however, the recession hit bottom, and expansion began once again.

In 1975 fiscal policy shifted sharply to expansion. Federal government purchases were constant in real terms, and tax cuts contributed to a shift in the full-employment budget—the level of government spending and taxation that would have existed had the economy been at full-employment—from a surplus of about $3 billion in 1974 to a $30 billion deficit in 1975. Monetary growth continued at about 5 percent, and with an expanding economy, the unemployment rate began to fall. The rate of inflation also declined, responding to the depth of the 1973–1974 recession. The recovery strengthened during 1976 as demand strengthened in the private sector. Fiscal policy remained neutral, with a small decrease in the full-employment deficit, while the monetary growth rate rose slightly, to about 6 percent. With policy still basically stimulative, the unemployment rate continued to fall, reaching 7.5 percent by year end. With oil prices more stable, and continued effects of stock demand and high unemployment, the rate of inflation fell to around 6 percent by the end of 1976.

The expansion continued in 1977. Fiscal policy remained neutral with no change in the full-employment budget deficit as real government purchases rose about 5 percent. The unemployment rate fell sharply to under 6.5 percent by year end, and the inflation rate persisted at about 6 percent with demand still rising strongly. The monetary growth rate increased to 8 percent to slow the rise in interest rates that tends to accompany rapid growth in demand.

In retrospect, it may be possible that the recovery continued too fast and too strong in 1978. Fiscal policy tightened with real government purchases falling slightly and the full employment deficit shrinking from $19 billion in 1977 to $12 billion in 1978. Money supply growth continued at 8 percent. The momentum of the recovery brought the unemployment rate to under 6 percent and the inflation rate to about 7 percent. Despite the fact that much of the inflation came from one-time price level adjustments to food and oil prices and fluctuations in the dollar exchange rate, it was clear that the inflation-unemployment trade-off had deteriorated.

During 1979 fiscal policy tightened again in an attempt to reduce demand and slow inflation. The full-employment budget shifted by $22 billion to a $10 billion surplus. Money supply growth slowed to 7.4 percent. The effect was a slowdown in real GNP growth to 2.3 percent, but there was no increase in unemployment as firms hoarded labor. The inflation rate continued to rise reaching almost 9 percent. In retrospect, we can see that policy should have shifted earlier than it did to decelerate the pace of recovery before the inflation rate increased again. The chance to move gradually to a sustainable expansion with steady but slow reduction of unemployment was missed again.

The tightening policy of 1979 continued into 1980. The full-employment surplus rose as social security taxes increased, inflation moved individuals into higher tax brackets, and money growth slowed substantially. The economy went into recession once more in January 1980 with the unemployment rising to around 7.5 percent by mid-year. During 1980 real GNP fell by 2 percent or more, but again the inflation rate responded slowly. The cycle of rapid recovery, tightening policy, and recession left the economy in its second-worst post-War recession as this was written in fall, 1980.

From our brief description of the main macroeconomic events of the period and from study of the data of Figure 1.1, certain relationships between the aggregate economic variables should be apparent. First, the relationship between actual output and the unemployment rate suggests that the level of output is a function of employment. This *production function* relationship is developed in Chapter 6 and is used throughout the rest of the book.

Second, as demand expands, there appears to be a positive relationship between the level of aggregate demand and the rate of inflation. This Phillips curve relationship is introduced in Chapter 15.

Finally, we have the notion of actual output regulated by the level of demand, which is, in turn, strongly affected by monetary and fiscal policy changes—movements in the money supply, government purchases, and tax rates. Much of Parts II and III focuses on the effects of changes in these variables, singly or in combinations, on the level of output, employment, and the price level.

AN ANALYTICAL APPROACH TO MACROECONOMICS

In Parts II and III, we use an aggregate general equilibrium approach to build a theory explaining movements in output, employment, and the price level. We introduce, in turn, a *product market* for goods and services, a *money market,* and a *labor market.* Together with the production function linking output and employment, demand-and-supply equilibrium conditions in these three markets jointly determine the equilibrium levels of four key variables—output, employment, the price level, and the interest rate.

In general, what happens in one market affects all markets in a general equilibrium framework; so in Part II, where we focus on the skeletal analytic framework of the system, the emphasis is on simultaneity and interaction between markets.

An example of simultaneity between markets

Consider a major increase in the efficiency of the transactions mechanism—the introduction of a widely held and accepted credit card system. This is "like" an increase in the money supply in that a given stock of money will finance an increase in annual transactions. This will tend to reduce interest rates, since people can reduce cash holdings and buy interest-earning bonds. The increase in bond demand bids bond prices up and interest rates down. The drop in interest rates essentially raises investment demand by making borrowing cheaper. Increased investment demand raises sales and income and pulls the price level up. The increase in output and the price level raises employment.

In the meantime, higher income and price levels tend to raise the demand for money, so that to a certain extent the effect of the original stimulus of the credit card is offset. Eventually, the system settles to a new equilibrium with higher levels of output, prices, and employment, and a lower interest rate. The initial disturbance in the money market has spread through the other markets in the "model," as it would spread through the entire economy in the real world. The important point in Part II is developing a intuitive understanding of this kind of simultaneity.

The discussion of empirical findings in Part III is designed to add richness or texture to the analytical framework of Part II. We see what both theory and practical experience with economic data tell us, for example, about how long it takes for one variable, say, investment demand, to react to changes in another variable, say, the interest rate. We also discuss whether temporary tax changes have different effects on the level of consumer spending than permanent ones.

While Part II is meant to help develop an understanding of the bare analytics of the macroeconomic system, Part III should help in developing a kind of quantitative intuition concerning the relationships between the basic macroeconomic variables: How long do things take to react and how large will the reactions be?

To begin at the beginning we need a brief review of the national income accounts, which both define many of our key macroeconomic variables—consumption, investment, and so on—and provide a social accounting framework for later analysis. This review is presented in Chapter 2. Part I then closes with a brief review in Chapter 3 of the basic income determination analysis from the initial economic principles course.

Connection to the "Real World" through empirical results

QUESTIONS FOR DISCUSSION AND REVIEW

1. As defined in the text, can actual output ever exceed potential output?

2. Total growth in output can be approximated by the sum of the growth in labor hours and the growth in output per labor hour. Why is this a useful division?

3. The cost of major social programs is often the major focus of debate on such programs. For example, in the mid-1970s a proposal to spend $100 billion to rebuild American cities was ridiculed as too expensive. What would you estimate the cost of producing at a level below potential output from 1970 to 1975 to have been?

SELECTED READINGS

Council of Economic Advisors, *Annual Reports* (Washington, D.C.: Government Printing Office), January 1962, pp. 39–56; January 1966, pp. 39–44; February 1971, chap. 3.

Council of Economic Advisors, "Measuring and Realizing the Economy's Potential," in R. L. Teigen, ed., *Readings in Money, National Income and Stabilization Policy,* 4th ed. (Homewood, Ill., Irwin, 1978).

W. W. Heller, *New Dimensions in Political Economy* (Cambridge, Mass.: Harvard University Press, 1966), chaps. 1–2.

A. M. Okun, *The Political Economy of Prosperity* (New York: Norton, 1970), chaps. 1–2 and appendix.

A. M. Okun, "Potential GNP: Its Measurement and Significance," in M. G. Mueller, ed., *Readings in Macroeconomics* (New York: Holt, Rinehart and Winston, 1971).

A REVIEW OF THE NATIONAL INCOME AND PRODUCT ACCOUNTS

The National Income and Product Accounts—frequently referred to as NIPA—are the official measurement of the flow of product and income in the economy. The accounts are maintained by the Office of Business Economics (OBE) of the Department of Commerce and are published in a monthly OBE publication called the *Survey of Current Business*. Many of the economic aggregates such as consumer expenditure, business investment, and so on, with which this book deals, are defined in the accounts, which also provide a framework for analyzing the level of economic activity. So we begin our analysis of income determination with a brief review of the accounts.

The *product* side of the national accounts measures the flow of *currently produced* goods and services in the economy. The *income* side of the accounts measures the *factor incomes* that are earned by U.S. workers in current production. On the product side, the flow of goods and services currently produced by U.S. workers is measured by expenditures on these goods and services by consumers, businesses, government, and foreigners. The counterpart to this flow of expenditures on final product is national income, which measures income received by factors of production—compensation of employees, profits paid to owners of capital, earnings of proprietors, and so on—in compensation for producing the final product.

This means that the product and income sides are two different measures of the same continuous flow. The product side measures expenditures on output. These expenditures then become payments compensating the factors that produced the output. These factor incomes then are disposed of in consumer expenditure, tax payments, saving, and transfer payments to foreigners. Thus, we can view gross national product (GNP) in three different ways—all measuring identically the same flow. The first is GNP measured by expenditure on final product; the second is GNP measured by the type of income generated in production; the third is GNP measured by the way this income is used, or disposed of. The first and third of these measurements give us the basic GNP *identity* that is fundamental to the study of economics on an aggregate—or "macro"—level:

$$C + I + G + (X + M) \equiv \text{GNP} \equiv C + S + T + R_f. \tag{1}$$

The left-hand side of this identity measures GNP by expenditures on final product. Here C is consumer expenditure; I is business expenditure on plant, equipment, inventories, and residential construction, all aggregated into gross private domestic investment; G is total (federal, state, and local) government purchases of goods and services; $(X - M)$ is net exports.

The right-hand side of equation (1) measures GNP by the way income earned in production is disposed of. Here C, again, is consumer expenditure; S is total saving by consumers and by businesses in the form of depreciation allowances and retained earnings; T is net tax payments (total tax receipts less transfer, interest, and subsidy payments by all levels of government); R_f is transfer payments to foreigners by private citizens, for example in private pension plans or donations to international relief efforts.

Much of this chapter shows how expenditures on final product, the left-hand side of equation (1), are translated into the disposition of income earned in production, the right-hand side of equation (1), through the income accounts. This exercise serves several purposes. First, it explicitly justifies the identity (1), which is basic to all the macroeconomic theory that follows, by showing the reader how the national income and product accounts "hang together." Second, it is designed to give the reader a feel for the quantities involved. Macroeconomic theory, like all theory, involves a great deal of abstraction, and it will be useful for the reader to be able to translate the theory, more or less continuously, back into the relevant national accounts categories. Finally, a review of the accounts introduces the reader to the categories of economic variables commonly dealt with in macroeconomic theory. The theory deals with aggregated variables; a tour through the accounts makes clear what these aggregated categories are.

The next section of this chapter discusses some basic principles underlying the accounts. We then introduce the idea of a circular flow of product and income behind the GNP identity (1). Next we describe the major expenditure aggregates on the product side of the accounts and trace the income flows back to the income side. We finish this description of the accounts by looking at the saving-investment balance in the economy and also at the distinction between nominal, or money, GNP measured in current prices, and real GNP measured in base-year prices. Next, since much of our later discussion of policy focuses on the government budget, we take a closer look at the government sector of the accounts and compare this to the federal unified budget that the president submits annually to Congress. Finally, we end the chapter by raising some questions about the use of GNP as a measure of national welfare.

SOME PRINCIPLES BEHIND THE ACCOUNTS

There are a few basic ideas underlying the construction of the accounts that should be kept in mind as we go through them. Here four of these ideas, which seem particularly relevant for our purposes, will be briefly discussed. Keeping an eye on them will help to prevent confusion in the later discussion.

The first point is that the accounts should aggregate economic variables in a way that is useful for economic analysis. In general, this means that "like" expenditures, or incomes, should be aggregated together, and "unlike" expenditures should be separated. On the product side of the accounts, this principle means that sectors of expenditure should be aggregated by who does the spending, that is, into expenditures by consumers, businesses, governments, and foreigners. This is a useful way to aggregate, since presumably each of these different kinds of expenditure is related to a different set of motivations, and thus to a different set of economic variables. For example, consumer spending is probably related to consumer income and perhaps wealth, as we see in some detail in Chapter 10; business investment may be related to such variables as expected sales, profits, and the cost of capital, as Chapter 11 shows; government spending is determined by a political process only distantly related to consumer and business spending decisions; and net exports depend to a great extent on foreign incomes and prices.

Second, the accounts measure the expenditure and income stream that comes from *current* production of goods and services. Transactions that transfer ownership of *existing* assets are, in general, not reflected in the accounts because they do not involve current production. For example, an individual's purchase of a used car will enter the accounts only insofar as the purchase price exceeds the sale price of the previous owner, reflecting some value added to the car by the services and facilities of the used car dealer, which presumably facilitate trading and thus add to output. In a case where the owner sells directly, the transaction involves only the trade of one existing asset—the car—for another, presumably cash or checking account deposits, with no value added by a used car dealer. The transaction *involving purely an asset exchange* has no *direct* effect on current production and thus does not enter into the national income accounts. Of course, it may have *indirect* effects on consumer expenditure since the mixture of assets on both sides has changed. The seller now has liquid funds which may increase his spending, while the buyer may reduce spending for just the opposite reason. But these are indirect effects that would be observed, to the degree they occur, in current consumer expenditure items.

The last two points are related to the orientation of the accounts toward the measurement of total output as an (obviously imperfect) indicator of welfare. Consistent with an individualistic view of welfare, consumer expenditure is counted as final demand, rather than as an input to the labor force. This treatment of consumer expenditure may seem obvious here. However, in any forced-labor economy, such as a slave state, the consumption by the labor force would be treated as a cost of maintaining the capital stock, just as is the cost of maintaining plant and equipment in the United States. Although the forced-labor economy example is an extreme case, arguments have been made, for example, to count the cost of transportation to and from work as a business cost rather than a consumer expenditure.

The other related point is that, where possible, output is valued at market price. This reflects the conclusion from microeconomics that, in a competitive economy, the market price of a good represents its marginal utility to the buyers, and the market price of a labor service represents its marginal disutility to the sellers.

The procedure of valuing output at market price even in a competitive economy can hold only for the output of the business sector; most government services are not sold and it is hard to measure output in the household sector. Thus, these two sectors measure output as equal in value to input, while the accounts measure business output, which is about 85 percent of GNP, at market price.

THE CIRCULAR FLOW OF PRODUCT AND INCOME

The flow of product and income in a simple two-sector economy with only households and firms is shown in Figure 2.1. The top pair of arrows represents *product* markets, in which the households exchange money for goods and services provided by the firms. The dashed "Product measure" line cutting these two arrows represents the product-side measure of GNP. This measures the flow of output by the total expenditure by households on that flow.

The bottom pair of arrows represents *factor* markets, in which the firms exchange money for the services provided by the households—wage payments for labor services, profits for capital services. Again, the dashed "Income measure" line represents the income side of GNP. It measures the flow of services provided by households by the factor incomes they receive. These two flow measures should give the same reading for GNP: output = GNP = income.

Here we should point out the importance of not double counting when we measure GNP, that is, of not adding the product and income measures together. The GNP loop of Figure 2.1 says that we can measure GNP by final output or by total input; intermediate goods must not be counted in the final output measure.

Another term for total input, measured by total factor income, is *value added*. GNP measured by final output should be equal to GNP measured

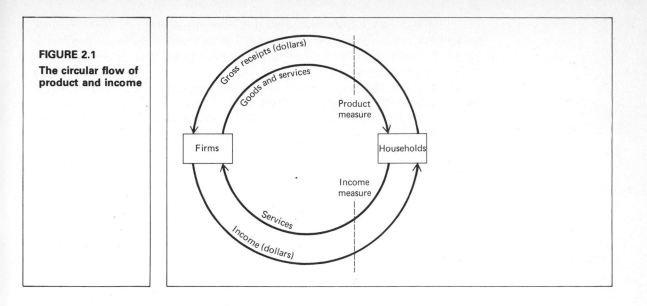

FIGURE 2.1

The circular flow of product and income

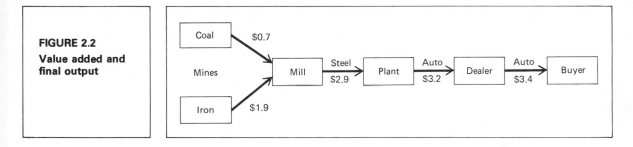

FIGURE 2.2

Value added and final output

by value added, as shown by the following example illustrated in Figure 2.2, which traces the steps from the coal and iron mines to the final sale of an (all steel?) car to a consumer. Suppose the manufacture of a $3.4 thousand car measured at retail value takes $2.9 thousand worth of steel, which in turn requires $0.7 thousand of coal and $1.9 thousand of iron to manufacture. Then we have the chain of events shown in Figure 2.2, in which the mines, using only capital and labor inputs, sell $2.6 thousand of output to the steel firm, which adds $0.3 thousand in capital and labor costs to produce $2.9 thousand of steel. The auto manufacturer adds another $0.3 thousand to make an auto for $3.2 thousand, and the dealer adds $0.2 thousand in services to sell it at $3.4 thousand to the consumer.

Now GNP in this case can be measured either by the value of the final sale, $3.4 thousand, which represents an upper loop transaction in Figure 2.1, or by value added in production, representing the lower loop in Figure 2.1. In the example total value added is $2.6 thousand by the mines, $0.3 thousand each by the steel and auto manufacturers, and $0.2 thousand by the dealer, for a total of $3.4 thousand, the same as the final output measure of GNP. Thus, when we look at the product-side measure of GNP, we should remember that we are looking at final output; the income side measures value added.

Figure 2.1 obviously could be expanded to include a government, which buys goods and services from firms and services from households in exchange for money, and receives tax receipts, implicitly in exchange for government services. We will not go into this expansion here, because the point on double counting can be made most easily in the context of Figure 2.1 as it stands. We now turn to a description of U.S. national income and product as actually measured in the official accounts, working toward a verification of the identity of equation (1).

GNP ON THE PRODUCT SIDE

On the product side of the accounts, GNP can be measured as total expenditure on final U.S. output, the upper loop of Figure 2.1. The accounts break down this expenditure by four major sectors—consumer expenditure, business investment, government purchases, and exports. U.S. output can go to U.S. consumers' purchases of consumption goods output, C_d; U.S. business purchases of plant and equipment output plus residential investment, I_d; U.S. federal, state, and local governments' purchases of U.S. output, G_d; and total exports, X. Thus, we have as an allocation of total output,

$$\text{GNP} = C_d + I_d + G_d + X. \tag{2}$$

But U.S. consumers' purchases of *domestic* output are equal to *total* consumer expenditure C less *imports* of consumer goods, M_c; U.S. business investment purchases of equipment are equal to total equipment purchases I less capital goods imports, M_i; and government purchases of U.S. output are equal to total government purchases, G, less purchases of foreign goods and, especially, services, such as maintaining U.S. embassies or armed forces abroad, for example, M_g. Thus, we also have as an allocation of total output,

$$\text{GNP} = (C - M_c) + (I - M_i) + (G - M_g) + X$$
$$= C + I + G + (X - M), \tag{3}$$

where M is total imports. Equation (3) is the basic product-side identity in which *total* consumer expenditure, investment, government purchases, and *net* exports add up to GNP. Another way to see the relation between the two identities in (2) and (3) is shown in Table 2.1, where $M_c + M_i + M_g$ add up to total imports. Read across, this table shows the relations between total expenditures, domestic expenditures, and imports by sector, and, read down, the table shows GNP.

The major product-side components of U.S. GNP for 1979 are shown in Table 2.2. Besides scanning the numbers to get an idea of the relative size of the sectors, the reader should notice several items. First, about 15

TABLE 2.1

GNP on the product side

$$
\begin{aligned}
C_d &= C - M_c \\
I_d &= I - M_i \\
G_d &= G - M_g \\
X &= X \\
\hline
\text{GNP} &= C + I + G + (X - M)
\end{aligned}
$$

TABLE 2.2

GNP and its major components, 1979 ($ billion)

Gross national product (GNP)	$2,369
Personal consumption expenditures	1,510
Durable goods	213
Nondurable goods	597
Services	700
Gross private domestic investment	387
Business fixed investment	255
Structures	93
Producers' durable equipment	162
Residential structures	114
Change in business inventories	18
Net exports of goods and services	−4
Exports	258
Imports	262
Government purchases of goods and services	476
Federal	167
National defense	108
Other	58
State and local	310

Source: *Survey of Current Business,* May 1980.

percent of consumer expenditures are on durable goods, with a lifetime over one year. There is some question concerning whether these should be treated as a separate investment category, with the output of the goods entered as investment goods, and consumer use of their services, measured by depreciation or an implicit rental price, entered in consumer expenditure on services. For example, if all consumer durables were owned by leasing firms, as is sometimes the case with autos, sales of the goods would enter into business investment and the rental price would enter into consumer expenditures.

A second related point is that almost 30 percent of total investment is in residential structures. Houses, of course, are the most important single consumer durable, and they are treated in the accounts in exactly the way suggested above for all consumer durables. All residential structures are entered in the accounts as investment as they are being built—the Census Bureau measures quarterly the value of residential construction put in place. In the case of rental housing, rents enter consumer expenditure on services. For owner-occupied housing the OBE imputes a gross rental value to the house and adds it to consumer expenditures on services; on the income side an imputed *net* rental income is added.

The last thing to notice about the investment component in this brief review is that it includes investment in business inventories. This is the *change* in the stock of inventories from the beginning of the accounting period to the end. The change in inventory component is perhaps the most volatile sector of the accounts, at least on the product side, and it is important in our discussion in Chapter 3 of the relationship between two interpretations of equation (1), as an *identity* which *always* holds and as an *equilibrium condition* that is true *only* when income and product are in equilibrium.

Finally, the breakdown of total government purchases of goods and services between the federal defense, federal nondefense, and state and local categories should be noticed. Total state and local government purchases are larger than total federal purchases. In addition, about 70 percent of federal purchases are for national defense. This is because almost all of federal *defense expenditures* are *purchases* of goods and services—such items as tanks and military pay—while less than 20 percent of nondefense expenditures are purchases. The rest of these expenditures are transfer payments, interest payments, and grants to state and local governments. These are *not* payments for currently produced goods and services, and thus do not enter GNP directly. Rather, they are recorded on the income side as offsets to tax receipts—as negative tax payments—as we shall see in the discussion of the disposition of national income.

GNP BY TYPE OF INCOME, AND NATIONAL INCOME

The translation from GNP at market price—the product-side measure of GNP as measured by expenditure—to national income (NI)—the sum of factor incomes earned in producing GNP—is shown in Table 2.3. Starting from GNP, capital consumption allowances (CCA)—depreciation of plant,

---

TABLE 2.3

GNP by type of income, 1979 ($ billion)

Gross national product (GNP)	$2,369
less Capital consumption allowances	243
Net national product (NNP)	2,126
less Indirect business taxes	189
Business transfer payments	10
Statistical discrepancy	4
plus Net subsidies to government enterprises	2
National income (NI)	1,925
Compensation of employees	1,459
Proprietors' income	131
Rental income of persons	27
Corporate profits	178
Net interest	130

Source: *Survey of Current Business,* May 1980.

equipment, and residential structures—are subtracted to obtain net national product (NNP). CCA, of course, are part of business cash flow and also are a major part of gross business saving, as we will see shortly. To state the basic identity (1), which is in terms of GNP, in terms of NNP, we could subtract CCA from I, making investment net, instead of gross, and from S, reducing the business saving component of S to net, instead of gross, business saving.

There are one major and three very minor items between NNP and NI. The major item is indirect business tax (IBT) payments. These represent the difference between what buyers pay for final product and what sellers receive—the receipts from excise and sales taxes. Since it is the amount that sellers receive, net of IBT, that is converted into factor payments, IBT must be subtracted from NNP to go to NI, which is essentially NNP measured at factor cost, rather than market price. IBT will enter the T component of the income side of the GNP identity (1).

The first of the minor items between NNP and NI, business transfer payments, is mainly business gifts to nonprofit foundations and writeoffs of bad debts. These must be subtracted because they are a part of business receipts from sales that are not passed on as factor incomes. Later, in Table 2.4, we will see that business transfers are added back in as we go from NI to personal income (PI).

The statistical discrepancy is the difference between GNP measured on the income and product sides due to the fact that the statistical bases for the two measurements are independent of, or at least different from, one another. The income-side measure comes from such items as personal and corporate tax returns and employment tax returns—payments into the social security and unemployment compensation funds. The product-side measure is built up from sales, inventory, and shipments data. The two measures will never exactly coincide. A negative discrepancy says that the income-side measure is greater than the product side. The statistical discrepancy is included in saving in the GNP identity; measured income that does not show up in product-side expenditures is assumed to be saved.

The other minor item between NNP and NI is net subsidies paid by governments to government enterprises, such as TVA or state liquor stores. These enterprises are in the business sector, so on the product side their output is measured at sales value. But if they incur losses, on balance, their payments to factor incomes for current production exceed the value of their output by the amount of the loss, which is, in turn, made up by a net subsidy from government. So these net subsidies must be added in to NNP to get NI. These net subsidies enter the basic GNP identity (1) as negative tax payments on the income side.

The last five lines of Table 2.3 show the breakdown of national income by factor shares, before direct tax payments. These are, then, gross factor incomes. The categories of factor incomes should be self-explanatory. In an effort to measure only real contributions to GNP, proprietors' income, rental income, and corporate profits are adjusted for depreciation through capital consumption allowances. Proprietors' income and corporate profits are also shown net of capital gains due to price increases on existing inventory holdings by including inventory valuation adjustments.

It is interesting to note that if we exclude proprietors' income, the share of national income going to compensation of employees in 1979 was about 80 percent, with 20 percent for property income, so that these would be the shares of national income to labor and capital if proprietors' income were divided proportionately to total national income. It is, however, very difficult to determine what fraction of proprietors' income is due to the store-owner's capital and what fraction is due to his labor. If it were all capital income, the labor share would have been about 75 percent in 1979; if it were all labor income, the labor share would have been about 82 percent.

THE DISPOSITION OF NATIONAL INCOME

The final step in our review of the accounts is to allocate GNP and NI among the income-side components of the GNP identity, consumer expenditure C, saving S, tax payments T, and private transfers to foreigners R_f. We do this by going down the income side from GNP to NI to PI to disposable personal income (DPI) to consumer expenditure (C), allocating each item that is taken out of GNP along the way to S, T, or R_f, so that at the end, when only C is left, we have a sum, $C + S + T + R_f$, that equals GNP.

The steps from GNP down to consumer expenditure on the income side are shown in Table 2.4, allocated among S, T, and R_f. The reader should notice that, since the components $C + S + T + R_f$ add up to GNP, the items that are *added* in going down the income side from GNP at the top of Table 2.4 to consumer expenditure at the bottom, are either *subtracted* in the allocation of the items to S, T, and R_f or *canceled out* by subtraction farther down in the progression to consumer expenditure.

The three items that are subtracted in allocation to an income-side category are net subsidies to government enterprises—"Net subsidies" in Table 2.4—government transfer payments, and government interest, which are all offsets to tax revenues T. Thus, the total for T on the income side is the *net* tax revenue—the *net* withdrawal from the income stream caused by the combined tax receipts less transfer payments of the federal, state, and local governments. Viewed another way, government transfer payments for such items as social security, unemployment compensation, and public assistance are *not* payments for current output, and therefore not in G, but rather negative tax payments to be included with a minus sign in T.

The other *plus* items going from GNP to C—personal interest payments and business transfer payments—are canceled by subtraction items elsewhere in the same chain from GNP to consumer expenditure. Thus, the sum $C + S + T + R_f$ does, in fact, add up to GNP.

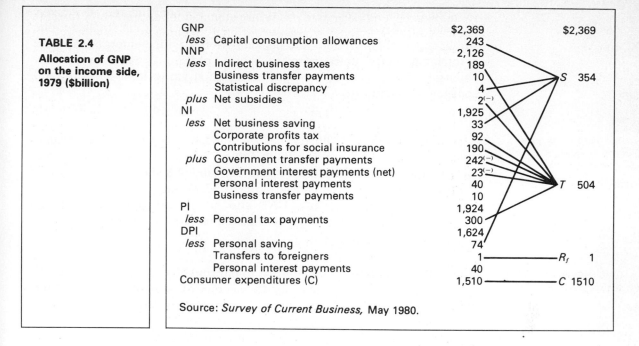

TABLE 2.4

Allocation of GNP on the income side, 1979 ($billion)

GNP		$2,369	$2,369
less	Capital consumption allowances	243	
NNP		2,126	
less	Indirect business taxes	189	
	Business transfer payments	10	*S* 354
	Statistical discrepancy	4	
plus	Net subsidies	2(−)	
NI		1,925	
less	Net business saving	33	
	Corporate profits tax	92	
	Contributions for social insurance	190	
plus	Government transfer payments	242(−)	
	Government interest payments (net)	23(−)	
	Personal interest payments	40	*T* 504
	Business transfer payments	10	
PI		1,924	
less	Personal tax payments	300	
DPI		1,624	
less	Personal saving	74	
	Transfers to foreigners	1	*R_f* 1
	Personal interest payments	40	
Consumer expenditures (C)		1,510	*C* 1510

Source: *Survey of Current Business,* May 1980.

In the last section we discussed the items between GNP and NI. Here we can briefly discuss the items in Table 2.4 between NI and C. Going from NI to PI involves subtracting factor incomes that do not get passed on to persons as gross before-tax income and adding items that enter PI but are not in NI. The first item under NI in Table 2.4, "Net business saving," is linked to the next item, "Corporate profits tax," by the following definition:

$$\text{Net business saving} \equiv \text{Corporate profits} - \text{Corporate profits tax} - \text{Dividends.} \qquad [4]$$

Thus, net business saving is the same as retained earnings, the fraction of profits not paid out in taxes or dividends. Net business saving plus CCA is gross business saving.

Contributions for social insurance (CSI) include both employer and employee payments of social security taxes, unemployment compensation taxes, and the like. These are taken out going from NI to PI and are part of government receipts in the accounts.

As shown above, government transfers and interest payments are added to NI and are treated as negative entries in *T*. These payments redistribute income between the (overlapping) groups who pay taxes, on the one hand, and receive transfer payments and interest on government debt, on the other hand.

The rest of the entries are straightforward. Personal interest and business transfers are both canceled elsewhere. Personal tax payments, allocated to T, take us from PI to DPI, which is personal income after taxes. Personal tax payments also include expenditures for such items as tolls and licenses. DPI is divided into personal saving, which enters S, transfers to foreigners—remittances to relatives in the old country, personal interest payments, which cancel the previous addition going from NI to PI, and consumer expenditure.

SUMMARY OF THE GNP IDENTITY

The final allocation of DPI finishes the allocation of GNP to the income-side components $C + S + T + R_f$. In Table 2.2 we show the composition of GNP on the product side of the accounts. Table 2.3 shows the translation from GNP to NI and the composition of NI by factor incomes. Finally, Table 2.4 demonstrates how GNP and NI are allocated between the income-side components. This verifies the basic GNP identity,

$$C + I + G + (X - M) \equiv \text{GNP} \equiv C + S + T + R_f, \qquad [5]$$

which plays an important analytical role throughout the rest of this book. Two other versions of this identity, the saving-investment balance and the real GNP identity, are also important in our analysis, so we will introduce them here.

The saving-investment balance

Implied in the GNP identity of equation (5) is another identity that shows the equality between, roughly speaking, saving and investment in the economy. This saving-investment identity will become an important analytical concept in Chapter 3, so it is useful to introduce it here as a natural derivative from the GNP identity.

If we subtract consumer expenditure C from both sides of the GNP identity (5), we obtain the saving-investment identity,

$$I + G + (X - M) \equiv S + T + R_f \qquad [6]$$

The sum on the left-hand side of (6) represents total output *not* going to consumer expenditure, and the right-hand sum gives total income of consumers that is not spent. If we loosely identify nonconsumed output as investment of one kind or another, and income not going to consumer expenditure as saving, then equation (6) can be interpreted as an investment = saving identity.

In a closed economy or one in which net exports and private transfer payments to foreigners are small, the $(X - M)$ and R_f terms can be dropped from equation (6) for analytical purposes. If we do this, and move government purchases G over to the right-hand side, we obtain

$$I \equiv S + (T - G), \qquad [7]$$

as another version of the saving-investment identity. This says that private investment I must be equal to the sum of private saving S plus net government saving, $T - G$. The latter is the total federal, state, and local government surplus. Output going to business investment plus residential construction must be equal to the sum of private saving—after-tax income not spent—plus the net government surplus.

Nominal and real GNP

GNP can be measured either at current prices, as we have assumed implicitly up to this point, or in *real* terms using some base-year prices. Nominal, or money, GNP, measured at current prices, is simply the total national output in dollar terms. Real GNP must be built up by dividing by the relevant price index each subsector of nominal GNP such as consumer expenditure on durables or business purchases of electrical equipment.

When each GNP component is thus "deflated" by the relevant price index, we have the real GNP identity.

$$gnp = c + i + g + (x - m). \tag{8}$$

Here we are establishing the convention of using capital letters to denote nominal values, while small letters denote real values. If P_I is the price index for investment, for example, then $I \equiv P_I \cdot i$, and real investment i in equation (8) is obtained by dividing nominal investment I by P_I.

Dividing real GNP from equation (8) into nominal GNP gives us the *implicit deflator* for GNP, the comprehensive price index P defined by

$$P \equiv \frac{GNP}{gnp}. \tag{9}$$

This relationship is extremely important to our analysis of income determination in Part II. There we explain movements in real output, gnp, and the price level, P. Changes in nominal GNP are determined analytically by the identity $GNP = P \cdot gnp$.

This completes our survey of the GNP accounts and the basic identities they contain. All three identities—income equals product, saving equals investment, and nominal GNP equals real gnp times the price index—are important for later analysis of employment level and price level determination. Now we can turn to another important aggregate in the accounts, the federal government budget.

THE GOVERNMENT SECTOR IN THE ACCOUNTS

Since much of our discussion of macroeconomic policy in the following chapters focuses on the results, under various conditions, of changing government spending and tax decisions, the next few pages of this chapter concentrate on the (total) government sector in the national income accounts and the relation between the federal NIPA sector and the unified budget that is presented to Congress by the president in January each year as the budget plan of the United States. First we take a closer look at the government sector and identify the G and T variables in the basic GNP identity,

$$
\begin{array}{ccccccccccccc}
C & + & I & + & G & + & (X - M) & \equiv & GNP & \equiv & C & + & S & + & T & + & R_f, \\
\$1510 & & 387 & & 476 & & -4 & & 2369 & & 1510 & & 354 & & 504 & & 1
\end{array}
$$
$$\tag{10}$$

where the values of the major GNP components in 1979 are shown.

TABLE 2.5

Government sector in the NIPA, 1979 ($ billion)

Expenditures		Receipts	
Purchases of goods and		Personal tax	$300
services	$476	Corporate profits tax	92
Transfer payments	246	Indirect business tax	189
To persons	242	Contributions for social	
To foreigners	4	insurance	190
Net interest	23		
Net subsidies	2		
Total expenditures	743	*Total receipts*	771

Source: *Survey of Current Business,* May 1980.

Table 2.5 shows the combined federal and state and local government sector in the accounts for 1979. The entries in Table 2.5 must be consistent with those of the product and income side Tables 2.2 and 2.4. Our focus here is on the definition of G and T in the basic GNP identity (10).

On the product side, measuring expenditure on current output of goods and services, the G entry is total government purchases of goods and services only—$476 billion in 1979—*not* total government expenditure. The reader should verify this in Table 2.2. On the income side, the tax entry, T, is *net* tax receipts—$504 billion in 1979. This number can be obtained by subtracting from gross tax receipts—$771 billion—the sum of transfer payments "to persons," net interest, and net subsidies—$267 billion. The reader should be able to locate each of these entries in Table 2.5. These items are government additions to the income stream, *not* in compensation for currently provided services. The tax item on the income side, T, thus measures *net withdrawals* by government from the income stream. Of the $771 billion gross tax receipts in 1979, $267 billion was returned to the public in a pure redistribution of income.

We should note here that the $4 billion government transfer payments to foreigners—foreign aid and retirement payments to foreigners—is *not* netted against gross tax receipts in calculating T. This is because transfers to foreigners are not payments returned to the U.S. income stream but are funds transferred abroad. While these funds may indirectly stimulate U.S. exports, the transfer itself does not enter the accounts.

The federal government sector of the accounts is shown in Table 2.6. With one exception, the items in Table 2.6 can be subtracted from those in Table 2.5 to get the state and local government sector. The one exception is the federal expenditure item, "Grants-in-aid," which are federal grants to state and local governments under such varied programs as the highway trust fund and public assistance. In general, under the grant programs, the federal government provides funds to "match" state and local expenditures for the specified program under a fixed formula. For example, the federal government provides about $90 for every $10 of state funds in the highway program. These grants, which are entered as expenditures in the federal account, are entered as receipts in the state and local account. When the two accounts are consolidated into the total government account, as is done in Table 2.5, this intragovernment transfer payment cancels out and the grants item disappears.

The federal sector in the national income accounts is not a budget in the legislative, accounting, or control sense. It is more a record of the economic activity of the federal government in the national accounts. However, the federal NIPA sector is very close, both in coverage and measurement, to the *expenditure account* of the *unified budget,* which is presented in January of each year for the fiscal year beginning the following October 1. The federal NIPA sector and the unified budget totals for fiscal year 1979, which ran from October 1978 to September 1979, are shown in Table 2.7.

The unified budget separates expenditures and tax receipts, in the expenditure account, from loan activities, in the loan account. This corresponds to the NIPA exclusion of asset transfers. The unified budget then records a total surplus which is the difference between the expenditure account surplus and net lending. The latter item is added to expenditures to make up "Outlays."

In general, the differences between the unified budget measure of federal receipts and expenditures and that of the federal NIPA sector are in

TABLE 2.6
Federal government sector in the NIPA, 1979 ($ billion)

Expenditures		Receipts	
Purchases of goods and services	$167	Personal tax	$230
Transfer payments	210	Corporate profits tax	78
To persons	206	Indirect business tax	30
To foreigners	4	Contributions for social insurance	159
Grants-in-aid	80		
Net interest	43		
Net subsidies	9		
Total expenditures	509	*Total receipts*	498

Source: *Survey of Current Business,* May 1980.

TABLE 2.7
Federal NIPA sector and unified budget, fiscal year 1979 ($ billion)

NIPA		Unified budget	
Receipts	$483.7	Receipts	$465.9
Expenditures	493.6	Outlays	493.7
Deficit	9.9	Deficit	27.8

Source: *Economic Indicators,* April 1980.

the timing with which various transactions are recorded. Both budgets ideally record expenditures as they accrue and receipts as they become liabilities to the government. In practice, a few differences remain.

Expenditures other than purchases of goods and services—transfers, interest, grants, and subsidies—are recorded in both budgets when checks are issued. However, purchases are recorded in the unified budget as they accrue, while in the NIPA sector they are recorded upon delivery, with the exception of construction, which is recorded as it is put in place. The accrual-delivery lag can make a significant difference in the case of items such as ships and other large hard goods.

In these cases, the unified budget records the accrual of expenditures through progress payments made to contractors. The federal NIPA sector, however, subtracts a factor related to progress payments from total purchases as the item is being built, and then records the total value as an expenditure upon delivery. Thus, while the item is under construction, it adds to inventories in the national income accounts through work-in-progress inventories. When it is delivered, inventories are reduced and federal purchases go up by the inventory reduction plus the addition to value in the final accounting period. Thus, the federal NIPA sector treatment does not affect the level of GNP, but it does affect the distribution of federal hard-goods purchases between inventory investment and federal purchases while items are under construction and progress payments are being made.

On the receipts side, both budgets record corporate profits taxes as the liabilities accrue. The unified budget, however, records personal taxes and contributions for social insurance as they are paid, while the federal NIPA sector estimates their accrual. This can make a difference when tax laws are changing, as was the case in 1968 with the income tax surcharge. Since the personal tax period is generally the calendar year, the federal sector in the accounts spread the 1968 personal tax liability due to the surcharge enacted in July 1968 over the entire year of 1968, while the unified budget counted the receipts in the second half of 1968 as all falling within fiscal year 1969 (this was, of course, during the period when the fiscal year ran from July to June).

Aside from these fairly small differences, the unified budget—the legislated financial control document—is now fairly close to the economic measure of the federal government's impact on the economy in the national income accounts. This is a major improvement in federal budgeting over the confusing system that prevailed as recently as 1967.

GNP AS A WELFARE MEASURE

There are difficulties on at least two levels in interpreting GNP as a welfare measure. The objective of this book is to describe the theory of the determinants of the level of employment and of national output and not to evaluate any particular indicator of social welfare. Since there are fairly clear statistical and analytical relationships between real GNP, the price level, and the unemployment rate, all as presently measured, real GNP as currently measured is a satisfactory concept for our purposes. But the subject of this book is not the only important subject in economics, and we should not leave the reader thinking that real GNP is a satisfactory general measure of economic welfare, even though it will adequately serve our analytical ends.

Market and nonmarket transactions

The most obvious deficiency of the accounts is that they exclude nonmarket transactions. If two people exchange services in a barter arrangement, the output involved is not measured in GNP. But if they incorporate and sell each other the services, the output is counted. Thus, the accounts are sensitive to the extent to which transactions are conducted through established markets in the monetary sector, as opposed to individual barter transactions.

The main instance of the exclusion of nonmarket transactions in the accounts is the fact that housewives' services are not counted, since no market transaction is involved in the provision of the services. Presumably housewives' services are worth the average wage in the economy in the absence of discrimination against women, so that if their services were correctly valued, the measured output of the household sector of the economy would rise by perhaps $180 billion—21 million women working 8 hours a day at home for an average wage of $4.36 an hour.

As long as the ratio between the volume of market and nonmarket transactions is fairly stable, a change in measured real GNP will correspond to a change in actual market and nonmarket output. But as a country develops with increasing labor specialization, the ratio of market to nonmarket transactions will rise. This will bring an increase in measured GNP due simply to the increase in the market sector of the economy. Real output will rise, but the extent of this increase will be overstated by the shift from a largely nonmarket economy to a largely market economy.

Externalities and the social value of output

The second problem involved in using real GNP as a welfare measure has to do with the assumption that market prices approximate the social value of output. Suppose a steel plant produces both steel, which enters GNP at market price, and smoke, which is given away free—that is, the steel company does not have to pay the consumers for its ill effects—and thus does not enter GNP. In this case the social value of the plant's output is less than the private value to the steel firm which enters GNP.

In the case of these *externalities* where undesirable output is produced but private costs are not assessed for it—it is not *internalized* to the producer—measured real GNP will overstate the social value of output. If firms were required to absorb the costs of not polluting, nominal GNP would not immediately change, but this would increase the costs and price of private output so that measured real GNP would fall. The drop in real GNP would correspond to the deduction from the value of private output that would come from recognizing the negative value of the output of pollution.

The measurement of real GNP in the case of externalities, as well as nonmarket transactions, could be adjusted to reflect true social values. The costs of pollution can be estimated, and a value can be imputed to nonmarket output, so that a rough adjustment to GNP can be made for these factors. As economic data are improved, the implicit value of housewives' work is recognized, and the costs of pollution are internalized, measured GNP should become a better approximation of social welfare.

This completes our brief survey of the national income and product accounts and the federal budget. We will now use the product = GNP = income identity expressed in equation (1) to begin analysis of the determination of the level of national output and income.

1. If the only economic activity in year 1 is the manufacture of a suit of clothes worth $100, and the only economic activity in year 2 is the sale of that suit of clothes for $100, fill in the following table:

Year	GNP	=	Consumption	+	Investment
1	____	=	_____	+	_____
2	____	=	_____	+	_____

2. What is the direct effect of an increase in social security payments on:

    a. Gross national product
    b. National income
    c. Personal income
    d. Disposable personal income

3. The following information about business activity is revealed to the Department of Commerce by the only three business firms in the economy:

Dewdrop Cookie Co.		Ace Oven Co.		Beta Flour Co.	
Sales	800	Sales	150	Sales	200
Wages	600	Wages	100	Wages	100
Flour inventory		Depreciation	20	Depreciation	30
Beg. of year	100			Rent	50
End of year	200				
Flour purchases	200				
Oven purchase	150				
Depreciation	50				

    a. Compute GNP by use of final output, flow of factor incomes, and value added. Hint: all three methods should yield the same answer.
    b. If Beta increases its sales by 200 and nothing else changes, how would your answers to (a) change?

4. If Gross national product increases from 2,000 billion dollars to 2,200 billion dollars while the GNP deflator grows from 1.40 to 1.60, would you estimate the output of real goods and services has risen, fallen, or remained the same?

5. How can one maintain that savings equals investment when a tax increase will reduce personal savings and the level of taxes can change at the whim of Congress?

SELECTED READINGS   G. Ackley, *Macroeconomic Theory* (New York: Macmillan, 1962), chaps. 1–4.

F. G. Adams, *National Accounts and the Structure of the U.S. Economy* (New York: General Learning Press, 1973).

P. A. Samuelson, *Economics,* 11th ed. (New York: McGraw-Hill, 1980), chap. 10.

P. A. Samuelson, "The Evaluation of Social Income," in F. Lutz and D. C. Hague, eds., *The Theory of Capital* (London: Macmillan, 1961).

U.S. Department of Commerce, *Survey of Current Business* (August 1965), National Income Account Revisions article.

3

INTRODUCTION TO INCOME DETERMINATION: THE MULTIPLIER

In the national income accounts, GNP can be viewed as a flow of either *product* or *income*. In either case the total value (at market prices) of goods and services produced in the economy is the same. This gives us the basic GNP identity,

$$C + I + G + (X - M) = \text{GNP} = C + S + T + R_f,$$ [1]

where

$$C \equiv \text{total value of consumption expenditure;}$$
$$I \equiv \text{total value of investment expenditure;}$$
$$G \equiv \text{government purchases of goods and services;}$$
$$(X - M) \equiv \text{net exports of goods and services;}$$
$$S \equiv \text{gross private saving (business saving + personal saving + depreciation);}$$
$$T \equiv \text{net tax revenues (tax revenue minus domestic transfer payments, net interest paid, and net subsidies); and}$$
$$R_f \equiv \text{total private transfer payments to foreigners.}$$

Since the foreign sector in the U.S. economy is small, as we saw in Chapter 2, for analytical purposes here we consider the United States to be a closed economy. The foreign sector is reintroduced in Chapter 16, both in terms of flows of goods and services and monetary flows. But for the present, eliminating the relatively minor foreign component from the GNP identity (1) gives us the following version of that identity,

$$C + I + G = Y = C + S + T,$$ [2]

where Y is the standard symbol for national income, national output, or GNP.

Depending on whether we include depreciation and value output at market price or factor cost, equation (2) can be interpreted as a GNP identity, a net national product (NNP) identity, or a national income (NI) identity. If Y is defined as GNP, then C, I, and G are valued at market prices, including indirect business taxes (IBT) which, on the other side of the identity, are included in T. Also, if Y is defined as GNP, I is gross private investment and S is gross private saving. If we subtract capital consumption allowances (depreciation) both from I to get net investment and from S to get net private saving, equation (2) is an identity for $Y = $ NNP. If, in addition, we value C, net I, and G at factor prices, subtracting IBT from both sides of the identity, equation (2) becomes an identity for $Y = $ NI. This chapter, all of Part II, and a good deal of Part III focus on the problem of the determination of the equilibrium level of national income and product (or output). For analytical purposes it will not matter much whether we define Y, national income and output, to include or exclude depreciation and IBT. Thus, in these chapters Y stands for both income and output.

National income, Y, is measured at current price levels and is frequently referred to as *money* or *nominal* GNP. Nominal Y can be broken down into a *price component*, P, and a *real output component*, y, so that $Y = P \cdot y$. In the national income accounts, discussed in Chapter 2, real output is measured on a disaggregated basis by dividing (or "deflating") the various components of output in nominal terms by the relevant price indices. These disaggregated real c, i, and g components then are added up to total real output y. This is then divided into total nominal output Y to obtain the *implicit price deflator* for GNP, P. Thus, we have a real GNP identity,

$$c + i + g = y = c + s + t, \qquad\qquad [3]$$

corresponding to the nominal GNP identity of equation (2). We will use this notation throughout Parts II and III: capital letters stand for nominal amounts, and small letters stand for real amounts, so that, for example, $Y = P \cdot y$.

This breakdown of nominal output into price and real output components is essential for the analysis of income determination in Parts II and III. Changes in employment and unemployment are related to changes in real output y, while changes in the price level P are what we mean by inflation or deflation. In this chapter, and in Chapters 4 and 5 in Part II, we look at the effects of shifts in demand factors on the level of real output assuming the price level P is fixed. In Chapter 6 we introduce the supply side and determination of the price level. Then in the rest of Part II, Chapters 7 through 9, we describe the factors determining equilibrium price level and output in the economy, so that by the end of Part II we have a fairly complete economic system that determines both P and y. In this chapter we review the simplest models of income determination and multipliers from the principles course starting with the basic identity.

$$c + i + g = y = c + s + t.$$

THE
SAVING-INVESTMENT
BALANCE

Subtracting the real consumption component from each side of equation (3) gives us

$$y - c = i + g \text{ and } y - c = s + t,$$

so that

$$i + g = s + t \qquad [4]$$

is just another way to express the basic real GNP identity (3). Equation (4) expresses the *saving-investment* balance implicit in the basic GNP identity. On the product side, $i + g$ is the amount of real output that does not go to consumer expenditure, while on the income side, $s + t$ is the amount of consumer income that is not spent. These two sums are the same by definition in the accounts. The use of resources in the private sector to produce output *not* for sale to consumers—$i + g$—must equal the amount of income that consumers do not spend—$s + t$.

By moving the g term to the right-hand side of equation (4) we obtain another expression for the saving-investment balance,

$$i = s + (t - g). \qquad [5]$$

Here i is total private investment (gross or net, depending on the definition of y), s is total private saving, and $(t - g)$ is the government surplus, which may be thought of as net government saving. The sum of private saving and the government's surplus must, by definition, equal private investment in the national income accounts.

PLANNED AND
REALIZED
INVESTMENT

The investment component of equations (3) and (4) includes both intended investment, that is, investment which is part of producers' plans, and unintended investment, that is, unforeseen changes in inventories, that come about because of unexpected changes in the level of consumption demand, or, in general, final sales. We will call *intended* investment $\bar{i}$ and *unintended inventory* investment Δinv. Intended investment i can, of course, include some *planned* amount of inventory accumulation; in a growing economy desired inventories would probably grow in line with final sales. But in addition to planned inventory accumulation, total investment will include an *unplanned* (and undesired) inventory change, Δinv, which can be positive, negative, or zero, depending on whether sales are smaller, greater, or no different than expected. This distinction between *planned* (or desired) and *unplanned* (or involuntary) inventory accumulation is the key to the analysis of the determination of equilibrium national income. The investment component in equation (4) can be broken into its two parts,

$$i = \bar{i} + \Delta inv. \quad [6]$$ [6]

Replacing the investment component in the saving-investment balance (4) by the sum of planned and unintended investment in equation (6) gives us

$$\bar{i} + \Delta inv + g = s + t,$$ [7]

and adding real consumer expenditure c back into equation (7) converts it back into the national income identity

$$C + \bar{i} + \Delta inv + g = y = c + s + t.$$ [8]

This is the first step toward converting the *accounting identities* of equations (3) and (4) into *equilibrium conditions* determining the level of income y.

The Δinv component is now a balancing item in the GNP identity (8). If, for example, people suddenly decide to reduce saving and increase consumer expenditure, the increase in spending would bring a drop in inventories as sellers meet the unexpected increase in demand by selling from inventory, so that Δinv is negative. This is an *unexpected* or *involuntary decumulation* of inventories. The negative Δinv entry in equation (8) would balance, initially, the c increase on the output side, while the c and s changes balance on the income side, maintaining the GNP identity at the preexisting level of income.

But this involuntary drop in inventories will cause sellers to increase orders to meet the higher sales level, leading to an increase in production and a change in y. Thus, the preexisting level of income is no longer an equilibrium level. It is only when producers and retailers are selling as expected, so that Δinv is zero, and realized investment i equals planned investment $\bar{i}$, that income is at an equilibrium level. In that case, there is nothing in the current situation to change producers' or sellers' behavior, and thus to change the level of income.

THE TAX, CONSUMPTION, AND SAVING FUNCTIONS

The next step in developing the conditions for income to be at equilibrium is recognition that tax payments, consumer spending, and saving are all likely to depend on the level of income. Each of these will be an increasing function of the level of income. In particular, tax revenue is a function of gross income y,

$$t = t(y),$$ [9]

and consumer expenditure and saving are functions of disposable (after-tax) income $y - t(y)$,

$$c = c(y - t(y));$$ [10]
$$s = s(y - t(y)).$$ [11]

These expressions are the first examples of the functional notation that will be used throughout this book. Equation (9), $t = t(y)$, is read "t is a function of y" and says that a particular relationship exists between taxes and gross income. More specifically it means that there is a rule or formula that will give us a level of taxes for each level of gross income. The reader should be careful to distinguish this functional notation from multiplication, by reference to the surrounding text.

The slope of the tax function, giving the change in tax revenue per unit change in income, is positive. That is, tax payments increase with increases in income. The fraction of an increase in income that goes to taxes, the *marginal tax rate*, will be called t'. This is the slope of the tax function.

Equations (10) and (11) give the split of disposable income between consumption and saving, both of which increase with disposable income. We will call the fraction of an increase in disposable income that goes to consumption the *marginal propensity to consume*, c', and the fraction that goes to saving the *marginal propensity to save*, s'. If saving and consumer spending exhaust disposable income, then $c' + s' = 1$, since all of a change in disposable income must be allocated between consumption and saving. The relationships between gross income, taxes, disposable income, and consumption and saving are shown in Figure 3.1. There taxes are subtracted from gross income to obtain disposable income, and the latter is distributed to consumption and saving.

The tax, consumption, and saving functions are shown in Figure 3.2, which plots total income on the horizontal axis and uses of income—t, c, and s—on the vertical axis. Since the sum of uses of income must equal income, for any income level in Figure 3.2 we can add up the uses of income to the 45° line where, by construction, uses = total income. Note that at low income levels, both tax revenue and saving are negative. Below income level y_1, people receive on balance transfer payments (social security, welfare, unemployment compensation) which are negative taxes, as we saw in Chapter 2. Below income level y_2, they also dissave (disposable

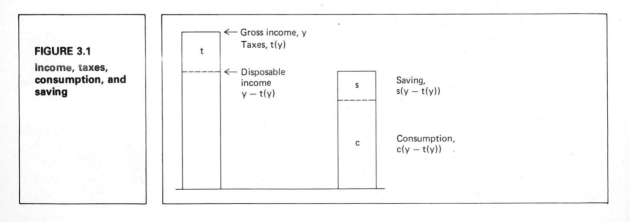

FIGURE 3.1

Income, taxes, consumption, and saving

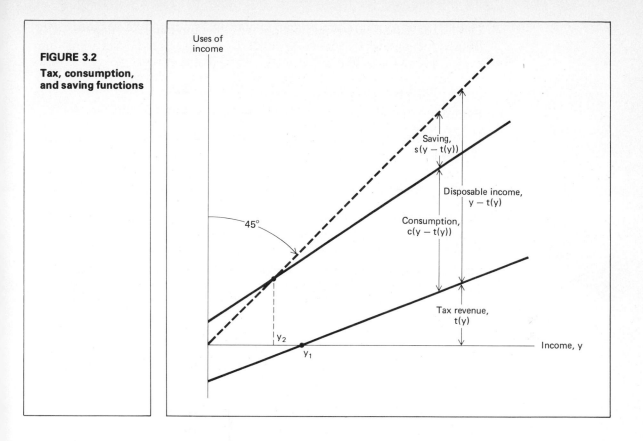

FIGURE 3.2

Tax, consumption, and saving functions

Uses of income

Saving, $s(y - t(y))$

Disposable income, $y - t(y)$

Consumption, $c(y - t(y))$

45°

Tax revenue, $t(y)$

Income, y

y_2

y_1

income is less than consumption), so saving is negative. The result is a level of consumption exceeding income, supported by negative tax payments and dissaving. As income increases along the horizontal axis, each of the wedges showing t, c, and s gets wider, so that, in general, an increase in y will increase t, c, and s.

One expression we will be interested in is the fraction of a change in gross income that goes into total social saving ($s + t$). This is the fraction of an increase in gross income that is not spent on c. This fraction, $\Delta(s + t)/\Delta y$, equals the slope of the ($s + t$) function that will be important in the multiplier analysis below. To compute it we cannot simply add the marginal tax rate $\Delta t/\Delta y$ and the marginal propensity to save $\Delta s/\Delta y$, since taxes are related to gross income while saving is a function of disposable income. In the example that follows, the correct expression for $\Delta(s + t)/\Delta y$ is derived.

As income rises by some amount Δy, say \$100, tax payments rise by $t' \cdot \Delta y$ (\$20 if the marginal tax rate t' is 0.2). This leaves an increase of disposable income of $(1 - t') \Delta y$, \$80 in the example. Of this, a fraction s' will be saved, so the increase in saving is $s' \cdot (1 - t') \Delta y$. If 20 percent of increases in disposable income are saved, this would be \$16 [$=0.2(1 - 0.2)$

· $100] in the example. Adding up the tax and saving increases then gives us

$$\text{Tax increase, } \Delta t, = \qquad t' \, \Delta y = \$20;$$

$$\text{Saving increase, } \Delta s, = \qquad s'(1 - t') \, \Delta y = \$16;$$

$$\text{Sum,} \Delta s + \Delta t = \Delta(s + t) = [s'(1 - t') + t'] \Delta y = \$36.$$

From the last line, the ratio of added saving and tax payments to increases in national income is given by

$$\frac{\Delta(s + t)}{\Delta y} = s' \, (1 - t') + t'. \qquad [12]$$

In the example this ratio is 0.36; we began with a y increase of $100 and ended up with an increase in $(s + t)$ of $36. With s' and t' both 0.2, we could have computed this directly:

$$s'(1 - t') + t' = 0.2(1 - 0.2) + 0.2 = 0.36.$$

Thus if total private saving is about 20 percent of national income less tax revenue, and tax revenue is also about 20 percent of national income, then the slope of this total social saving function is 0.36, that is, about 36 percent of an increase in income will go to taxes and saving. The important point here, though, is just that as y rises $(s + t)$ also increases. This fact is crucial for the stability of equilibrium income.

DETERMINATION OF EQUILIBRIUM INCOME

We can now bring together the material developed in the last two sections into a simple model of the determination of equilibrium income. The national income accounts identity (7) gave us the saving-investment balance equation,

$$\bar{\imath} + \Delta inv + g = s + t,$$

where Δinv represents unexpected, or involuntary, inventory changes. This equation is true, by definition, all the time. But income is at its *equilibrium* level—that is, sales are going as expected—only when Δinv is zero, and

$$\bar{\imath} + g = s + t = s(y - t(y)) + t(y). \qquad [13]$$

Here we introduce the dependence of saving and tax revenues on y, from the previous discussion. Equation (13) is an *equilibrium* condition for income y. When income is at the level where saving plus tax revenue (as functions of income) equal *planned* investment plus government spending, then unexpected Δinv equals zero, sales expectations are being realized, and there is no tendency for income and output to change. If income is higher than that level which satisfies equation (13), $(s + t)$ will exceed planned $(\bar{\imath} + g)$, sales will be low, and Δinv will be positive. The identity (7) will still hold with $\Delta inv = (s + t) - (\bar{\imath} + g)$, but income will not be at its equilibrium level because sellers will be cutting back orders to reduce unwanted inventory stocks, and production and income will be falling. This will continue until income falls enough to bring $(s + t)$ down to $(\bar{i} + g)$ and reduce Δinv to zero, bringing sales expectations and realizations back in line with each other.

Thus, from equation (7), if at an initial level of income y_0, $(s + t)$ exceeds $(\bar{i} + g)$, Δinv is positive. If this is the case, the economy is not in equilibrium because final sales are less than producers and sellers expected. Therefore, producers will reduce their expectations and begin to reduce production. As they do that, income will fall. Conversely, if $(s + t)$ is less than $(\bar{i} + g)$, Δinv must be negative, producers will expand output to meet the unexpected increase in demand, and income will rise.

The stability of equilibrium income

The determination of the equilibrium level of income is shown graphically in Figure 3.3. In Figure 3.3, $s + t$ has a positive slope because of the assumption that both s and t are increasing functions of y, described in the previous section. We have also assumed that $\bar{i}$ and g are fixed independently of the level of y, so that the $\bar{i} + g$ line is horizontal. The point at which $s + t = \bar{i} + g$, that is, where the two lines cross, determines the equilibrium level of income y_E that satisfies equilibrium condition (13).

We can further see that this equilibrium is a *stable* one. In other words, if outside forces cause the system to move away from the equilibrium point, it will tend to settle back to equilibrium at y_E. At a level of income y_0 in Figure 3.3, to the right of y_E, saving plus tax revenue is greater than planned $\bar{i} + g$. This means that people are buying less than sellers expected at that level of income, causing an unexpected inventory accumulation of amount Δinv_0. The inventory accumulation is just enough to maintain the saving-investment balance in the national income accounts, since at y_0,

$$\bar{i} + g + \Delta inv_0 = s(y_0 - t(y_0)) + t(y_0).$$

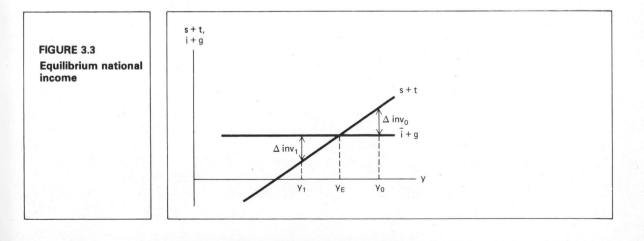

FIGURE 3.3

Equilibrium national income

But since Δinv_0 is positive, producers will cut back on production, causing income to decrease toward y_E. Conversely, to the left of y_E, where income is at y_1, saving plus tax revenue is less than $\bar{i} + g$. This means that people are buying more than sellers anticipated, causing an unexpected reduction of inventories of amount Δinv_1. Producers will then expand production to satisfy this greater demand, causing income to increase toward y_E. Thus, the equilibrium level of income, y_E, is stable. When actual income is below equilibrium y_E, Δinv is negative and production and income are rising. When actual income exceeds y_E, Δinv is positive and income is falling. Only at y_E is there no tendency for income to change.

This explanation of the equilibrium level of income contains one important oversimplification. At y_0 unexpected inventories accumulated, causing producers to decrease their production until there was no further unexpected inventory accumulation at y_E, where Δinv is zero. However, although no new unwanted inventories are accumulated at y_E, producers and sellers are still faced with that unwanted stock of inventories that accumulated before they made their adjustments. In order to work off that stock, they may cut *intended* inventory accumulation slightly, shifting the $\bar{i} + g$ line of Figure 3.3 down a bit as excess inventories are reduced. Eventually, though, the desired level of inventory accumulation included in $\bar{i}$ will return to its original level, and equilibrium income will be restored at y_E.

Shifts in the saving function

Now that we have seen that the equilibrium level of income determined by equation (13) is stable, it is useful to look at the effects of shifts in the saving function to see better how this simple model of income determination works. For example, consider the effect of an increase in the desire to save. This can be shown graphically as an upward shift in the $s + t$ function to $s_1 + t$ in Figure 3.4. At any given level of income people now want to save more than before. In Figure 3.2, this shift would be shown by a widening of the saving wedge at the expense of the consumption wedge. At the initial equilibrium level of income y_0, with the new saving function, $s + t$ exceeds planned $\bar{i} + g$, which results in an unin-

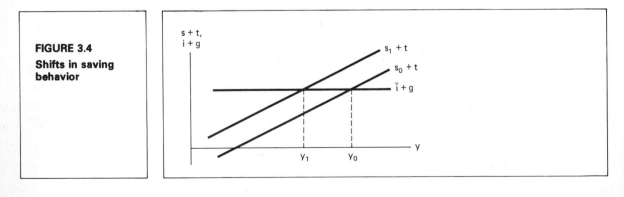

FIGURE 3.4

Shifts in saving behavior

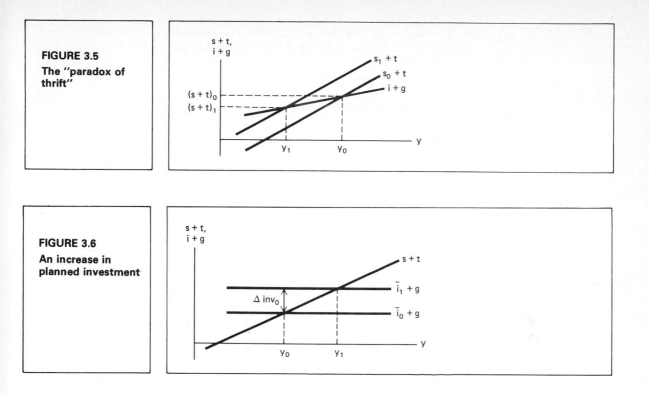

FIGURE 3.5

The "paradox of thrift"

FIGURE 3.6

An increase in planned investment

tended increase in inventories of Δinv_0. As we have seen, this will cause producers to cut production until Δinv is zero, where y reaches a new equilibrium at y_1, which brings a return to the original level of saving, but at a *lower* level of income. Thus, in a situation where $\bar{i} + g$ is fixed exogenously, an exogenous increase in the desire to save leads to an unchanged level of $s + t$ but at a lower level of income. Income must fall to reduce saving enough to restore equilibrium $s + t = \bar{i} + g$ with the higer saving function.

If we change the assumption that $\bar{i}$ and g are fixed independently of y, we can observe the possibility of what has been called the *paradox of thrift*. Suppose that, as shown in Figure 3.5, $i + g$ is an increasing function of income. That is, as the level of income increases, planned investment and/or government purchases rise. This gives the $i + g$ line a positive slope in Figure 3.5. Now we can see that an autonomous shift upward in saving to $s_1 + t$ causes not only a decrease in the level of income from y_0 to y_1, but also brings a *decrease* in the level of realized $s + t$. Thus, we have the result that an *increase* in the desire to save can lead ultimately to a *decrease* in the realized level of $s + t$ since the drop in income reduces planned investment. This is the so-called paradox of thrift.

Finally, suppose that it is not the saving function that shifts autonomously but the level of planned investment, $\bar{i}$. In Figure 3.6, this is rep-

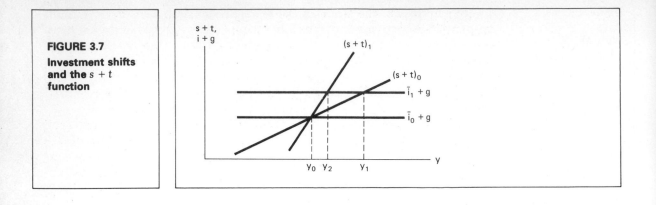

FIGURE 3.7

Investment shifts and the $s + t$ function

resented by an upward shift in the $\bar{i} + g$ line to $\bar{i}_1 + g$. This shift causes $s + t$ to be less than planned $\bar{i} + g$ at the initial equilibrium level of income y_0 by the amount $(-\Delta inv_0)$, representing an unexpected sell-off of inventory. As a result, orders and production increase, bringing an increase in the level of income toward the new equilibrium level y_1. (The same effect would occur, of course, as a result of a *downward* shift in the saving or tax function.) The size of the increase in income caused by an autonomous increase in $\bar{i}$ or g depends on the slope of the $s + t$ function. In Figure 3.7, with the flat $(s + t)_0$ function, income rises from y_0 to y_1 with an investment shift from $\bar{i}_0$ to $\bar{i}_1$. With the very steep $(s + t)_1$ function, implying a large increase in saving plus tax revenue with a change in y, the investment shift raises y only to y_2. This relationship between the slope of the $s + t$ function and the size of the increase in equilibrium income following from a given increase in exogenous investment demand or government purchases takes us to consideration of the multiplier.

DERIVATION OF THE EXPENDITURE MULTIPLIER

We have just seen how a change in planned investment from $\bar{i}_0$ to $\bar{i}_1$ changes equilibrium y from y_0 to y_1, and that the relationship of the change in y, $\Delta y = y_1 - y_0$, to the initial change in investment $\Delta\bar{i} = \bar{i}_1 - \bar{i}_0$, depends on the slope of the $s + t$ schedule. The change in y is $\Delta y = y_1 - y_0$; the initial change in investment is $\Delta\bar{i} = \bar{i}_1 - \bar{i}_0$. *The ratio* $\Delta y/\Delta i$, which gives the change in equilibrium y per unit change in $\bar{i}$, is the *multiplier* for investment expenditure. Here we will develop the multipliers for changes in investment and government purchases, and also for shifts in the tax schedule, beginning with the simplest economy in which taxes are levied as lump-sum amounts, not sensitive to the level of income. This analytical abstraction would be observed, for example, in an economy that raises public revenue only from a head tax.

Lump-sum taxes

In order to make the analytics of the multiplier process as clear as possible, we begin with a case where tax revenues are a fixed sum, $\bar{t}$. This is the real tax revenue to be collected, regardless of the level of income.

In Figure 3.8, the slope of the $s + \bar{t}$ line is simply s', the marginal propensity to save out of disposable income. This is because we are here assuming taxes are fixed; so, for example, a $100 increase in income becomes a $100 increase in disposable income of which the fraction s' is saved. Suppose now that from the initial equilibrium position in Figure 3.8, with investment $\bar{i}_0$ and income y_0, investment increases by $\Delta\bar{i}$. This shifts the $\bar{i} + g$ line up by that distance in Figure 3.8, moving equilibrium income to y_1. As we saw in Figure 3.7, the ratio of the income increase, $\Delta y = y_1 - y_0$, to the increase in investment $\Delta\bar{i}$ depends on the slope of the $s + \bar{t}$ line. The ratio $\Delta\bar{i}/\Delta y$ is equal to that slope, which in this case is simply s'. Thus in this case with taxes fixed, $\Delta\bar{i}/\Delta y = s'$, and the multiplier relationship is given by solving for Δy:

$$\Delta y = \frac{1}{s'} \Delta\bar{i}. \tag{14}$$

The *multiplier* that relates the final change in national income to the initial increase in investment is $1/s'$. If s' in this case were 0.2, the multiplier would be 5.

The multiplier can also be written as $1/(1 - c')$, since we saw earlier that $c' + s' = 1$. Thus if the marginal propensity to consume is 0.8 so that, with taxes fixed, 80 percent of an addition to income goes to consumption, the multiplier $1/(1 - c')$ is $1/0.2 = 5$. A $1 billion increase in investment demand will yield a $5 billion increase in income.

We can also view the multiplier in a dynamic setting as the sum of a stream of expenditure increases following from a $\Delta\bar{i}$ increase. When expenditure is first raised by $\Delta\bar{i}$, output rises directly by the amount $\Delta\bar{i}$, as more investment goods are produced, and the incomes of the factors producing them go up. With taxes fixed, the *net* income of these factors rises by $\Delta\bar{i}$. But they, in turn, spend $c' \cdot \Delta\bar{i}$—in the previous example, 0.8 $\Delta\bar{i}$—for groceries, shoes, and so on, so that the output and income of the grocers go up by $c' \cdot \Delta\bar{i}$. This adds another term to the income increase generated by the initial investment change. Again, the recipients of this

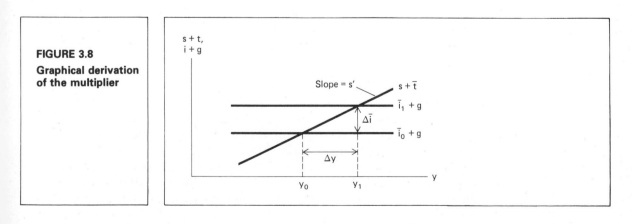

FIGURE 3.8

Graphical derivation of the multiplier

increment of spending $c' \cdot \Delta \bar{i}$ will spend c' of it, adding a term of $c'^2 \cdot \Delta \bar{i}$ to the income increase. This will go on indefinitely with the increments becoming smaller and smaller as c'^n tends toward zero as n gets large. The increase in output and income, Δy, given by this process is

$$\Delta y = \Delta \bar{i} + c' \Delta \bar{i} + c'(c' \Delta \bar{i}) + \cdots,$$

or

$$\Delta y = \Delta \bar{i} \cdot (1 + c' + c'^2 + c'^3 + \cdots). \tag{15}$$

From elementary algebra, we know that dividing $1 - c'$ into 1 will give us the expression in parentheses in equation (15), that is,

$$\frac{1}{1 - c'} = 1 + c' + c'^2 + c'^3 + \cdots,$$

so that we can replace the expansion term in equation (15) by $1/(1 - c')$ to obtain the multiplier given in equation (14) with $1 - c' = s'$. We can now understand why the ratio $\Delta y/\Delta i$ is called a *multiplier*. The equilibrium increase in y is a *multiple* of the initial unit increase in i, as the exogenous increment in aggregate demand (here investment) is coupled with successive endogenous increments in consumer spending.

This is essentially all there is to the multiplier. It can be viewed as the result of a convergent expansion (or contraction) of income as the economy adjusts to an exogenous increase (or decrease) in expenditure, and it can be derived by careful consideration of the slope of the curve along which the economy adjusts from one equilibrium position to the next. In the rest of this section we first see what happens to the multiplier as we allow g and $\bar{t}$ to change and then look at a multiplier for tax *rate* changes. This manipulation of the basic equilibrium model should bring out a few interesting relationships and also make the reader more familiar with the type of analysis to be used in Part II.

A general expenditure multiplier

We have just seen that the multiplier giving the effect on national income of a change in investment expenditure, holding government spending and tax revenues fixed, is $1/s'$ or $1/(1 - c')$. It should be easy to see in Figure 3.8 that the same multiplier holds for an increase in government purchases g, holding investment and tax revenues fixed. Suppose in Figure 3.8 we replaced the $\Delta \bar{i}$ shift in the $\bar{i} + g$ line with a Δg shift of the same amount. This would shift the $\bar{i} + g$ line up as much as in Figure 3.8, giving the same y increase from y_0 to y_1. So the multiplier for government expenditure is the same as that for investment expenditure—$1/s'$.

This makes good intuitive sense. The key factor in each example is an exogenous increase in expenditure—in one case by business firms buying capital goods and in the other by the government. If the amounts of increase are the same in both cases, the outcome for national income should be the same. To take an easy example, compare the purchase of an additional \$1 million of automotive vehicles—trucks, cars, and so on—by industry with the same purchase by governments, holding tax revenues constant. The initial impact on the auto industry is the same in both cases, and the multiplier expansion should also be the same as workers spend extra earnings, and so on.

This line of argument should lead us to expect that something similar holds for the results of a tax cut. Suppose a tax cut reduces tax revenues by $\Delta \bar{t}$. With lump-sum taxes, this increases disposable income, $\Delta \bar{t}$, and consumer spending rises by $c' \cdot \Delta \bar{t}$. This increase in consumer spending, induced by the tax cut, will have the same multiplier effect on national income as the other kinds of exogenous expenditure changes. That is, if tax revenues are reduced by $\Delta \bar{t}$ and consumer spending as a result initially rises by $c' \cdot \Delta \bar{t}$, the resulting increase in y is given by

$$\Delta y = \frac{1}{s'} (c' \cdot \Delta \bar{t}).$$

To go back to the previous example, if a tax cut induces consumers to spend an additional $1 million on autos, the net result for national income should be the same as if business or government bought the additional autos. If the initial expenditure change is the same in all three cases, the final result for the change in y should be the same, that is, the multiplier is the same, regardless of where the expenditure change originated.

The multiplier for tax changes is shown in Figure 3.9. The tax reduction shifts the $s + \bar{t}$ line down, but not by the entire tax cut $\Delta \bar{t}$. Why not? The tax reduction $\Delta \bar{t}$ increases disposable income by the same amount, increasing saving by $s' \cdot \Delta \bar{t}$. Thus the sum of saving and tax revenues at the initial income level is decreased by $\Delta \bar{t} - s' \cdot \Delta \bar{t} = (1 - s) \Delta \bar{t} = c' \cdot \Delta \bar{t}$, as shown.

The ratio of this initial shift in $s + \bar{t}$ to the resulting change in y is as usual given by the slope of the $s + \bar{t}$ line: $-c' \Delta \bar{t} / \Delta y = s'$. So the multiplier of the initial expenditure effect of the tax cut, $-c' \cdot \Delta \bar{t}$, on y is given by $1/s'$.

The general point here is that the multiplier for an initial expenditure change, whether exogenous or induced by some policy action, is going to

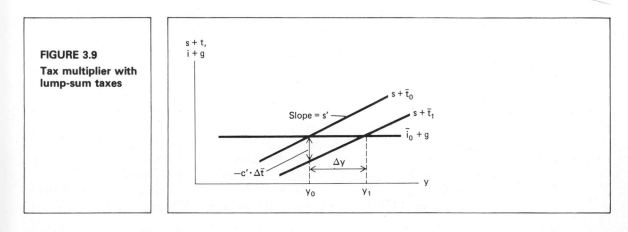

FIGURE 3.9

Tax multiplier with lump-sum taxes

be the same as that for any other initial expenditure change of the same amount, at least in the simple models we are dealing with at this stage. Once we know the size of the initial change in expenditure, $\Delta \bar{i}$, Δg, or $-c' \cdot \Delta \bar{t}$ induced by a tax change, it is multiplied by $1/s'$ to get the effect on income, with lump-sum taxes.

The balanced budget multiplier

One interesting application of the general expenditure multipliers is the theorem of the balanced budget multiplier. This theorem says that if government purchases and tax revenues are increased by the same amount, $\Delta g = \Delta \bar{t}$, with investment held constant, national income will rise by the amount of the government purchase increase. The name of the theorem comes from the fact that this is a balanced *change* in the budget; whatever the initial surplus or deficit, it is unchanged by this move.

This theorem follows directly from the expenditure multipliers. Suppose both g and $\bar{t}$ are increased by the same amount, $\Delta g = \Delta \bar{t}$. The g increase alone would increase NI by the multiplier $1/s' = 1/(1 - c')$. The tax increase would give an initial reduction in consumer spending of $-c' \cdot \Delta \bar{t}$, and this taken alone would reduce NI by the same multiplier. Summing these two effects gives the net change in national income:

$$\Delta y = \frac{1}{1 - c'} \Delta g - \frac{1}{1 - c'} c' \Delta \bar{t} = \frac{1}{1 - c'} \Delta g - \frac{c'}{1 - c'} \Delta \bar{t}.$$

If $\Delta g = \Delta \bar{t}$, then this effect is

$$\Delta y = \frac{1}{1 - c'} \Delta g - \frac{c'}{1 - c'} \Delta g = \frac{1 - c'}{1 - c'} \Delta g = \Delta g.$$

The increase in y equals the increase in g (and $\bar{t}$), so the multiplier for a balanced change in the budget, holding investment constant, is unity ($\Delta y/\Delta g = 1$).

One explanation for this comes from the income expansion chains considered earlier. In the case of government purchases, Δg raises national income by the amount Δg *directly* and then *indirectly* through the multiplier chain, giving a Δy effect of

$$\Delta y = \Delta g \cdot (1 + c' + c'^2 + \cdots).$$

But the tax increase only enters national income when the cut in disposable income by $\Delta \bar{t}$ reduces consumer expenditure by $c' \Delta \bar{t}$. Thus, the Δy effect of the tax increase is given by

$$\Delta y = -\Delta \bar{t} \cdot (c' + c'^2 + \cdots).$$

The difference between the two, which gives the net effect on y, is Δg ($= \Delta \bar{t}$), since the initial direct increase in NI is missing from the tax multiplier. A \$10 billion increase in g has an immediate \$10 billion impact on national income, while a \$10 billion increase in $\bar{t}$ affects NI only after consumers reduce their spending in reaction to the change.

This result, surprising as it is at first glance, makes good intuitive sense. The driving force behind the multiplier is that as output increases in response to demand this generates additional disposable income and hence additional demand. In the case where output responds to an increase in government demand *and* taxes increase by an equal amount, there is no increase in disposable income and no induced increase in demand. The multiplier chain is cut off after the first round.

Next we can return to the original specification of the tax function, which is $t = t(y)$; tax revenues are an increasing function of income. In this more realistic case, the basic equilibrium condition for income determination is

$$c(y - t(y)) + \bar{i} + g = y = c(y - t(y)) + s(y)) + t(y), \qquad [16]$$

and subtracting $c(y - t(y))$ from each part of equation (16) gives us the alternative form

$$\bar{i} + g = y - c(y - t(y)) = s(y - t(y)) + t(y). \qquad [17]$$

The $s + t = i + g$ diagram of Figure 3.10 shows the determination of equilibrium income in this case, as compared with the previous analysis with tax revenues fixed.

Earlier, in expression (12), we saw that the slope of the $s + t$ function with tax revenues dependent on income is $s' \cdot (1 - t') + t'$, where t' is the slope of the tax function alone. In this case, if investment rises by $\Delta \bar{i} = \bar{i}_1 - \bar{i}_0$ in Figure 3.10, the ratio of the investment increase $\Delta \bar{i}$ and the resulting increase in national income Δy is $s' \cdot (1 - t') + t'$, combining the slopes of the saving and tax functions. The multiplier, as usual, is given by

$$\Delta y = \frac{1}{s' \cdot (1 - t') + t'} \Delta \bar{i}.$$

This same multiplier would hold for any other exogenous or direct policy-induced change in expenditure. It should be clear that the multiplier here is less than the simple $1/s'$ in the case with fixed tax revenues. The denominator of the multiplier expression is $s' - s't' + t' = s' + t'(1 - s')$. This is larger than s' as long as the marginal propensity to save is less than unity.

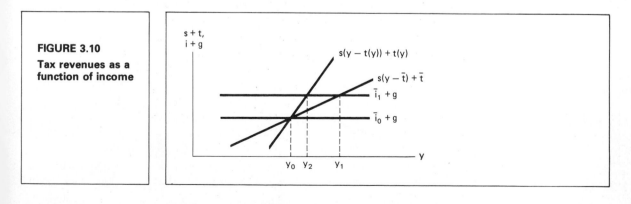

FIGURE 3.10

Tax revenues as a function of income

Introducing a tax function has *reduced* the multiplier. As tax revenue rises with income (with fixed tax *rates*), the increase in disposable income which a person can either save or spend is smaller than the increase in total income. A little is thus siphoned off of each round of expenditure by the existence of the tax schedule, thereby reducing the size of the multiplier.

With tax revenue fixed at $\bar{t}$ in Figure 3.10, an increase in investment demand from i_0 to i_1 raises equilibrium income from y_0 to y_1. If tax revenues are an increasing function of income, that is, $t = t(y)$, then the same $\bar{i}$ increase only raises y to y_2 from y_0. The presence of the tax function reduces the increases in disposable income relative to those in total income at each stage in the expansion, reducing the eventual increase in y from y_1 to y_2 in Figure 3.10. The tax system thus functions as a *built-in stabilizer*, reducing the changes in income that are induced by exogenous changes in investment. If investment demand had shifted down, the steeper $s(y - t(y)) + t(y)$ function would have cushioned the fall in y since disposable income would fall less than total income with a reduction in tax payments.

The tax rate multiplier

To conclude our discussion of multipliers, we can develop the multiplier for a *tax rate* change. This is the model most relevant to stabilization policy decisions involving tax changes; the government controls the tax rates, and their relation to the state of the economy determines the level of tax revenues.

Here we simplify the tax function by assuming that tax revenues are proportional to income, so that $t(y) = \tau y$, where τ is a proportional tax rate, such as, perhaps, 20 percent. This proportional tax schedule is shown in Figure 3.11.

Now suppose the government reduces the tax rate, say from 0.20 to 0.18. This 10 percent variation in the rate is about the order of magnitude that we have seen in the United States in the 1960s and 1970s. To see what happens to national income, we first go back to the tax multiplier discussed earlier (p. 45). There we saw that once we calculate the initial effect on consumption spending, the multiplier is the same as for any other expenditure change, $1/[s'(1 - t') + t']$ with tax revenues endogenous. With the proportional tax function $t(y) = \tau y$, the slope t' is given by τ.

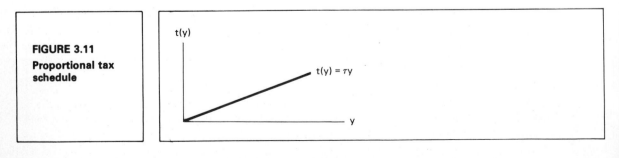

FIGURE 3.11
Proportional tax schedule

$t(y)$

$t(y) = \tau y$

y

Thus in this special case the expenditure multiplier is $1/[s'(1 - \tau) + \tau]$, replacing t' by τ.

The change in tax *rates* changes tax revenues by the change in rate times income: if national income is $1 billion and the tax rate changes by 0.02, the change in revenues at the initial income level is $20 million. Thus the initial change in revenues, equal to the change in disposable income, is $y \cdot \Delta\tau$ where τ is the proportional tax rate. The initial change in consumption spending is then $-c' \cdot y \cdot \Delta\tau$, the disposable income change times the marginal propensity to consume. Note that the minus sign converts a tax cut ($\Delta\tau$ is negative) to a spending increase. Putting this through the expenditure multiplier with tax revenues proportional to income gives

$$\Delta y = \frac{1}{s'(1 - \tau) + \tau} (c'y \, \Delta\tau)$$

for the resulting change in national income. Again, the expression $-c'y \, \Delta\tau$ simply gives the exogenous consumer expenditure change, analogous to $\Delta\bar{i}$ and Δg changes, that comes from a tax rate change. If tax rates are raised by $\Delta\tau$, then $(-y \, \Delta\tau)$ gives the drop in disposable income that comes directly from the tax change, and c' times $-y \, \Delta\tau$ gives the direct effect on consumer expenditure. This is a direct, policy-induced change in consumer expenditure c, as opposed to the endogenous changes that result from changes in income with a given tax structure. From this point on, we refer to this type of expenditure change, which comes as a *direct* effect of a policy change before any adjustment to a changing level of income is considered, as a *policy-induced* change in expenditure. Thus, the tax rate multiplier just translates a tax rate change into a direct impact on consumer spending and then multiplies it by the usual multiplier, $1/[s'(1 - t') + t']$. The difference between the multipliers is in the source of the exogenous expenditure change.

CONCLUSION TO PART I These introductory three chapters have reviewed the basics of income determination as they generally appear under the name "Keynesian model" in introductory texts. This chapter has shown the changes in equilibrium income and output that follow changes in investment demand, savings behavior, government purchases, and tax rates in a world in which investment is given exogenously, the money supply plays no role, and real output y can change with no effect on the price level P. In Part II we first introduce the money supply and interest rates and then the labor market and the price level. At each additional level of complexity we will pause to reassess the effects of policy changes on these key variables.

QUESTIONS FOR DISCUSSION AND REVIEW **1.** "Savings must always equal investment. Consequently, an increase in the desire to save will lead to an increase in investment and an increase in national income." Evaluate this statement.

2. Many continue to believe a balanced increase in the government's budget will leave equilibrium output unchanged. They reason that if the government gives with one hand (increased government spending) what it takes away with the other (increased taxes), the equilibrium flow of income should be unchanged. Why would you disagree with this logic?

3. Assume that the marginal propensity to consume is .9 and that taxes do not vary with the level of income. How would an increase of 10 in investment alter equilibrium income? If a new tax system is introduced in which taxes always equal ⅓ of the national income, how would your answer to the above change?

4. Contrast the impact on national output of a national policy to provide every low income citizen with $50 worth of food each week and a policy that provides $50 directly with which to buy food.

5. A given change in national income can be accomplished by a change in government spending or by a change in taxes, albeit larger and with the opposite sign. On what basis do you feel a policy maker might choose between these policies?

SELECTED READINGS   R. G. D. Allen, *Macroeconomic Theory* (New York: St. Martin's Press, 1967), chaps. 1–2.

W. A. Salant, "Taxes, Income Determination, and the Balanced Budget Theorem," in R. A. Gordon and L. R. Klein, eds., *Readings in Business Cycles* (Homewood, Ill.: Irwin, 1965).

P. A. Samuelson, "The Simple Mathematics of Income Determination," in *Income, Employment, and Public Policy: Essays in Honor of Alvin Hansen,* reproduced in M. G. Mueller, ed., *Readings in Macroeconomics* (New York: Holt, Rinehart and Winston, 1971).

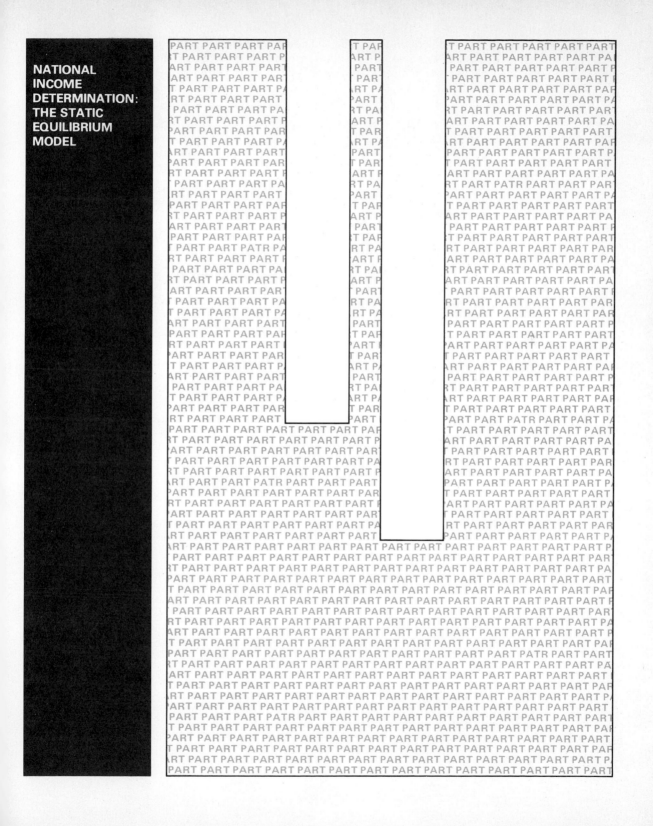

NATIONAL
INCOME
DETERMINATION:
THE STATIC
EQUILIBRIUM
MODEL

CHAPTER CHAPTER CHAPTER CHAPTER CH
HAPTER CHAPTER CHAPTER CHAPTER CHA
HAPTER CHAPTER CHAPTER CHA
IAPTER CHAPTER CHAPTER CHA
HAPTER CHAPTER CHAPTER CHAPTER CH
APTER CHAPTER CHAPTER CHAPTER CH
HAPTER CHAPTER CHAPTER CHAPTER CH
HAPTER CHAPTER CHAPTER CHAPTER CHA
APTER CHAPTER CHAPTER CHAPTER CHA
HAPTER CHAPTER CHAPTER CHAPTER CHA
HAPTER CHAPTER CHAPTER CHAPTER CHA
HAPTER CHAPTER CHAPTER CHAPTER CH
HAPTER CHAPTER CHAPTER CHAPTER CHA
APTER CHAPTER CHAPTER CHAPTER CHA
HAPTER CHAPTER CHAPTER CHAPTER CH
APTER CHAPTER CHAPTER CHAPTER CHAP
HAPTER CHAPTER CHAPTER CHAPTER CH
APTER CHAPTER CHAPTER CHAPTER CHAP
APTER CHAPTER CHAPTER CHAPTER CHAP

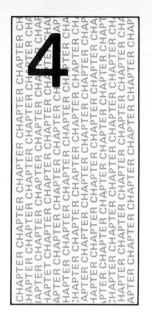

4

DEMAND-SIDE EQUILIBRIUM: INCOME AND THE INTEREST RATE

In Part II we develop, step by step, the basic model of income determination. This shows how the price level, the interest rate, and the levels of output and employment are determined in an economy that typically operates with more or less full employment. Most of the industrial economies of North America, Europe, and Japan fit into this category. The various pieces of this model—the consumption function, the investment function, and so on—are kept as simple as possible here, so that we can focus on how the various sectors of the economy interact. Further investigation of the details of these various sectors, then, is the subject of Part III.

Since macroeconomics is really just aggregated microeconomics—the trick being to aggregate the zillions of micro activities and markets in a way that improves our understanding of how the economy works—it is only natural that we approach determination of equilibrium values of the interest rate, the price level, output, and employment by identifying supply and demand functions in the various markets and then finding equilibrium price and quantity in each. What we find, as we might expect, is that changing conditions in one market, for example, shifting the demand for money, changes the outcomes in the other markets—equilibrium output and employment, for example. The point of Part II is to see just how this system hangs together.

In this chapter we develop the *demand side* of the economy. This involves finding the equilibrium values of the interest rate and of *output demanded* by consumers, business, and government, given the price level. At the end of the chapter, we are able to develop a *demand curve* for the economy that shows how these equlibrium demand-side variables change as the price level changes.

53

After introducing monetary and fiscal policy and its effect on demand conditions in the economy, we then go on to develop, in Chapter 6, the *supply side* of the economy. This shows how the equilibrium values of *output produced* and employment are determined, again given the price level. Varying the price level then gives us an economy-wide *supply curve*. Combining the demand curve and the supply curve in Chapter 7 then gives us the equilibrium price level which equates the quantity of output demanded, from the demand side, to that produced, on the supply side.

This can all be put very simply in mathematical terms. On the demand side we have two equations, expressing equilibrium conditions in the *product* and *money* markets, in three variables: the level of income (or real national product) y; the interest rate r; and the price level P. On the supply side we have two equations, a production function and a labor market equilibrium condition, in three variables: y, P, and the level of employment N. Combining these gives us four equations in four variables: y, N, P, and r. The task of Part II is to expose, as simply as possible, the relationships between these variables (the equations) and just how their equilibrium values are determined.

EQUILIBRIUM INCOME AND THE INTEREST RATE IN THE PRODUCT MARKET

In Chapter 3 we reviewed the simplest model of income determination, in which both the price level and the level of investment are taken as given. That model is essentially one equilibrium condition—total expenditure as a function of income equals income—in one variable, income. This equilibrium condition can be written as an equation:

$$y = c(y - t(y)) + i + g, \qquad\qquad [1]$$

or

$$y - c = s(y - t(y)) + t(y) = i + g,$$

where y is real GNP, c is real consumer expenditure as a function of real disposable income, and s is real saving, t is real tax revenue as a function of real GNP, i is real investment demand, and g is real government purchases of goods and services.

Investment demand and the interest rate

In equation (1) each element is at a *planned* level. Thus, i is the level of *planned* fixed investment and inventory investment. In Chapter 3, we took i as exogeneously given. Now we turn to the question of what determines investment i. To begin with, we can speculate that the level of fixed investment planned by a firm might depend on the market interest rate, r. Intuitively this seems reasonable because, in order to invest, a firm must either borrow or use its own funds. In either case, the cost of borrowing can be measured by the interest rate the firm has to pay or to forego receiving in case it uses its own funds.

In deciding whether to invest in a given project, a firm can utilize a concept known as the *present discounted value* (PDV) of future income from the investment. To compute the *PDV* of any investment project, a firm discounts the project's stream of future net returns or net incomes, R_t, by the rate of interest r and weighs the discounted value of this stream, that is, $R_{t+i}/(1 + r)^i$, and so on, against the cost, C, of the project, using the formula

$$PDV_t = -C + R_t + \frac{R_{t+1}}{1 + r} + \frac{R_{t+2}}{(1 + r)^2} + \cdots + \frac{R_{t+n}}{(1 + r)^n}. \qquad [2]$$

In this calculation of the present value of the future income stream, the interest rate r is used in evaluating the "worth" of each future return at the present time. For example, if A were to offer B $108, payable in one year, in exchange for cash now, B would have to decide how much that $108 a year from now is worth to him now. If he knew that he could lend money in the market and receive a 8 percent return on it, he would decide that $108 in one year is worth $100 now. Therefore, he would give A $100 now in exchange for $108 in a year. This is his way of valuing future payments at the present time. This can be expressed mathematically as in equation (2).

PDV of $108 now: $\quad PDV_t = \dfrac{\$108}{1.08} = \dfrac{R_{t+1}}{1 + r}.$

If the money were to be returned in two years, the present discounted value of this repayment would be

$$PDV_t = \frac{R_{t+2}}{(1 + r)^2},$$

and so on. It can be seen that the further in the future B expects to be paid, the less that payment is worth to him now.

This description simplifies reality somewhat. In the first place, returns (R's) are *expected future returns*. While we take these as given, in reality future returns will vary with changes in current business conditions. This additional complication is added in Chapter 11, where we discuss investment demand in more detail. Furthermore, a firm is faced, in reality, with several interest rates in different kinds of bond and securities markets. These different interest rates, however, will probably move together when there are changes in monetary conditions so that for simplicity we can treat them as one generalized interest rate r.

Now firms can rank various projects in order of their *PDV*'s, as shown in Figure 4.1. With an elastic supply of investment funds, firms will invest in all projects with a positive *PDV* (that is, having positive net returns). This would push the level of investment shown in Figure 4.1 to i_0. If a firm had only limited investment funds, it would invest them in the most productive projects (highest *PDV*'s) until its funds ran out, at a point somewhere to the left of i_0.

Thus, in Figure 4.1, applying the *PDV* formula of equation (2) to its potential investment projects using r_0, the firm comes to an investment

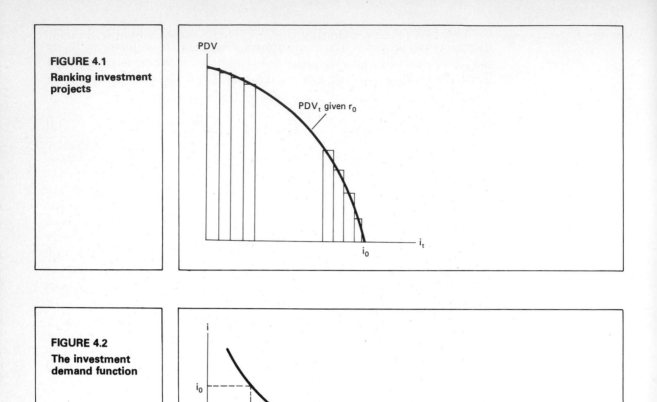

FIGURE 4.1

Ranking investment projects

FIGURE 4.2

The investment demand function

level i_0. If the interest rate were higher, all the entries in the PDV formula for each project would have a larger denominator, so the PDV of each project would be smaller. So as interest rates rise, all PDV's fall and the PDV curve of Figure 4.1 shifts down, reducing the level of planned investment.

This gives us the simplest investment model,

$$i = i(r),$$ [3]

with investment falling as the interest rate rises, as shown in Figure 4.2. Increasing the interest rate r from r_0 to r_1 reduces the level of planned investment i from i_0 to i_1. Now, substituting the investment function (3) into the original equilibrium equation gives us the product market equilibrium condition,

$$y = c(y - t(y)) + g + i(r).$$ [4]

Derivation of the IS curve

Equation (4) now describes pairs of y and r values which will maintain equilibrium in what we will call the "product market." Any given value of r will determine a level of investment i, and this will in turn determine an equilibrium level of income y. We can analyze the nature of these equilibrium pairs of y and r graphically. Figure 4.3(a) is by now familiar, with a fixed level of i + g and with s + t increasing with the level of income. From Figure 4.2 we know that an increase in r from r_0 to r_1 will cause a decrease in i; this decrease is represented in Figure 4.3(a) as a downward shift in the i(r) + g line by the amount $\Delta i = i_1 - i_0$. At the original level of i(r) + g, with r = r_0, equilibrium income was at y_0. With the increase in r to r_1, equilibrium shifts to y_1, a lower level of income, due to the drop in planned investment. This relationship between equilibrium r and y can be represented directly as shown in Figure 4.3(b). As the interest rate r rises, the level of investment in Figure 4.3(a) falls, reducing equilibrium income through the multiplier. Thus, the line describing equilibrium pairs of r and y must be negatively sloped, as in Figure 4.3(b). This curve, showing equilibrium r, y points in the product market, is labeled IS. It describes the infinite number of r, y combinations that maintain equality between planned i + g and planned s + t. The label IS comes from the fact that along this curve, planned *investment* equals planned *saving*, including both private sector and government. In the product market we have a whole series of equilibrium income levels, each corre-

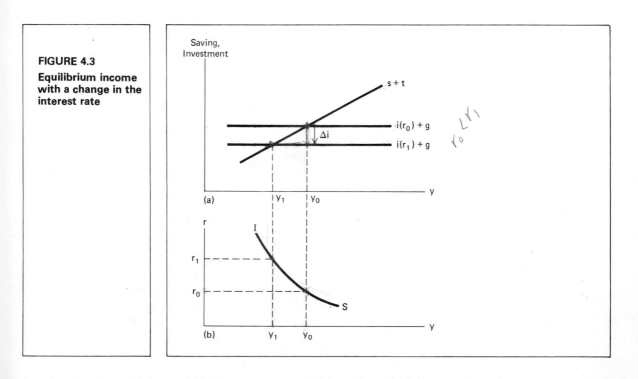

FIGURE 4.3

Equilibrium income with a change in the interest rate

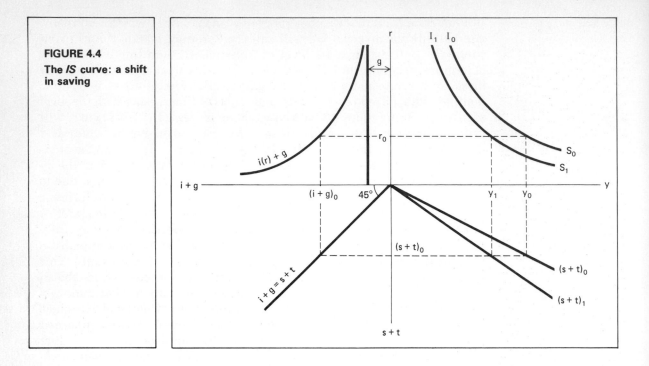

FIGURE 4.4

The *IS* curve: a shift in saving

sponding to a given interest rate. We cannot find the equilibrium value for r or y without positing a value for the other.

All of the relationships which contribute to the location of equilibrium pairs of r and y in the product market are summarized in the four-quadrant diagram in Figure 4.4. The southeast quadrant in Figure 4.4 is an "upside down" version of a graph similar to that shown in Figure 4.3(a) giving saving plus tax revenues as a function of income. In the northwest quadrant we have plotted government spending, which is fixed by the budget and therefore a vertical line, plus investment, which is a decreasing function of r. The $i(r)$ line is similar to the one shown in Figure 4.2, but rotated 90°. The values of g and $i(r)$ are summed horizontally in this quadrant to give the $i(r) + g$ lines, which represent total expenditure on i plus g as a function of r. In the southwest quadrant we have drawn a 45° line from the origin. This line is used to equate $s + t$ from the southeast quadrant to $i + g$ in the northwest quadrant. It thus directly represents the equilibrium condition in the product market, given by equation (1).

It is the line in the northeast quadrant, the *IS* curve, representing equilibrium pairs of r and y, which we can now derive from these three other relationships. If we choose a level of income on the y-axis, we can trace through the three quadrants following the dashed line to locate the equilibrium interest rate for that level of income. For example, at income y_0 in equilibrium we would have planned $s + t$ at $(s + t)_0$. To generate an equal amount of $(i + g)_0$ the interest rate would have to be at r_0. This can be done for any level of y to give a corresponding level of r. Or, conversely, we could take the level of r as given and locate the equilibrium income level associated with that interest rate.

In other words, *the IS curve represents the pairs of r and y that will keep the product market in equilibrium, in the sense that planned investment plus government purchases equal planned saving plus tax revenue.*

Shifting the *IS* curve

The four-quadrant diagram is useful for studying the effects of changes in exogenous variables like g, or shifts in the investment, saving, or tax functions, on the product market equilibrium r and y levels.

For example, an increase in the desire to save, that is, a decrease in consumption demand at any given income level, can be shown as a downward rotation of the $s + t$ function to the $(s + t)_1$ function in Figure 4.4. This gives a higher level of $s + t$ for any given y. At the original level of the interest rate r_0, and planned $(i + g)_0$, this decrease in consumption demand will reduce equilibrium income through the multiplier process. Graphically, at the initial equilibrium r_0 and thus the initial level of $i + g$, with the new $s + t$ function we will trace out a new, lower equilibrium y_1 in Figure 4.4. Thus, the increase in the desire to save, reducing total demand at any given interest rate level, has shifted the *IS* curve to the left, giving a lower equilibrium y for any given r, or lower equilibrium r for any given y.

As another example of the use of the *IS* four-quadrant diagram, consider the effects of increasing government purchases, g, on the equilibrium r, y pairs, shown in Figure 4.5. The increase in g can be shown as an

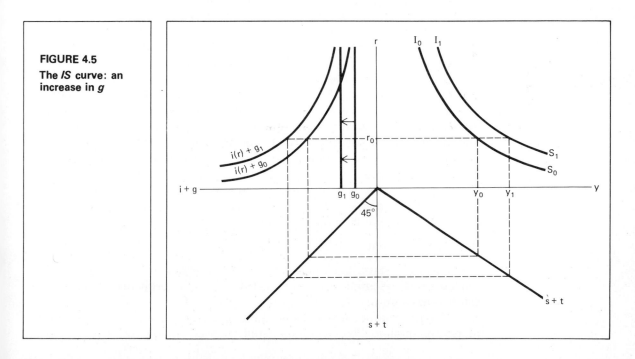

FIGURE 4.5

The *IS* curve: an increase in *g*

outward shift in the $i + g$ function in the northwest quadrant. This increase in g, as we saw in Chapter 3, will increase y through the multiplier, assuming investment is unchanged. Thus, in Figure 4.5, the increase in g from g_0 to g_1 ($= \Delta g$) would raise y from y_0 to y_1 ($= \Delta y$) at the initial interest rate r_0. Since $i = i(r)$, holding r constant here holds i constant.

For any initial level of r, the g increase has increased equilibrium y, shifting the IS curve to the right, as shown in Figure 4.5. At any given r, implying again an unchanged i, the ratio of the increase in y to the increase in g, $\Delta y / \Delta g$, is simply the government purchases multiplier of Chapter 3.

EQUILIBRIUM INCOME AND THE INTEREST RATE IN THE MONEY MARKET

So far we have developed one equilibrium condition in two variables, y and r, which gives us an infinity of potential equilibrium points known as the IS curve. In order to be able to locate a single equilibrium level of income and the interest rate we need another relationship between the same two variables. This relationship, or equation, can then be solved simultaneously with our product market equilibrium condition. In order to obtain this second equation we will now introduce the *money market*.

We begin by defining money, M, as currency in circulation plus demand deposits, that is, checking account deposits in commercial banks. A more thorough and detailed analysis of the money supply is to be found in Chapter 13. Both kinds of money share the features of being an accepted medium of exchange and bringing no return, that is, earning no interest. On the other hand, most other kinds of assets, which we will lump into a general category called *bonds*, do bring a return to the holder and cannot be used directly as a medium of exchange. Wealth is thus defined as consisting of two categories, money and bonds, and a person chooses the allocation of his wealth between money and bonds.

Demand for money and real balances

The money market has, like all other markets, both a demand side and a supply side. We will first examine the demand side. Since a person allocates his wealth between money and bonds, we might expect that an increase in the interest rate, or the rate of return on bonds, would tempt him to put more of his assets into bonds and less into money. Conversely, a decrease in the interest rate should induce him to shift some assets out of bonds and into money.

This inclination to hold more or less money depending on the interest rate on bonds we will call the *speculative demand* for money, based on a *speculative motive* for holding money:

Speculative demand $\equiv l(r)$.

Hence l might stand for *liquidity preference*, as discussed in Chapter 12. Because the speculative demand for money will probably go down as interest rates go up, l' is negative.

There is another reason to hold money, creating another kind of demand for money. People hold money in order to bridge the time gap between their receipt of income and the payments they have to make, for example, to smooth out the difference between monthly pay checks and daily payments for food and other items. As incomes rise, income and expenditure streams both grow, and these balances held to smooth out the cash flow must also grow. Therefore, this second kind of demand for money, which we call a *transactions demand*, increases with the level of income, or

Transactions demand $\equiv k(y)$,

and k' is positive.

Both components of the demand for money, the transactions demand and the speculative demand, should be stated as demand for real money balances, $M/P = m$. This is fairly evident in the transactions balance case. Suppose with a given real income y, the price level P doubles overnight so that money income Y and money expenditures also double. In this case, we should expect the transactions demand for money balances M also to double, since the money transactions these balances are financing have doubled. Thus, the transactions demand $k(y)$ is for *real* balances; the demand for *money* balances is $P \cdot k(y)$.

Speculative demand should also be a demand for real balances. This is a little less obvious than the transactions balance case, but perhaps the following thought experiment will make things clear. Suppose one night you go to bed holding a given amount of money depending on present interest rates and your expectations concerning the bond market. Overnight the government changes currency units from old francs to new francs, with 10 old francs = 1 new franc. When you wake up in the morning, you find your salary is now 1,000 new francs, where it was previously 10,000 old francs, all prices in new francs are $1/10$ of old franc prices, and your new franc money balances are $1/10$ of their old franc value. Is there any reason for you to change your demand for money? No. All prices, incomes, and wealth values have changed proportionately, reduced to $1/10$ their former values. Nothing real has changed.

But this is the same as if the price level just changed overnight by the same amount! With all prices changed, your income, in (new) money terms, is smaller, your expenditures are smaller, and your wealth is smaller; again, no real change has occurred. Thus, the speculative demand $l(r)$ is also a demand for real balances; the demand for money balances would be $P \cdot l(r)$.

Summing the two components of the demand for money, we have the demand function for real balances,

$$\frac{M}{P} = l(r) + k(y). \tag{5}$$

In general, we should recognize that the speculative and transactions demands cannot be separated. For example, as the interest rate on bonds rises, we would expect transactions balances to be reduced as people recognize the increasing opportunity cost of holding idle cash balances and squeeze them down. So the amount of transactions balances people hold should be sensitive to the interest rate. Thus, the demand-for-money function, in general, should be written as

$$\frac{M}{P} = m(r, y), \tag{6}$$

where the slope with respect to y is positive and the slope with respect to r is negative, removing the separation of speculative and transactions demands. We should point out here that the demand for money has been developed in a model with two assets, bonds and money. The problem facing the individual portfolio manager is to allocate his fixed wealth between the two assets. In this situation, the demand for bonds is simply the inverse of the demand for money. With wealth fixed, an increase in the interest rate that reduces the demand for money also increases the demand for bonds. Similarly an increase in income that increases the demand for money must also reduce the demand for bonds. Thus a reduction in the speculative demand for money implies an increase in the speculative demand for bonds; similarly for the transactions demand for money and bonds.

Figure 4.6 shows the money demand function of either equation (5) or (6). When we plot the demand for real balances against the interest rate r, we get a different curve for each level of income y. At any given level of y, say, y_0, which (more or less) fixed transactions demand, as r rises the speculative demand falls, reducing total demand. Also, at any given r, say, r_0, fixing speculative demand, as y rises transactions demand also rises, increasing total demand.

It may be useful here to discuss a bit the probable shape and curvature of the demand-for-money function. These will play an important role in the discussion of the relative effectiveness of monetary and fiscal policy in the next chapter. It also relates to the discussion in Chapter 7 of the infamous liquidity trap. At very high interest rate levels, money balances should

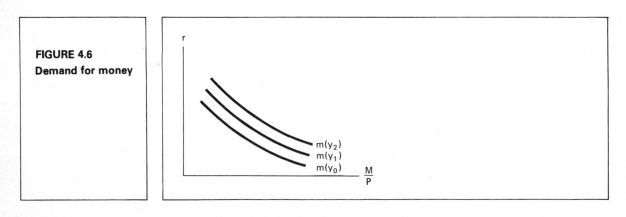

FIGURE 4.6
Demand for money

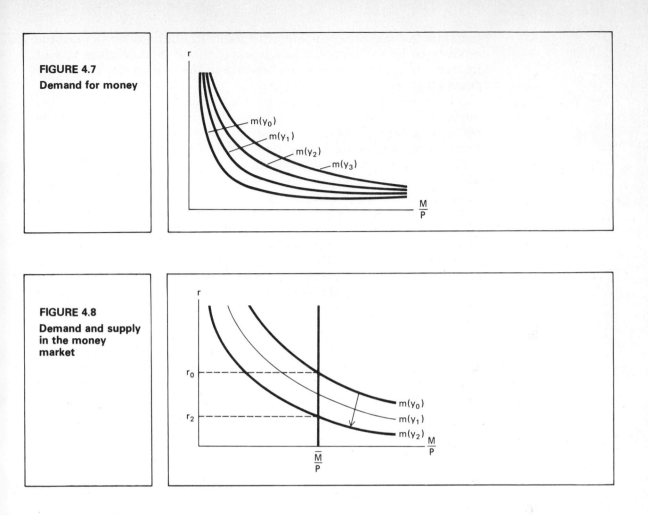

FIGURE 4.7
Demand for money

FIGURE 4.8
Demand and supply in the money market

be squeezed down to some irreducible minimum, giving a minimum demand for money with rising interest rates. At the other end, as interest rates fall lower and lower, people may become indifferent between holding, for example, 2 percent bonds and 0 percent money. Thus, the demand for money may become very flat at low interest rates. So the demand-for-money map of Figure 4.6 might be drawn as in Figure 4.7, with the demand curves converging at both extremely high and extremely low interest rate levels.

On the supply side of the money market, we will assume that the amount of currency and demand deposits in the economy are fixed by institutional arrangements between the commercial banking system and the Federal Reserve Board. This is discussed in much more detail in Chapter 13. Thus, the money supply is fixed exogenously: $M = \bar{M}$.

Figure 4.8 is a graphic representation of the demand and supply situation we have so far described. Given the price level, the real-money supply is fixed at the level $\bar{M}/P$. As in Figures 4.6 and 4.7, the demand for money is represented by the functions $m(y_0)$, $m(y_1)$, $m(y_2)$. At any given rate of interest, say r_2, the total demand depends on the level of income (in this case $y_0 > y_1 > y_2$).

From Figure 4.8 we see that as income falls from y_0 to y_1 to y_2, the money market equilibrium interest rate also falls, given the level of the real-money supply. When income drops off, there is a decrease in the transactions demand for money. Some present holders of money want to shift it into interest-earning bonds due to their lower transactions needs. This increase in demand in the bond market drives bond prices up and interest rates down. This happens because with bond coupon yields fixed in dollar amounts (a bond with face value of $100 may carry a $5/year coupon), an increase in bond prices produces a drop in their percentage yields, or interest rates. For example, a bond with a $5 coupon selling at $100 yields 5 percent. If the price rises to $125, the percentage yield falls to 4 percent. Thus, the excess supply of money at the old interest rate r_0 and the new income level y_2 drives interest rates down until supply equals demand at the new, lower, level of income y_2 and interest rate r_2.

Equating the money demand function to the exogenously fixed supply gives us the equilibrium condition in the money market:

$$\frac{\bar{M}}{P} = m(r,y) \approx l(r) + k(y). \tag{7}$$

For any given level of y and the supply of real balances $\bar{M}/P$, the money market equilibrium condition (7) gives us the interest rate that clears the money market. Separating the speculative and transactions balances gives us a convenient way to represent money market equilibrium in another four-quadrant diagram that summarizes the money market relationships we have just discussed.

Derivation of the *LM* curve

In the southeast quadrant of Figure 4.9, the line $k(y)$ gives transactions demand as an increasing function of income, measured downward. In the northwest quadrant is the curve representing the speculative demand as a function of the interest rate. This curve has a negative slope l', as we have seen in Figures 4.6 to 4.8. In the southwest quadrant we have used another geometric "trick," which represents the equilibrium condition (7), equating total supply of money to total demand. This time we have drawn a line between the transactions demand axis and the speculative demand axis, at a 45° angle to each axis. The line is drawn at a distance from the origin on each axis equal to the total exogenously given real-money supply, $\bar{M}/P_0$. Because of the geometric nature of the 45° triangle, the two components of demand always add up to the total money supply on each axis, so that this 45° line directly represents money market equilibrium condition (7). Any point on this 45° line gives a speculative component $l(r)$ plus a transactions component $k(y)$ which just add up to the total money supply.

FIGURE 4.9

The *LM* curve:
equilibrium *r* and *y*
in the money market

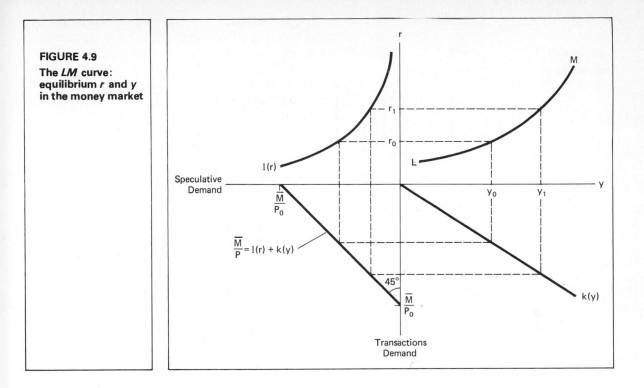

We can now locate in the northeast quadrant of Figure 4.9 the r, y pairs that maintain the money market in equilibrium. At a given level of income such as y_0 we can find the transactions component of the demand for money from the $k(y)$ function. By following the dashed line we subtract this from supply, $\bar{M}/P_0$, to see what level of the speculative component this implies if the money market is to be in equilibrium. This shows us, in turn, the level of interest rate r_0 that will maintain the money market in equilibrium with income level y_0. Having located one money market equilibrium pair, (r_0, y_0), we can locate another by beginning with y_1 in Figure 4.9. Repeating this process traces out the line that describes the set of r, y pairs that maintain money market equilibrium. This is the *LM* curve in Figure 4.9, giving r, y pairs where *liquidity* demand equals *money* supply.

Thus, we can see that *the LM curve represents the pairs of r and y that will keep the money market in equilibrium with a given level of the money supply, M, and a given price level, P.*

Shifting the *LM* curve

This four-quadrant diagram is useful in analyzing the effects of changes in exogenous variables or shifts in the speculative demand or transactions demand functions on the equilibrium values of r and y in the money market. Looking back to Figure 4.8, for example, we see that an increase in the money supply creates an excess supply of money at the old

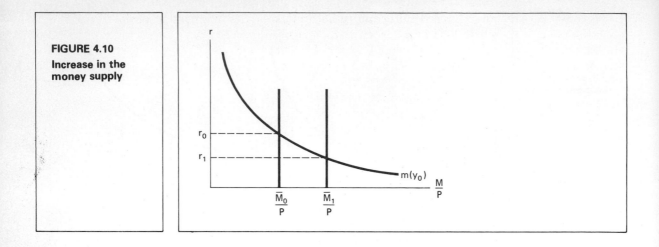

FIGURE 4.10

Increase in the money supply

level of income and interest rate. This excess supply pushes the equilibrium interest rate down, given the income level.

In terms of Figure 4.9, an increase in the money supply will shift the $\bar{M}/P_0$ line out. In Figure 4.10, at a given level of income y_0 and interest rate r_0, an increase in the money supply from $\bar{M}_0$ to $\bar{M}_1$ creates an excess supply of money. People will attempt to shift into interest-earning assets, that is, bonds, and hence exercise an upward pressure on bond prices. This, in turn, will have the effect of driving the interest rate down from r_0 to r_1 (see our discussion on p. 64). An increase in the real-money supply, therefore, would imply, for money market equilibrium, a lower interest rate at each income level and thus a shift to the right of the LM curve of Figure 4.9.

Here we should point out that a change in the price level, P, works symmetrically opposite to a change in the money supply, $\bar{M}$. For example, an increase in P reduces the supply of real balances, shifting the $\bar{M}/P$ line in Figure 4.10 to the left and the $\bar{M}/P$ line in Figure 4.9 in toward the origin. This reduction in the real-money supply creates excess demand in the money market at the initial income and interest rate levels, causing interest rates to rise to clear the market. Thus, for any given level of income y, an increase in P raises the money market equilibrium r, shifting the LM curve to the left. This movement can be traced out in the four-quadrant diagram of Figure 4.9; it will play an important role in the derivation of the economy's demand curve later in this chapter.

EQUILIBRIUM IN THE PRODUCT AND MONEY MARKETS

We have now derived two pieces of geometric apparatus. One gives the equilibrium pairs of r and y in the product market—the IS curve—and the other gives the equilibrium pairs of r and y in the money market—the LM curve. By placing these two curves in the same quadrant, that is, by solving equations (4) and (6) simultaneously, we can find the single r, y pair that gives equilibrium in both markets, the intersection of the *IS* and *LM* curves. This is shown as r_0, y_0 in Figure 4.11.

Consider what happens if income and the interest rate are at a point other than the equilibrium point. At point r_1, y_1 in Figure 4.11, the product market is in equilibrium; r_1, y_1 is the *IS* curve. But this point lies off the *LM* curve; the money market is not in equilibrium. In the money market, r_1 is lower than the equilibrium r, given y_1, as shown in Figure 4.11. There is an excess demand for money at r_1. This means that people are trying to "buy" money, or sell bonds, and are finding it difficult to do so. In order to get money they have to offer a higher yield, or interest rate, on bonds. Thus, r begins to rise, throwing the product market out of equilibrium, that is, off the *IS* curve. In the product market this rising r reduces investment demand and final sales. Thus, the product market is thrown into disequilibrium, inventories accumulate, producers slow down production, and income falls. As r is rising and y is falling the economy moves toward equilibrium r_0, y_0 in Figure 4.11.

This sequence can be shown as follows:

$$\begin{array}{l} \text{excess} \\ \text{demand in} \\ \text{money market} \end{array} \rightarrow \text{rising } r \rightarrow \text{falling } i \rightarrow \text{falling } y \rightarrow \begin{array}{l} \text{reduced} \\ \text{demand in} \\ \text{money market} \end{array}$$

In other words, we now have a dynamic process occurring in the background behind the equilibrium conditions. The excess demand in the money market directly raises the interest rate, and, through the investment function, indirectly reduces income. This, in turn, reduces the transactions demand for money, working to eliminate the initial excess demand. Eventually the economy settles toward the equilibrium r_0, y_0 point.

Effect of an increase in *g*

In the above example we assumed that the process began from a point of disequilibrium and moved toward equilibrium r_0, y_0. Now assume that

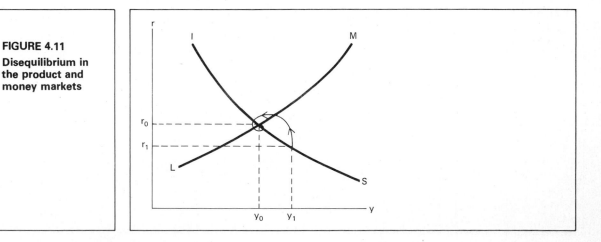

FIGURE 4.11

Disequilibrium in the product and money markets

4. DEMAND-SIDE EQUILIBRIUM: INCOME AND THE INTEREST RATE

we begin at an initial point of equilibrium and that the government decides to increase spending in order to raise incomes. By using a diagram such as Figure 4.5, we can see that this shifts the IS curve out, giving a higher product market equilibrium y for any given r. This shift is represented by the shift to I_1S_1 in Figure 4.12. At the initial level of the interest rate r_0, income begins to rise through the multiplier process. The increase in income causes an increase in the demand for transactions balances. This creates excess demand in the money market, raising r. First one market and then the other is thrown out of equilibrium causing a spiral effect as seen in Figure 4.11. Eventually, a new equilibrium is reached at r_1, y_1.

Because investment is a function of r and falls as r rises, the increase in equilibrium r leads to a reduction in equilibrium i. In other words, the increase in government spending causes a partial displacement or "crowding out" of private investment. This displacement is smaller than the magnitude of the original increase in g, because both r and y rise from their initial equilibrium position.

Another way to look at the effect of the increase in g is that the government decision to spend more means it will have to increase borrowing. It does this by selling government bonds. Because the money supply is fixed and the government raises the level of its demand for money, demand exceeds supply in the money market. Interest rates go up along with incomes and the movement shown in Figure 4.12 begins. We see in Figure 4.12 that equilibrium income goes up due to the increase in g. This means that more tax revenue will accrue to the government than at the earlier equilibrium level. This increase in tax revenue will cover part of the increased government expenditure, so that the amount the government borrows will be less than the increment to expenditure.

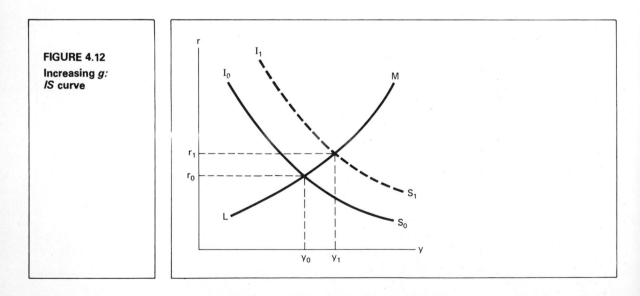

FIGURE 4.12

Increasing *g:*
IS curve

As an alternative to increasing g to increase income, the government might increase the money supply. By examination of Figure 4.9, we can see that this will result in an outward shift of the *LM* curve, which will move the economy toward lower interest rates at each level of income. The increase in the money supply therefore creates excess supply in the money market, pushing r down. This, in turn, increases investment demand, raising y. The increase in income will, of course, increase the demand for money. But the increase in demand will not offset the increased supply, so that interest rates will still go down. Thus, the main difference between the effects of increasing g or increasing M to raise the level of income in the economy is where the interest rate ends up. An increase in government spending raises interest rates, while an increase in the money supply lowers interest rates. For this reason, the two "tools"—fiscal policy changes in g or tax rates and monetary policy changes in M—are usually used together to achieve a desired mix of income expansion and control of interest rates. Chapter 5 looks at the effects of monetary and fiscal policy on the demand side of the economy in more detail. First, we will derive the economy's aggregate demand curve from the *IS-LM* apparatus.

INCOME AND THE PRICE LEVEL ON THE DEMAND SIDE

In the previous section we saw how the intersection of the *IS* and *LM* curves determines the equilibrium level of income and the interest rate, *given the price level* P_0. Now we can derive the economy's demand curve by varying P and seeing what happens to the equilibrium real income level, y.

The two equilibrium conditions we have developed so far, for the product and money markets, are

$$s(y - t(y)) + t(y) = i(r) + g \tag{8}$$

and

$$\frac{\bar{M}}{P} = l(r) + k(y). \tag{9}$$

There are two equations in three variables, y, r, and P. In the *IS-LM* analysis we assumed P to be given exogenously, eliminating one variable, and then solved for the equilibrium values of y and r at the intersection of the *IS* curve—equation (8)—and the *LM* curve—equation (9).

To analyze the effects of price level changes on equilibrium y on the demand side of the economy we can use Figure 4.13. This reproduces the money market four-quadrant diagram behind the *LM* curve and then superimposes on it the *IS* curve of equation (8) to locate equilibrium r_0, y_0, given the initial price level P_0. We use the complete *LM* diagram with a given *IS* curve here because the price level P does not enter into equation (8), the *IS* product-market equilibrium condition, but it does enter equation (9). Thus, a change in P will not affect the position of the *IS* curve in this model, but it will shift the *LM* curve.

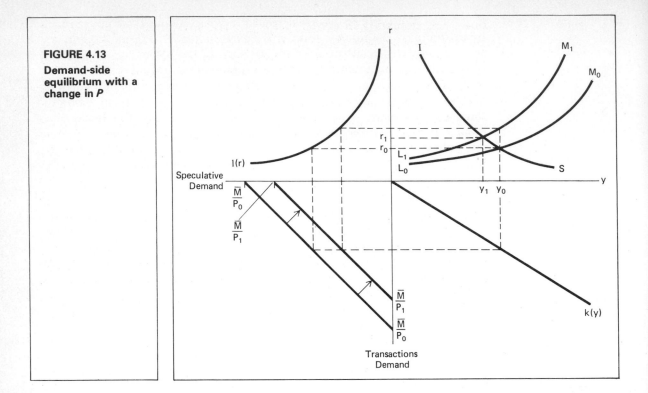

FIGURE 4.13

Demand-side equilibrium with a change in *P*

Suppose, now, from the initial price level P_0 in Figure 4.13, which gives equilibrium r_0, y_0, the price level *increases* to P_1, reducing the real-money supply to M/P_1. As can be seen in Figure 4.13, this shifts the *LM* curve to the left to $L_1 M_1$ and moves the equilibrium point to r_1, y_1. Why is this?

The price level increase reduces the real money supply. This means that at any given real income level, there is an excess demand for money because the supply of *real* balances was reduced. Another way to put this is that with *real* income constant, the price increase increases *nominal* income, increasing the demand for money balances. In both cases, for the market to clear, interest rates must be higher for any given income level than they were with the initial price P_0. So, with a given value of the money stock $\bar{M}$, when the price level increases—for whatever reason—the real-money supply shrinks and excess demand is created in the money market. This can be seen by increasing P in Figure 4.8. This excess demand raises interest rates, reducing investment demand and equilibrium income. Gradually the economy settles toward a new r_1, y_1 equilibrium with the new higher price level P_1. As Figure 4.13 shows, the new equilibrium y_1 is smaller than the initial y_0 due to the increase in P from P_0 to P_1.

If, from P_0, we had reduced the price level in Figure 4.13, increasing the real-money supply, the equilibrium r, y point would have moved down the stationary *IS curve, increasing the equilibrium y* level. Thus, varying the (exogenously given, for the time being) price level produces opposite variations in the equilibrium level of output demanded in the economy: As P rises, y falls, and vice versa. This relationship is shown as the *economy's demand curve* of Figure 4.14. Figure 4.14(a) describes the outward shift in the LM curve caused by the reduction in the price level from P_0 to P_1. Plotting the initial and subsequent levels of prices against income in Figure 4.14(b) gives us the economy's demand curve. The Figure 4.14(b) demand curve shows therefore that *as the price level P decreases, the equilibrium output y demanded in the economy increases, and vice versa.*

The demand curve is derived by asking what happens to equilibrium output demanded as the price level changes, allowing other variables, such as the interest rate, also to adjust to their equilibrium levels. This brings out an important point. Changes in equilibrium variables on the demand side of the economy as a result of price changes are *movements along the demand curve.* Changes in exogenous variables on the demand side, such as g or M of the tax schedule, or shifts of functions like the saving function or the transactions demand for money, *shift the demand*

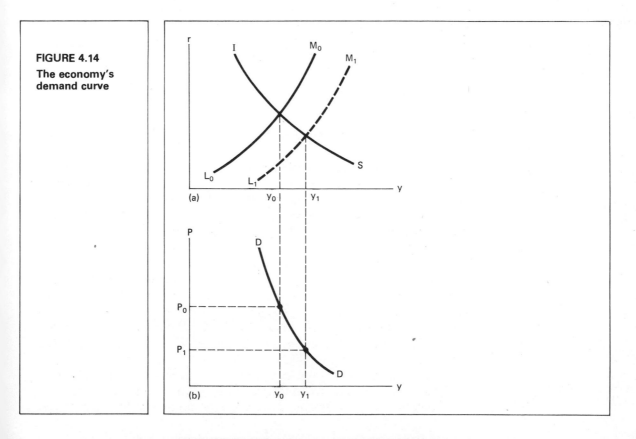

FIGURE 4.14

The economy's demand curve

curve. This distinction will become important when we have developed the supply side of the economy and can analyze how changes in exogenous variables *shift* the demand or supply curve, creating excess demand (or supply), and causing price changes that bring further adjustments *along* the demand and supply curves.

The other important point to notice about the Figure 4.14(b) demand curve is that it does *not* reflect the ordinary substitution effect of a rising price reducing demand. Rather, the rising aggregate price level P reduces equilibrium output demanded, y, by tightening the money market, raising the interest rate, and thus reducing investment.

In the next chapter we use the graphical representations of demand-side equilibrium to discuss the effects of monetary and fiscal policy changes. This offers us a chance to give our simple model a "work-out," which is really the only way to learn the workings of the economy thoroughly.

QUESTIONS FOR DISCUSSION AND REVIEW

1. The *IS* curve describes the set of interest rate—income level combinations at which the volume of savings determined by income matches the volume of investment demanded at a given interest rate. Show how a balanced change in government expenditures and taxes which leaves government saving unchanged will shift the *IS* curve.

2. If interest rates have no effect on the level of investment demand, what will the *IS* curve look like?

3. What will the *LM* curve look like if the demand for money does not vary with changes in the interest rate?

4. If the money supply is always increased when interest rates are above a target level and is always decreased when interest rates are below the target, what will the *LM* curve look like?

5. An increase in investment will shift out the *IS* curve. In the process of adjusting to this, interest rates will rise as the increased level of income increases the demand for money. The rise in interest rates causes a reduction in the level of investment. Can one be sure the induced fall in investment will not offset the initial increase in investment?

SELECTED READINGS

R. G. D. Allen, *Macroeconomic Theory* (New York: St. Martin's Press, 1967), chaps. 6–7.

J. R. Hicks, "Mr. Keynes and the Classics," in M. G. Mueller, ed., *Readings in Macroeconomics* (New York: Holt, Rinehart and Winston, 1971).

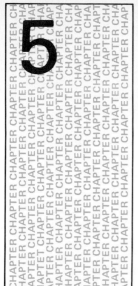

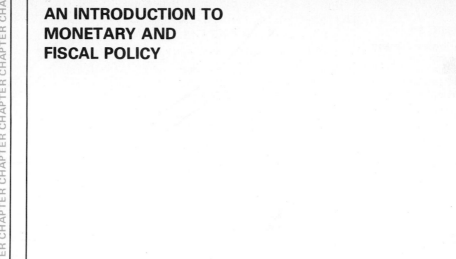

5

AN INTRODUCTION TO MONETARY AND FISCAL POLICY

Monetary and fiscal policies are generally thought of as *demand-management* policies. Since they deal with *demand* management, we can discuss their effects fairly thoroughly now before we go on to the supply side in Chapter 6. The purpose of monetary and fiscal policy, taken together, is to maintain demand roughly equal to supply in the economy and to maintain the existing price level. The appearance of excess demand will probably cause inflation, while an insufficiency of demand will bring at least temporary unemployment and deflation.

In Chapter 4 we derived the economy's demand curve by finding, in the *IS-LM* diagram, the equilibrium level of output demanded at each price level. This demand curve is shown as $D_0 D_0$ in Figure 5.1(a). Thus, if the initial price level is P_0, the equilibrium output demanded will be y_0. Now suppose the economy has a full-employment output level, y_F, which is determined by the existing labor force and capital stock. (The determination of the level of y_F is discussed at some length later in Chapter 8.) If, as shown in Figure 5.1(a), equilibrium output demanded, y_0, is more than full-employment output, y_F, there will be excess demand in the economy, measured by $y_0 - y_F$, and the price level will be pulled up. This would be inflation. In this case the object of demand management (monetary and fiscal) policy would be to shift the demand curve down to $D_1 D_1$ to eliminate the excess demand and prevent the inflation.

The case of deficient demand is shown in Figure 5.1(b). Suppose the demand curve $D_0 D_0$ is initially lower than was shown in Figure 5.1(a) due, perhaps, to lower investment demand. Then at the initial price level P_0, equilibrium output demanded could be less than full-employment output y_F, creating excess supply, or deficient demand, in the economy. This

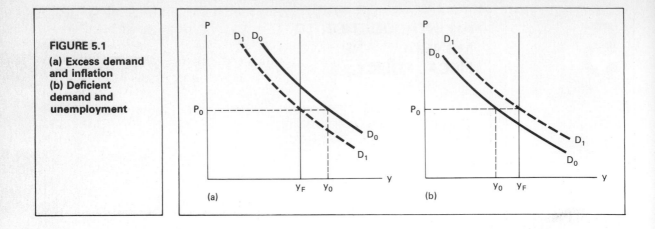

FIGURE 5.1

(a) Excess demand and inflation
(b) Deficient demand and unemployment

would tend to push prices down, and, at least temporarily, cause unemployment corresponding to the shortfall in demand measured by $y_F - y_0$ in Figure 5.1(b). In this case the objective of demand management policy would be to shift the demand curve up to $D_1 D_1$ eliminating the deflationary gap and maintaining full employment.

The government can shift the economy's demand curve by manipulating its monetary and fiscal *policy instruments*. In the case of deficient demand in Figure 5.1(b), the demand curve can be shifted up by (a) a fiscal policy increase in government purchases, g; (b) a fiscal policy cut in the tax rate; (c) a monetary policy increase in the money supply, $\bar{M}$; or some combination of purchases, tax, and money supply changes. Thus, in this analysis, the instrument of monetary policy is the money supply, and the instruments of fiscal policy are the level of government purchases of goods and services and the tax rate.

In Chapter 4 we briefly described how changes in the money supply shift the *LM* curve, while changes in the fiscal policy instruments shift the *IS* curve. Each of these changes also shifts the demand curve. Here we describe in more detail the effects of monetary and fiscal policy changes on the level of demand. We see how the simple multipliers of Chapter 3 are modified by the introduction of the money market and how the size of these multipliers depends on whether the economy is initially near full employment or in a recession. We also discuss the effects of changes in monetary and fiscal policy on the composition of output at full employment—the division of output between c, i, and g—and take an initial look at some current issues in macroeconomic stabilization policy.

FISCAL POLICY EFFECTS ON DEMAND

In analyzing the effects of fiscal policy changes in g or tax rates on equilibrium output demanded, we use the four-quadrant diagram for the *IS* curve, shown in Figure 5.2. Since fiscal policy changes do not initially affect any of the curves underlying the *LM* curve, we can just add a fixed *LM* curve to the r, y quadrant in Figure 5.2, giving an initial equilibrium point r_0, y_0, corresponding to an initial price level. With the LM curve fixed, fiscal policy changes will then shift the IS curve along the given LM, changing equilibrium output demanded and the interest rate as well at the initial price level. Since the initial price level is held constant throughout, these changes in equilibrium output demanded, at a given price level, represent horizontal shifts in the demand curve equal to the change in equilibrium output. Thus, in analyzing fiscal policy shifts, we will also refer to Figure 5.3, which shows the demand curve D_0D_0 which corresponds to the initial

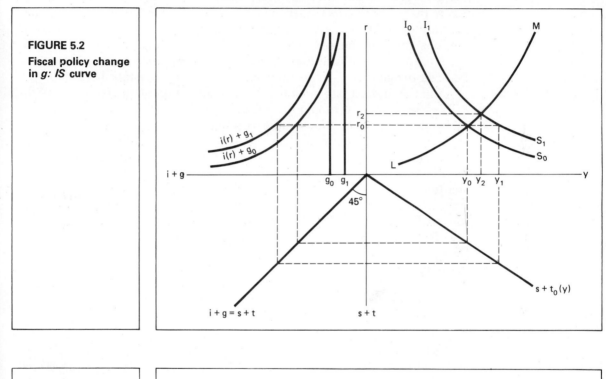

FIGURE 5.2

Fiscal policy change in g: IS curve

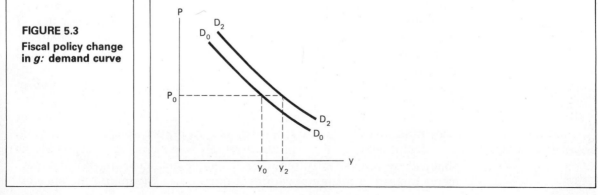

FIGURE 5.3

Fiscal policy change in g: demand curve

IS curve in Figure 5.2, $I_0 S_0$, with initial P_0 and y_0 corresponding to y_0 in Figure 5.2.

Now suppose with the initial level of government purchases g_0 and tax schedule t_0 in Figure 5.2, the resulting output level y_0 is below full employment. Then fiscal policy can increase equilibrium output, shifting the demand curve to the right, either by increasing g, or by shifting the tax schedule down, that is, reducing tax rates.

Changes in government spending, g

Consider first an increase in government purchases by Δg from g_0 to g_1 with the tax schedule unchanged at $t_0(y)$, as shown in Figure 5.2. The increase in g adds directly to real GNP and, through the multiplier, further increases y. If the interest rate did not rise from the initial level r_0 in Figure 5.2, so that investment $(i = i(r))$ was not affected, equilibrium y would rise from y_0 to y_1. This measures the outward shift in IS, since y_1 is the new equilibrium y if the old interest rate had been maintained. The ratio $(y_1 - y_0)/\Delta g$ is the multiplier of Chapter 3, which assumed investment to be fixed exogenously, the equivalent of holding r constant here.

But the interest rate must rise from r_0 following the increase in g. With a fixed level of real-money balances ($= \bar{M}/P_0$), the increase in income raises the demand for money, pulling interest rates up along the LM curve. In the background, the g increase raises the government deficit, increasing the amount of bonds the government sells. To sell more bonds in order to obtain more money to finance the Δg increase, the government must raise the interest rate it pays. In general, the increase in bond supply raises interest rates in the bond market, the other side of the coin to the money market rise in r shown in Figure 5.2.

The increase in interest rates, along the fixed LM curve, reduces the level of investment demand, tending partially to offset the increase in government spending. Again, in the bond market the increase in government borrowing squeezes out borrowing by corporations buying plant and equipment and especially borrowing by house builders, reducing the level of investment. The reduced level of investment moves the new equilibrium level of output demanded down from y_1 to y_2, with the interest rate rising from r_0 to r_2. This increase in equilibrium demand-side y is reflected in the shift in the Figure 5.3 demand curve from $D_0 D_0$ to $D_2 D_2$, with y rising from y_0 to y_2 at the initial price level P_0.

Here we can summarize the results of the fiscal policy increase in g on the demand side. With income increased and the tax rate unchanged, disposable income and consumer spending are both higher. Government purchases have risen, and with an interest rate increase, the level of investment has fallen, partially offsetting the g increase. We know the offset is only partial because for y to go up in the end, the $i + g$ sum must have risen. Thus, increasing g to raise equilibrium y shifts the mix of output away from investment and toward g, and also raises consumer spending.

Changes in the tax schedule, t(y)

Much the same effects on the level of y and r (and thus $i(r)$) could be obtained by permanently reducing tax rates or increasing transfer payments instead of raising government purchases. The main difference be-

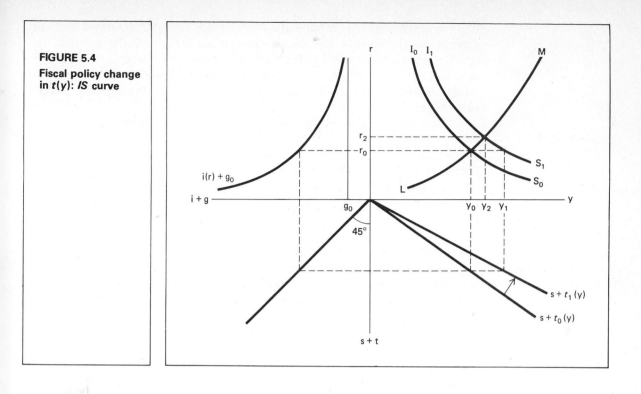

FIGURE 5.4

Fiscal policy change
in $t(y)$: *IS* curve

tween these two expansionary fiscal policy steps is in the resulting mix of output: With an equal effect on y, r, and investment, a tax reduction favors consumer expenditure while a g increase obviously increases the government share of output.

The result of a tax reduction is shown in the four-quadrant diagram of Figure 5.4. Here for simplicity we assume that the tax schedule is proportional, that is,

$$t(y) = \tau \cdot y, \tag{1}$$

so that tax revenues $t(y)$ are a given fraction, τ, of y. Then the tax cut just reduces the proportional tax rate from τ_0, say, 25 percent, to τ_1, say, 20 percent.

The downward rotation of the tax schedule increases the level of equilibrium income at any given interest rate. The alert observer might notice that since the Δg increase was the same regardless of the y level while the $t(y)$ change is bigger at higher y levels, the tax change will result in a slightly flatter slope of the *IS* curve.

From the basic equilibrium condition

$$i(r) + g = y - c(y - t(y)) = s(y - t(y)) + t(y), \tag{2}$$

we can see that if $i(r_0)$ and g are unchanged, and the tax cut raises disposable income $y - t(y)$, raising consumption, y must increase to maintain

$y - c$ equal to $i(r) + g$. Essentially, with a given r_0 maintaining i fixed, the change in disposable income at the initial income level y_0, that is, $\tau_0 \cdot y_0 - \tau_1 \cdot y_0$, generates a policy-induced increase in consumer spending that has the same effects as the Δg considered earlier. If r_0 were maintained, equilibrium output demanded would rise to y_1 through the multiplier effect.

But the increase in income again creates excess demand in the money market, raising r along LM. In the bond markets, the increase in the deficit generated by the tax cut increases the supply of bonds as the government increases borrowing. This squeezes out borrowing for plant and equipment investment and house building, reducing investment to offset partially the exogenous increase in consumer spending. In the end, equilibrium demand-side output rises to y_2 and the interest rate rises to r_2. The demand curve shifts out much the same as in Figure 5.3, with equilibrium y increasing from y_0 to y_2 at the initial price level P_0.

The multiplier for fiscal policy changes

The last sections described the effects of government purchases and tax rate changes using mainly the IS-LM diagram. These changes yield implicit multipliers—the ratio of the changes in equilibrium y to the initial change in fiscal policy. These can be traced, and compared with the multipliers of Chapter 3, through Figure 5.5. Figure 5.5(a) shows the IS shift and the change in equilibrium output demanded due to a g increase or a tax cut. Figure 5.5(b) shows the shift in the economy's aggregate demand curve, given the price level P_0. This is the same as Figure 5.3.

An increase in government spending g, or a tax cut that gives an equal increase in consumer spending, $-c'y\Delta t$ from Chapter 3, shifts the IS curve from I_0S_0 to I_1S_1 in Figure 5.5(a). At the initial value of the interest rate r_0, this would raise equilibrium output demanded to y_1. The ratio $(y_1 - y_0)/\Delta g$ is the simple multiplier of Chapter 3. Remember that investment there was held constant as g changed. Here with investment depending on the interest rate, the equivalent is holding the interest rate constant. But in fact, the interest rate will rise along the fixed LM curve. As

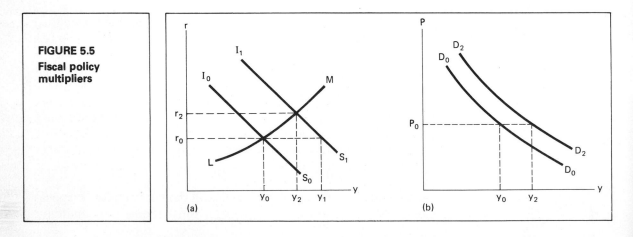

FIGURE 5.5

Fiscal policy multipliers

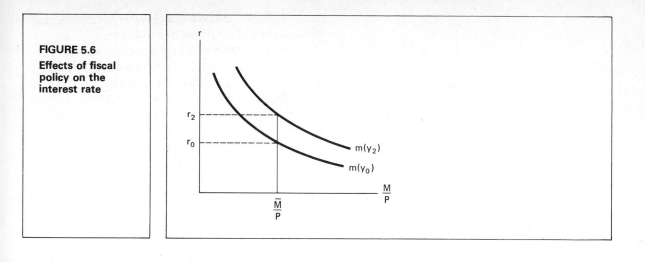

FIGURE 5.6

Effects of fiscal policy on the interest rate

income rises, the transactions demand for money increases, pulling up the interest rate, as shown in Figure 5.6. This is the movement of the interest rate up along LM in Figure 5.5(a). The increase in the interest rate cuts back investment, partially offsetting the fiscal policy stimulus. So in equilibrium, income rises only to y_2 instead of y_1; the money market effects reduce the multiplier from $(y_1 - y_0)/\Delta g$ to $(y_2 - y_0)/\Delta g$.

The increase in equilibrium output demanded at the fixed price level P_0 is shown as a shift in the demand curve of Figure 5.5(b). There again, the fiscal policy stimulus increases output from y_0 to y_2 in the final equilibrium, which includes the money market effects of Figure 5.5(a).

In Chapter 3 we saw that a balanced increase in both government purchases and tax revenue would increase income by an amount equal to the Δg. This gave us a *balanced-budget multiplier* of unity $(\Delta y/\Delta g = 1)$. Again, that assumed no change in investment as income rose. But now we see that the increase in income increases the demand for money in Figure 5.6, pulling up the interest rate along the LM curve of Figure 5.5(a). This reduces investment somewhat, reducing the size of the balanced-budget multiplier below 1. Using Figure 5.5 as an illustration of the balanced-budget multiplier, in Chapter 3 an increase of government purchases and tax revenues by an equal amount $\Delta g = \Delta t (= y_1 - y_0)$ gave an increase in y from y_0 to y_1. Here it would increase y only to y_2 due to the money market effects. So the balanced-budget multiplier is $(y_2 - y_0)/(y_1 - y_0)$, less than one but still greater than zero.

The effectiveness of fiscal policy

It should be clear from Figure 5.5 that the size of the fiscal policy multiplier itself, or the effectiveness of fiscal policy, depends on whether the fiscal policy change is initiated at a low or high level of output relative to full-employment output. This point is illustrated in Figure 5.7, which shows the differing effect on y of a given IS shift, depending on where on the LM curve the action begins.

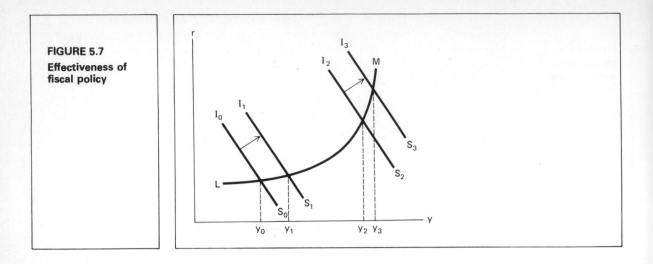

FIGURE 5.7

Effectiveness of fiscal policy

At the initial equilibrium y_0, the LM curve is relatively flat, so that its slope is nearly zero. This gives a large fiscal policy multiplier, nearly equal to the simple value without any money market effects. But at the initial equilibrium point y_2, the LM curve is nearly vertical, with a slope that is very large. In this case the fiscal policy multiplier is extremely small, approaching zero as the LM curve becomes vertical.

Thus, the size of the fiscal policy multiplier depends on the slope of the LM curve at the initial equilibrium point. A given increase in g and shift in IS will yield a large increase in y if the economy begins at a point of high unemployment and low interest rates. But if the g increase comes in a tight economy near full employment, there will be little effect on y, with a large increase in r squeezing out an amount of investment demand nearly equal to the g increase.

The economic explanation of this difference is easy to see. With a given supply of real-money balances $\bar{M}/P_0$ (which fixes the position of the LM curve), at the low level of y there is, loosely speaking, a low demand for transactions balances and hence a lot of money in speculative balances; these can be drawn out to finance a higher level of transactions, that is, a higher y, by a small increase in interest rate. But at the higher level of r and y, at y_2 in Figure 5.7, the amount of funds in speculative balances is very small, and the increase in demand for money from a rising y serves mostly to raise r, reducing investment, rather than bringing funds out of speculative balances in any substantial amount.

From an alternative perspective, at low interest rates portfolio holders expect the interest rate to rise sooner or later and, hence, bond prices to fall; therefore, their speculative balances of money are large and, as before, can be used to finance an increase in y with only a small change in interest rates.

At very high levels of interest rates, however, expectations of a gradual decline in interest rates are widespread and as a consequence portfolio holders shift more into bonds. This results in low speculative balances of money and high transaction balances.

The main point here is that the size of the fiscal policy multiplier itself depends on the initial cyclical position of the economy. Thus, it is not surprising that some investigators have found the multiplier "unstable" looking at data, say, since World War II. Of course it is unstable; the data include the initial conditions of the 1958 recession with unemployment at 7 percent and short-term interest rates at 1.8 percent, as well as the conditions of 1979 with unemployment at 6 percent and short-term rates at 12 percent. But the conclusion should not be that fiscal policy is not effective because the multiplier seems unstable. Rather, its effectiveness varies over the cycle, and in anticipating the effects of any given Δg at any given time, a prudent analyst must take into consideration the initial state of the economy rather than simply relying on a simple multiplier like those in Chapter 3.

Comparison of government purchases and tax rates as fiscal policy instruments

We have seen that the effects of equivalent fiscal policy changes in g or t on the level of total output y will be the same. But there are two major differences between fiscal policy change in g and in tax rates. First, there will be a difference in the composition of the new equilibrium output. Expanding output by increasing g also will increase the government's share of output. But a tax cut shifts the initial stimulus to a policy-induced increase in consumer spending, raising the share of output going to consumers. Thus the choice between cutting taxes or increasing government purchases to expand output and reduce unemployment will in part depend on a judgment on the relative social benefits of more consumer expenditure as opposed to more resources going into the production of public goods. This was one of the points of debate within the Kennedy administration prior to the proposal of the 1964 tax cut. With unemployment near 6 percent and the economy expanding too slowly, the debate was whether to increase government purchases g, increasing the provision of public goods, or to cut taxes, placing more emphasis on consumer spending.

The other major difference between g and t changes stems from the fact that a tax cut will affect the economy only if consumers increase their spending as a result, so that the direct policy-induced consumption stimulus does, in fact, appear. There is always the possibility that consumers will save the additional disposable income, leaving the total $s + t(y)$ schedule unchanged with no effect on y. To a certain extent, but in the other direction, this happened with the income tax surcharge in 1968; when the surcharge was passed, raising taxes, consumers paid about two-thirds of the additional tax out of saving and only one-third out of consumption, thus reducing the effect on y.

This problem does not occur with g changes though, since the government can make sure that g changes by the desired amount. Thus, there is more certainty of achieving the desired effect on y if fiscal policy changes come in government purchases, rather than in tax and transfer payment changes. Also, it seems likely that permanent tax rate changes will have a greater effect than temporary changes that may well be compensated by temporary changes in saving.

MONETARY POLICY EFFECTS ON DEMAND

To analyze the effects of monetary policy changes in the money supply, $\bar{M}$, we will use the four-quadrant LM diagram, shown in Figure 5.8. Since in this section we will be holding the fiscal policy variables and the saving and investment functions behind the IS curve constant, we can add a fixed IS curve to Figure 5.8. This establishes initial equilibrium values of y_0 and r_0, given the price level P_0 and the initial level of the money supply $\bar{M}_0$.

Monetary policy changes in $\bar{M}$ will now shift the LM curve along the given IS curve, changing the interest rate and the equilibrium output demanded. These changes in output demanded, *at the given price level*, produce horizontal shifts in the economy's demand curve. This was shown in Figure 5.3, and is reproduced here as Figure 5.9. The $D_0 D_0$ demand curve corresponds to the fixed IS in Figure 5.8 and the initial level of the money supply, $\bar{M}_0$. The initial y_0 and P_0 of Figure 5.9 are the same as those of Figure 5.8.

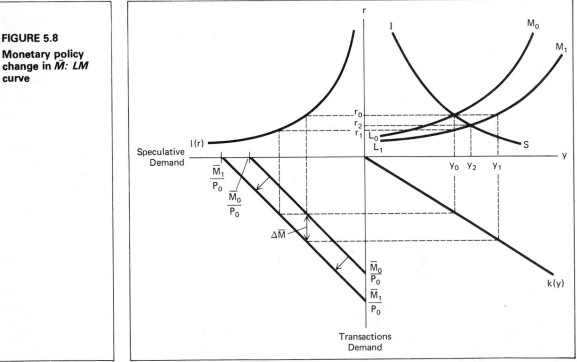

FIGURE 5.8
Monetary policy change in $\bar{M}$: LM curve

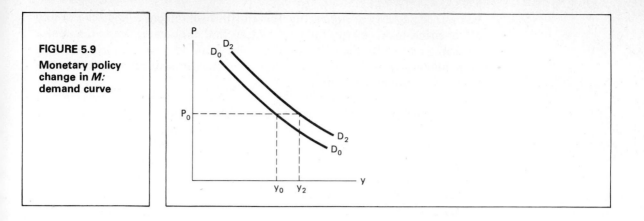

FIGURE 5.9

Monetary policy
change in M:
demand curve

**Changes in the money
supply, $\bar{M}$**

If the initial equilibrium value of real output y_0 is below full-employment output, the demand curve can be shifted to the right by fiscal policy changes, as we have seen above, or by an increase in the money supply. This is illustrated in Figure 5.8, where the money supply is increased by $\Delta \bar{M}$ from $\bar{M}_0$ to $\bar{M}_1$. At the initial equilibrium level of output and income, y_0, this increase in the money supply would push the interest rate down to r_1 to maintain equilibrium in the money market. Thus the $\Delta \bar{M}$ shifts the LM curve down (or to the right) by an amount measured by $r_0 - r_1$ at the initial y_0 level.

Another way to measure the LM shift is to assume that the interest rate remains at r_0, fixing the level of speculative demand for money. In this case, all of the $\Delta \bar{M}$ increase would be available for transactions balances to support a higher level of y. The increase in y that would absorb the money supply increase into transactions balances at the old r_0 is shown in Figure 5.8 as $y_1 - y_0$. Thus, the point r_0, y_1 would also maintain the money market in equilibrium and is on the new LM curve, $L_1 M_1$. The distance $y_1 - y_0$ measures the outward shift in LM at the initial interest rate r_0.

When the money supply is increased, initially the interest rate will tend to fall toward r_1 at the initial y_0 in Figure 5.8. But this drop in r increases investment demand, raising the level of output and income, moving the economy from r_1, y_0 toward the IS curve. The income increase, in turn, raises the transactions demand for money, pulling the interest rate back up. In the end, the economy comes to the equilibrium point r_2, y_2 with both the product market and money market in equilibrium.

In the bond market in the background, the central bank increases the money supply by buying bonds (selling money). This increase in bond demand raises bond prices, reducing interest rates. Firms find it easier (and cheaper) to borrow to finance investment projects, so investment demand goes up, moving the economy toward equilibrium at r_2, y_2.

The movement from the old equilibrium y_0 to the new y_2 at the original price level P_0 is also reflected in a shift of the demand curve in Figure

5.9 to D_2D_2, giving a higher level of equilibrium output demanded at any given price level. Here monetary policy has shifted the demand curve; back in Figure 5.3 it was fiscal policy. The same increase in income could be achieved by an appropriately sized change in any of the three major policy instruments: g, t, or $\bar{M}$.

The monetary policy increase in $\bar{M}$ has reduced the interest rate and raised investment and equilibrium output and income. The income increase, with a given tax schedule, has increased consumer spending, while government purchases remain unchanged. Thus, monetary policy has a different effect on the composition of output than do fiscal policy changes in g or $t(y)$. Here the policy-induced expenditure effect comes through a change in investment demand. Government purchases remain unchanged and consumer expenditure goes up only endogenously. We can summarize these compositional effects by looking at the basic national income identity,

$$y = c + i + g. \tag{3}$$

For a given increase in income and output, y, each of the policies gives about the same endogenous consumption increase through the multiplier. The difference lies in the source of the policy-induced expenditure change. An increase in government spending raises g and reduces i somewhat, raising the proportion of g in the use of output relative to c or i in the final equilibrium position. A tax cut gives a direct c increase and also reduces i somewhat, raising the proportion of c. Finally, a money supply increase gives a policy-induced increase in i, raising the fraction of investment in the final equilibrium position. Thus, a choice of which policy instrument to use to *expand* (or contract) output will, in part, depend on how the policy maker wants the *composition* of output to change.

The multiplier for monetary policy changes

The multiplier for changes in the money stock in the *IS-LM* model, compared with the simple investment multiplier of Chapter 3, is shown in Figure 5.10. This figure is the same as Figure 5.5, which illustrated the

FIGURE 5.10

Monetary policy multiplier

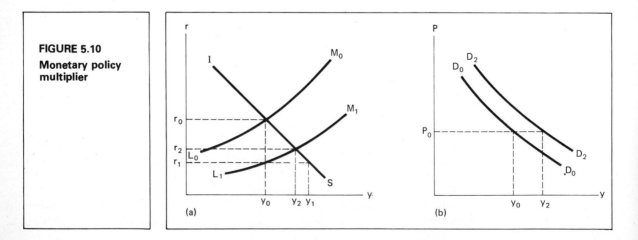

(a) (b)

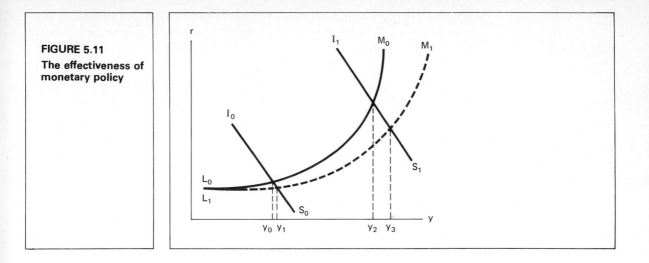

FIGURE 5.11

The effectiveness of monetary policy

fiscal policy multipliers, except here the *LM* curve shifts, whereas there the *IS* curve shifted.

In Figure 5.10(a), an increase in the money supply shifts the *LM* curve out. At the initial level of income y_0, this excess supply of money would drive the interest rate down to r_1. This drop in the interest rate, in turn, would stimulate investment demand, increasing income toward y_1 at interest rate r_1. The ratio of the increase in income $y_1 - y_0$ to the rise in investment Δi coming from the drop in the interest rate from r_0 to r_1 is the Chapter 3 multiplier $(y_1 - y_0)/\Delta i$.

However, the interest rate will not fall all the way to r_1 and the level of income will stop short of y_1 with the money market in the picture. As income rises, the demand for money increases, absorbing some of the increased supply that started the movement away from r_0, y_0. With the demand for money rising with income, the economy will settle at r_2, y_2. The interest rate has fallen, but not to r_1, and equilibrium output demanded rises less than the Chapter 3 multiplier would suggest, to y_2 instead of y_1.

The increase in the money supply shifts the demand curve of Figure 5.10(b) out at the initial price level. Note that Figure 5.10(b) is exactly the same as Figure 5.5(b). With a given price level P_0, equilibrium output demanded rises from y_0 to y_2 with the money market adjustment along the new $L_1 M_1$ curve taken into account.

The effectiveness of monetary policy

As was the case with fiscal policy, the effectiveness of monetary policy will vary with the cyclical position of the economy. As Figure 5.11 shows, with a given slope of the *IS* curve, a given shift in the *LM* curve due to an increase in the money supply will have a greater effect on y at high levels of y and r than at low levels.

From the four-quadrant diagram of Figure 5.12, it is clear that when the $l(r)$ curve is very flat, the *LM* curve is flat. If the economy is in equilib-

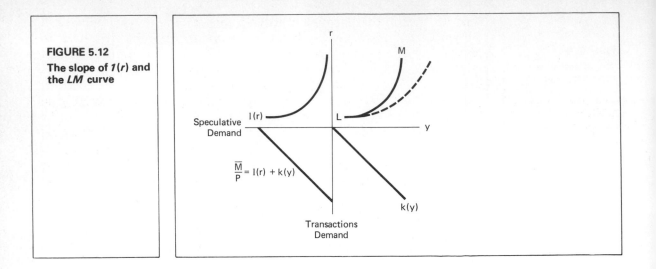

FIGURE 5.12

The slope of $1(r)$ and the *LM* curve

Speculative Demand

$1(r)$

r

M

L

y

$$\frac{\overline{M}}{P} = 1(r) + k(y)$$

Transactions Demand

$k(y)$

rium at a low level of y and r, on the flat segment of the *LM* curve, people may be relatively indifferent between holding money and bonds, so that speculative balances absorb an increase in $\overline{M}$ with little effect on r, thus little effect on i and y.

On the other hand, when the $1(r)$ curve is steeper, at a higher rate of interest, the *LM* curve is also steeper. With interest rates and bond demand high, speculative and transactions money balances get squeezed to a minimum, and the limit on expansion of y is the availability of money $\overline{M}$ to finance transactions. In this area of the *LM* curve, an increase in the money supply eases this constraint, permitting an increase in y. Thus an increase in $\overline{M}$ shifts the *LM* curve out as shown in Figures 5.11 and 5.12. The result, as shown in Figure 5.11, is that monetary policy is more effective when the LM curve is more vertical, at relatively higher levels of r and y, than when it is flat. So monetary policy has its maximum effectiveness when the economy is at high r, y levels and is utilizing almost all of the money supply to finance transactions, that is, to support y.

THE INTERACTION OF MONETARY AND FISCAL POLICIES

In the previous sections of this chapter we discussed the relative effectiveness of monetary and fiscal policies in relation to the cyclical position of the economy. The likelihood that the policy instruments g, $t(y)$, and $\overline{M}$ differ in the certainty of their results was also mentioned. In addition, it should by now be apparent that changes in these policy instruments can be combined in many different ways to achieve a desired position of the economy's demand curve. We end this introductory chapter on monetary and fiscal policy as demand-management tools first by summarizing what has already been said on relative effectiveness and certainty of results.

Then we look at the interaction between monetary and fiscal policies in two important cases: first, where they work in opposite directions to change the interest rate and the composition of output at a given level of output; and, second, where they work in the same direction to achieve a desired shift in the demand curve and change in y, given P_0.

The effectiveness and certainty of monetary and fiscal policy

The relative effectiveness of monetary and fiscal policy, depending on the shape of the LM curve and the economy's initial position, can be summarized by reference to Figure 5.13. If the economy is in an initial position such as r_1, y_1 of Figure 5.13, an expansionary monetary policy, shifting LM right, may have little effect on y, since at that low interest rate the additional money would be absorbed by speculative balances without a further drop in the interest rate and thus provide no stimulus to investment. On the other hand, at r_1, y_1, a shift in the IS curve will be relatively effective in raising y, since a small increase in the interest rate will release a substantial amount of funds from speculative balances to support an increase in y.

At the other extreme, where the economy is very taut with high r and y at r_2, y_2, a fiscal policy shift in IS will be relatively ineffective in changing equilibrium demand-side y. With interest rates very high, money balances will be squeezed to the minimum that is needed to finance transactions. An increase in demand by, say, an increase in g will raise the interest rate enough that the initial g increase will be nearly fully offset by a drop in investment demand, giving little increase in y. This would be a case of nearly full "crowding-out" of investment by an increase in g. In this case, however, an expansion of the money supply will be very effective in shifting the economy's demand curve. With the level of output and income y limited by the money available for transactions purposes, an $\bar{M}/P_0$ increase will permit a commensurate increase in y. Thus, when the economy is near full employment with very tight credit conditions, monetary policy will be most effective in shifting the demand curve.

FIGURE 5.13

The effectiveness of monetary and fiscal policy

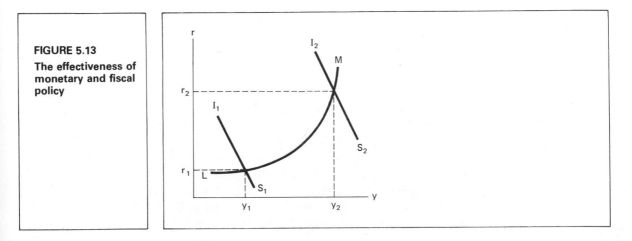

The three instruments of fiscal and monetary policy act on demand through different channels. In the case of government purchases, the initial change in expenditures comes directly through the change in g, which is in itself a change in GNP. In the case of a change in the tax rate τ, the initial policy-induced expenditure change comes in the reaction of consumer spending to the change in disposable income $(-y\,\Delta\tau)$. In the case of a change in M, the initial expenditure change is in investment, which reacts to the interest rate changes that follow an exogenous increase or decrease in the money supply. These three channels can be used to rank the policy instruments in terms of the certainty of the results.

The highest degree of certainty seems to come in the Δg case, since here the government exogenously changes spending by its own decision. In the two other cases, the direct expenditure effect depends on the reaction of private spending to a change in one of its determinants. Tax changes will be effective only if consumer spending reacts. Since it is possible that consumers will offset tax changes, particularly temporary ones, by changing saving behavior, the results of tax changes are not as certain as those of g changes.

Money supply changes will be effective only if (a) the change affects the interest rate and credit conditions facing investors, and (b) if these changes affect investment spending. Since both of these steps are uncertain, it seems likely (although this would be hard to prove) that the effects of M changes may be less certain than those of tax changes. This is very likely the case for permanent tax changes, less likely for temporary tax changes.

These considerations of uncertainty might lead to the following kind of stabilization policy formula. First, keep M growth fairly smooth, since the results of M changes in the short run may be pretty unpredictable. Second, use permanent tax changes to set the IS curve at a desired *long-run normal level*, depending on the long-run desired level of g. Third, use small g changes for short-run *fine-tuning* stabilization policy since their results are most certain.

The monetary-fiscal policy mix

From the discussion of the effects of monetary and fiscal policy changes in this chapter it should be clear that changes in the policy variables can be used to change the level of the interest rate and the composition of output without shifting the demand curve, that is, without changing equilibrium demand-side y at the given P_0.

For example, in Figure 5.14 it may be that at the going price level P_0, the level of output y_0 yields roughly full employment. But the r_0 level may be too high because it gives a level of investment, especially in housing, that is too low. In this case, the interest rate may be reduced by putting in a permanent tax increase, shifting IS to $I_1 S_1$, and reducing consumption demand. This could be balanced by a money supply increase, lowering the interest rate and stimulating investment demand, bringing the economy back to y_0 at the lower interest rate r_1. This shift in the *monetary-fiscal policy mix*, tightening the budget and easing the money supply, has

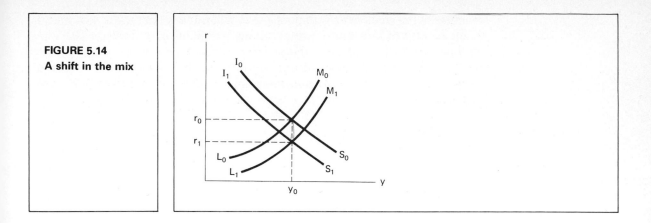

FIGURE 5.14
A shift in the mix

shifted the composition of the equilibrium y_0. With g fixed, consumer expenditure has been reduced and investment increased. Thus, the policy variables can be changed in opposite directions to change the composition of demand without shifting the demand curve.

Working the policy variables against each other in this way creates substantial uncertainty about the outcome, especially since the *amount* of change in each variable will depend on the initial position of the economy. For example, in mid-1968 a mix shift was attempted, with the imposition of an income tax surcharge and a shift to monetary ease. With the economy running at very low unemployment and historically high interest rates, we might say that it was in the *vertical* region of the *LM* curve when the mix change began. Then the imposition of only a temporary surcharge shifted the *IS* curve down only slightly, while the monetary expansion shifted *LM* out substantially, resulting in a shift of the economy's demand curve to the right, increasing output and the rate of inflation and pushing unemployment down even more. Thus, while the policy instruments can be used against each other to change composition, the amounts by which the instruments should change will depend on the economy's position and this should be carefully taken into account before such a mix shift is attempted.

The various levels of uncertainty associated with the policy instruments also suggest that if the objective is to shift the demand curve, it might be best to use all the instruments in the same direction, giving the highest probability of success in changing y. This strategy, of course, maximizes the uncertainty as to where r will come out, since if, for example, in a restrictive move, the fiscal policy change "bites" but the monetary policy change does not, r will fall, while if the monetary change bites but the fiscal does not, r will rise.

This section is meant to temper, at least a bit, the air of determinateness and certainty that the calculation of multipliers gives stabilization policy. The theory is fairly clear, as the multipliers show. But the actual reaction in the economy to changes in g, $t(y)$ and $\bar{M}$ is uncertain, so that the exact results of any given policy change will be hard to forecast. The chapters of Part III discuss the sectors of the economy in more detail, trying to reduce this level of uncertainty. But first we must turn to the supply side of the economy and relax the assumption that the price level P_0 is fixed.

MULTIPLIERS IN THE *IS-LM* MODEL

It is useful to relate specific changes in policy to specific changes in output. In the more general model, this involves a degree of mathematics that may prove difficult for some readers. Consequently, we have separated this section from the main text. For most readers, we think the effort is justified.

SLOPE OF *IS*

The *IS* curve has been defined as the combinations of interest rate and income that satisfy

$$i(r) + g = s(y - t(y)) + t(y) = y - c(y - t(y)). \tag{1}$$

The slope of the *IS* curve is the ratio of the change in interest rate to the change in income required so that (1) remains satisfied.

FIGURE 5A.1

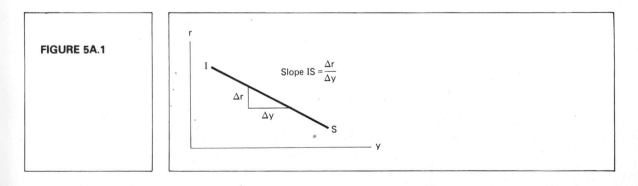

A change in interest rates of Δr will change the left-hand side of equation (1) by $\Delta r \cdot i'(r)$. For clarification purposes it should be noted that if a variable z is a function of x, or $z = z(x)$, differentiating z with respect to x, or $z'(x)$, gives the *incremental* change in z attributed to an *incremental* change in x while $\Delta x \cdot z'(x)$ gives the *total* change in z as a result of a specific change Δx of variable x. In our case, $i = i(r)$ and, hence, $\Delta r \cdot i'(r)$ gives the change in investment attributed to a change in the interest rate.

A change in y of Δy will change the right-hand side of equation (1) in three steps. Taxes will rise by

$$\Delta t(y) = \Delta y \cdot t'(y),$$

and disposable income will rise

$$\Delta(y - t(y)) = \Delta y - \Delta t(y) = \Delta y - \Delta y \cdot t'(y) = \Delta y \cdot (1 - t'(y)).$$

Thus, consumption will rise by

$$\Delta c(y - t(y)) = c' \cdot (1 - t'(y)) \cdot \Delta y,$$

and the total change in the right-hand side of (1) from a change in y of Δy will be

$$\Delta y - c' \cdot (1 - t'(y)) \cdot \Delta y = [1 - c' \cdot (1 - t'(y))] \cdot \Delta y.$$

Since (1) must remain satisifed along the IS curve, the change in the left-hand side must equal the change in the right-hand side or

$$i'(r) \cdot \Delta r = [1 - c' \cdot (1 - t'(y))] \cdot \Delta y,$$

so

$$\Delta y = \frac{i'(r) \cdot \Delta r}{1 - c' \cdot (1 - t'(y))};$$

thus

$$\left.\frac{\Delta r}{\Delta y}\right|_{IS} = \frac{1}{\dfrac{1}{1 - c'(1 - t'(y))} \cdot i'(r)}.$$

Since $i'(r)$ is negative and $c'(1 - t'(y))$ is less than one, it follows that the slope of the IS curve is negative.

We have defined the LM curve as the combinations of interest rate and income that satisfy

$$\frac{\bar{M}}{P} = m = l(r) + k(y). \tag{2}$$

The slope of LM is the ratio of the change in interest rate to the change in income necessary to keep equation (2) satisfied.

A change in interest rate will change the right-hand side of equation (2) by $l'(r) \cdot \Delta r$. A change in income changes this side by $k'(y) \cdot \Delta y$. Since

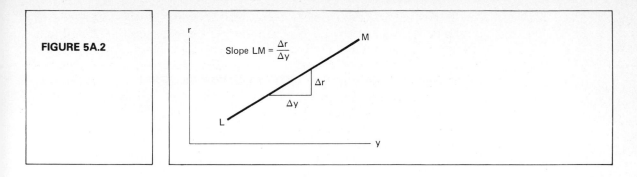

the left-hand side is fixed, the changes in the right-hand side must add to zero for equation (2) to remain satisfied.

$$0 = l'(r) \cdot \Delta r + k'(y) \cdot \Delta y$$

or

$$\Delta y = \frac{-l'(r) \, \Delta r}{k'(y)} \, ;$$

thus

$$\left. \frac{\Delta r}{\Delta y} \right|_{LM} = - \frac{1}{\dfrac{l'(r)}{k'(y)}} = - \frac{k'}{l'} \, .$$

Since k' is positive and l' is negative, it follows that the slope of the LM curve is positive.

A GENERAL
MULTIPLIER

Equilibrium values of the interest rate and income are determined by the intersection of the IS and LM curves. We have seen that fiscal or monetary policy shifts one of these curves creating a discrepancy between IS and LM at the old equilibrium interest rate.

For example, a change in fiscal policy might cause a shift from $I_1 S_1$ to $I_2 S_2$. If (r_1, y_1) had been an equilibrium, there is a discrepancy of $y_3 - y_1$ at r_1 after the shift.

FIGURE 5A.3

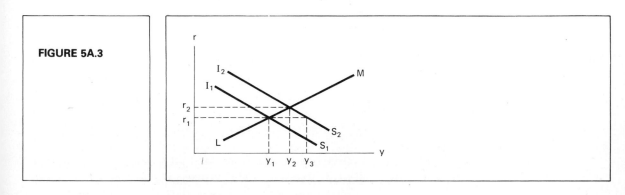

Now

$$\frac{r_2 - r_1}{y_2 - y_1} = \frac{\Delta r}{\Delta y}\bigg|_{LM},$$

so the change in equilibrium income can be expressed as

$$y_2 - y_1 = \frac{r_2 - r_1}{\dfrac{\Delta r}{\Delta y}\bigg|_{LM}}.$$

We can express $r_2 - r_1$ in terms of the shift $y_3 - y_1$ as follows: We know that

$$y_3 - y_1 = (y_2 - y_1) + (y_3 - y_2),$$

where

$$y_2 - y_1 = \frac{r_2 - r_1}{\dfrac{\Delta r}{\Delta y}\bigg|_{LM}} \quad \text{and} \quad y_3 - y_2 = -\frac{r_2 - r_1}{\dfrac{\Delta r}{\Delta y}\bigg|_{IS}}.$$

The negative sign before the ratio $\dfrac{r_2 - r_1}{\dfrac{\Delta r}{\Delta y}\big|_{IS}}$ is needed because $y_3 - y_2$ is a positive number while the slope of the IS curve is negative. So,

$$y_3 - y_1 = \frac{r_2 - r_1}{\dfrac{\Delta r}{\Delta y}\bigg|_{LM}} - \frac{r_2 - r_1}{\dfrac{\Delta r}{\Delta y}\bigg|_{IS}} = (r_2 - r_1) \cdot \left[\frac{1}{\dfrac{\Delta r}{\Delta y}\big|_{LM}} - \frac{1}{\dfrac{\Delta r}{\Delta y}\big|_{IS}} \right]$$

or

$$= (r_2 - r_1) \cdot \frac{\dfrac{\Delta r}{\Delta y}\big|_{IS} - \dfrac{\Delta r}{\Delta y}\big|_{LM}}{\dfrac{\Delta r}{\Delta y}\big|_{LM} \cdot \dfrac{\Delta r}{\Delta y}\big|_{IS}}$$

and

$$r_2 - r_1 = \frac{\dfrac{\Delta r}{\Delta y}\big|_{LM} \cdot \dfrac{\Delta r}{\Delta y}\big|_{IS}}{\dfrac{\Delta r}{\Delta y}\big|_{IS} - \dfrac{\Delta r}{\Delta y}\big|_{LM}} \cdot (y_3 - y_1).$$

The change in equilibrium income, then, for a change in fiscal policy, can be expressed as

$$y_2 - y_1 = \frac{\dfrac{\Delta r}{\Delta y}\big|_{IS}}{\dfrac{\Delta r}{\Delta y}\big|_{IS} - \dfrac{\Delta r}{\Delta y}\big|_{LM}} \cdot (y_3 - y_1). \qquad [3]$$

If, now, the LM curve had shifted from one that passed through (r_1, y_3) to the one shown with $I_2 S_2$ fixed, a similar process would lead to

$$y_3 - y_2 = -\frac{\left.\dfrac{\Delta r}{\Delta y}\right|_{LM}}{\left.\dfrac{\Delta r}{\Delta y}\right|_{IS} - \left.\dfrac{\Delta r}{\Delta y}\right|_{LM}} \cdot (y_3 - y_1).$$

[4]

Equations (3) and (4) differ only in the numerator term.

Substituting into equation (3) the slope formulas we derived earlier, we have

$$y_2 - y_1 = \frac{\dfrac{1 - c' \cdot (1 - t'(y))}{i'(r)}}{\dfrac{1 - c' \cdot (1 - t'(y))}{i'(r)} + \dfrac{k'(y)}{l'(r)}} \cdot (y_3 - y_1).$$

We saw on p. 47 that if the shift is due to a change in government spending,

$$y_3 - y_1 = \frac{1}{1 - c' \cdot (1 - t'(y))} \cdot \Delta g.$$

This implies

$$y_2 - y_1 = \frac{\dfrac{1 - c' \cdot (1 - t'(y))}{i'(r)}}{\dfrac{1 - c' \cdot (1 - t'(y))}{i'(r)} + \dfrac{k'(y)}{l'(r)}} \cdot \frac{1}{1 - c' \cdot (1 - t'(y))} \cdot \Delta g$$

or

$$y_2 - y_1 = \left[\frac{1}{1 - c' \cdot (1 - t'(y)) + \dfrac{i'(r) \cdot k'(y)}{l'(r)}} \right] \cdot \Delta g.$$

The term in brackets is the multiplier for a change in government spending or an autonomous shift in the investment or consumption schedule.

If, now, the LM schedule had shifted we know that at the original rate of interest,

$$y_3 - y_1 = \frac{1}{k'(y)} \cdot \Delta m.$$

Substituting into (4) the above expression as well as the formula for the LM slope we arrived at earlier, we get

$$y_3 - y_2 = \left[-\frac{-\dfrac{k'(y)}{l'(r)}}{\dfrac{(1 - c' \cdot (1 - t'(y)))}{i'(r)} + \dfrac{k'(y)}{l'(r)}} \cdot \frac{1}{k'(y)} \right] \cdot \Delta m$$

$$= \left[\frac{\dfrac{i'(r)}{l'(r)}}{1 - c' \cdot (1 - t'(y)) + \dfrac{k'(y) \cdot i'(r)}{l'(r)}} \right] \cdot \Delta m$$

or

$$= \left[\frac{\dfrac{i'}{l'}}{1 - c' \cdot (1 - t') + \dfrac{k' \cdot i'}{l'}} \right] \cdot \Delta m.$$

The term in brackets gives the multiplier for a change in the amount of real-money balances supplied.

QUESTIONS FOR DISCUSSION AND REVIEW

1. The following equations describe an economy:

$c = .9(1 - t)y$
$i = 300 - 600r$
$g = 600$
$t = \frac{1}{3}y$
$m(r, y) = .25y - 1500r$
$\dfrac{M}{P} = 375$

    a. Derive the equation for the *IS* curve.
    b. Derive the equation for the *IM* curve.
    c. What are the equilibrium levels of income and interest rates?

2. Using the same equations:

    a. By how much will equilibrium income increase if the government increases its expenditures from 600 to 610?
    b. Why does your answer to 2(a) differ from the answer to question 3 in Chapter 3?

3. Using the same equations, assume the policy makers wish to reduce equilibrium income by 100.

    a. What lump-sum tax change would be required to accomplish this?
    b. By how much would real balances have to change to accomplish this?

4. To move an economy from a less than full employment level of income to a full employment level, a number of choices are available. Relying on fiscal policy alone will yield high interest rates. Using only monetary policy will result in low interest rates. Using both types of policies will yield interest rates between these two extremes.

    a. Is it possible to develop a policy mix that yields interest rates at full employment outside this range?
    b. What concerns would motivate policy makers in adopting such policy mixes?

5. How would an increase in tax rates alter the *IS* curve? Would this effect the potency of monetary policy?

SELECTED READINGS   E. C. Brown, "Fiscal Policy in the '30's." *American Economic Review*, December
1956.

A. P. Lerner, "Functional Finance and the Federal Debt," *Social Research*,
February 1943, also in M. G. Mueller, ed., *Readings in Macroeconomics*
(New York: Holt, Rinehart and Winston, 1971).

P. A. Samuelson, "The Simple Mathematics of Income Determination," in
Income, Employment, and Public Policy, reproduced in M. G. Mueller, ed.,
Readings in Macroeconomics (New York: Holt, Rinehart and Winston, 1971).

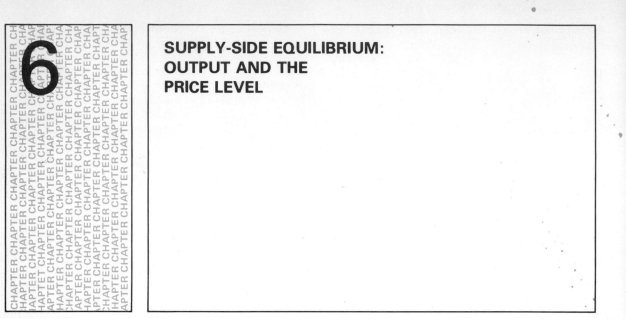

SUPPLY-SIDE EQUILIBRIUM: OUTPUT AND THE PRICE LEVEL

The last two chapters developed the demand side of the economy taking the price level P as exogenously determined. The product market equilibrium condition,

$$IS: \quad y = c(y - t(y)) + i(r) + g, \qquad [1]$$

and the money market equilibrium condition,

$$LM: \quad \frac{\bar{M}}{P} = l(r) + k(y), \qquad [2]$$

determine the equilibrium values of the level of output y and the interest rate r for any given value of P. Changing the price level changes equilibrium y and r through changes in real-money supply, $m = (M/P)$. This effect comes through shifts in the LM curve. Varying the exogenous price level gave us the economy's demand curve, shown in Figure 6.1 as DD.

This chapter develops the supply side of our skeletal macroeconomy. This gives us a supply curve to add to Figure 6.1, so that equating supply and demand in the economy we obtain endogenously determined equilibrium values of the price level and output.

THE SIMPLE DEPRESSION MODEL

To begin with, let us look for the moment at an economy such as that of the Depression in the 1930s, in which the unemployed labor supply is more or less unlimited so that a demand increase can expand output y and employment N without raising the price level. This essentially gives us as a supply curve a horizontal line at P_0 in Figure 6.1, with equilibrium output then at y_0. We can next introduce a short-run production function for real output,

$$y = y(N; \bar{K}),$$ [3]

which says simply that in the short run the level of real output y depends on labor input N only, with output increasing as employment rises. All other factor inputs, included in $\bar{K}$ (K for *Kapital*) are either fixed in the short run, like the capital stock, or vary in direct proportion to labor input, like materials input. For any given level of y, the production function gives the level of employment N needed to produce this y.

This gives us a complete, if somewhat unsatisfactory, *depression model*. The presence of massive unemployment means that a demand increase can increase output and employment without pulling up wages and prices to any significant degree. This situation is represented by the horizontal supply curve at P_0 in Figure 6.1. Production of the resulting equilibrium output y_0 gives employment to N_0 persons in Figure 6.2, pre-

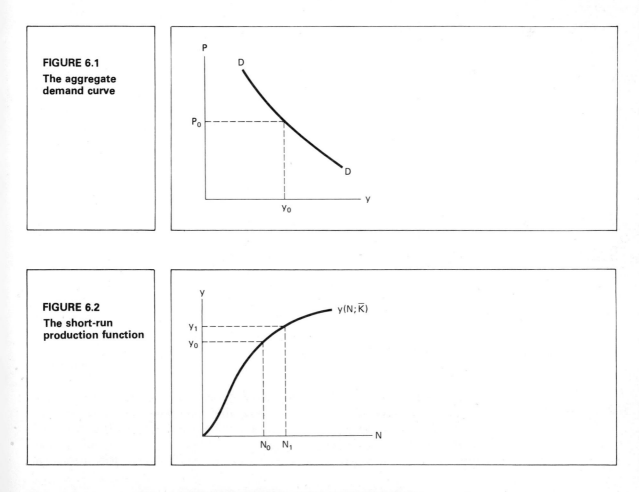

FIGURE 6.1

The aggregate demand curve

FIGURE 6.2

The short-run production function

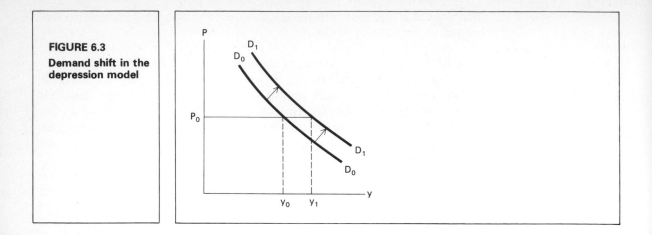

FIGURE 6.3

Demand shift in the depression model

sumably far less than the total labor force. (Unemployment peaked at 25 percent in 1933.) In this case, if government purchases were increased, the *IS* curve would shift out and the demand curve of Figure 6.1 would shift to $D_1 D_1$ in Figure 6.3; equilibrium output would rise to y_1, and employment would rise to N_1 in Figure 6.2.

The main difficulty with this analysis is that the assumption of a fixed price level is not acceptable if labor supply is not perfectly elastic. We know this from empirical observation. In the 1930s, when widespread unemployment prevailed, an increase in demand could have expanded production without resulting in much of a price increase. Even after 1961, when unemployment was about 7 percent, demand increases expanded output without causing much of an increase in prices. After 1965, however, with unemployment below 4 percent, the continued expansion of demand brought a rise in prices, which has continued through three inflationary cycles to the present (1980).

We should be able to imagine intuitively the qualitative relationship between prices, wages, and the level of employment that would occur when an economy is at or near full employment. If the demand for goods should suddenly rise above the available supply, prices would begin to rise. Higher prices would mean increased profits for producers, and they would expand their production in order to make even greater profits. To do so they would try to hire more labor; thus, higher prices would lead to an increased demand for labor. The increased demand for labor would take the form of employers offering higher money wages to attract more labor.

Presumably, however, workers are interested in the purchasing power of their wages—what they can buy with their income. What they can buy depends not only on the level of money wages but also on the prices of goods and services. Thus, an increase in prices would lower the real wages earned by workers and might cause a reduction in the supply of labor offered at a given money wage. Another way to look at this is that the effect of an increase in demand for labor on employment, stimulated by an increase in the price level, is likely to be dampened by the reduction in labor supply caused by the falling real wage. Thus, common sense tells us that there is a close relationship between prices, wages, and the level of employment, and that this relationship is more complicated than the simple depression model outlined above.

We have already developed the product market and money market equilibrium conditions, equations (1) and (2):

$$y = c(y - t(y)) + i(r) + g$$

and

$$\frac{\bar{M}}{P} = l(r) + k(y),$$

and introduced the production function, (3):

$$y = y(N; \bar{K}).$$

These three equations have four endogenous variables: y, r, P, and N. So the system as it stands is *underdetermined*; it has one too many unknowns. In order to find equilibrium solutions for y, r, P, and N, we have to find another relationship that includes at least some of these variables and is a bit more sensible than the fixed P assumption in the simple depression model. We will find this equation by looking at a third market, the *labor market.*

THE DEMAND FOR LABOR

We have already introduced a simple production function, equation (3), which describes real output y as a function of labor input N, with the level of the capital stock and of other inputs held constant or varying in direct proportion to labor in the short run. This function is shown graphically in Figure 6.4(a). The shape of the production function $y(N; K)$ shows y; increasing with each increase in labor input. However, y increases at an increasing rate with the first additions of labor to the fixed capital stock. But after some level of employment, shown as N_1 in Figure 6.4, y begins to increase at a decreasing rate—showing diminishing marginal returns—as the capital stock is spread over more and more men. Eventually a point may be reached where no addition to output would come from added labor (where $y(N; \bar{K})$ would flatten out) or even where output would be diminished by adding labor (where $y(N; \bar{K})$ would turn down).

There are some interesting functions to be derived from this production function, shown in Figure 6.4(b). One is average labor productivity, y/N, also known as the average product of labor (APL). This is represented by the slope of a line from the origin to any point on the production function. It can be seen that as employment increases, the average product of labor first increases and then decreases. This relationship between APL

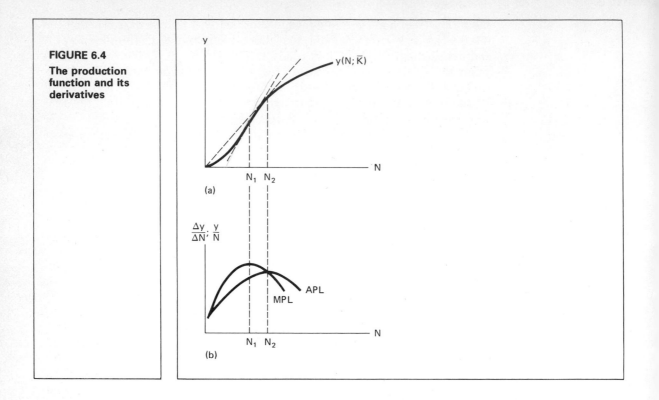

FIGURE 6.4

The production function and its derivatives

and the level of employment is shown in Figure 6.4(b). The other curve in Figure 6.4(b), derived from the production function, is the marginal product of labor (*MPL*). This is the slope of the production function at each point, and in Figure 6.4(a) would be shown by the slope of a tangent to the production function at each point *N*.

Three points about the *APL* and *MPL* curves should be apparent from Figure 6.4. With the production function first convex, showing increasing returns, and then concave, showing diminishing returns, the *MPL* curve will reach a maximum at the *N* level where the production function has an inflection point, that is, changes from convex to concave. This is shown as N_1 in Figure 6.4. The maximum *APL* comes at the *N* level where a ray from the origin in Figure 6.4(a) is just tangent to the production function N_2 in Figure 6.4. Since *MPL* is given by the slope of $y(N; \bar{K})$, at maximum *APL*, *MPL* = *APL*. Finally, to the left of maximum *APL*, *MPL* is greater than *APL*; to the right, *MPL* is less than *APL*.

Now as a firm increases employment, the resulting increase in output per unit increase in employment is given by the *MPL*. For a competitive firm, facing a given price level, the revenue increase from employment increase is

$$\Delta R = P \cdot MPL \cdot \Delta N,$$

where $P \cdot MPL$ is the marginal value product of labor, that is, the value of the product generated by each additional hired worker. In turn, the marginal value product of labor times the increase in the number of people employed gives us the value of the additional output generated or, in other words, the additional revenue to the firm. The increase in cost, ΔC, to the firm hiring additional labor is simply the money wage rate W times ΔN. This gives us the firm's equilibrium employment condition and the demand-for-labor function, as follows. If an addition to the labor force is such that ΔR is greater than ΔC, a profit-maximizing firm will hire the additional labor. If ΔR is less than ΔC, the firm will not hire. The firm will continue to hire labor until $\Delta R = \Delta C$,

$$P \cdot MPL \cdot \Delta N = W \cdot \Delta N.$$

Cancelling the ΔN terms gives us the labor market equilibrium condition,

$$W = P \cdot MPL, \tag{4a}$$

or

$$w \equiv \frac{W}{P} = MPL, \tag{4b}$$

where w is the *real-wage rate*.

We can develop the demand-for-labor function from equations (4) in the following way. Suppose the competitive firm is faced with market wage W_0. It will then extend employment until $P \cdot MPL = W_0$. If W falls, the firm will increase employment, reducing the MPL, to maintain condition (4). This gives us the interpretation of equations (4) as (a) the money wage the firm is willing to pay, $W = P \cdot (MPL)$, or (b) the real wage the firm is willing to pay, $w = MPL$, for employment N. These relationships are shown in Figure 6.5.

If the real wage W_0/P is less than the MPL or W_0 is less than $P \cdot MPL$, the firm will hire additional labor. If the direction of the inequality is reversed, firms will reduce the amount of labor hired.

The monopolistic case

The monopolistic firm's demand for labor will be qualitatively similar to that of the competitive firm, and we can develop it briefly here. The difference between the two cases is that, where the competitive firm faces a given price determined by the market, so that the marginal revenue product of labor $= P \cdot MPL$, the monopolist can choose the price-quantity combination that maximizes profit along the demand curve.

Figure 6.6 shows the monopolist's demand curve relating the quantity Q he sells to the price P he charges. To increase sales by ΔQ from Q_0 to Q_1, the monopolist must reduce price by ΔP from P_0 to P_1. Thus, the net revenue gain, ΔR, is the increased sales at P_0, the original price level, *less* the reduction in price at the initial sales level:

$$\Delta R = P \cdot \Delta Q + Q \cdot \Delta P.$$

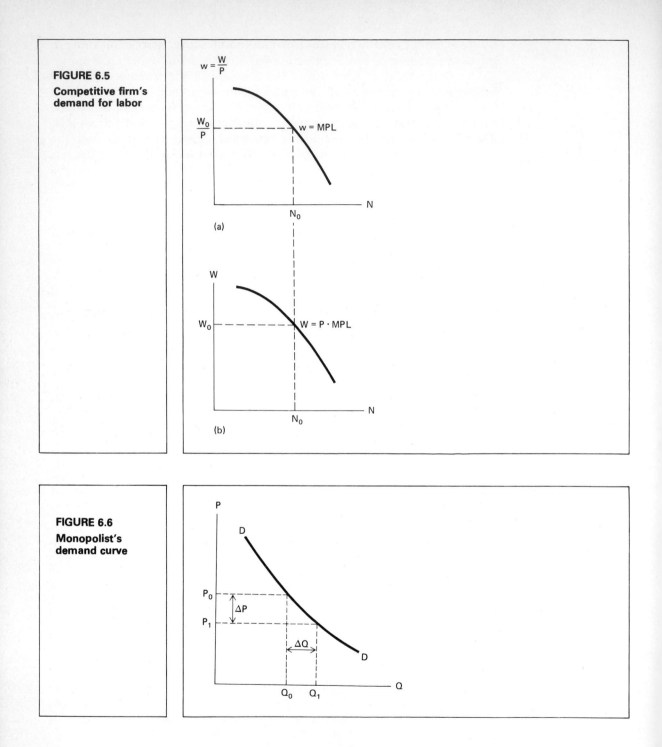

FIGURE 6.5
Competitive firm's demand for labor

$w = \dfrac{W}{P}$

$\dfrac{W_0}{P}$

$w = MPL$

N_0

N

(a)

W

W_0

$W = P \cdot MPL$

N_0

N

(b)

FIGURE 6.6
Monopolist's demand curve

P

D

P_0

ΔP

P_1

ΔQ

D

Q_0 Q_1

Q

Thus, the monopolist's *marginal* revenue from an increase in sales ΔQ is given by

$$MR = \frac{\Delta R}{\Delta Q} = P + Q \cdot \frac{\Delta P}{\Delta Q}.$$

For a unit increase in output, the monopolist gains P but loses the drop in price, $\Delta P/\Delta Q$, times the initial level of output Q.

By factoring P out of the MR expression, we can obtain

$$MR = P \cdot \left(1 + \frac{Q}{P} \cdot \frac{\Delta P}{\Delta Q}\right) = P \cdot \left(1 + \frac{1}{e}\right),$$

where e is the (negative) price elasticity of demand.

If we now multiply the MR $(= \Delta R/\Delta Q)$ by the MPL $(= \Delta Q/\Delta N)$, we will get the gain to the monopolist from hiring a new worker:

$$\frac{\Delta R}{\Delta N} = \frac{\Delta R}{\Delta Q} \cdot \frac{\Delta Q}{\Delta N} = MR \cdot MPL = P \cdot \left(1 + \frac{1}{e}\right) \cdot MPL,$$

It follows that the increase in revenue ΔR from an increase in employment ΔN is simply

$$\Delta R = P \cdot \left(1 + \frac{1}{e}\right) \cdot MPL \cdot \Delta N.$$

The marginal cost of hiring a new worker in this simple model is still W, the wage rate, and the monopolist will maximize profit by hiring additional labor until the marginal revenue, $\Delta R/\Delta N$, is reduced to the level of marginal cost, or

$$W = P \cdot \left(1 + \frac{1}{e}\right) \cdot MPL. \qquad [5]$$

This gives the monopolist's demand for labor curves shown in Figure 6.7.

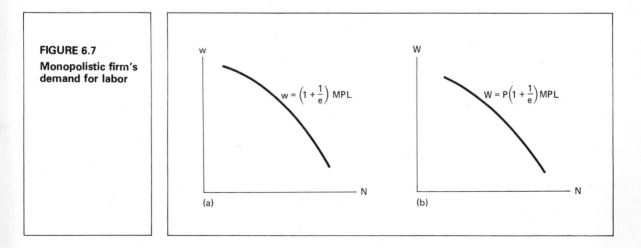

FIGURE 6.7

Monopolistic firm's demand for labor

These are simply the competitive firm's curves of Figure 6.5 shifted left by the factor $1 + (1/e)$. A value of -1.5 for e would make the monopolist's wage offer W one-third of the competitive firm's for any given level of employment N.

The aggregate demand for labor

In an economy with a mixture of monopolistic and competitive elements, the aggregate demand for labor will be a horizontal sum of many individual demand curves, some looking like Figure 6.5, some like Figure 6.7. With a given technology, so that each firm's MPL curve is stable, this aggregate labor demand curve will be fairly stable if product market demand changes do not substantially alter either the output mix between the monopolistic and competitive sectors, or the average elasticity of demand within the monopolistic sector. Under these conditions, the aggregate demand for labor is given by

$$w \equiv \frac{W}{P} = f(N), \qquad\qquad\qquad [6a]$$

or

$$W = P \cdot f(N), \qquad\qquad\qquad [6b]$$

where the slope of the demand curve, f', is negative. The aggregate demand curve (6) is shown in Figure 6.8, following the same format as Figures 6.5 and 6.7.

There are two important things to notice about the aggregate labor-demand curve. First, its negative slope is due to diminishing marginal productivity of labor as more labor is added to a fixed capital stock. In a perfectly competitive economy with a fixed output mix, the demand curve would be the aggregate MPL. Second, since profit-maximizing firms are interested in the real wage they pay—the price of the labor input relative to the price of output—the price level enters the money wage version of the demand function, (6b), multiplicatively. We write $W = P \cdot f(N)$, rather than $W = f(P, N)$. This distinction will be important when we examine the effects on equilibrium employment and output of price changes shifting the labor demand and labor supply curves.

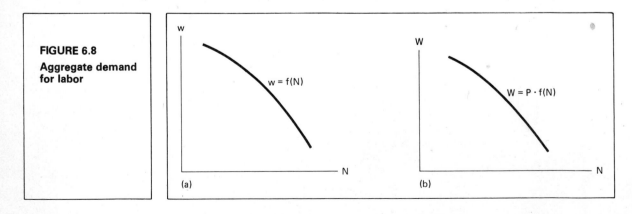

FIGURE 6.8

Aggregate demand for labor

FIGURE 6.9

Fixed-coefficients production function

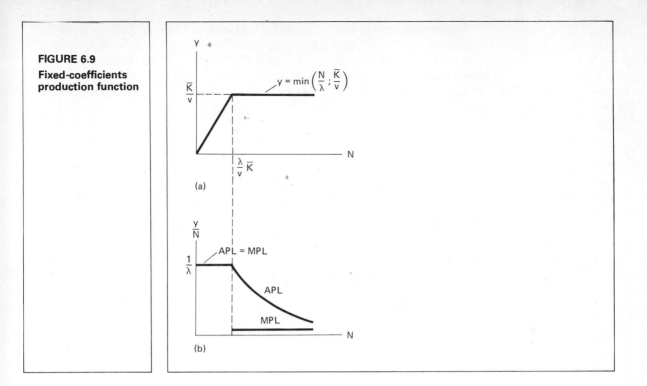

(a)

(b)

The fixed-coefficients production function

Before moving on to discussion of the labor supply curve, we should briefly examine one special production function that implies a fixed relationship between capital and labor inputs and output. This *fixed-coefficients production function* is introduced here because it has obvious implications for the equilibrium level of employment.

The fixed-coefficients production function assumes that there is no possibility for substitution between capital and labor, once the capital stock is put into place. Each machine requires a given man-hour input to produce a given stream of output, and there is no room for varying the output per machine-hour by varying the labor input per machine-hour. With a fixed capital stock in the short run, this production function, shown in Figure 6.9(a), is written as

$$y = \min \left(\frac{N}{\lambda} ; \frac{\bar{K}}{\nu} \right).$$

This says that to produce one unit of y, at least λ units of N and ν units of K are required; λ and ν are the *fixed coefficients*. Thus, in production the ratio of N to K is λ/ν, or $N = (\lambda/\nu)K$. If K is fixed at the level $\bar{K}$, the maximum productive employment is $(\lambda/\nu)\bar{K}$. As employment grows from zero to $(\lambda/\nu)\bar{K}$, output per unit of labor increases at the rate $1/\lambda$; $MPL = 1/\lambda$, as shown in Figure 6.9(b). But at $(\lambda/\nu)\bar{K}$, the capital stock is fully utilized, and the marginal productivity of additional labor falls to zero.

The demand for labor in this case is shown in Figure 6.10. Since the marginal productivity of labor is constant at $1/\lambda$ as N is increased from zero to $(\lambda/\nu)\bar{K}$, the demand curve is flat in that region. At the point where the fixed capital stock becomes fully utilized, the marginal productivity drops to zero. The importance of this case should be clear. The maximum level

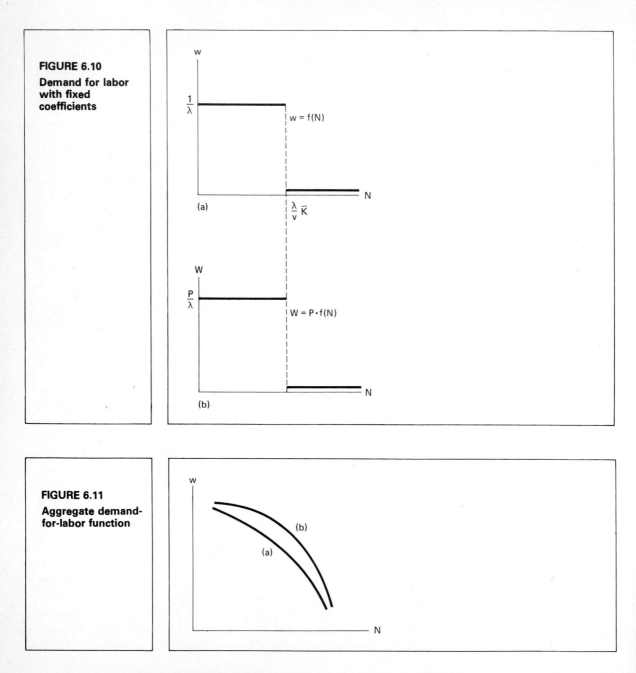

FIGURE 6.10

Demand for labor with fixed coefficients

FIGURE 6.11

Aggregate demand-for-labor function

of employment is $(\lambda/\nu)\bar{K}$; any labor supplied beyond that will be unemployed. If the supply curve crosses the demand curve to the left of $(\lambda/\nu)\bar{K}$, the real wage will be $1/\lambda$; if it crosses the demand curve to the right of $(\lambda/\nu)\bar{K}$, there will be excess labor, and the wage rate will be indeterminate.

To the extent that some firms in the economy operate with fixed-coefficients production functions, the aggregate labor demand curve will be more concave, or *bowed*, with a more or less flat initial segment as those firms increase employment without reducing the *MPL*, and then a steep drop as the firms hit full utilization of capital stock. Figure 6.11 shows two aggregate labor demand functions: (a) with no fixed-coefficients production functions in the economy, and (b) with a significant proportion of fixed-coefficients functions.

THE SUPPLY OF LABOR In developing the aggregate demand for labor, we make no mention of the ability of employers to perceive correctly changes in prices or wages. Employers obviously have good information on, if not control over, the particular prices charged and the wage rate paid. Thus, for the employer, the real wage is simply the money wage paid deflated by the employer's particular product price. The worker, however, has a more difficult time determining the real-wage rate or the real-wage income received. He or she must deflate the known money wage in a way that reflects the prices of the wide range of products available for consumption. Obtaining and digesting price information is a difficult and time-consuming process; individuals probably cannot perceive changes in the price index for their particular baskets of consumer goods nearly as well nor as quickly as employers can perceive changes in individual product prices. The importance of this asymmetry between firms on the demand side and workers on the supply side will become evident as we proceed with the analysis of aggregate supply.

In developing the supply side of the labor market, two important questions must be considered.

1. How quickly or completely does labor respond to changes in the price level?
2. Is the money-wage rate rigid or flexible?

The assumptions made regarding the correct answers to these questions will be important for the operation of our skeletal macro model. In Chapter 8 we will explore the implications of wage rigidity. In the remainder of Chapter 6, we will analyze labor market equilibrium and derive the aggregate supply curve under a range of assumptions about labor's response to changes in the price level. We will be particularly concerned with the two polar case assumptions of (a) a correct perception of and an immediate response to changes in P, and (b) no response to a change in P. Assumption (a) can be described as the *classical* case in which the supply of labor depends only on the real wage, w. The polar case is called *classical* because it stems from the traditional theory of consumer behavior and dominated pre-Keynesian macroeconomic thinking. Assumption (b), which makes the labor supply a function of the money wage rate, we will call the *Keynesian* case. Although the assumption the labor supply responds only to the real-wage rate seems more rational and may indeed be correct (although difficult to verify) in the long run, assumption (b) may be a more useful hypothesis for explaining actual short-run variations in employment.

The individual work-leisure decision

To develop the labor supply function, we must again borrow some basic ideas from microeconomics. We assume that the worker wants to achieve the mix of real income and leisure that is most satisfactory. For our initial discussion of individual behavior, we will treat income, y^*, as that level of real income the worker perceives he is receiving. It does not matter, at the outset, for individual behavior whether the worker has correctly perceived the existing price level. Similarly, we will use w^* to denote the real-wage rate the worker perceives he is receiving. This is the actual nominal wage W deflated by the perceived price level P^*; it will differ from the true real-wage rate to the extent the worker's perception of the price level, P^*, differs from the actual price level. Assuming he can allocate hours to work, thus earning real income y, or to leisure S, the limits or constraints on his ability to achieve maximum satisfaction, or, as we will refer to it, *utility U*, are the number of hours in the day and his real-wage rate. Thus, his utility function is

$$U = U(y^*, S).$$

The worker wants to maximize his (or her) utility subject to the constraint that his real income *is* his real wage times his hours of work. In turn his hours of work n equal his total hours available H less the number he allocates to leisure S. Thus the worker's perceived *budget constraint* is

$$y^* = \frac{W}{P^*} \cdot (H - S) = w^* \cdot (H - S).$$

These relationships are shown in Figure 6.12. Each U (indifference) curve shows all the combinations of y^* and S which yield the same level of satisfaction or utility. The points on U_1 represent a higher level of utility than those on U_0. The entire y^*, S space is filled with such curves, none crossing any other. The worker-consumer wants to reach the highest indifference curve possible. The limit to his ability to move toward the northeast in the y^*, S space is given by the straight line; its location is determined by the number of hours available to the person, and the real wage he faces. Thus if he has H hours at his disposal and he chooses to have no income at all, he will have H hours of leisure. At real-wage rate w_0^*, if he chooses to have no leisure at all, he will have $w_0^* \cdot H$ income, and he can trade leisure for income along the *budget line* connecting these two points. All points on or below the budget line are attainable, or *feasi-*

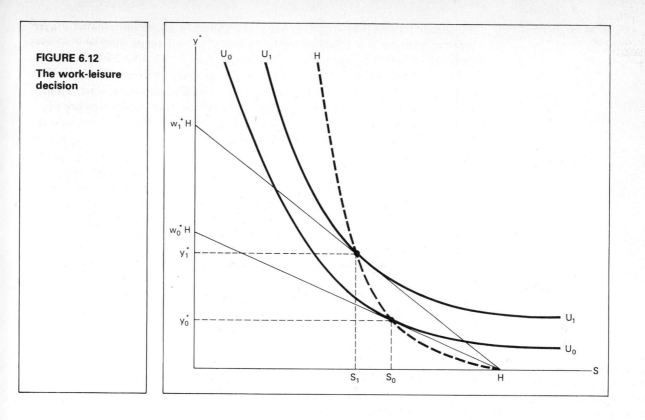

FIGURE 6.12

The work-leisure decision

ble, those above it are not. From the budget constraint $y^* = w^* \cdot (H - S)$, with w^* and H fixed, reductions in leisure time ΔS yield increases in income given by $\Delta y^* = -w^* \cdot \Delta S$, so that the slope of the budget line is $\Delta y^*/\Delta S = -w^*$.

With a given perceived real-wage rate, the worker will reach maximum utility at the point where the straight line is just tangent to an indifference curve, such as y_0^*, S_0 is Figure 6.12. This will be the highest indifference curve, and thus the highest level of utility, he can reach. As the real-wage rate changes, the slope of the budget line changes. For example, if the wage rate were increased to w_1^*, the budget line would swing up to meet the y-axis at w_1^*H, and the equilibrium point would move to y_1^*, S_1.

As we have drawn the indifference curves, it can be seen that increasing the wage rate, that is, increasing the slope of the budget line from an initial low level, initially reduces the amount of leisure consumed by the individual, or conversely, increases the number of hours he works, $n = H - S$. By connecting all the points of tangency of the budget line and indifference curves for various real-wage rates with H held constant, we get the dashed labor supply curve HH of Figure 6.12.

Since leisure S is just H minus the number of hours of labor offered n, we can redraw the relationship between the real-wage rate w and the amount of labor n_i offered by individual i as in Figure 6.13(a), which shows an individual labor supply curve that eventually bends backward. This suggests that once wage rates reach a certain high level, increases in wages may cause some workers to begin to increase leisure rather than working time, as the income effect of higher wages overcomes the substitution effect. If we assume a homogeneous labor force with a single wage rate which is perceived in the same way by all members of the labor force, we can sum the individual labor supply curves to generate the aggregate labor supply curve for the economy. This is shown in Figure 6.13(b). The assumption of a homogeneous labor force with identical wage perceptions does not limit the general usefulness of our conclusions: its usefulness, of course, is in the ease of exposition that a single labor supply curve makes possible. In Chapter 8, we drop the assumption of a homogeneous labor supply and deal with problems associated with a labor force disaggregated both by geography and skills. This does not change our qualitative conclusions about the aggregate level of unemployment, but it does help to explain the distribution of unemployment.

An additional step is required to yield a labor supply curve comparable to the labor demand curve developed earlier in this chapter. We require a labor supply curve that relates the quantity of labor supplied to the real-wage rate, w, instead of the real-wage rate as perceived by labor, w^*. The aggregate labor supply curve of Figure 6.13(b) gives the amount of employment the labor force will offer at any perceived real wage. It also gives the perceived real wage the labor force requires for any given amount of employment and can be represented as $w^* = g(n)$, or

$$w^* \equiv \frac{W}{P^*} = g(N), \tag{7a}$$

or

$$W = P^* \cdot g(N). \tag{7b}$$

The difference between the real-wage rate w and the *perceived* real-wage

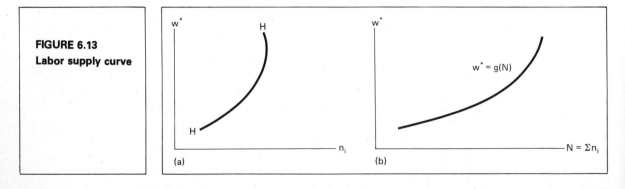

FIGURE 6.13

Labor supply curve

(a)

(b)

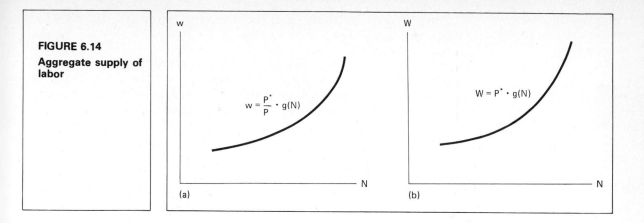

FIGURE 6.14

Aggregate supply of labor

(a)

(b)

rate w^* is due to labor's *perception* of the price level P^* differing from the actual price level P. That is, the ratio of w to w^* can be written as

$$\frac{w}{w^*} = \frac{\dfrac{W}{P}}{\dfrac{W}{P^*}} = \frac{P^*}{P},$$

so that

$$w = \frac{P^*}{P} \cdot w^*.$$

Thus we can rewrite (7a) as

$$w = \frac{P^*}{P} \cdot w^* = \frac{P^*}{P} \cdot g(N), \qquad\qquad [8a]$$

and

$$W = P^* \cdot g(N). \qquad\qquad [8b]$$

These supply curves are shown in Figure 6.14, which follows the same format as our illustrations of the demand for labor.

EQUILIBRIUM IN THE LABOR MARKET

We have now derived equations for both the demand and the supply of labor.

Demand: $w = f(N)$ or $W = P \cdot f(N)$; $\qquad\qquad [9]$

Supply: $w = \dfrac{P^*}{P} \cdot g(N)$ or $W = P^* \cdot g(N)$. $\qquad\qquad [10]$

Equating demand to supply gives the labor market equilibrium condition,

$$f(N) = \frac{P^*}{P} \cdot g(N), \qquad\qquad [11a]$$

or

$$P \cdot f(N) = P^* \cdot g(N).$$ [11b]

That is, for any price level, P, and price level perceived by labor, P^*, wages will adjust to equate the demand for labor with the supply of labor. The graphical solution of labor market equilibrium is represented by the intersection of the two curves in Figure 6.15. For given values of the actual price level, P_0, and the perceived price level, P^*, equilibrium employment is N_0, and the nominal- and real-wage rates are W_0 and w_0, respectively.

Let us now examine what happens as the price level changes under the extreme classical and Keynesian assumptions regarding labor's ability to perceive price level changes, namely, (a) a correct perception of and immediate response to P (classical case), or (b) no response to changes in P (extreme Keynesian case).

In the classical case, P^* is identical to P or $P^*/P = 1$. It is clear from Figure 6.15(a) that a movement in P under this assumption would leave the initial labor equilibrium values, w_0 and N_0, unchanged. This is the classical result in which movements of the price level do not influence equilibrium employment. The same results, of course, can be obtained from Figure 6.15(b). If P^* and P increase in the same proportion, both labor demand and labor supply shift up by the same amounts leaving N_0 undisturbed. The nominal-wage rate, W, will rise by the same proportion as P leaving the real-wage rate unchanged. To repeat, in the classical case a price level change will not alter the real-wage rate nor the level of employment.

In the Keynesian no-adjustment case, as P rises from P_0 there is no change in P^*. Examining Figure 6.15(b) under the extreme Keynesian assumption, we see that the demand for labor shifts up along an unchanged supply curve. Equilibrium employment and the nominal-wage rate will increase. However, the real-wage rate will fall as the increase in the wage rate will not match the increase in the price level. This is clear in Figure 6.15(a). The increase in the price level means P^*/P will fall so that the supply curve shifts down, yielding higher employment at a reduced real-wage rate. In the extreme Keynesian model, the inability of labor to

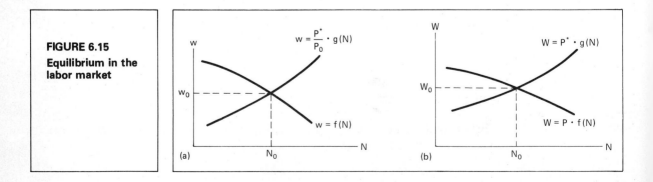

FIGURE 6.15
Equilibrium in the labor market

perceive a price change means a price increase will reduce real wages inducing firms to hire more labor.

It is clear the relation of perceived price level changes to movements in actual price levels is crucial. Our assumptions about this relationship will determine the effect of a change in the price level on aggregate supply.

AGGREGATE SUPPLY As noted on page 107, it is no easy task to obtain or digest price information on the wide range of products available for consumption. The process is not only difficult but it is time consuming. In the short run, the classical assumption that labor correctly perceives and immediately responds to price level changes does not seem realistic. On the other hand, in a period of unusually rapid price changes, such as we have experienced in the 1970s, the extreme Keynesian assumption of no adjustment to price changes is similarly unrealistic. The most useful assumption under which to develop our aggregate supply curve is that labor does adjust its perception of the price level to movements in the actual price level. As the actual price level P rises, the perceived price level P^* also increases, but at most by as much as P. This could be written as

$$P^* = p(P); \quad 0 < p' < 1.$$

Here the perceived price level is an increasing function of the actual price level. The extreme case where $p' = 0$ is the extreme Keynesian case; $p' = 1$ defines the classical case where $P^* = P$. The intermediate case of incomplete adjustment has p' between zero and one.

We could also formulate the relationship between P^* and P in terms of adjustment over time of P^* as P changes. The adjustment of P^* to a change in P between time $(t-1)$ and time t could be written as

$$P_t^* - P_{t-1} = \lambda \, (P_t - P_{t-1}); \quad 0 < \lambda < 1.$$

Here the perceived price level P_t^* differs from the price level in the preceding period by the fraction λ of the actual change in P. This could result, for example, from workers being uncertain as to the permanence of a short-run change in the price level, and revising the perceived price level P^* by only a fraction of the actual changes. Our extreme assumptions correspond to $\lambda = 0$ (extreme Keynesian) and $\lambda = 1$ (classical case). Our intermediate case of incomplete adjustment $(0 < \lambda < 1)$ we will describe as the general Keynesian case. In this chapter, we will not make explicit use of the difference equation described above; however, this formulation will allow us in Chapter 15 to deal with dynamic models of inflation.

Aggregate supply curve: General Keynesian model Our assumption of incomplete adjustment to price changes by labor simply means that P^* will not rise by as much as P when P changes. Labor market equilibrium as described in equation (11b) is

$$P \cdot f(N) = P^* \cdot g(N)$$

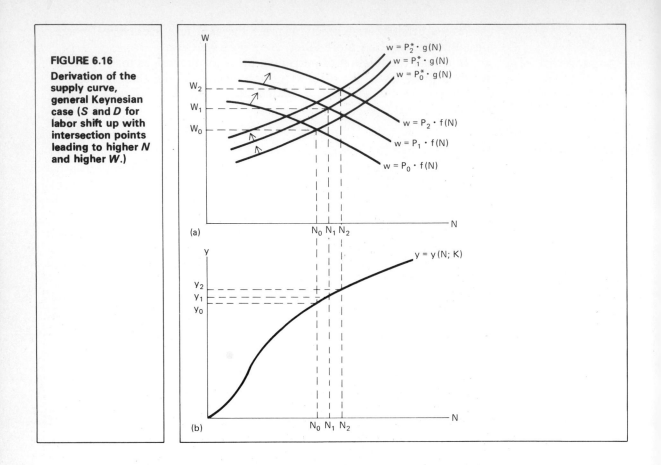

FIGURE 6.16

Derivation of the supply curve, general Keynesian case (*S* and *D* for labor shift up with intersection points leading to higher *N* and higher *W*.)

In figure (a):

$w = P_2^* \cdot g(N)$
$w = P_1^* \cdot g(N)$
$w = P_0^* \cdot g(N)$
$w = P_2 \cdot f(N)$
$w = P_1 \cdot f(N)$
$w = P_0 \cdot f(N)$

W_2, W_1, W_0

(a) N_0 N_1 N_2

In figure (b):

$y = y(N; \bar{K})$

y_2, y_1, y_0

(b) N_0 N_1 N_2

and our assumption means that when P rises demand will exceed supply and labor market equilibrium will only be achieved at a higher level of employment and at a lower real-wage rate since this is the only way employers can be induced to increase their hiring. Figure 6.16 makes clear that for each level of P there is a corresponding level of real output, y.

As the price level increases, the demand for labor increases and the supply of labor shifts up but by a smaller amount. Equilibrium is achieved at a higher level of employment, N, which through our production function $y = y(N; \bar{K})$ yields a higher level of output. Money wage rates increase but not to the extent prices have risen, so real-wage rates fall. Aggregate supply corresponding to Figure 6.16 is shown in Figure 6.17.

Aggregate supply:
Extreme Keynesian case

Our polar case of no adjustment to price changes by labor leads to a supply curve similar to that of Figure 6.17; however, it is flatter. Under the extreme Keynesian assumption the supply curve in Figure 6.16(a) will not shift as prices change. Consequently, the increase in employment required to establish equilibrium in the labor market as prices change will be

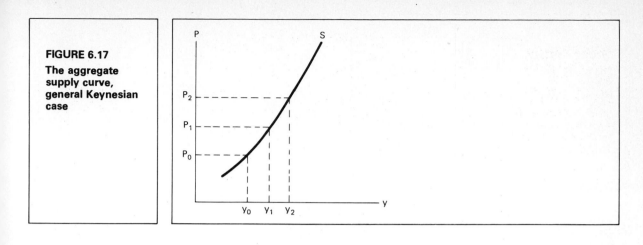

FIGURE 6.17

The aggregate supply curve, general Keynesian case

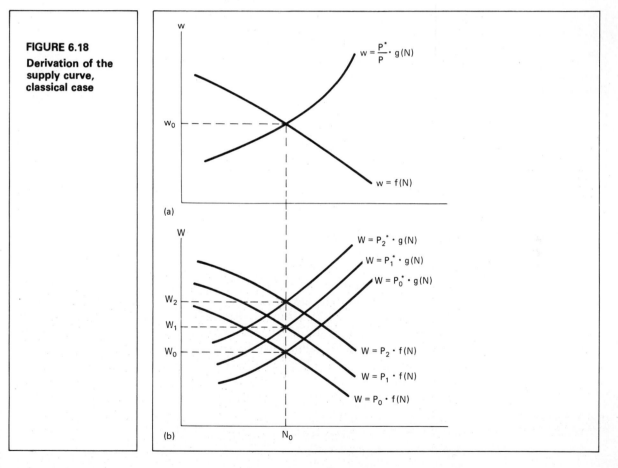

FIGURE 6.18

Derivation of the supply curve, classical case

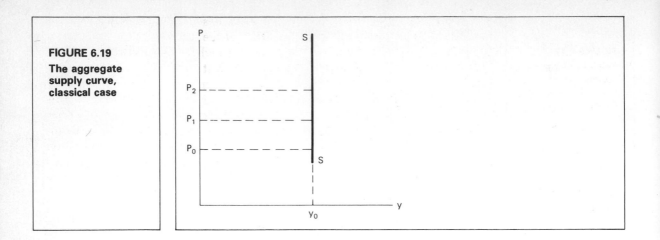

FIGURE 6.19

The aggregate supply curve, classical case

greater. This in turn will yield a greater increase in output for a given price increase.

Aggregate supply: Classical case

To derive the aggregate supply curve in the case of complete adjustment to price changes we consider the labor market equilibrium described in equation (11a)

$$f(N) = \frac{P^*}{P} \cdot g(N).$$

This classical equilibrium is illustrated in Figure 6.18(a). Again, we can derive the aggregate supply curve by asking what happens to equilibrium employment as the price level is increased exogenously.

With P^* moving identically to P, Figure 6.18(a) shows no effect on equilibrium employment as P rises. The mechanism holding employment constant is seen more clearly in Figure 6.18(b). The demand curve shifts up as P changes; however, the change in P leads to an equal change in P^* so the supply curve shifts up proportionately to the demand curve.

The resulting aggregate supply curve is shown in Figure 6.19. With employment fixed at N_0 in Figure 6.18, output is fixed at $y_0 = y(N_0;\bar{K})$ as P rises from P_0 to P_1 to P_2. In the classical case, the aggregate supply curve is vertical. On the supply side, equilibrium employment and output do not vary with movements in the price level.

SUPPLY-SIDE DISTURBANCES

Before turning to an integration of aggregate demand and aggregate supply, it is worthwhile to examine briefly the sources of shifts in the supply curve. As we have developed it, the supply curve depends on two basic relationships, the production function, $y = y(N; \bar{K})$, and the supply of labor, $w^* = g(N)$. A change in either of these relationships will cause the supply curve to shift. Let us consider three "pure" cases of shifts as this will point the way for more complicated cases. Supply shifts will be important in understanding the inflation of the 1970s.

Shifts in the production function
We can distinguish between two ways in which a shift in the production function will alter aggregate supply. A shift in the *level* of the production function will mean that a given equilibrium level of employment will yield a higher level of output. Figures 6.20 and 6.21 demonstrate this effect. Such a change might result from a technical change improving only the efficiency of capital or an increase in the capital stock in a fixed-coefficient model. We have been careful to keep the slope of the production function constant at the initial level of employment. This means the mar-

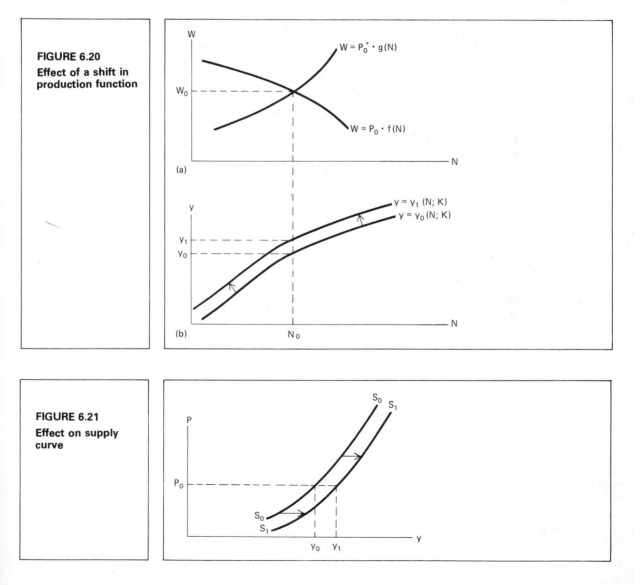

FIGURE 6.20

Effect of a shift in production function

FIGURE 6.21

Effect on supply curve

ginal product of labor will be unchanged and consequently the demand for labor, $f(N)$, is unchanged. Labor market equilibrium remains unchanged and aggregate supply shifts out at the given price level.

A shift in the production function might also result in a shift in the *slope* of the production function. Such a change would cause $f(N)$ to shift disturbing the initial equilibrium in the labor market. An increase in the demand for labor would yield a higher level of employment for any price level. Higher employment, through the (unshifted) production function, would yield higher output. Again Figure 6.21 describes the shift in the aggregate supply curve from an increase in the demand for labor.

Shift in labor supply   The effect of an upward shift in the labor supply function is illustrated in Figures 6.22 and 6.23. In Figure 6.22(a), the labor supply curve shifts from $g_0(N)$ to $g_1(N)$. This could be the result of a change in labor force tastes between income and leisure, an increase in real-wage demands by strong unions, or an increase in unemployment benefits. The upward shift reduces equilibrium employment from N_0 to N_1 in Figure 6.22(a) at the preexisting values of actual and perceived price levels. In Figure 6.22(b) the reduction in employment reduces output supplied from y_0 to y_1 again at the preexisting values of P_0 and P_0^*.

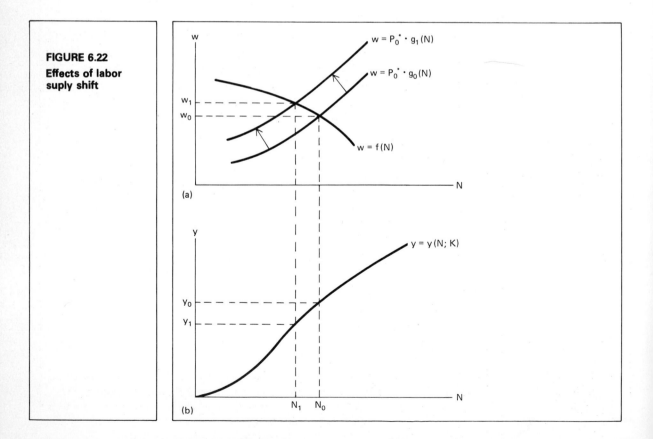

FIGURE 6.22

Effects of labor suply shift

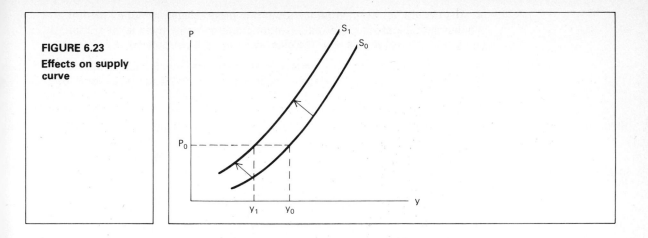

FIGURE 6.23
Effects on supply curve

The shift in aggregate supply is shown in Figure 6.23. At the initial price level P_0, equilibrium output supplied falls from y_0 to y_1. For any initial price level, equilibrium output is reduced by the shift in labor supply.

These examples conclude our analysis of the supply side of our skeletal macro model. They illustrate shifts in output supplied, given P, while earlier sections showed movements along the supply curve due to changes in P and given the underlying relationships. In Chapter 7 we combine the demand analysis of Chapters 4 and 5 with the supply analysis of this chapter to study general equilibrium determination in this basic model.

QUESTIONS FOR DISCUSSION AND REVIEW

1. How will an increase in the capital stock affect each of the following?

   a. The demand curve for labor
   b. The real-wage rate
   c. The level of employment
   d. The aggregate supply curve

2. How will a decrease in the size of the work force effect each of the following?

   a. The demand curve for labor
   b. The real-wage rate
   c. The level of employment
   d. The aggregate supply curve

3. Labor's inability to perceive correctly particular price level change and thus its real wage most likely diminishes with the passage of time. Accepting this, how would long-run and medium-run aggregate supply curves appear relative to the short-run aggregate supply curve?

4. The United States' income tax system is progressive on money income. Thus inflation increases the real level of taxation at any given level of real income. How would this alter the classical aggregate supply curve?

5. Output supplied will only increase with the price level if labor is deceived into accepting a lower real wage. Why is the lower real-wage rate required?

SELECTED READINGS

M. Friedman, "A Monetary Theory of Nominal Income," *Journal of Political Economy*, March/April 1971.

M. Friedman, "A Theoretical Framework for Monetary Analysis," *Journal of Political Economy*, March/April 1970.

F. Modigliani, "The Monetary Mechanism and Its Interaction with Real Phenomenon," *Review of Economics and Statistics*, Supplement, February 1963.

D. Patinkin, *Money, Interest and Prices*, 2nd ed. (New York: Harper & Row, 1965), chaps. 9–10.

D. Patinkin, "Price Flexibility and Full Employment," in M. G. Mueller, ed., *Readings in Macroeconomics* (New York: Holt, Rinehart and Winston, 1971).

W. L. Smith, "A Graphical Exposition of the Complete Keynesian System," in M. G. Mueller, ed., *Readings in Macroeconomics* (New York: Holt, Rinehart and Winston, 1971).

EQUILIBRIUM IN
THE STATIC MODEL

In Chapters 4 and 5 we developed the demand side of our skeletal macro model by taking the price level P as exogenous and deriving the equilibrium output demanded y. In Chapter 6, we examined the labor market and developed the economy's supply curve. Again, we took the price level as exogenous and derived the equilibrium output that results from labor market equilibrium. Now, in Chapter 7, we combine demand and supply to determine the equilibrium value for the price level and, simultaneously, the equilibrium values for output and income, y, for employment, N, and for the interest rate, r. In Figure 7.1, the intersection of the supply and demand curves gives us equilibrium P_0 and y_0. We can take these values to the IS or LM curves on the demand side to find equilibrium r_0, and to the production function on the supply side to find equilibrium N_0.

This chapter analyzes the process by which equilibrium values of these four important variables are reached, and the reaction of these equilibrium values to exogenous changes. The changes may be the result of a government pursuing policies designed to alter the equilibrium values or the result of "shocks" to the system such as an oil embargo or exogenous shifts in demand or technology. Working carefully through the analysis of reactions to exogenous disturbances will give the student an intuitive understanding of how the macroeconomy "hangs together." In Chapter 9, we will consider more carefully the effects of policies designed to offset exogenous changes.

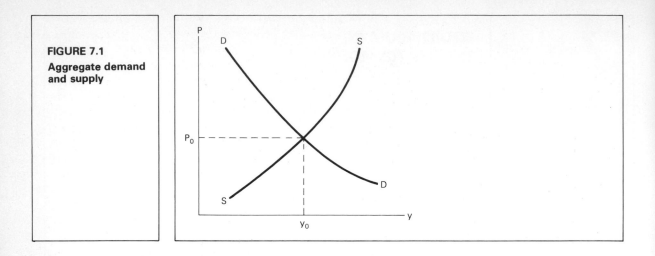

EQUILIBRIUM IN THE GENERAL KEYNESIAN MODEL

We now have four equations in our four unknown variables: y, N, r and P. Three equations represent the equilibrium conditions in the product market, the money market, and the labor market, and the fourth equation is the production function. These are shown below as:

Product market: $y = c(y - t(y)) + i(r) + g;$ [1]

Money market: $\dfrac{\bar{M}}{P} = l(r) + k(y);$ [2]

Labor market: $P \cdot f(N) = P^* \cdot g(N);$ [3]

Production function: $y = y(N; \bar{K}).$ [4]

We leave unquantified the assumption that P^* relates to P such that it increases as P increases, but by a lesser amount. We are accepting neither the extreme Keynesian assumption that labor supply does not respond to a change in the price level nor the classical assumption that labor responds to a change in the price level just as it responds to a change in the money wage rate; that is, that labor supply depends only on the real-wage rate.

It should be noted the model is indeed a simultaneous one. That is, substituting N for y through the production function, we see that the product market equilibrium condition includes the variables N and r; the money market includes N, P and r; and the labor market equilibrium includes N and P. No market is sufficient to determine any single variable. When we reconsider the classical assumption, we will see that it allows us to dichotomize the labor market from the other markets.

To understand how the system reaches equilibrium, let us consider a system that is out of equilibrium. In Figure 7.2(a) we see that at an initial equilibrium price level P_0, equilibrium in the product market and the money market requires an interest rate r_0 and a level of income (= output) of y_0. Figure 7.2(b) shows that at price level P_0, equilibrium in the labor market requires a level of employment N_0. If we have aligned the two diagrams so that the level of output lies directly above the corresponding level of employment as determined by the production function, we can see that the level of output supplied at P_0 is below the level of output demanded. The system is not in equilibrium. Since the demand for output exceeds the supply of output, prices will begin to rise. This begins the process that will bring us to equilibrium.

An increase in prices is equivalent to a reduction in the real-money supply. That means that the LM curve will begin to shift upwards. Tightness in the money market will increase interest rates. This in turn will reduce the level of investment leading to an even larger decrease in the level of equilibrium income and output in the product market.

Simultaneously, an increase in the price level increases the demand for labor. Firms will offer higher money wages in an effort to attract more labor. As prices rise, labor will insist on higher money wages, implying that the supply of labor curve shifts up. However, under our assumption of incomplete adjustment, the increase in P^* is less than the increase in P, and the supply curve does not shift up to the same extent as the demand curve. Thus, the real-wage rate is reduced and the level of employment is increased. Through the production function, the level of output supplied increases.

FIGURE 7.2

Equilibrium in the general Keynesian model

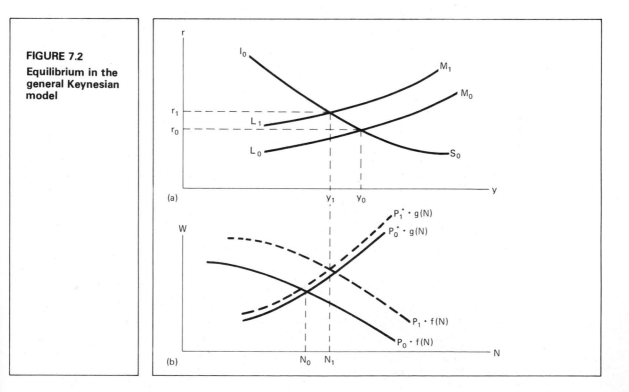

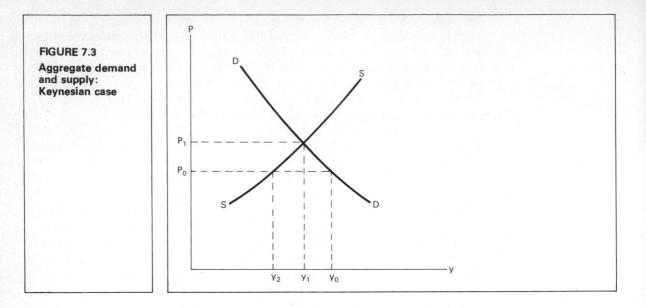

FIGURE 7.3

Aggregate demand and supply: Keynesian case

Figure 7.3 demonstrates that prices will continue to increase until price level P_1 is reached. At this level, output supplied has increased and output demanded has fallen until the initial excess demand has been eliminated. Labor market equilibrium yields a level of output y_1 equal to the level of income corresponding to equilibrium in the product and money markets.

This description of the process by which equilibrium is reached from an initial disequilibrium points the way towards analyzing the impact of macroeconomic policies or exogenous shocks. An initial equilibrium becomes a disequilibrium position as a result of a shift in one of our underlying relationships. For example, P_0 and N_0 might have represented an initial equilibrium which was disturbed by an increase in the desire of business to invest which shifted upwards the *IS* curve to the position shown in Figure 7.2.

This process of adjustment can be shown in terms of aggregate demand and aggregate supply in Figure 7.3. At price level P_0, there is excess demand of $y_0 - y_2$. As prices rise, output demanded falls by $(y_0 - y_1)$ and output supplied increases by $(y_1 - y_2)$. These changes eliminate the excess demand at equilibrium price level P_1 and output (= income) level y_1.

EQUILIBRIUM IN THE CLASSICAL MODEL

Although the process through which equilibrium is reached under the classical assumption of complete adjustment in labor supply is similar to the process described above, the result differs in one significant aspect. The classical assumption is equivalent to setting $P = P^*$ and consequently equilibrium condition (3) is replaced by,

Classical labor market: $f(N) = g(N)$. [3a]

The classical labor market equilibrium condition (3a) represents one equation in one unknown, N. This determines equilibrium N_0 and, through the production function, equilibrium income y_0 with no reference to the product and money markets. The model becomes dichotomized in that supply conditions determine output while demand determines prices and interest rates. Indeed, with y_0 determined, the product market, or the IS curve, determines interest rates r_0 and the money market, or the LM curve, determines the price level.

Figure 7.4 depicts the process through which equilibrium is reached in the classical model. Again we begin from a condition of disequilibrium. At the initial disequilibrium price level P_0, output demanded y_1 again exceeds output supplied y_0. This leads to an increase in prices, which reduces the real-money supply, increases interest rates, and reduces investment and thus output demanded. The story is identical to that told in the Keynesian model. The increase in prices again leads employers to offer

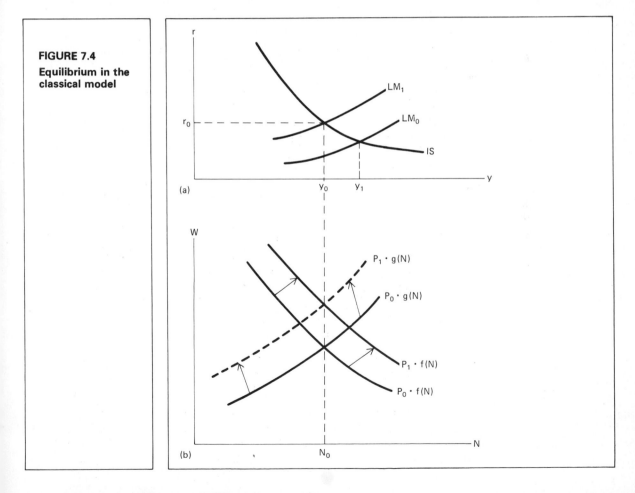

FIGURE 7.4
Equilibrium in the classical model

higher money wages in an effort to attract more labor; however, the increase in prices leads labor to demand a corresponding increase in money wages. The change in the price level has no effect on labor market equilibrium N_0: money wages increase, but real wages remain constant. The model achieves equilibrium when the price level has risen to P_1. The entire adjustment to the initial excess demand takes place on the demand side, as output demanded is reduced to the level of output supplied.

This result is summarized in Figure 7.5. Excess demand of $y_1 - y_0$ is eliminated by the decrease in output demanded as the price level rises to P_1. Figures 7.5 and 7.3 should be compared. In the latter, an aggregate supply curve slopes up and to the right so that some of the excess demand is eliminated by an increase in the quantity supplied. In Figure 7.5 with the vertical supply curve that results from the classical assumption, there is no change in the quantity supplied as the price level rises.

New support for the classical model

The determination of output in the classical model is in sharp contrast to that in the Keynesian models. In the classical model, output and income are determined without reference to aggregate demand. Demand adjusts through price changes to equal the output determined by the vertical supply curve. In the Keynesian models, both demand and supply adjust to changes in the price level and thus the determination of output requires consideration of both sides of the market. This difference is the result of the different assumptions about the labor supply function as we discussed in Chapter 6.

A reasonable question to ask is which set of assumptions is appropriate. For the past 40 years, most economists have held that the classical assumption that the supply of labor depends only on the real wage was of little use in explaining short-run behavior. Variations in output that appeared to be in response to changes in demand cast doubt on the usefulness of the classical model. Why then do we spend so much time developing such a model?

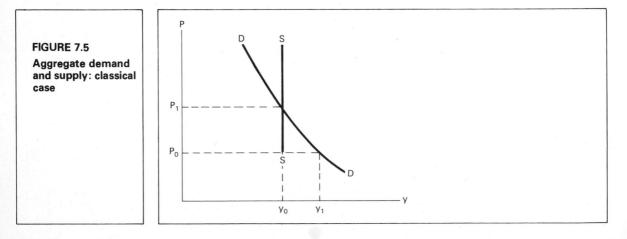

FIGURE 7.5

Aggregate demand and supply: classical case

We believe there are two good reasons for dealing with the classical model in detail. Many economists suggest the assumptions of the classical model may hold in the long run. In particular, the extreme Keynesian assumption that labor responds to the money-wage rate and not to price levels is not acceptable in the long run. We will return to this issue later in this chapter.

In addition, the classical model has been resurrected in the 1970s as descriptive of the short run. It is argued that short-run variations in demand will lead systematically to variations in output only if labor systematically errs in its estimate of real wages. Proponents of the new classical school argue that for labor to be systematically wrong in its expectations, particularly as to the effects of policy, is for them to be irrational. They will adjust the way expectations are formed to eliminate any systematic error. We will evaluate this "rational expectations" argument in some detail in Chapter 14. For now, it is important to note that there exists new support for aggregate supply curves that are vertical even in the short run and that the workings of the classical model are consequently important to understand.

<table>
<tr><td>SOURCES OF
DISEQUILIBRIUM:
DEMAND SHIFT</td><td>Changes in any of the basic relationships underlying the product market or the money market will shift the IS curve or the LM curve. For example, a change in the desire of people to consume or a change in the desire of business to invest will shift the IS curve. A change in the demand for money will cause the LM curve to shift. These changes will mean that at a given price level a new demand side equilibrium y will be determined that will be inconsistent with the initial level of y that still yields equilibrium in the labor market. The effects of such changes are seen in the results of the process by which P and y adjust to reestablish general equilibrium. That is, the process of adjustment to a disequilibrium described above is sufficient to explain how the economy responds to changes in the product market or money market. Once the disturbance is translated into an impact effect on expenditure, the results can be analyzed independently of the source of the disturbance.</td></tr>
</table>

This is also true for shifts in the fiscal and monetary variables under the government's control. As explained in Chapter 5, a shift in government purchases g or net taxes t will shift the IS curve, and a change in the nominal stock of money M will shift the LM curve. These changes create a disequilibrium at the initial levels of P and y and the impact of policy is felt as the process of establishing a new equilibrium is played out independently from the source of disequilibrium.

Expansionary policy creates excess demand and, in the general Keynesian model, this excess demand is eliminated as price increases reduce output demanded and increase output supplied. The net change is an increase in equilibrium income price level. In the classical model, the real adjustment is entirely on the demand side. An increase in M, for example, leads to an offsetting increase in P as equilibrium is reestablished at the initial level of y.

SOURCES OF DISEQUILIBRIUM: SUPPLY SHIFT

For supply-side disturbances the analysis is not quite as simple as it was on the demand side. This is because shifts in the production function may change both the *slope* ($= MPL$), and the *level* of the production function. A shift in the MPL will change the demand curve for labor resulting in a new equilibrium level of employment N. Changes in the level of the production function give a change in the level of output y produced by any given level of employment N. Analysis of the impact on output y will proceed as above; however, the impact on employment is more difficult to determine.

Let us consider a shock that reduces the supply of a factor that cooperates with capital and labor in producing output. This could be a run of bad weather, a shift in supply curve of an intermediate good, such as would result from an oil embargo or Iranian revolution, or even a reduction in the capital stock due to a war.

The effects of a reduction in supply of a cooperating factor are shown in Figures 7.6 and 7.7. In Figure 7.6(b) the loss of a cooperating factor shifts the production function down. In Figure 7.6(a) the demand for labor also shifts down on the assumption that the marginal product of labor falls. Output supplied falls from y_0 to y_2 at the initial equilibrium price level. The fall from y_0 to y_1 is due to the fact that less output can be produced with initial employment N_0 and the fall from y_1 to y_2 is due to

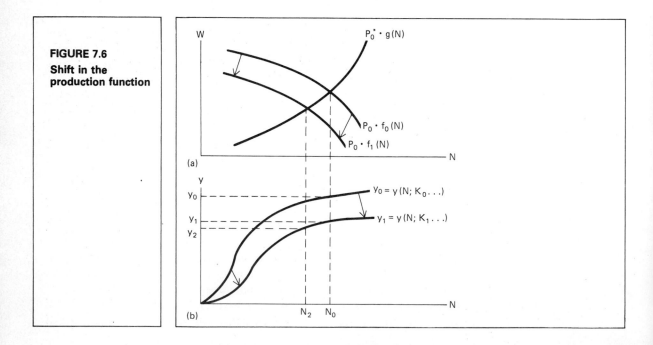

FIGURE 7.6

Shift in the production function

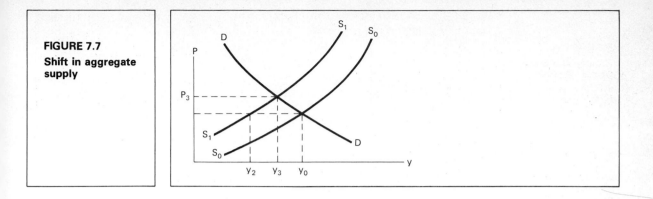

FIGURE 7.7

Shift in aggregate supply

the fall in MPL which reduced employment from N_0 to N_2. Thus, the supply curve shift in Figure 7.7 comes from two sources: the production function shift and the change in employment.

The shift in the supply curve has created disequilibrium at the initial price level P_0 and level of output (= income) y_0. We have a situation of excess demand that will lead to adjustment. As in the previous section, it should be noted—once it is established whether a given shock has created excess demand (pulling P up) or excess supply (pushing P down)—the analysis of adjustment is independent of where the shock originates. In the case at hand, as with all cases of excess demand, prices will begin to rise. On the supply side, this will increase the demand for labor and, to a lesser extent (since P^* does not adjust fully to P), shift upwards the supply of labor. Employment will increase as real wages fall, and output will rise along the new production function. The increase in prices will reduce the real-money supply, leading to upward pressure on interest rates, a decline in real investment, and a multiplied decrease in the level of income demanded. These changes are implicit in the movement along the old demand curve and the new supply curve in Figure 7.7 to the new equilibrium. From our initial equilibrium, output has fallen and prices have risen.

Although the net effect on output y is unambiguous, the net impact on employment could be positive or negative. If the reduction in MPL is very large (as it would be in a production function similar to a fixed coefficient model in which substitution of between factors of production is difficult), there would be a large initial change in N. If the aggregate demand curve were very flat, price adjustment would be small and output adjustment large in the process of reaching a new equilibrium. In either case, it is probable that the net effect of a reduction in the supply of a cooperating factor would be to reduce equilibrium employment. If substitution of factors were easy or the adjustment to a new equilibrium involved large price changes and minor output changes, employment would rise. In the extreme, if substitution were so easy that the production function could fall

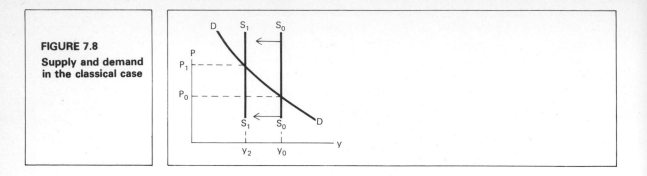

FIGURE 7.8

Supply and demand in the classical case

with no change in *MPL,* the shift would not initially alter employment. Excess demand, which is partially eliminated by an increase in output on the supply side, would then require an increase in employment.

The reaction to a supply disturbance in the classical model includes no similar ambiguity. The initial impact of the loss of a cooperating factor of production is a reduction in employment N and a fall in output supplied y. This creates the usual excess demand gap y_0–y_2 in Figure 7.8. As prices rise in reaction to excess demand, however, the equilibrium level of employment and output supplied remain at N_2 and y_2. All the adjustment comes from the demand side as prices rise until output demanded has been reduced to y_2. The ambiguity has been eliminated because there is no effect on employment beyond the impact effect.

ADJUSTMENT OVER TIME: LONG-RUN AND SHORT-RUN SUPPLY CURVES

The failure of labor to perceive correctly the change in the price level in the Keynesian model means that real wages change in the process of adjusting to disequilibrium and, consequently, that equilibrium employment and output adjust in response to demand disturbances. The rationale for this in the previous chapter was that it is difficult and time consuming to perceive and digest changes in prices of the wide range of products available. As time passes, however, it is reasonable to expect the price level perceived to more closely approximate the actual price level. This in turn implies that the long-run response to a demand disturbance will differ from the short-run response.

Figure 7.9 shows the adjustment to a given shift in demand over time. Assume, for example, demand is increased by an increase in the level of government purchases. In the short run this leads to an increase in equilibrium output to y_1 and causes some inflation as prices rise to P_1. Labor adjusts supply incompletely to the change in prices and although money wages have risen, the real-wage rate falls. As time passes, the increase in prices is more completely perceived and labor insists on a higher money wage to compensate for the price increase. This shift in the labor supply curve leads to a further increase in prices to P_2 and a fall in real output to y_2. Eventually, the more complete perception of price increases, and consequent demand for higher money wages to compensate, means the economy moves along a supply curve such as S_2, which is close to the vertical supply curve of the classical model. In the long run, the increase in demand has led to larger price increases and limited increases in real output.

This is a good way to view the U.S. experience of the late sixties and early seventies. Prices rose initially, due to a sharp increase in defense spending. In subsequent years, prices continued to increase as labor perceived the fall in real wages and demanded higher money wages to offset the higher price level. The price increases initiated by a demand shift led to subsequent price increases occasioned by labor supply shifts.

THE LIQUIDITY TRAP The liquidity trap suggested by Keynes is a special case in which the classical case has no equilibrium solution, and monetary policy becomes completely ineffective. Keynes used the liquidity trap to score a debating point on the classical model; we can use it here to illustrate a conceptual difference between the classical model and the general Keynesian model.

We saw in Chapter 5 that the speculative demand for money may become very elastic, or flat, at low interest rates. If $l(r)$ becomes horizontal at some low r_{min}, the LM curve will also be horizontal at that value of r. The theoretical importance of this point in the classical model is shown in Figures 7.10 and 7.11. If, from initial equilibrium y_0 in Figure 7.10(a), investment demand collapses so that the IS curve shifts to I_1S_1, the price level will begin to fall. In the classical labor market of Figure 7.10(b), the price drop will not change equilibrium N_0; the price change affects labor supply and demand symmetrically, since both depend on the real wage alone.

FIGURE 7.9

Supply reactions over time

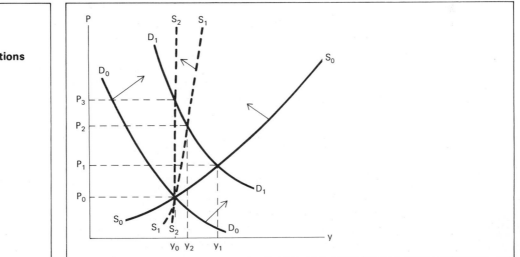

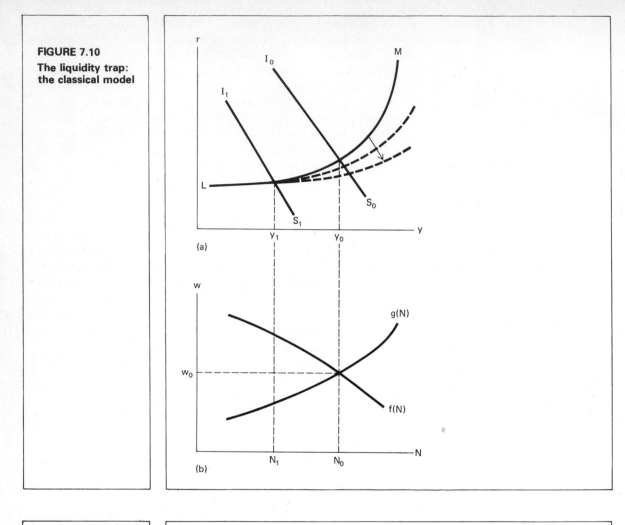

FIGURE 7.10
The liquidity trap: the classical model

(a)

(b)

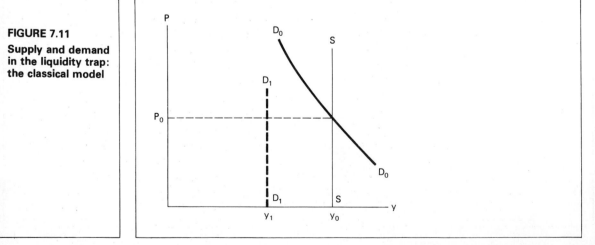

FIGURE 7.11
Supply and demand in the liquidity trap: the classical model

On the demand side, in Figure 7.10(a), the price drop shifts the LM curve out. But since IS has fallen to an intersection with the horizontal segment of the LM curve, the price change does not increase demand-side equilibrium output from y_1, so that excess supply $y_0 - y_1$ remains. Thus, as Keynes pointed out, the classical model may be *inconsistent* at low interest rates. This inconsistency is brought out in Figure 7.11, which shows the demand curve shifting to D_1D_1, corresponding to the IS shift to I_1S_1. With no intersection of the supply and demand curves, the classical model has no equilibrium solution, and seems to suggest that wages and prices would fall continuously if the economy were to get stuck in this liquidity trap where people are indifferent between holding bonds that earn r_{min} and money that earns nothing.

Various writers since Keynes have removed this inconsistency in the classical model. Pigou suggested that falling prices would increase consumers' real wealth, increasing consumer spending and reducing saving, shifting $s(y - t(y))$ down. This would shift IS up to eventual demand-side equilibrium. This wealth effect has been confirmed by subsequent research, as discussed in Chapter 10 on the consumption function. Also,

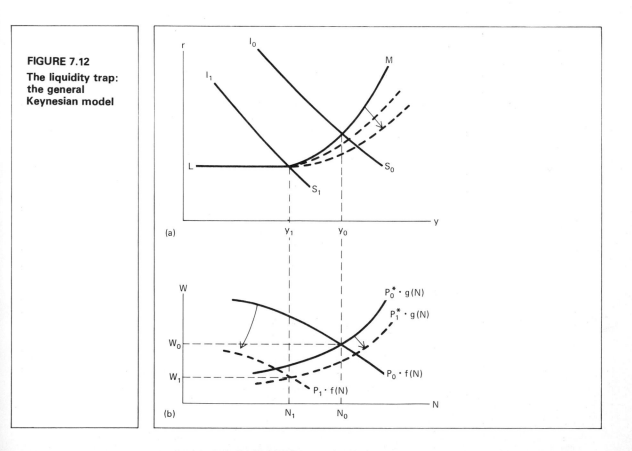

FIGURE 7.12

The liquidity trap: the general Keynesian model

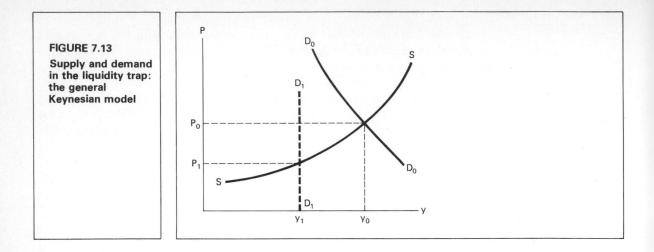

FIGURE 7.13

Supply and demand in the liquidity trap: the general Keynesian model

empirical work on the demand for money has found no evidence that it does, indeed, become absolutely flat at very low interest rates, as we discuss in Chapter 12 on the demand for money.

These solutions to the "inconsistency" in the classical model generally imply that, after a long period of falling wages and prices, equilibrium will be reestablished at the original N_0, y_0 point. But in the 1930s, the U.S. economy seemed to reach a different result: a fairly stable low level of employment with wages and prices dropping to a fairly stable level.

This result is possible in the general Keynesian model, which does not have the liquidity trap inconsistency. The problem in the classical model was that neither equilibrium output supplied nor demanded responded to the price drop in the liquidity trap case. In the Keynesian model of Figures 7.12 and 7.13, the price drop reduces the demand for labor, reducing equilibrium supply-side output from y_0 to y_1, along the positively sloped SS curve of Figure 7.13.

Thus, in this depression case, the general Keynesian model establishes a new equilibrium at y_1, N_1, P_1, W_1, with a drop in employment, as experienced in the 1930s, and new, lower but equilibrium, price and wage levels. The general Keynesian model seems to be a better framework for understanding the events of the 1930s than the classical model with the liquidity trap.

This concludes our discussion of general equilibrium in the skeletal macro model. In this chapter we have proceeded on the assumption that prices and wages are perfectly flexible. In Chapter 8, we consider a somewhat different approach to the labor market and consider the complications of the more common assumption that prices and wages are "sticky," at least in the downward direction.

REAL-LABOR INCOME
AND AVERAGE PRODUCTIVITY

The demonstration in the general Keynesian model that an increase in aggregate demand will lead to an increase in employment with a falling real-wage rate $w = W/P$ as labor market equilibrium moves along the negatively sloped demand function leads to two interesting questions. What will be the effect on total labor income? How will the average productivity of labor change? As the answers to these two questions require a rather lengthy and detailed digression from our main task, we deal with them in an appendix.

Whether the increase in employment outweighs the decrease in the real wage as employment rises, thus increasing total labor income, will depend on the elasticity of the demand curve for labor, that is, the elasticity of $f(N)$ with respect to changes in N. This will tend to be more elastic if excess capacity is available, which is also likely to be the case if expansionary fiscal or monetary policy is in order.

In addition, although w falls as N rises, average productivity—output per man-hour—may rise, mainly due to the existence of *overhead labor*—foremen, office staff, and others—who have more stable employment than production workers. As N expands from a point of low plant utilization, the overhead labor staff will be used more efficiently, raising output per man-hour even though the marginal productivity of production labor is falling.

Real-labor income and changes in N

To begin with, consider a competitive firm producing a given output q, using the following inputs:

capital $\equiv K$;
raw materials $\equiv M$;

"production" labor $\equiv N$;
"overhead" labor $\equiv X$.

In the short run, both K and X are fixed; $K = \bar{K}$, and $X = \bar{X}$. The firm can utilize the existing capacity of the plant and overhead labor as it chooses by applying varying amounts of production labor and raw materials.

The costs of the firm will be of two kinds, fixed and variable.

Fixed costs $= c\bar{K} + W_x\bar{X}$,

where c is the unit cost of fixed capital and W_x is the wage rate for overhead labor.

Variable costs $= P_mM + W_nN$,

where P_m is the unit price of raw materials and W_n is the wage rate for production labor.

We will assume here that the firm's production activity has two aspects: First,

$q = q(N; \bar{K}, \bar{X})$.

This says that the firm's output q in the short run depends on the amount of production labor man-hours employed, given $\bar{X}$ and $\bar{K}$. Production labor has diminishing marginal productivity as shown in Figure 7A.1. Second,

$M = M(q)$,

which says that the amount of raw materials required depends on the level of output as shown in Figure 7A.2. The slope of the $M(q)$ function is simply $\Delta M/\Delta q$. Finally, we will assume that the firm follows normal profit-maximizing behavior. The firm has the following conditions:

Revenue: $R = P \cdot q(N; \bar{K}, \bar{X})$;
Cost: $C = P_mM + W_nN + c\bar{K} + W_x\bar{X}$.

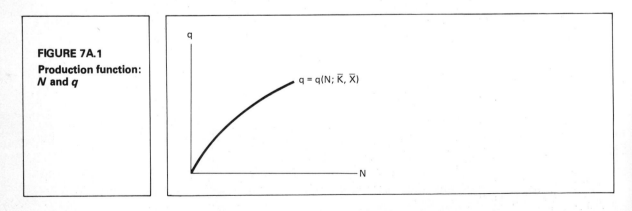

FIGURE 7A.1

Production function: N and q

$q = q(N; \bar{K}, \bar{X})$

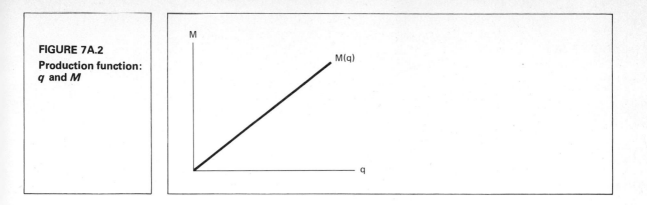

FIGURE 7A.2
Production function:
q and *M*

By adding an extra unit of labor N the firm sees the change in revenue that should be familiar from Chapter 6 (p. 102):

$$\Delta R = P \cdot MPL \cdot \Delta N.$$

The increase in cost includes both the wage paid to the additional workers and the increased materials costs. If we represent the increased materials used per unit of additional output by $\Delta M/\Delta q$, we then have the increment to cost:

$$\Delta C = \left(W_n + P_m \frac{\Delta M}{\Delta q} \cdot MPL \right) \cdot \Delta N.$$

To maximize profit, the firm will continue to hire labor as long as the increase in revenue from doing so is greater than the increase in cost. Thus, the firm will reach equilibrium employment where

$$P \cdot MPL = W_n + P_m \cdot \frac{\Delta M}{\Delta q} \cdot MPL.$$

Moving the expression containing P_m to the left-hand side of the equality sign and factoring MPL out gives

$$W_n = \left(P - P_m \frac{M}{\Delta q} \right) \cdot MPL.$$

Factoring out P from the expression in parentheses gives us the firm's demand function for production labor man-hours:

$$W_n = P \left(1 - \frac{P_m}{P} \cdot \frac{\Delta M}{\Delta q} \right) \cdot MPL.$$

This function, shown in Figure 7A.3, should be fairly familiar. The new factor is the term $\Delta M/\Delta q$. We may now ask, what happens if demand for the firm's output increases, driving prices up?

If there is excess capacity in the firm, that is, if the firm is using few workers relative to the number that could be employed with its fixed

FIGURE 7A.3

Firm's demand for labor

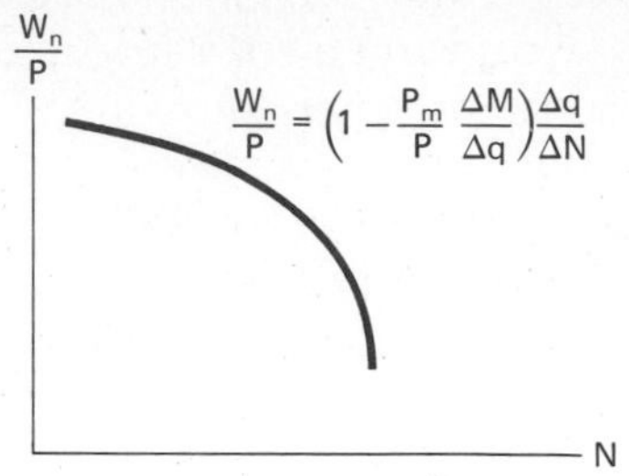

$$\frac{W_n}{P} = \left(1 - \frac{P_m}{P}\frac{\Delta M}{\Delta q}\right)\frac{\Delta q}{\Delta N}$$

capital, as production increases the marginal productivity of labor, MPL, decreases slowly at first. In the case of the fixed-coefficients production function MPL drops not at all with the initial increment of labor. But in general as production increases further, older, less efficient machines have to be activated and MPL drops faster. Furthermore, these older, less efficient machines may need more raw materials, causing $\Delta M/\Delta q$ to go up, and possibly raising P_m relative to P. Thus as the firm approaches full-capacity operation, the term $(P_m/P)(\Delta M/\Delta q)$ is increasing, perhaps at an increasing rate, adding to the effect of a falling MPL in making the slope of the labor demand curve decrease.

The effect on the real-wage rate and on total real-labor income depends on the steepness of the demand curve. If the curve is very steep, the drop in the real wage might result in a decrease in total real-labor income. This is illustrated in Figure 7A.4. There the labor supply function is the money wage function $W = h(N)$. To draw this in the w, N space, we divide both sides of this equation by P, giving $h(N)/P$ as the supply function of Figure 7A.4. There an increase in the price level shifts the labor supply function down along the labor demand function. In the illustration of the Keynesian model, the price increase also raised money wages, but reduced the real wage, similar to the movement shown in Figure 7A.4 from w_0, N_0 to w_1, N_1.

At real wage w_0, production labor's real income is equal to the area $w_0 0 N_0 O$ under the demand curve. If the real wage decreases to w_1, real income to labor becomes the area $w_1 1 N_1 O$. Whether the real income in the second case is greater than, equal to, or less than it was to start with depends on the elasticity of the demand curve. The total real income of production labor will increase with an increase in employment if the elasticity of demand for labor is greater than unity.

As we have seen, the existence of initial excess capacity will tend to flatten out the labor demand curve and will therefore lead to increases in aggregate real-labor income with increasing employment. If the economy is initially at full employment of its resources, the demand for labor curve will have a steeper slope, and decreases in real wages could lead to a decrease in total real-labor income with an elasticity of demand less than unity. Thus, an expansionary demand policy in a period of excess capacity will tend to reduce the real wage only a little and raise employment enough to substantially increase aggregate real-labor income. But an expansionary policy in the face of full-capacity plant utilization may reduce aggregate labor income by reducing the real wage.

Average productivity and employment

We can end this appendix by looking at the behavior of average productivity of the total labor force, both production and overhead:

$$APL_T = \frac{q}{N + \bar{X}}.$$

We can think of the utilization of overhead labor in much the same way as we regarded excess capacity. If there is a large surplus of overhead labor relative to the amount that is normally required for an initial level of production labor, more production workers can be employed with the overhead labor force being "spread out" over them. Thus, although increasing the production man-hour input will reduce the output per production man-hour beyond peak APL, it is possible that the average productivity over the whole labor force will continue to increase because the productivity of the overhead labor force goes up as output rises. Therefore, in a cyclical upswing, we may see average labor productivity rising as the marginal productivity and real wage of production workers fall, due to the overhead labor phenomenon. If the economy begins with substantial excess capacity, this will also be accompanied by rising aggregate real-labor income.

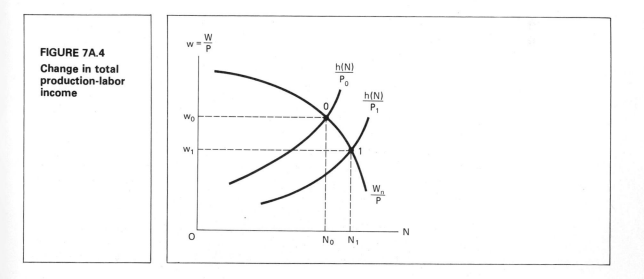

FIGURE 7A.4

Change in total production-labor income

1. The percentage change in money national income can be approximated by the rate of growth in real output plus the rate of price change. For a given change in money income, would you expect the division of the change into its "real" and "price" components to differ in the short run and the long run?

2. It has been stated that demand shifts that lead to increased levels of output must also lead to some increases in prices. Do you agree? If so, what is the explanation for this?

3. Describe the effect of increased pessimism by investors—that is, a reduced desire to invest at any given level of interest rates and income—on the *IS* and *LM* curves and, consequently, on aggregate demand. How will this affect equilibrium income, real wages, and money wages?

4. In the classical model, how will an increased desire by the public to hold money balances affect prices, income, and employment? How would your answers differ in an extreme Keynesian model?

5. In the classical model, how would a decision by OPEC to supply more oil at a lower price affect prices, income, and employment? How would your answers differ in an extreme Keynesian model?

SELECTED READINGS

M. Friedman, "A Monetary Theory of Nominal Income," *Journal of Political Economy*, March/April 1971.

M. Friedman, "A Theoretical Framework for Monetary Analysis," *Journal of Political Economy*, March/April 1970.

F. Modigliani, "The Monetary Mechanism and Its Interaction with Real Phenomenon," *Review of Economics and Statistics*, Supplement, February 1963.

D. Patinkin, *Money, Interest and Prices,* 2nd ed. (New York: Harper & Row, 1965), chaps. 9–10.

D. Patinkin, "Price Flexibility and Full Employment," in M. G. Mueller, ed., *Readings in Macroeconomics* (New York: Holt, Rinehart and Winston, 1971).

T. L. Sargent and N. Wallace, "Rational Expectations and the Theory of Economic Policy," in P. Korliras and R. J. Thorn, eds., *Modern Macroeconomics* (New York: Harper & Row, 1979).

W. L. Smith, "A Graphical Exposition of the Complete Keynesian System," in M. G. Mueller, ed., *Readings in Macroeconomics* (New York: Holt, Rinehart and Winston, 1971).

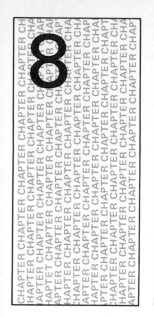

UNEMPLOYMENT AND WAGE RIGIDITY

The last chapter combined aggregate demand and aggregate supply completing our development of a skeletal macroeconomic model. In this general Keynesian model, changes in aggregate demand affect the level of equilibrium output and employment in the economy. This naturally leads us to the questions: How is the unemployment rate related to this equilibrium level of employment, and how does it change when demand conditions change? As we see in this chapter, there are several ways to answer these questions.

First, we interpret movements in employment in the general model as changes in the proportion of those seeking work who are in fact employed. If we accept an unemployment rate of 5–5.5 percent as being "full employment," then at any given time there will be something in excess of 5 million unemployed persons in the United States seeking employment. About half of these people will find jobs within a month or so; an equivalent number of workers will give up or lose their employment. Our hypothesis is that shifts in aggregate demand affect how rapidly individuals who are seeking work will find employment.

Next we develop a statistical explanation of unemployment by defining the labor force L as the level of employment at which the labor supply curve becomes nearly vertical. Movements of actual employment N relative to L give us an explanation of how measured unemployment might change as demand conditions change. Then we introduce wage ridigities into the picture, both in the sense of an economy-wide average wage floor and in the sense of local labor market rigidities. While the relevance of an economy-wide wage floor is questionable, the hypothesis of local wage rigidity is useful. Finally, we summarize a view of unemployment that

143

draws on all of these elements, as well as on the fixed-coefficients production function of Chapter 6.

Even when the economy has achieved an equilibrium position, there is continuous change in the labor market. As noted above, a full-employment unemployment rate of about 5 percent with a labor force of about 100 million persons means that even in good times we should expect that over 5 million people will be actively looking for work in any full-employment month. Moreover, these are not the same people every month; some job seekers will find employment while others join the ranks of active job seekers. Thus, the monthly average unemployment rate does not give even a reasonable estimate of the rate of job search and turnover.

In 1973, our last full-employment year, half of the unemployed in any given month found jobs after less than five weeks of unemployment; less than 20 percent remained unemployed more than 15 weeks. Thus, with a monthly average of 5 million unemployed job seekers at full employment, we can expect 2.5 million to find jobs within a month or so and 2.5 million new people to enter the ranks of unemployed job seekers. The labor market is characterized by constant turnover with workers searching for better, or at least different, jobs and employers continuously screening applicants for newly opened positions. It is within this context that we must understand employment and unemployment in the Keynesian model of Chapter 7.

**Aggregate demand
and employment**

In Chapters 6 and 7 we have seen that variations in aggregate demand will cause variations in employment in the general Keynesian model. This view is entirely consistent with a view of the labor market as consisting of a stock of unemployed job seekers that is turning over frequently. In Figure 8.1 we see the labor market results of an increase in aggregate demand. As in previous examples, an increase in aggregate demand generates excess demand in the product market leading to an increase in the price level.

In Figure 8.1 the price increase alters the labor market by shifting up demand and, to a lesser extent, supply. Excess demand at the former wage rate W_0 leads to an increase in the money wage rate to W_1. This increase in the wage rate is greater than the increase in prices as perceived by labor. As a result, workers searching for employment perceive an improvement in the opportunities available to them, that is, W/P^* rises. An increased fraction of the job seekers accept employment and total employment increases to N_1. The effect of the perceived improvement in W/P^* on job seekers is the movement along the labor supply schedule from N_0 to N_1.

A fall in aggregate demand in this job search model would have the opposite effect to that shown in Figure 8.1. The fall in money wages would exceed the perceived fall in prices so W/P^* would decrease. This deterioration in the value of job offers would lead to a smaller fraction of job seekers accepting employment and thus a drop in equilibrium N.

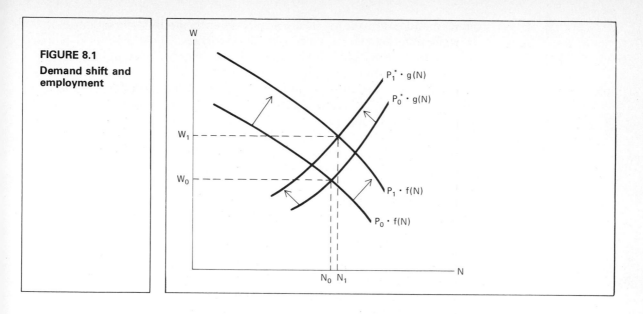

FIGURE 8.1

Demand shift and employment

Alternative
job search
models

This search model has two key features. First, there is the existence of a stock of job seekers evaluating employment opportunities at any point in time. Second, there is a lack of accurate awareness of the true price level. If workers correctly perceived and adjusted to the price level, we could use the classical model and we would see no change in employment. Thus, our search model again relies on incomplete adjustment to movement in the price level as originally discussed in Chapter 6.

There are numerous alternative descriptions of search in the labor market that make employment sensitive to variations in aggregate demand. One can develop models that focus on workers who are uncertain about alternative wage offers. Or one can focus on employers who are uncertain about alternative wage offers available to their workers or who are uncertain about the price at which they can sell their product. Many such models can be found in the books edited by Phelps and by Brunner and Meltzer. The key ingredient common to all the models is that one side, either worker or employer, is searching and is uncertain about W or P.

As an example of an alternative job search theory, consider a worker who is considering a job offer and is uncertain about wages paid in alternative jobs. If demand for the potential employer's output rises, the wage offered by the firm will rise. If the job seeker does not expect other wage rates or the price level to rise, he or she will perceive an improved opportunity and this will increase the probability the job under consideration will be accepted. If this situation characterizes a substantial fraction of all job seekers, we again have an explanation of employment increasing as aggregate demand increases.

Search models connect the analytics of Chapter 6 and Figure 8.1 to the real world of the labor market, which has constant search on both demand and supply sides. There are many such models corresponding to different situations facing employers and workers. These models also provide a structure within which the costs and benefits of searching, or the cost of gaining more complete and accurate information as against the expected value of such information, can be included more formally in the calculus of whether a job opportunity will be accepted. The general Keynesian supply-side model of Chapter 6 is meant to be representative of these search and uncertainty-based models within the context of our skeletal static macroeconomic model.

EQUILIBRIUM UNEMPLOYMENT

In Chapter 6 we developed a labor supply function that gave employment N as a function of the money wage W and the perceived price level P^*. In that chapter N was measured in man-hours of employment, the product of the number of people employed E and the average number of hours worked $\bar{n}$. That is,

$$E \cdot \bar{n} = N,$$

and changes in man-hours worked N are generally reflected in changes in both E and $\bar{n}$. Thus the slope of the labor supply curve combines two effects. As the wage rate rises, persons already employed will offer increasing hours of work. More importantly here, a wage rate increase will also increase the number of people employed E and reduce the number of workers unemployed, $U = L - E$, with a given size of the labor force L.

The supply of workers and hours

The change in both $\bar{n}$ and E along the labor supply function as N goes up can be explained by the existence of a customary minimum number of working hours n_{min} that is acceptable to employers. For example, employers may require at least 35 hours per week of their employees, and not be willing to hire anyone offering less. The effect of this institutional, rigidity on labor supply is shown in Figures 8.2 and 8.3.

The work-leisure decision for the individual maximizing utility $U = U(Y, S)$ subject to the budget constraint $Y = W \cdot (H - S)$, and the further requirement that if he (or she) works, he works at least some minimum $n_{min} = H - S_{min}$ hours, is shown in Figure 8.2. H, again, is total hours available, to be divided between work n and leisure S. With the minimum n_{min} constraint, only points with at most S_{min} are permissible; the worker has to sacrifice at least S_{min} hours of leisure to get a job. At a high wage level such as W_0 in Figure 8.2, the worker maximizes utility by working more than n_{min} hours. As the wage rate falls to W_1, his maximizing hours of work fall to n_{min}. As the wage falls further through W_2 toward W_{min}, the worker still provides n_{min} hours rather than be fully unemployed, even though he would prefer less than n_{min} hours. As the wage rate gets low enough, the wage line intersects an indifference curve that is tangent to the S-axis. This level of the wage rate is shown as W_{min} in Figure 8.2. At this wage rate the worker will jump discontinuously from n_{min} hours to zero hours of employment. This individual labor supply curve is shown in the W, n_i space in Figure 8.3. Below W_{min} the worker supplies zero hours of labor. At W_{min} the labor supply function jumps discontinuously to

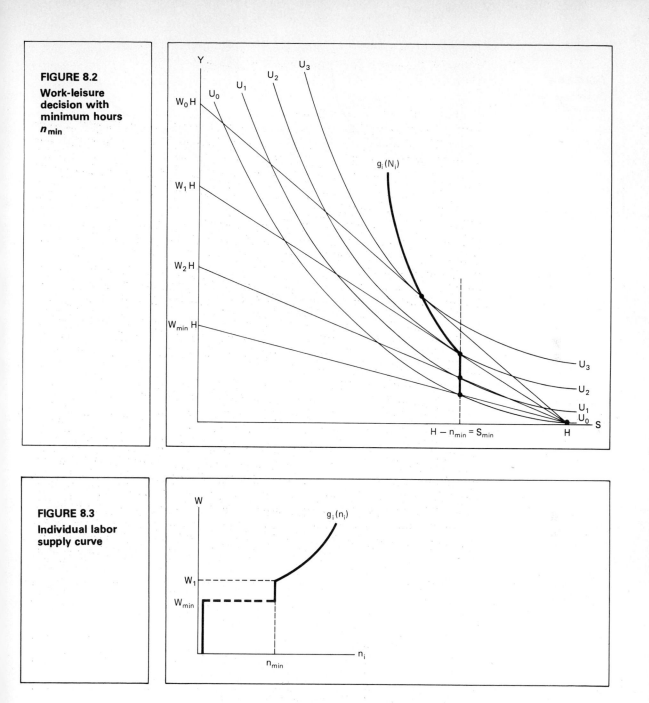

FIGURE 8.2
Work-leisure decision with minimum hours n_{min}

FIGURE 8.3
Individual labor supply curve

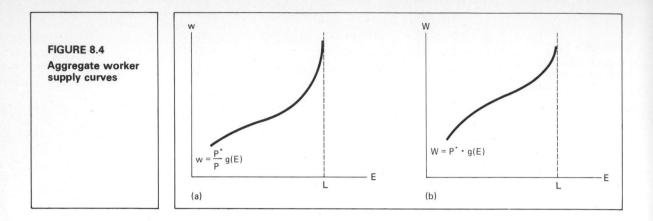

In the figure: (a) $w = \dfrac{P^*}{P}\, g(E)$; (b) $W = P^* \cdot g(E)$.

W_{min}, n_{min} and then rises vertically to W_1, n_{min}. With wage rates above W_1, the labor supply function takes on the normal shape of the $g_i(n_i)$ function in Figure 8.3.

When the individual labor supply curves of Figure 8.3 are aggregated over the labor force, the slope of the resulting aggregate supply curve, then, has the two components pointed out at the beginning of this section: as W rises, first more workers' W_{min} thresholds are passed, and E rises; and second, the number of hours worked by those employed rises, raising $\bar{n}$, average hours worked. The first of these effects gives us the supply curve of workers shown in Figure 8.4(a).

The shape of the worker supply curve can be explained as follows. As the wage rate rises from very low levels, increasing numbers of workers become employed as their W_{min} (or w_{min}) thresholds are passed, so that at low wage levels, the curve is concave. But after most of the primary workers—working heads of households and single males—are employed, further W or w increases call forth diminishing increases in the supply of workers, so that the curve turns convex and becomes nearly vertical at a high wage level where virtually all potential workers are employed.

The labor force and unemployment

The aggregate worker supply curves of Figure 8.4, with positive and increasing slopes in the range that is relevant for our analysis, provide a natural definition of full employment. As wages rise, the labor supply curves become vertical at some maximum level of feasible employment, which we will identify as the labor force. Thus, in Figure 8.4 we can define the labor force L as that level of employment at which the labor supply curve becomes vertical. The difference between the total labor force L and the equilibrium level of employment, E_0 in Figure 8.5, is then the level of unemployment—the number of unemployed people who would be willing to work if a suitable job were available:

$$U_0 = L - E_0.$$

The difference between the classical model and the Keynesian model should be noticed in Figure 8.5. The classical model sets $P^* = P$ so that the worker supply function reduces to $w = g(E)$. Since both supply and demand are then given in terms of the real wage, the labor market equilibrium condition in terms of workers is

$$g(E) = f(E),\qquad\qquad [1]$$

one equation in one variable, determining the level of employment in the labor market alone. With a given level of the labor force, this means that the equilibrium level of unemployment U_0 is also determined in the labor market alone, without reference to demand conditions, in the classical real wage model. This is, again, the dichotomy of the classical model that we saw in Chapter 6: The equilibrium level of unemployment is determined by labor market conditions alone and will not be affected by monetary or fiscal policy changes.

The situation is different when P^* responds less than equally to changes in P as in the general Keynesian model. Here the market equilibrium for workers is

$$\frac{P^*}{P} \cdot g(E) = f(E).\qquad\qquad [2]$$

Here the equilibrium level of employment E_0 and unemployment U_0 depend on conditions in the product market which partially determine the price level. Thus, as we saw in Chapter 7, the general Keynesian model links unemployment to the demand side of the economy. An expansionary monetary or fiscal policy will raise P, and P^* will rise, under our Keynesian assumption, by a lesser amount. The supply curve of labor in Figure 8.5 will shift down indicating an increase in the supply of labor at any real wage as labor *perceives* the real wage to be higher.

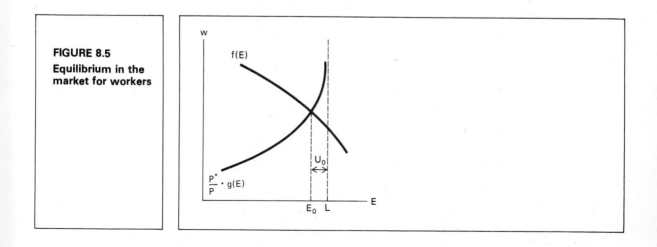

FIGURE 8.5

Equilibrium in the market for workers

This will increase E and decrease U, given L. The Keynesian model gives us an explanation of how demand changes can affect the level of unemployment. (The reader should compare Figure 8.5 to Figure 6.16 which illustrates the same effect, but in a money wage diagram).

We now have a reasonable explanation of fluctuations in unemployment in an economy that is generally operating near full employment, such as the U.S. economy since World War II with unemployment rates between 3 and 9 percent, as compared with the 15 to 25 percent of the 1930s. Even so, there is one troublesome aspect about this explanation: It implies that the unemployed are unemployed more or less by choice. Looking back to Figure 8.2, the cause of their unemployment is that the wage rate (for their skill class and geographical area) is below their threshold W_{min}. In a way, it is their definition of what is a suitable job—one paying at least W_{min}—that keeps them unemployed. In an economy with a relatively homogeneous labor market, operating near full employment, we would observe such voluntary changes in unemployment. Changes in labor force participation as the wage rate changes can be partially explained by this mechanism.

However, in an economy generally operating near full employment, we can also see pockets of local involuntary unemployment running as high as 15 percent. Examples of these are Appalachia, many areas in our major central cities, and, in general, areas where there has been a major drop in industry output. When industry declined in Boston and central-city jobs disappeared, unemployment in the ghetto rose. The reappearance of industry along Route 128 circling the city did not help the central-city workers much because of the lack of public transportation from Roxbury to Route 128. This kind of large-scale local structural unemployment is due to local labor market rigidities, the lack of job information, and the cost of moving, and can, in time, be alleviated by government action to remove these impediments. It is still consistent with our Figure 8.5 explanation of unemployment in an economy that is, in the aggregate, operating near full employment.

But this view of unemployment will not hold up well in a case in which there is clearly widespread involuntary unemployment, such as in the 1930s when people would take work at almost any wage, but no work was available. The labor market equilibrium picture of Figure 8.5 includes unemployment of people who cannot find *suitable* work, not of people who cannot find *any* work. So the model of Figure 8.5 cannot, by itself, explain the massive involuntary unemployment of the 1930s, although it does represent the operation of the postwar economy fairly well.

To explain aggregate, or economy-wide, involuntary unemployment, we can introduce the notion of *wage rigidity*—when labor market demand falls, wages do not fall, so that the equilibrium labor market outcome is off the labor supply curve. In the next section we look at the aggregate labor markets with rigid wages and then in the following section use the notion of wage rigidities in local markets to explain unemployment changes with demand shifts.

**WAGE RIGIDITY
IN THE AGGREGATE
LABOR MARKET**

The possibility that the money wage rate is "sticky" or "rigid" in a downward direction—that is, once it reaches a given level, it cannot fall—was introduced in the 1930s as an explanation for unemployment within the framework of the classical real-wage model. It provides a rationalization for the existence of large-scale aggregate unemployment. Suppose that once the money wage rate rises to an equilibrium level W_0, it cannot fall from that level due to institutional imperfections in the labor market. Perhaps employers do not like the idea of wage cuts, or perhaps labor contracts make it impossible to reduce wages. This downward wage rigidity will give us an explanation of involuntary unemployment on an economy-wide scale.

**Wage rigidity in the
classical model**

In the classical real-wage model, downward wage rigidity is shown in Figure 8.6. There the labor supply function is the real-wage labor supply $g(N)$, drawn to become vertical at full-employment man-hours employed N_F, corresponding to the employment of the entire labor force L at average hours $\bar{n}$. Inclusion of N_F in Figure 8.6 will aid in a comparison of the view taken of unemployment in the last section and the rigid-wage view.

Figure 8.6 shows an initial equilibrium at real wage w_0 with money wage W_0, price level P_0, and equilibrium employment N_0. By the view of unemployment in the last section, $N_F - N_0$ measures unemployment in the initial equilibrium. But strictly speaking, there is no aggregate *involuntary* unemployment since, on aggregate, the people in the labor force out of work are in that circumstance by choice.

Now suppose the money wage rate is fixed at W_0, and aggregate demand drops due to, say, a collapse in investment demand and a large shift of the IS curve to the left. This creates excess supply in the economy and the price level falls to P_1. In Figure 8.6(a), the real wage, with W stuck at W_0, rises to w_1, creating an excess supply of labor equal to $N^S - N^D$. Similarly, in Figure 8.6(b) both the supply and demand curves of labor shift down, giving the same excess supply. If there is no mechanism to force employers to hire more labor than they want to, employment will fall to N^D in Figure 8.6. If P_1 is the new equilibrium price level, assuming that W_0 is fixed, then employment has dropped to N^D and output has dropped to $y_1 = y(N^D; \bar{K})$. This is shown in the supply and demand diagram of Figure 8.6.

The "true" supply curve SS is, as usual in the real-wage model, vertical in Figure 8.7, fixed in the labor market at $y_0 = y(N_0; \bar{K})$. The intersection of the original demand curve D_0D_0 and the supply curve determined the initial equilibrium price level P_0 of Figure 8.6, and, given w_0, this determined the initial, and now rigid, money wage rate W_0.

Now if W_0 is rigid downward, as the price level falls in Figure 8.6

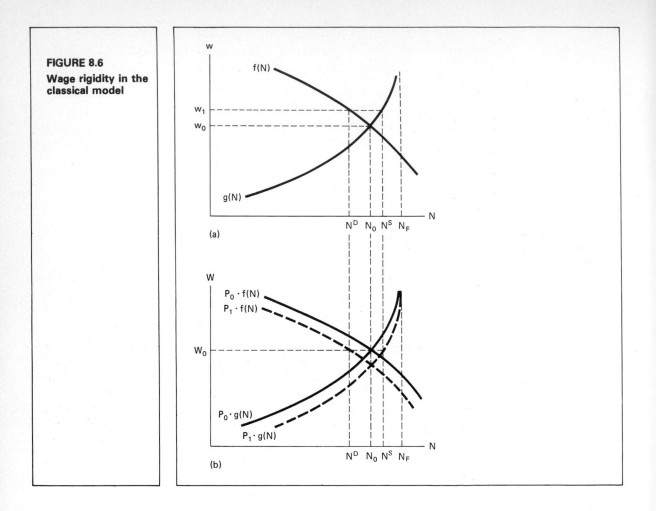

FIGURE 8.6

Wage rigidity in the classical model

raising the real wage, employment and output will fall along the labor demand curve. This is best illustrated in Figure 8.6(a); as P falls from P_0 with W fixed at W_0, employment falls along the $f(N)$ demand curve. This gives us the dashed ss segment of the supply curve in Figure 8.7, which replaces the segment of the true supply curve below the initial equilibrium. The downward shift in the demand curve from D_0D_0 to D_1D_1 creates excess supply and reduces the price level to P_1 with observed output $y_1 = y(N^D; \bar{K})$. Whether this is an equilibrium position is a question debated in the economics literature since the 1930s.

From Figure 8.6(a) it is clear that at the new quasi-equilibrium point W_0, P_1, N^D, y_1, the labor force is off its supply curve. This is just another way of saying that points on ss in Figure 8.7 are not on SS. If the definition of equilibrium requires that all economic actors are on their relevant supply and demand curves, then the quasi-equilibrium P_1, y_1 of Figure 8.7 is an outcome, but not an equilibrium outcome. It seems more reasonable, however, to define an equilibrium situation as one which will not change of itself if it is left undisturbed. Is there a tendency in the model for the point P and y to move from P_1, y_1? The answer has to be "no" if the money wage is really rigid. Once the economy is at P_0, y_0 in Figure 8.7, if W_0 really cannot fall, then the true supply curve below P_0 becomes ss in this definition of equilibrium. Thus, whether P_1, y_1 is an equilibrium position depends on your definition of equilibrium. The view taken here is that the better definition is one that focuses on whether the situation tends to change if left alone, so that P_1, y_1 is an equlibrium outcome.

If we now ask how many more man-hours would be offered at the going wage than are employed, the answer is $N^S - N^D$, the measure of aggregate involuntary unemployment. Thus, introduction of the rigid wage provides an explanation for truly involuntary unemployment in the classical real-wage model.

Several points should be noticed here. First, unemployment in the sense of an externally measured labor force minus actual employment has risen from $N_F - N_0$ to $N_F - N^D$ in Figure 8.6, while truly involuntary unemployment has risen from zero to $N^S - N^D$ at real wage w_1. This is emphasized because, second, $N^S - N^D$ does not measure the "effect" of the wage rigidity. If the rigidity were removed, employment would return to N_0 in this model, an increase of $N_0 - N^D$, not $N^S - N^D$, which overstates the effect of the rigidity by $N^S - N_0$. The latter is the supply effect of the price change.

Finally, from the supply and demand diagram of Figure 8.7, it should be clear that the rigid-wage hypothesis provides another solution to the liquidity trap problem, if the trap exists in the first place. If the demand curve shifts to the left and becomes vertical because price decreases will

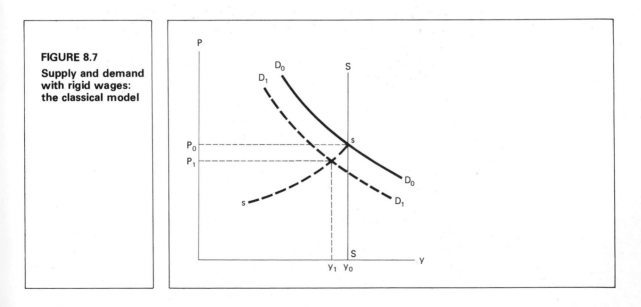

FIGURE 8.7

Supply and demand with rigid wages: the classical model

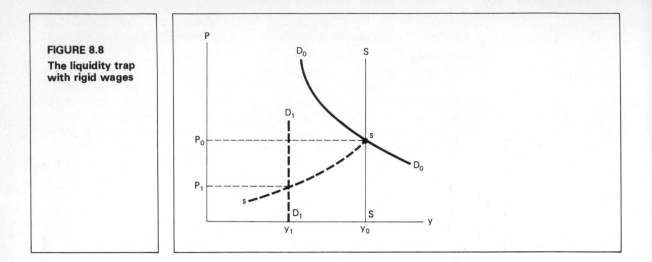

FIGURE 8.8

The liquidity trap with rigid wages

not increase equilibrium output demanded, in the classical real-wage model an inconsistency appears; there is no intersection between the demand and supply curves, and prices and wages can fall continuously without restoring equilibrium. With a rigid wage rate, however, the original vertical supply curve below the initial equilibrium point is replaced by the positively sloped supply curve ss. Now if the economy falls into the liquidity trap, equilibrium will be reached at a new P_1, y_1 point as shown in Figure 8.8, at the intersection of ss and the vertical D_1D_1 demand curve.

Wage rigidity in the Keynesian model

Downward wage rigidity in the Keynesian model is shown in Figure 8.9. In the initial equilibrium situation employment is at N_0, with equilibrium unemployment of $N_F - N_0$. The money wage rate is W_0 and, by hypothesis, it cannot fall from W_0.

If, starting from the initial equilibrium W_0, N_0, demand falls off creating excess supply in the product market, prices will fall. This will, in turn, shift the demand curve for labor down in Figure 8.9 and the supply curve for labor will shift down as well but by a lesser amount. If P_1 is the new equilibrium price level in the sense that the product and money markets come into equilibrium at P_1, employment will drop to N_1 at wage rate W_0. If the wage rate were able to fall, the price level drop to P_1 would have reduced equilibrium employment only to N_2 along the supply curve, although, as we will see shortly, a further price drop would actually have been required to restore equilibrium.

The wage rigidity would replace the segment of the labor supply curve below W_0, N_0 with the horizontal line at W_0. As the price level falls, equilibrium employment falls along the W_0 horizontal line instead of along the supply curve in Figure 8.9, so that a given price level drop causes a bigger drop in N (to N_1, for example) with the wage rigidity than without it (to N_2, for example).

This is shown in the supply and demand diagram of Figure 8.10. The segment of the supply curve SS below the initial equilibrium P_0, y_0 point is replaced by ss, which corresponds to the horizontal line at W_0 in Figure 8.9. When demand drops from $D_0 D_0$ to $D_1 D_1$ with wage rigidity, the price level falls from P_0 to P_1, and output falls from $y_0 = y(N_0; \bar{K})$ to y_1. Without wage rigidity at P_1, equilibrium output supplied would have been y_2, corresponding to N_2 in Figure 8.9. There would have been excess supply measured by $y_2 - y_1$ in the product market, requiring the price level to fall to P_3 to establish a new equilibrium at y_3.

Thus, with the wage rigidity in the Keynesian model, the downward shift in demand gives a new equilibrium at P_1, y_1, W_0, N_1 in Figures 8.9 and 8.10, with y falling along ss. Without the wage rigidity, the new equilibrium would be P_3, y_3 in Figure 8.10. N would be between N_1 and N_2 in Figure 8.9, and the price level would be at P_3 in Figure 8.10, lower than P_1. Introduction of the wage rigidity has increased the magnitude of the decrease in y and reduced the magnitude of decrease in P needed to restore equilibrium with a given downward demand shift. In other words, the supply curve has been flattened by the substitution of ss for the lower segment of SS in Figure 8.10.

The wage rigidity gives aggregate involuntary unemployment of $N_4 - N_1$ in Figure 8.9, with measured total unemployment of $N_F - N_1$. Again, the involuntary unemployment of $N_4 - N_1$ is not a measure of the effect of the wage rigidity. With flexible wages, employment would have fallen to N_2; the wage rigidity has caused an additional drop in man-hours employed of $N_2 - N_1$.

Two points of contrast should be noticed about the effects of wage rigidity in the classical and Keynesian models. First, the wage rigidity

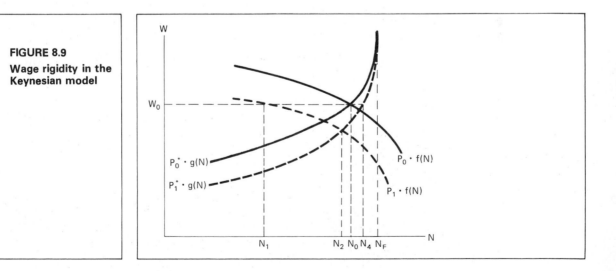

FIGURE 8.9

Wage rigidity in the Keynesian model

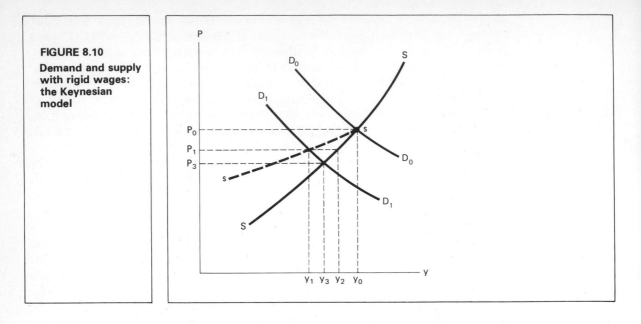

FIGURE 8.10

Demand and supply with rigid wages: the Keynesian model

changed the fundamental character of the classical model. Without wage rigidity the labor market equilibrium condition in the real-wage model is

$$f(N) = g(N),\qquad\qquad\qquad\qquad [3]$$

and employment is determined in the labor market alone; (3) is one equation in one unknown. Wage rigidity replaces the equilibrium condition by

$$W_0 = P \cdot f(N),\qquad\qquad\qquad\qquad [4]$$

one equation in two unknowns, P and N. This eliminates the dichotomy of the classical model. It makes the supply curve in Figure 8.7 the positively sloped ss instead of a vertical SS, and the model becomes simultaneous, with interaction between demand and supply sides.

In the Keynesian model, replacing (4) with the flexible-wage equilibrium condition,

$$P^* \cdot g(N) = P \cdot f(N),\qquad\qquad\qquad\qquad [5]$$

does not change the fundamental character of the model. Both equations (4) and (5) include the variables P and N; both SS and ss in Figure 8.10 have positive slopes. Wage rigidity just changes the slope of the supply curve in an already simultaneous model.

A second point of contrast that should be noted is in the amount of involuntary unemployment. In the Keynesian model the shift down in the supply curve is less than the shift of the supply curve in the classical model. Thus, the increase in involuntary unemployment is less under the Keynesian assumption because labor supply increases by a lesser amount.

This again is the result of money illusion on the part of labor which does not perceive real wages W/P^* to have increased by as much as they have.

The previous section analyzed the effects of wage rigidity in our two basic models partially to take advantage of an opportunity to look at those models from a new angle. The best way to understand how the economy "hangs together" is to look at it from several different aspects, and asking how wage rigidity affects its operation is one useful way to do this. But these labor market models with an economy-wide rigid wage probably have little relevance to the actual explanation of unemployment in the United States. This is because, at least in the short run, labor mobility between local labor markets, disaggregated by geography or skill class, is very low. Thus, the notion of an economy-wide downward rigid wage has to be based on the assumption that all local wage rates—for steelworkers in Pittsburgh, rubber workers in Akron, electricians in Los Angeles, and so on—are rigid downward. But if this is the case, for an economy-wide wage index literally not to fall as demand and employment fall implies both that every local market where demand falls has a wage rigidity, and that demand falls the same proportion in each, so that the wage index is not reduced by a shift in the mix of employment from high-wage to low-wage areas. Since one major cause of a downward rigid wage, at least in the short run, would be the existence of a union contract, the fact that only 20 percent of the U.S. labor force is unionized suggests that local rigidities are not so frequent that the first of these conditions is very likely to be met.

One might expect the economy-wide labor supply curve to have a horizontal rigid-wage floor at the level of the minimum wage, or at the average unemployment or public assistance benefit level. But the minimum wage—the highest of these three levels(!)—is $2.90 (in 1979), compared to average gross hourly earnings in manufacturing of over $5.00. So this floor is so far below the normal operating range of the economy that it cannot explain existing economy-wide unemployment, although it might explain some unemployment among marginal workers such as teenagers.

A more plausible role for wage rigidity to play in explaining unemployment is in the presumption that some local labor markets have rigid wages, particularly those most unionized in the manufacturing and mining sectors, and some have flexible wages, particularly those in services. If this is the case, as aggregate demand rises, the money wage rate and employment will generally rise with the impact on particular local labor markets depending on the source of the demand increase. But when demand falls, W and N fall along the supply curve in markets with flexible wages, and in markets with rigid wages, N falls along the initial W_0 line. This would give us a positively sloped economy-wide labor supply curve, but the supply curve would be steeper as W and N rise to any point W_0, N_0 than it is as W and N fall from that point.

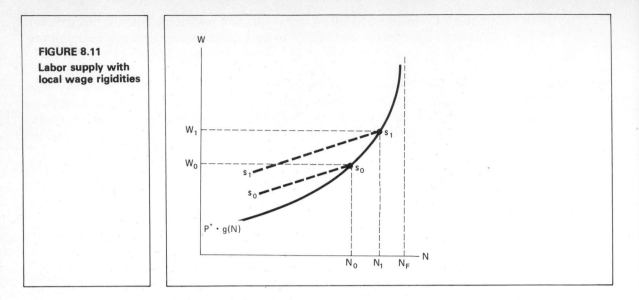

FIGURE 8.11

Labor supply with local wage rigidities

This kind of local-wage-rigidity curve is shown in Figure 8.11. There $P^* \cdot g(N)$ is the usual supply curve. As demand increases W and N rise to an equilibrium point like W_0, N_0. If demand falls from that level, W and N will fall along $s_0 s_0$, not along $P^* \cdot g(N)$, due to rigid wages in some local markets. If demand rises beyond W_0, N_0, W and N increase along $P^* \cdot g(N)$ to the new equilibrium, say, W_1, N_1, establishing a new, higher, rigid wage. If demand then falls from W_1, N_1, it falls along $s_1 s_1$, not along $P^* \cdot g(N)$. Thus, as demand expands, an ss curve is established at each equilibrium point, replacing the supply curve $P^* \cdot g(N)$ below that point. When demand does fall, then, literal involuntary unemployment appears (or increases) in the markets with rigid-wage rates.

Another feature of this kind of partial, local-wage-ridigity model is interesting. Suppose demand shifts from a product that is manufactured in rigid-wage market i, to any other product (since all markets are assumed to have upward flexible wages) manufactured in, say, market j, with no drop in aggregate real demand. Then, in the rigid-wage market N_i will fall but W_i will not. But in the other market j both N_j and W_j will rise, and since W_j rises, N_j will probably rise less than N_i fell. Thus, the demand shift would raise average W and reduce total employment while maintaining the same level of aggregate demand. As long as all markets have upward flexible wage rates, but some have downward rigid wages, as demand continually shifts there may be a bias toward both wage and unemployment increases.

SUMMARY: AN ECLECTIC VIEW OF UNEMPLOYMENT

In an economy operating at fairly high levels of resource utilization, unemployment can be explained without appeal to wage rigidity, as the first part of this chapter showed. With the labor market in equilibrium in the sense that demand and supply are equal, there will be some people who are on the supply curve above the equilibrium point. They would accept suitable employment if it were offered, but are counted as unemployed. The Keynesian model seems superior to the classical model here because it also offers an explanation of how changes in demand conditions affect this level of unemployment.

While this explanation of aggregate unemployment might be sufficient when the economy is operating at high levels of employment, it needs help in cases of widespread involuntary unemployment. Here the hypothesis that wages are rigid in the downward direction in some local labor markets seems more useful than a hypothesis that there is an economy-wide rigid wage. The hypothesis of local wage rigidity can explain the appearance of widespread involuntary unemployment as demand drops substantially. In addition, combined with shifting industrial mix and immobility between labor markets—due largely, in the cases of central cities, to racial discrimination—the hypothesis of local wage rigidity can explain the existence of local high-unemployment areas in a generally full-employment economy.

Furthermore, as we suggest in Chapter 6, the existence of firms with fixed co-efficients production functions will lead to layoffs as demand drops and capital utilization falls off. Thus, a demand change in the short run will change aggregate unemployment relative to the measured labor force, because to some extent labor is supplied as a function of the money wage instead of the real wage, to some extent because of local wage rigidities and to some extent because of fixed coefficients of production.

QUESTIONS FOR DISCUSSION AND REVIEW

1. How might a sharp increase in unemployment benefits alter the aggregate supply curve? How would this affect income, prices, and employment?

2. Why would you expect rigid wages downward to lead to a lack of price flexibility in a downward direction?

3. In what way might decreased expectations about wages and employment in the future lead to less unemployment in the present?

4. The chapter distinguishes between voluntary and involuntary unemployment. Do you consider the former a social problem requiring public policy?

5. How does the recognition of wage rigidities alter the distribution of a change in money income into its price component and its output component?

SELECTED READINGS

R. Gordon, "Recent Developments in the Theory of Inflation and Unemployment," in P. G. Korliras and R. J. Thorn, eds., *Modern Macroeconomics* (New York: Harper & Row, 1979).

R. E. Hall, "Why is the Unemployment Rate So High at Full Employment?" *Brookings Papers on Economic Activity*, vol. 3, 1970.

E. Kuh, "Unemployment, Production Functions, and Effective Demand," *Journal of Political Economy*, July 1966.

D. Patinkin, *Money, Interest, and Prices* (New York: Harper & Row, 1965), chaps. 12–14 and appendices.

D. Patinkin, "Price Flexibility and Full Employment," in M. G. Mueller, ed., *Readings in Macroeconomics* (New York: Holt, Rinehart and Winston, 1971).

E. S. Phelps, "Money-Wage Dynamics and the Labor Market Equilibrium," in P. G. Korliras and R. S. Thorn, eds., *Modern Macroeconomics* (New York: Harper & Row, 1979).

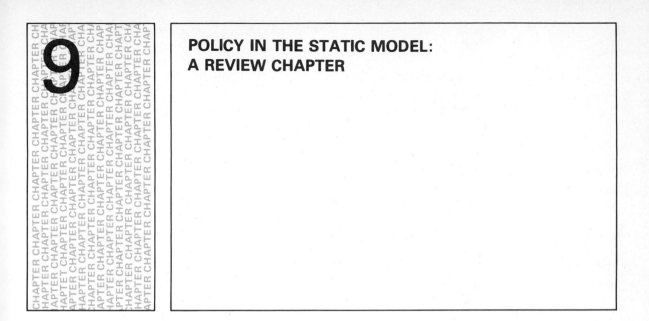

POLICY IN THE STATIC MODEL:
A REVIEW CHAPTER

In Chapter 7 we joined the demand side of the economy developed in Chapters 4 and 5 with the supply side of Chapter 6 to study the general equilibrium determination of the key variables y, P, r and N. Then in Chapter 8 we examined more carefully the nature and causes of unemployment in the model of Chapter 7. We now turn to an analysis of aggregate demand and supply policies in the basic static model.

Suppose the government decides the existing equilibrium levels of y, P, r, and N are not satisfactory. For example, demand may be deficient with a level of output and employment yielding an unemployment rate of 9 percent as in mid-1975. Alternatively, there could be an excess demand gap caused by an upwards shift in the supply curve in response to shifts in oil supply with the result that prices are being pulled (or pushed) up as in early 1979.

Chapter 5 provided an initial indication of how policies might alter equilibria to avoid such difficulties. Chapter 7 returned briefly to these issues. It is useful now to deal with them in some detail as a bridge between Part II and Part III. Reviewing how policy changes work through the economy will provide the reader with a good test of his or her understanding of the model developed in Part II. Detailed discussion will make clear the relative importance of specific parameters in our basic relationships; Part III is concerned with quantifying these parameters.

The approach in most of Part II has been to take policy instruments such as $\bar{M}$ or g as given, positioning the relevant demand or supply curves, and then to solve for the equilibrium values of our key variables. In Chapter 5 and again below, we then study the effects on these key variables of changes in the policy instruments. In the formal study of the theory of policy, this procedure is inverted. Desired values for key endogenous variables are given as policy *targets*. The model is then inverted to solve for the values of the policy *instruments*. This analysis has been expanded to allow for uncertainty in the impact of policies within the model and to recognize that goals or targets may conflict requiring the policy maker to make explicit a social welfare function to guide in the trade-off between goals. A full discussion of the theory of policy would take too much time to develop here, but the student who has followed the analysis carefully to this point should be able to see how the four-equation system of Chapter 7, repeated below, can be inverted to solve, given policy targets, for appropriate instrument levels.

MONETARY AND FISCAL POLICY IN THE STATIC MODEL

On the demand side of the economy, the equilibrium conditions for the product market,

$$IS: \quad y = c(y - t(y)) + i(r) + g, \tag{1}$$

and for the money market,

$$LM: \quad \frac{\bar{M}}{P} = l(r) + k(y), \tag{2}$$

are shown in the r, y space of Figure 9.1(a) as $I_0 S_0$ and $L_0 M_0$. The investment and saving functions and level of government purchases fix the position of the IS curve. The demand-for-money function and the level of real balances $m = \bar{M}/P$ fix the position of the LM curve. Varying the price level shifts the LM curve in Figure 9.1(a), tracing out the demand curve $D_0 D_0$ in Figure 9.2.

On the supply side of the economy, we have the labor market equilibrium condition.

$$P \cdot f(N) = P^* \cdot g(N) = p(P) \cdot g(N), \tag{3}$$

shown in Figure 9.1(b). Again, we assume that P^* reacts incompletely to changes in P, that is, $0 < p' < 1$. This gives equilibrium employment N as a function of the price level. Employment is translated into output y by the production function,

$$y = y(N; \bar{K}). \tag{4}$$

Changes in P shift both the demand and supply curves in Figure 9.1(b), changing equilibrium employment N. This, in turn, changes equilibrium output on the supply side through the production function, tracing out the supply curve $S_0 S_0$ of Figure 9.2. Thus, the IS and LM equations give us a demand relationship between P and y, and the labor market equation and the production function give us a supply relationship between the same two variables. On the most aggregate level we have two equations in the two unknowns, P and y, shown in Figure 9.2. The solution to those two equations—the intersection of the demand and supply curves of Figure

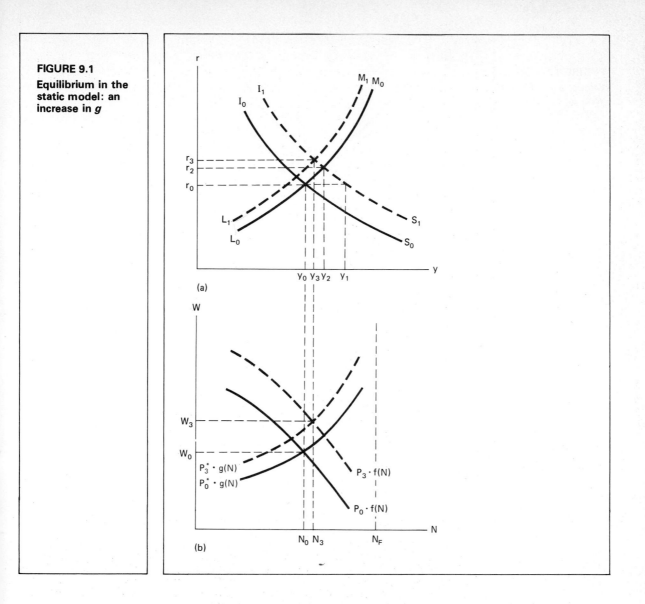

FIGURE 9.1

Equilibrium in the static model: an increase in _g_

(a)

(b)

The effects of a fiscal policy stimulus

9.2—is equilibrium P_0, y_0, which we can trace back to W_0, N_0 in Figure 9.1(b) and r_0, y_0 in Figure 9.1(a).

In the initial equilibrium position, employment is at N_0 in Figure 9.1(b). Suppose the political judgment is made that unemployment $N_F - N_0$ is excessive, so government purchases g are increased by $\Delta g = g_1 - g_0$ to increase employment. This shifts the IS curve up to $I_1 S_1$ in Figure 9.1(a). The increased government purchases increase GNP directly, and, through the multiplier process, increase GNP indirectly by increasing consumption. At the initial price level P_0 and interest rate r_0, equilibrium output on the demand side would rise to y_1 in Figure 9.1(a).

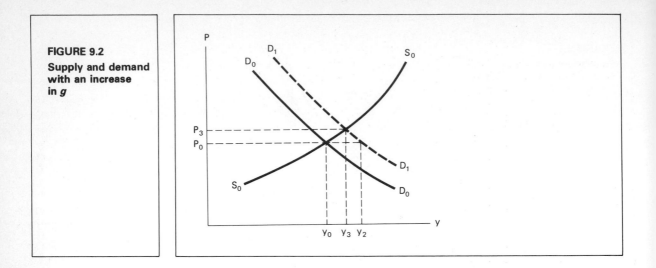

FIGURE 9.2

Supply and demand with an increase in g

The ratio of $y_1 - y_0$ to Δg is given by the simple g multiplier of Chapter 3, which assumes investment, and thus implicitly the interest rate, is fixed.

But the increase in output, even with the price level unchanged, will increase the demand for money, raising the interest rate along $L_0 M_0$ and reducing investment demand. This partially offsets the g increase, so that at the initial price level, equilibrium output on the demand side would rise to y_2 in Figures 9.1(a) and 9.2, with the interest rate rising to r_2. Thus, the g increase has shifted the demand curve to $D_1 D_1$ in Figure 9.2, creating excess demand $y_2 - y_0$ in the economy. At the initial price level P_0, consumers, businesses, and government would demand y_2 output, but producers are supplying only y_0, so prices rise.

On the demand side of the economy, the price increase tightens the money market by increasing the demand for money or, what is the same thing, reducing the supply of real balances m. This shifts the LM curve up toward $L_1 M_1$ in Figure 9.1(a), reducing equilibrium output demanded from y_2 along the new demand curve $D_1 D_1$ in Figure 9.2. Again, the reader should notice that the price increase reduces equilibrium output demanded *indirectly*; it tightens the money market, raising r and reducing investment.

On the supply side, the price increase raises the demand for labor, shifting the demand curve in Figure 9.1(b) up toward $P_3 \cdot f(N)$. It also shifts the labor supply curve up toward $P_3^* \cdot g(N)$, but the supply shift is smaller than the demand shift, so equilibrium employment increases from N_0 toward N_3. This is represented in Figure 9.2 by a movement along the supply curve $S_0 S_0$ from y_0 toward y_3.

The price increase continues until excess demand has been eliminated at P_3, y_3 in Figure 9.2. Employment rises to N_3 and the money wage rises to W_3. The real-wage rate is reduced somewhat, but if the elasticity of demand for labor was greater than one at the initial equilibrium point, real-labor income rises. Presumably this was the point of the g increase in the first place.

The interest rate rises from r_0 to r_3 following the g increase. The increase in government spending is partially offset by an increase in tax revenues as both P and y rise, but the government has to increase its borrowing in the bond market somewhat to finance the increase in its deficit. This increased supply of bonds reduces bond prices and raises yields, giving the bond market counterpart to the money market increase in r. The r increase reduces investment demand with $i = i(r)$, but by less than the initial g increase, so that on balance the g increase directly induces an increase in expenditure, raising y from y_0 to y_3.

A permanent tax cut would have much the same effect as the g increase, assuming that consumers react by spending a large fraction of the increase in disposable income. The tax cut would shift the IS curve and demand curve out, raising the price level and the interest rate. Employment and output would rise, and the tax cut would yield the same y increase as the alternative Δg increase if tax rates are reduced by an amount that gives a direct policy-induced consumer expenditure increase equal to Δg.

The difference between a tax cut and a g increase, as usual, is in the composition of final output. The tax cut favors increased consumer spending, while the g increase favors increased output of public goods.

The effects of a money supply increase

Instead of a fiscal policy stimulus through an increase in government purchases or a tax cut, employment could be raised from the initial level N_0 by the monetary policy stimulus of an increase in $\bar{M}$. Putting aside the problem of the certainty of results, discussed in Chapter 5, a desired increase in equilibrium output and employment can be achieved with an $\bar{M}$ change equivalent to the necessary g change if fiscal policy were to be used. The difference in outcomes will be in the composition of final output. An $\bar{M}$ increase pushes down interest rates, stimulating investment, whereas the fiscal policy stimuli either increase g or consumer spending directly and raise interest rates indirectly.

The effects of a money supply increase are shown in Figures 9.3 and 9.4. Figures 9.3(b) and 9.4 are exactly the same as Figures 9.1(b) and 9.2; the only difference between the analyses of a g increase and an $\bar{M}$ increase lies in the origin of the demand shift in Figure 9.3(a).

The increase in the money supply shifts the LM curve from L_0M_0 to L_1M_1 in Figure 9.3(a). At the initial income level y_0, the interest rate would be pushed down to r_1 by the appearance of excess supply in the money market. This drop in the interest rate would stimulate investment demand, increasing equilibrium demand-side y. This, in turn, would increase the demand for money, pulling the interest rate back up again. At the initial price level P_0, equilibrium output demanded after the $\bar{M}$ increase would be y_2 with the interest rate at r_2. This is shown in Figure 9.4, where the money supply increase has shifted the demand curve out and created excess demand $y_2 - y_0$ in the economy. In equilibrium with the price level at the initial P_0, consumers, business, and government would purchase y_2 level of output, but producers are still supplying only y_0, employing N_0 man-hours.

The excess demand raises the price level in Figure 9.4 toward P_3. On the demand side of the economy, the price level increase tightens the money market, shifting LM back up toward $L_2 M_2$. This brings an increase in r and a drop in equilibrium demand-side output toward y_3. In Figure 9.4, equilibrium output on the demand side falls along the new demand curve, $D_1 D_1$ toward y_3.

On the supply side, the situation is exactly the same as with the

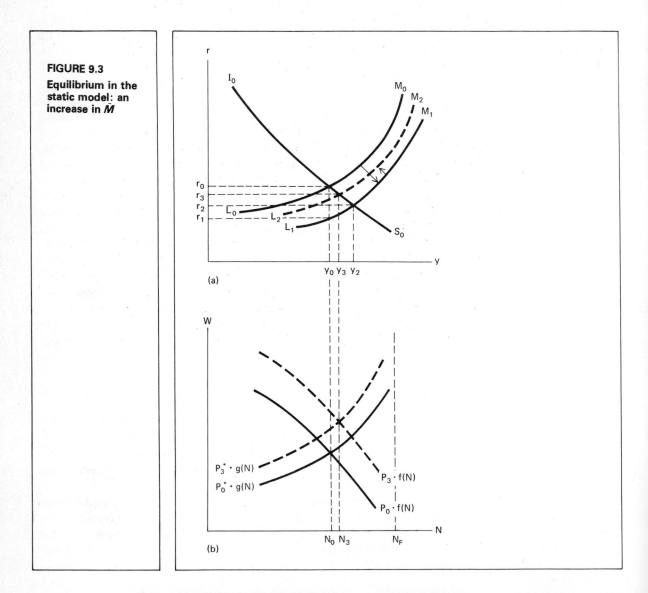

FIGURE 9.3

Equilibrium in the static model: an increase in $\bar{M}$

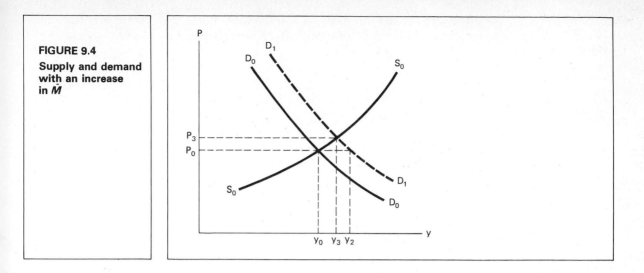

FIGURE 9.4

Supply and demand with an increase in $\dot{M}$

increase in g. The price increase shifts the labor demand curve up toward $P_3 \cdot f(N)$ and the labor supply curve up toward $P_3^* \cdot g(N)$. The latter supply shift is smaller than the demand shift by hypothesis, so employment rises toward N_3. In Figure 9.4, the employment increase is represented by a movement of equilibrium supply-side output up the supply curve $S_0 S_0$ from y_0 toward y_3.

The price level stops rising when the excess demand gap has been eliminated at P_3, y_3 in Figure 9.4. Employment has risen to N_3 in Figure 9.3(b). The interest rate first fell from r_0 to r_1 in Figure 9.3(b) under the initial monetary stimulus, and then rose back to r_3, still below the initial r_0. With g constant, and i higher due to the drop in r from r_0 to r_3, output and income have risen and consumer expenditure, with tax rates unchanged, has risen endogenously. Again, the difference between equivalent doses of monetary or fiscal policy stimuli is in the composition of final output.

MULTIPLIERS IN THE STATIC MODEL

In Chapter 5 we studied the effects of monetary and fiscal policy—changes in the policy instruments $\bar{M}$, g, and tax rates t—on equilibrium output under the assumption that the price level was fixed. This was equivalent to assuming that the supply curve of Figure 9.5 is horizontal at the initial price level P_0. Then a shift in the demand curve from $D_0 D_0$ to $D_1 D_1$ induced by a change in a policy instrument would yield an increase in output from y_0 to y_2.

But if the supply curve is positively sloped, like $S_0 S_0$ in Figure 9.5, the same policy change would raise equilibrium output only to y_3. Thus introduction of the supply side of the economy and a price response to changes in demand reduces the multiplier effect of policy changes on output.

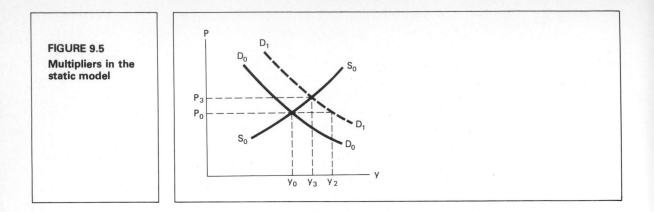

FIGURE 9.5

Multipliers in the static model

Two general points should be noted about the modification of the Chapter 5 analysis to include a price response. First, changes in the policy variables *shift* the aggregate demand curve, and then the price level rises *along* the supply curve. The change in price along the supply curve affects demand through its effect in the money market on interest rates and then on investment demand. This is shown graphically by the secondary shift in the *LM* curve in Figures 9.1(a) and 9.3(a). So the price change affects demand through the following chain:

$$\Delta P \rightarrow \Delta r \rightarrow \Delta i \qquad \text{(endogenous investment change).}$$

The second point is that, as we suggested in the previous section, the difference between the effects of the three policy instruments is in where the initial *policy-induced* expenditure stimulus appears. Once the excess demand is created, for example $y_2 - y_0$ in Figures 9.2 and 9.4, the adjustment of the model through the price mechanism is the same in all cases.

In the following sections we will compare the effects of fiscal and monetary policy on equilibrium output in the basic static model with the Chapter 5 results which assumed a constant price level.

Fiscal policy multipliers

The effects of an expansionary fiscal policy increase in government purchases g or cut in tax rates t are summarized in Figure 9.6. An increase in g, for example, shifts the IS curve out from $I_0 S_0$ to $I_1 S_1$ in Figure 9.6(a). If *both* the interest rate and the price level remained constant, equilibrium output would rise from y_0 to y_1. The ratio $(y_1 - y_0)/\Delta g$ is the simplest multiplier of Chapter 3.

In Chapter 4, we saw that as equilibrium output rises, the transactions demand for money rises, pulling up the interest rate. Thus with the interest rate adjusting to maintain equilibrium in the money market but with the price level still constant, equilibrium output would increase along the LM curve to y_2, instead of y_1. The ratio $(y_2 - y_0)/\Delta g$ is the Chapter 5 multiplier.

The increase in equilibrium output demanded from y_0 to y_2 at the original price level P_0 is shown as a shift in the aggregate demand curve in

Figure 9.6(b). With output demanded at P_0 equal to y_2, while output supplied is still at y_0, we have excess demand equal to $y_2 - y_0$ and the price level rises toward P_3. The price increase increases output supplied from y_0 toward y_3 by shifting the LM curve up in Figure 9.6(a), raising the interest rate and reducing investment.

When the economy reaches a new equilibrium at P_3, y_3 in Figure 9.6, the excess demand has been eliminated so there is no further tendency for the price level to rise. The final result of an initial Δg increase is an increase in the interest rate to r_3, in the price level to P_3, and on equilibrium output to y_3. The ratio $(y_3 - y_0)/\Delta g$ is the final multiplier, including both interest rate and price adjustments.

The same results could have been obtained with an appropriately sized tax cut instead of the increase in g. The only difference would be in

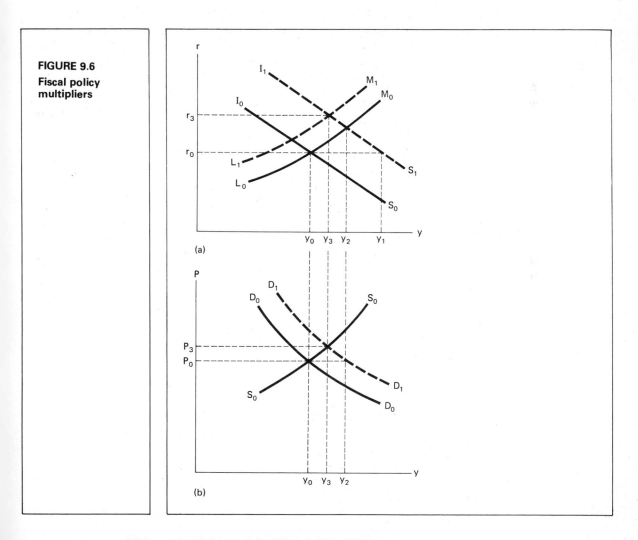

FIGURE 9.6

Fiscal policy multipliers

the composition of output. With the same interest rate, r_3, in both cases, investment would be the same. But instead of increased government spending Δg and an indirect increase in consumption, through the multiplier, the tax cut case would give an *initial* increase in consumption of $(-c'y\Delta t)$ plus the multipler increase, with g unchanged. So the tax cut would result in more consumption in the final equilibrium.

The effects of an equivalent expansionary monetary policy increase in $\bar{M}$ are summarized in Figure 9.7. The increase in M shifts the LM curve out from L_0M_0 to L_1M_1 in Figure 9.7(a). This reduces the interest rate and raises investment, moving equilibrium output demanded at the initial price level P_0 along the IS curve to y_2. The increase from y_0 to y_2 is the effect of an expansionary monetary policy as described in Chapter 5 before taking into account any supply restrictions.

The increase in equilibrium output demanded to y_2 at the initial price level P_0 is shown as the shift in the demand curve from D_0D_0 to D_1D_1 in Figure 9.7(b), which is exactly the same as Figure 9.6(b). Again, the differ-

Monetary policy multipliers

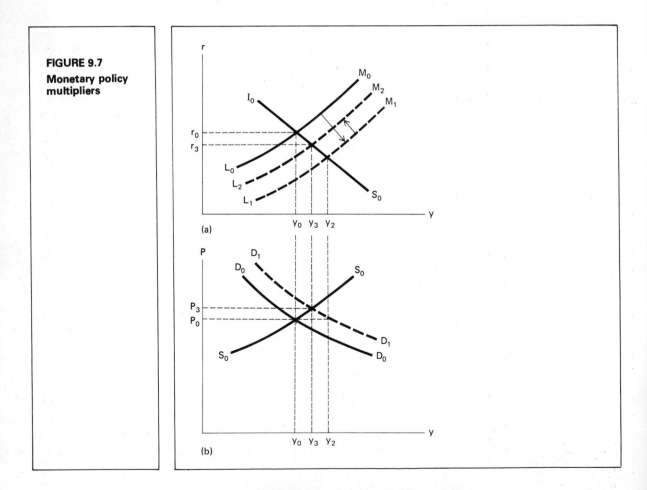

FIGURE 9.7

Monetary policy multipliers

ence between y_2 and equilibrium output supplied at P_0, y_0 is excess demand. This pulls the price level up toward P_3.

The increase in the price level increases equilibrium output supplied from y_0 to toward y_3. It also shifts the LM curve back up toward L_2M_2, reducing equilibrium output demanded from y_2 toward y_3. When the economy reaches the new equilibrium point P_3, y_3, excess demand has been eliminated and the price level comes to rest. The final result of the $\Delta \bar{M}$ increase is the increase of output from y_0 to y_3, with the price level rising to P_3 and the interest rate falling to r_3.

The results of the expansionary monetary policy are the same for P and y as those of the alternative fiscal policy. A comparison of Figures 9.6(b) and 9.7(b) will show that the increment from P_0, y_0 to P_3, y_3 is the same in both. The difference between the effects of monetary and fiscal policy is, again, in the composition of final output. With the interest rate falling under expansionary monetary policy, investment increases, resulting in more investment in final output y_3 than in the fiscal policy case.

INCOMES POLICY IN THE STATIC MODEL

One clear implication of our analysis of monetary and fiscal policy is that expansionary aggregate demand policy will pull up the price level as a side effect. This result has led policy makers to search for additional policy instruments that could shift the aggregate supply curve to eliminate the price (inflationary) effects of movements in aggregate demand. The Council of Economic Advisers' guideposts for wage and price behavior in 1962 were an early example of incomes policy.

The search for policies that might shift down the aggregate supply curve has intensified in the 1970s as it has been recognized that many of our difficulties have resulted from exogenous supply disturbances as well as supply shifts in response to price changes initiated on the demand side. The 1974–1975 recession, which resulted, in part, from an unhappy concurrence of supply shifts involving oil, crops, and even anchovies, featured rising unemployment *and* rising prices. The United States had tried wage and price controls in 1971–1973, and most European countries had been experimenting with incomes policies for decades. But the recession of 1974–1975, so widely viewed as supply induced, brought incomes policy to the front ranks of economic policy.

In essence, incomes policy is a euphemism for wage restraints. Although applied in many forms, the government induces labor to accept lower nominal wages in exchange for some other benefit. This benefit usually involves the promise of lower prices in the future but may also involve something more concrete. For example, in late 1978, President Carter proposed that if specific labor groups agreed to wage increases of less than 7 percent, such workers would receive a tax rebate, should inflation exceed the target level. This put some substance—although not very much—behind the promise of lower inflation in return for restricted wage increases. What is desired, as with all incomes policies, is a downward shift of the labor supply curve. Most attempts at incomes policy have been unsuccessful because the promise of a future slowdown in the rate of price increases has not been believed and correctly so.

Here we analyze incomes policy in the static model as policy that shifts the labor supply curve down. This translates into a downward shift in the aggregate supply curve and a downward pressure on the price level. If the policy began from an initial situation of excess demand disequilibrium, it would be aimed at stopping or slowing an incipient inflation.

Aggregate supply shift
To represent incomes policy in the labor supply curve, we add a shift parameter γ to the supply function so that it becomes $W = P^*(\gamma) \cdot g(N)$. A reduction in γ, representing a successful incomes policy, means that labor will be supplied as if prices were perceived to be lower for any actual level of P. This could be due to the government successfully convincing labor to expect lower rates of price increase, inducing labor to accept lower increases of money wages in return for payroll tax reductions or successfully introducing a real-wage insurance scheme that protects labor from a higher rate of inflation. Our concern in this chapter is to demonstrate the *effect* of a successful incomes policy rather than to demonstrate that it is possible. The difficulties in developing a successful incomes policy (a task so vital that a successful solution by economists will equal in importance the solution to issues of demand management developed in the 1930s) will be discussed in Chapter 15's treatment of inflation.

The effect of a reduction in γ is shown in Figures 9.8 and 9.9. P^* is reduced from P_0^* to p_1^* directly by the incomes policy. This would shift the labor supply curve down at any initial price level P_0 in Figure 9.8(a), increasing equilibrium employment at the initial value P_0 from N_0 to N_1. This in turn increases equilibrium output supplied from y_0 to y_1 in Figure 9.8(b).

The increase in equilibrium output supplied at the initial price level P_0 is shown as an outward shift in the aggregate supply curve in Figure 9.9. The objective of incomes policy is generally stated as shifting the supply curve down, but with the positively sloped SS we can interpret the shift as down in terms of P for a given y_0, or out in terms of y for a given P_0.

Incomes policy and excess demand
Incomes policies are usually tried during periods of excess demand to forestall incipient price increases. Frequently an incomes policy is added to expansionary aggregate demand measures, to eliminate the inflationary consequences of demand expansion. For example, both in 1962 and in 1971 the economy was beginning to come out of recession, and monetary and fiscal policy were being used to stimulate demand. In 1962 the Council of Economic Advisers published the wage-price guideposts as an attempt to shift the supply curve in order to get the expansionary effects on N and y without prices increasing. In 1971, the administration applied a wage-price freeze as an extreme measure to control inflation as demand was expanded.

The coupling of incomes policy with expansionary demand policy is illustrated in Figure 9.10. An expansionary monetary or fiscal policy

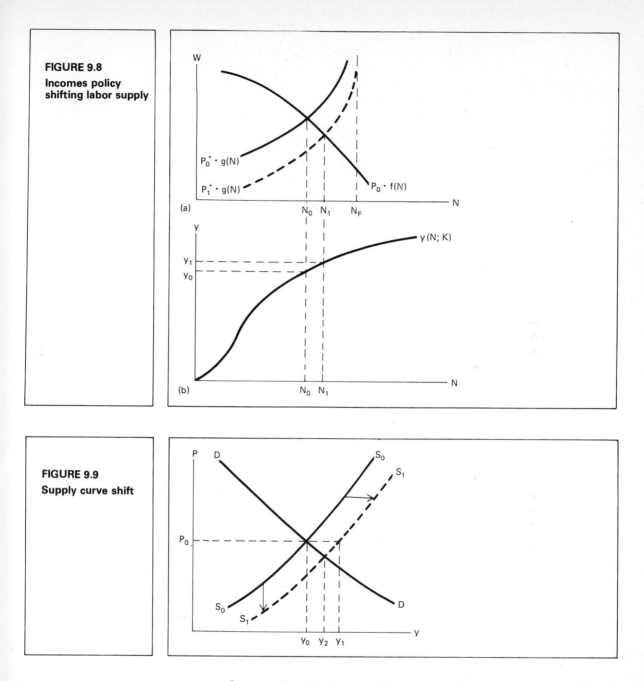

FIGURE 9.8
Incomes policy shifting labor supply

FIGURE 9.9
Supply curve shift

move, as discussed earlier in this chapter, would shift the demand curve out to $D_1 D_1$. This would increase equilibrium output in the general Keynesian model to y, but would also pull the price level up to P_1. To eliminate the price increase, incomes policy could attempt to shift the supply curve out to $S_1 S_1$, taking the economy to the new equilibrium P_0, y_2. The in-

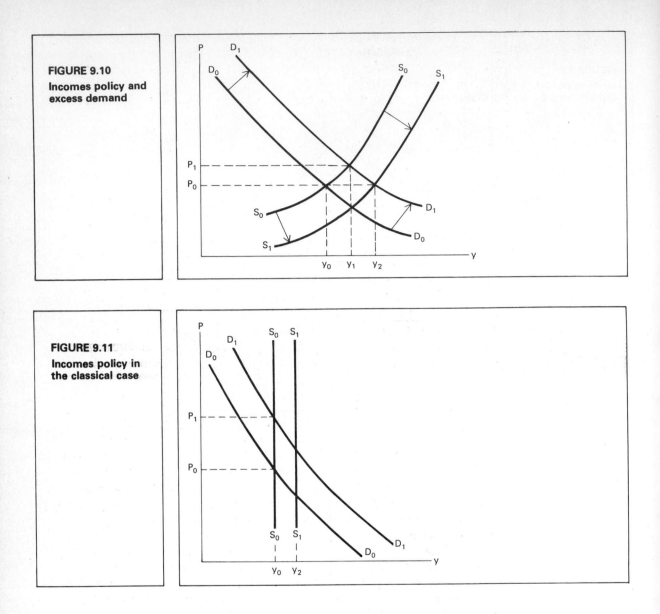

FIGURE 9.10

Incomes policy and excess demand

FIGURE 9.11

Incomes policy in the classical case

comes policy in this case would increase the change in equilibrium output while holding the price level constant. Clearly, if y_1 were the target for income, a smaller dose of both policies could take the supply-demand intersection to P_0, y_1.

In the classical case, incomes policy would have effects somewhat different from those in the general Keynesian model. In Figure 9.11 we show an excess demand gap eliminated by the shift in the vertical classical supply curve. At the initial price level P_0, aggregate demand shifts to D_1D_1. As we saw earlier, in the classical case this would result in the price level rising to P_1 with no change in output. To obtain a change in output, the vertical supply curve must shift; incomes policy is one way to do this. In Figure 9.11 it is incomes policy that moves equilibrium output, while demand policy controls the price level. Thus, in the classical case, movements in aggregate demand move the price level, and incomes policy offers one way to move equilibrium output.

CONCLUSION TO PART II

In Part II we have developed a skeletal model of the economy based on varying assumptions on how the parts of the economy interact. We have focused on the most basic structure of the economy, using the various multiplier expressions to analyze how the economy is interconnected rather than to give quantitative estimates of reaction coefficients. In particular, we have stressed that the size of the multipliers depends on one's estimate of the values of the slopes of all the functions involved, and these estimates themselves vary with economic conditions.

Thus, the models of Part II give a sense of how the parts of the economy are interconnected and in what direction the key variables (y, N, P, and r) will change as the exogenous variables—particularly the instruments of monetary, fiscal, and incomes policies—are changed. The equilibrium equations do not tell us, however, how long an adjustment to a policy change takes or what sequence it follows. To know this, we have to estimate empirically the equations of the model with the appropriate lags built in. This is one of the major ongoing tasks of economic research, and much of Part III investigates how this work is going.

QUESTIONS FOR DISCUSSION AND REVIEW

1. Why does the introduction of both interest rate and price adjustments reduce the effectiveness of policy weapons?

2. A change in the supply of money will shift the *LM* curve and consequently the aggregate demand curve. Will all shifts in the *LM* curve cause the aggregate demand curve to shift?

3. Contractionary monetary policy usually leads to an increase in the real rate of interest. What would you expect the path of the interest rate to look like in the movement from an equilibrium level to another?

4. Economists frequently seek to establish numerical values for policy multipliers. Are different values at different points in time an indication that underlying behavioral relations have shifted?

5. The new "supply side" school of economists has made much of the potential for shifting the supply curve through selective tax cuts. Such reductions, it is alleged, will increase the incentive to invest and perhaps shift out the supply of labor schedule. What is the likely result of such actions on the aggregate demand curve? Can one ascertain the overall effects on income, employment, and prices?

SELECTED READINGS

A. S. Blinder, "Can Income Tax Increases Be Inflationary? An Expository Note," *National Tax Journal*, June 1973.

M. Friedman, "A Monetary Theory of Nominal Income," *Journal of Political Economy*, March /April 1971.

M. Friedman, "A Theoretical Framework for Monetary Analysis," *Journal of Political Economy*, March/April 1970.

F. Modigliani, "The Monetary Mechanism and Its Interaction with Real Phenomenon," *Review of Economics and Statistics*, Supplement, February, 1963.

D. Patinkin, *Money, Interest and Prices*, 2nd ed. (New York: Harper & Row, 1965), chaps. 9–10.

D. Patinkin, "Price Flexibility and Full Employment," in M. G. Mueller, ed., *Readings in Macroeconomics* (New York: Holt, Rinehart and Winston, 1971).

W. L. Smith, "A Graphical Exposition of the Complete Keynesian System," in M. G. Mueller, ed., *Readings in Macroeconomics* (New York: Holt, Rinehart and Winston, 1971).

SECTORAL DEMAND FUNCTIONS AND EXTENSIONS OF THE BASIC MODEL

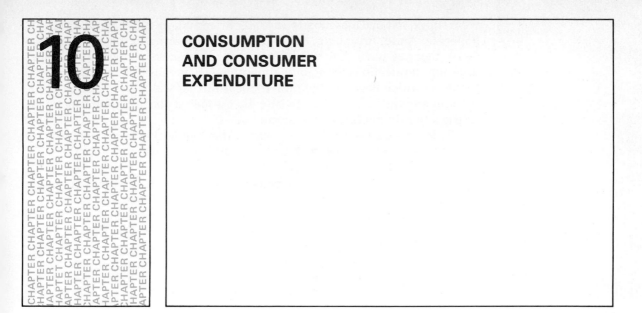

CONSUMPTION AND CONSUMER EXPENDITURE

In Part II, consumer expenditure is simply assumed to be a function of income less taxes. As disposable income increases, consumption increases, but by a lesser amount. Symbolically,

$$c = c(y - t(y)), \qquad 0 < \frac{\Delta c}{\Delta(y - t(y))} < 1, \qquad [1]$$

where c is real consumer expenditure, y is real income, and $t(y)$ is the tax function. This general formulation is sufficient for the qualitative analysis of income determination introduced in Part II. We turn now to a closer examination of the nature of the consumption function.

The consumption function provides an excellent illustration of a typical sequence in the development of knowledge in economics. This sequence involved first a conceptual breakthrough by Keynes in 1936, after which it was fairly obvious that a key relationship in macroeconomic analysis for some time to come would be the relationship between income and consumer expenditure. The importance of this relationship should be clear from Part II. The second step in the sequence involved the development of statistical information about consumer behavior and the relationships between consumption, saving, and income. This work, reasonably complete by the end of World War II, turned up an interesting and seemingly contradictory fact: The ratio of consumer expenditure to income varies inversely with the level of income both cyclically and across families at any given time, but on average this ratio does not tend to fall as income rises over a long period. The next step in the sequence of research into the consumption function was the development of more rigorous and elaborate theories which could explain the facts. Three different theories

179

were suggested by Duesenberry in 1949, Friedman in 1957, and a series of papers by Ando, Brumberg, and Modigliani beginning in the early 1950s. These theories have their similarities and differences, among which are differing implications for stabilization policy. The most recent step in this sequence which began in the mid-1930s is further statistical testing of the theories and the inclusion of statistically estimated consumption functions in econometric models of the economy.

This chapter traces that sequence. After we look at the background and the facts as they were known around 1945, we develop the microeconomic basis for the consumption function. Then we study the three principal theories of consumer behavior. Here the distinctions between labor and property income, current and permanent income, and consumption and consumer expenditure will be seen. The next section discusses some current empirical work on the consumption function, especially concerning the lag of consumer expenditure behind changes in income. The last two sections of the chapter draw the implications of the theoretical and empirical work, first for the operation of the basic static model of Chapter 9, and second for economic policy.

BACKGROUND: CROSS SECTIONS, CYCLES, AND TRENDS

Consumer expenditure runs about 65 percent of GNP in the United States, so any analysis of the factors determining the level of GNP must be concerned with consumer expenditure at some point. Analytically, in 1936 Keynes made the consumption function the basic element in the income-expenditure approach to the determination of national income. We have seen in Part II that the consumption function is the principal building block in multiplier analysis.

The short-run consumption function that Keynes introduced is shown in Figure 10.1, which plots real consumer expenditure c, against real income y. This function reflects the observation that as incomes increase people tend to spend a decreasing percentage of income, or conversely tend to save an increasing percentage of income. The slope of a line from the origin to a point on the consumption function gives the *average propensity to consume (APC)*, or the c/y ratio at that point. The slope of the

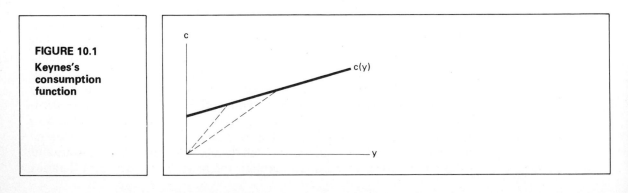

FIGURE 10.1
Keynes's consumption function

consumption function itself is the *marginal propensity to consume (MPC)*. Using the notation of Part II, if $c = c(y)$, the *MPC* is c'. From the graph it should be clear that the marginal propensity to consume is less than the average propensity to consume. If the ratio c/y falls as income rises, the ratio of the increment to c to the increment of y, c', must be smaller than c/y. Keynes saw this as the behavior of consumer expenditure in the short run—over the duration of a business cycle—reasoning that as income falls relative to recent levels, people will protect consumption standards by not cutting consumption proportionally to the drop in income and, conversely, as income rises, consumption will not rise proportionally.

The same kind of reasoning can also be applied to cross-sectional budget studies. Given a social standard of consumption, one would expect the proportion of income saved to rise as income rises. In the late 1930s cross-sectional budget studies were examined to see if Keynes' assumption that "rich people save proportionally more" was borne out. In general, these budget studies seemed to verify the theory.

Acceptance of the theory that $MPC < APC$, so that as income rises c/y falls, led to the formation of the *stagnation thesis* around 1940. It was observed that if consumption follows this pattern, the ratio of consumption demand to income would decrease as income grew. The problem that the stagnation thesis poses for fiscal policy can be seen as follows. If

$$y = c + i + g \quad \text{or} \quad 1 = \frac{c}{y} + \frac{i}{y} + \frac{g}{y}$$

is the condition for equilibrium growth of real output y, and there is no reason to assume that i/y will rise as the economy grows, then g/y must increase to balance the c/y drop to maintain full-employment demand as y grows. In other words, unless government spending increases at a faster rate than income, the economy would not grow but would stagnate.

During World War II, as government purchases soared, the economy did expand rapidly. However, many economists, following the stagnation thesis, feared that when the war ended and government spending was reduced, the economy would plunge back into depression. Yet precisely the opposite occurred. Private demand increased sharply when the war ended, causing an inflation rather than recession. Why did this happen? One plausible explanation is that during the war people had earned large increases in income but consumer expenditure was curbed by rationing. Consumers put their excess funds, the savings "forced" by rationing, into liquid assets in the form of government bonds. When the war ended, people had an excess stock of liquid assets which they converted into increased consumption demand. This phenomenon suggested that assets, as well as level of income, have something to do with consumption. In other words, for a given level of income, consumption may also be a function of *assets* or *wealth*.

In 1946 Simon Kuznets published a study of consumption and saving behavior dating back to the Civil War. Kuznets's data pointed out two

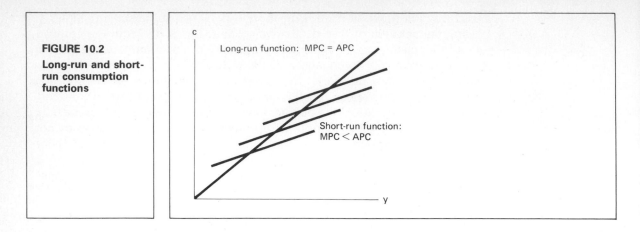

FIGURE 10.2

Long-run and short-run consumption functions

c

Long-run function: MPC = APC

Short-run function:
MPC < APC

y

important things about consumption behavior. First, it appeared that on average over the long run the ratio of consumer expenditure to income, c/y or APC, showed no downward trend, so the marginal propensity to consume equaled the average propensity to consume as income grew along trend. This meant that along trend the $c = c(y)$ function was a straight line passing through the origin, as shown in Figure 10.2. Second, Kuznets's study suggested that the c/y ratio was below the long-run average during boom years and above the average during periods of economic slump.

This meant that the c/y ratio varied inversely with income during cyclical fluctuations, so that for the short period corresponding to a business cycle empirical studies would show consumption as a function of income to have a slope like that of the short-run functions of Figure 10.2 rather than the long-run function.

Thus by the late 1940s it was clear that there were three observed phenomena for which a theory of consumption must account.

1. Cross-sectional budget studies show s/y increasing and c/y decreasing as y rises, so that *in cross sections of the population, MPC < APC.*
2. Business cycle, or short-run, data show that the c/y ratio is smaller than average during boom periods and greater than average during slumps, so that *in the short run, as income fluctuates, MPC < APC.*
3. Long-run trend data show no tendency for the c/y ratio to change over the long run, so that *as income grows along trend, MPC = APC.*

In addition, a theory of consumption should be able to explain the apparent effect of liquid assets on consumption which was observed after World War II.

THREE THEORIES OF THE CONSUMPTION FUNCTION

The theories that were developed by Duesenberry, Friedman, and Modigliani et al. to explain these phenomena all have a basic foundation in the microeconomic theory of consumer choice. In particular, both Friedman and Modigliani begin with the explicit common assumption that observed consumer behavior is the result of an attempt by rational consumers to maximize utility by allocating a lifetime stream of earnings to an optimum lifetime pattern of consumption. So we can begin a discussion of these theories at their common point of departure in the theory of consumer behavior, and then follow them individually as they diverge.

Consumption and the present value of income

Along with Friedman and Modigliani—and before them, Irving Fisher—we can begin with a single consumer with a utility function

$$U = U(c_0, \ldots, c_t, \ldots, c_T), \tag{2}$$

where lifetime utility U is a function of his real consumption c in all time periods up to T, the instant before he dies. The consumer will try to maximize his utility; that is, obtain the highest level of utility, subject to the budget constraint that the present value of his total consumption in life cannot exceed the present value of his total income in life. This budget constraint can be written symbolically as

$$\sum_0^T \frac{y_t}{(1+r)^t} = \sum_0^T \frac{c_t}{(1+r)^t}, \tag{3}$$

where T is the individual's expected lifetime. The notion of present discounted value is discussed in Chapter 4, pp. 54–56. This constraint says that the consumer can allocate his income stream to a consumption stream by borrowing and lending, but the present value of consumption is limited by the present value of income. For this restriction to hold as a strict equality, we assume that if the person receives an inheritance, he passes on a bequest of an equal amount.

We thus have an individual with an expected stream of lifetime income who will want to spread that income over a consumption pattern in an optimum way. We might imagine that his expected income stream begins and ends low, with a rise in midlife, and he wants to smooth it out into a more even consumption stream.

To formulate this problem in a workable manner, let us consider a two-period case in which the individual has an income stream y_0, y_1, and wants to maximize $U(c_0, c_1)$ subject to the borrowing-lending constraint

$$c_0 + \frac{c_1}{1+r} = y_0 + \frac{y_1}{1+r}.$$

In Figure 10.3 the income stream y_0, y_1 locates the point A. This point shows the amount of income the individual will earn in period 0, y_0, and the amount of income he will earn in period 1, y_1. We assume that he can either lend or borrow money at the interest rate r. Thus, if his income in period 0 is greater than the value of goods and services he wants to consume in that period he can lend, that is, save, his unspent income:

$$s_0 = y_0 - c_0 \equiv \text{income lent in period 0.} \tag{4}$$

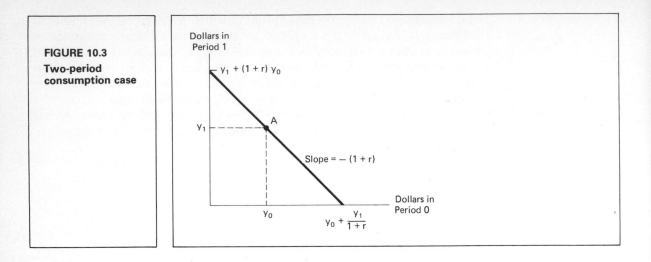

FIGURE 10.3

Two-period
consumption case

Dollars in
Period 1

$y_1 + (1 + r) y_0$

y_1

A

Slope $= -(1 + r)$

Dollars in
Period 0

y_0

$y_0 + \dfrac{y_1}{1+r}$

By lending this amount at the interest rate r, he will receive in period 1 an amount equal to $s_0(1 + r)$, so that his consumption in period 1 can exceed his income by that amount, which is his period 1 *dissaving*, s_1:

$$s_1 = -(1 + r)s_0 = y_1 - c_1. \tag{5}$$

The minus sign enters equation (5) because the dissaving in period 1 is of the opposite sign to the saving in period 0, and $c_1 > y_1$. Dividing the expression for s_1 by that for s_0 yields the trade-off between present and future consumption,

$$\frac{s_1}{s_0} = -\frac{s_0(1 + r)}{s_0} = \frac{y_1 - c_1}{y_0 - c_0}. \tag{6}$$

From the right-hand equality in (6), by cancelling the s_0's and multiplying through by $(y_0 - c_0)$, we obtain

$$y_1 - c_1 = -(1 + r)(y_0 - c_0). \tag{7}$$

This says that by reducing consumption in period 0 below income by the amount $s_0 = y_0 - c_0$, the consumer can enjoy in period 1 consumption in excess of income, $c_1 - y_1$, by the amount $(1 + r)s_0$. In other words, the consumer can trade from a y_0, y_1 income point in Figure 10.3 to a c_0, c_1 consumption point along a budget constraint that has a slope of $-(1 + r)$.

Another way to construct this budget line is to suppose that the individual wants to consume 100 percent of his income stream in period 0, by borrowing against his period 1 income. The maximum amount he can consume in period 0 will then be $y_0 + y_1/(1 + r)$, which is the intercept of the budget line on the period 0 axis. Conversely, if he decides that he will consume nothing in period 0, putting off all consumption until period 1, the maximum he can consume in period 1 will be $y_1 + (1 + r)y_0$, which is the intercept of the budget line on the period 1 axis. Thus the budget line in Figure 10.3 bounds the consumption possibilities open to the individual with an income stream y_0, y_1 facing an interest rate r. His consumption point c_0, c_1 cannot be above the budget line.

From the individual's utility function $U = U(c_0, c_1)$, we can obtain a set of indifference curves that show the points at which he is indifferent between additional consumption in period 1 or period 0 at each level of utility. These curves—U_0, U_1, U_2 in Figure 10.4—are conceptually similar to those introduced in chapter 6, pp. 110–111. Movement from U_0 to U_1 to U_2 raises the individual's level of utility.

Now, as pointed out above, all points on or below the budget line in Figure 10.4 are attainable. That is, the individual may consume at any level in either period up to the budget constraint. In order to maximize utility he will consume at a point on the budget line where it is just tangent to an indifference curve, such as point B in Figure 10.4. At point B, the individual's consumption pattern is c_0, c_1. Since his income flow is skewed toward period 1 (y_1 is much greater than y_0), he borrows $c_0 - y_0$ in period 0 at interest rate r. In period 1, he pays back $y_1 - c_1 = (1 + r)$ $(c_0 - y_0)$. The consumer's pattern of consumption, including present consumption c_0, is determined by the position of his budget line and the shape of his indifference curves.

The position of the budget line in Figure 10.4 is determined by two variables—the income in each period and the interest rate. This can be seen by noting that point A on the budget line has coordinates (y_0, y_1), the value of income in each period. The slope of the budget line, $-(1 + r)$, is determined by the interest rate. If the consumer's income should increase in *any* period, the present value (PV) of his income stream will increase; point A would move horizontally or vertically, moving the period 0 intercept and the budget line out with an unchanged slope. Thus, any increase in income will shift the budget line up parallel to the

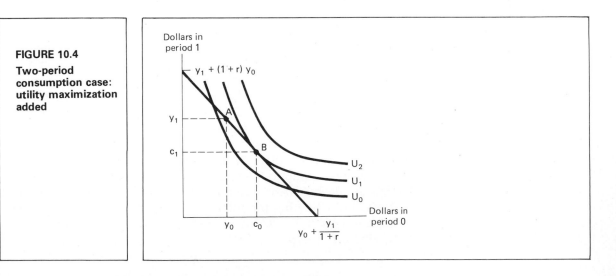

FIGURE 10.4

Two-period consumption case: utility maximization added

old budget line. This will make it possible for the consumer to reach a new, higher level of utility at a new c_0, c_1 point.

If consumption is not in any period an *inferior good*, that is, one with a negative income effect, then whenever *any* period's income rises, *all* periods' consumptions rise. For example, an increase in y_1 in Figure 10.4, shifting the budget line up, would raise both c_0 and c_1. The level of present consumption rises with a rise in future (expected) income.

One implication of this analysis is that current period consumption will vary less than does income. In the two-period case of Figure 10.4, an increase in y_0 would be spread across an increase in both c_0 and c_1. The change in c_0 would equal that in y_0 only if point B moved directly to the right with the y_0 increase. If we extend the analysis to many periods, say, 25 years, spreading a y_0 increase over 25 years of consumption increments would give a c_0 increase that is very small relative to the y_0 increase. If, for example, the consumer allocates his income to equal consumption in each of 25 years—in the two-period case this would put point B of Figure 10.4 on a 45° line from the origin, so that $c_0 = c_1$—the c_0 increment would be only 4 percent ($= \frac{1}{25}$) of the y_0 increment.

The relationship between the present value of the income stream and current consumption from Figure 10.4 gives us the first general formulation of the consumption function,

$$c_0 = f(PV_0); \qquad f' > 0, \tag{8}$$

where PV_0, the present value of current and expected future income at time 0, is

$$\sum_0^T \frac{y_t}{(1 + r)^t}.$$

This says simply that an individual's consumption in time 0 is an increasing function of the present value of his income in time 0. Symbolically, f' is the slope of this consumption function.

Both Ando-Modigliani and Friedman begin their analyses of the consumption function with the general form of the function given in equation (8). Their analyses differ in the treatment of the PV term, especially in how they relate this to observable economic variables for the statistical testing of their hypotheses. We first discuss the approach of Ando and Modigliani, and then that of Friedman. We will compare the results from these two approaches before discussing Duesenberry's analysis.

The Ando-Modigliani approach: The life-cycle hypothesis

To explain the three observed consumption function relationships discussed earlier in this chapter, Ando and Modigliani postulate a *life-cycle* hypothesis of consumption. According to this hypothesis, the typical individual has an income stream which is relatively low at the beginning and end of his life, when his productivity is low, and high during the middle of his life. This "typical" income stream is shown as the y curve in Figure 10.5, where T is expected lifetime.

On the other hand, the individual might be expected to maintain a more or less constant, or perhaps slightly increasing, level of consumption, shown as the c line in Figure 10.5, throughout his life. The constraint on this consumption stream, equation (3), is that the present value of his total consumption does not exceed the present value of his total income. This model suggests that in the early years of a person's life, the first shaded portion of Figure 10.5, he is a net borrower. In the middle years, he saves to repay debt and provide for retirement. In the late years, the second shaded portion of Figure 10.5, he dissaves.

Now if the life-cycle hypothesis is correct, if one were to undertake a budget study by selecting a cross-sectional sample of the population at random and classifying the sample by income level, the high-income groups would contain a higher-than-average proportion of persons who are at high-income levels *because* they are in the middle years of life, and thus have a relatively low c/y ratio. Similarly, the low-income groups would include relatively more persons whose incomes are low *because* they are at the ends of the age distribution, and thus have a high c/y ratio. Thus, if the life-cycle theory holds, a cross-sectional study would show c/y falling as income rises, explaining the cross-sectional budget studies showing $MPC < APC$.

Next, it seems reasonable to assume that in the absence of any particular reason to favor consumption in any one period over any other, for a representative consumer if PV rises, his consumption in each period rises more or less proportionately. The fraction of present value that each individual decides to consume in each period will depend on the consumer's preferences and interest rates.

If the population distribution by age and income is relatively constant, and tastes between present and future consumption (that is, the average shape of indifference curves) are stable through time, we can add up all the individual consumption functions to a stable aggregate function in which the population consumes k percent of the present value of its income stream in each period:

$$c_0 = k(PV_o). \tag{9}$$

FIGURE 10.5

"Life-cycle" hypothesis of consumption

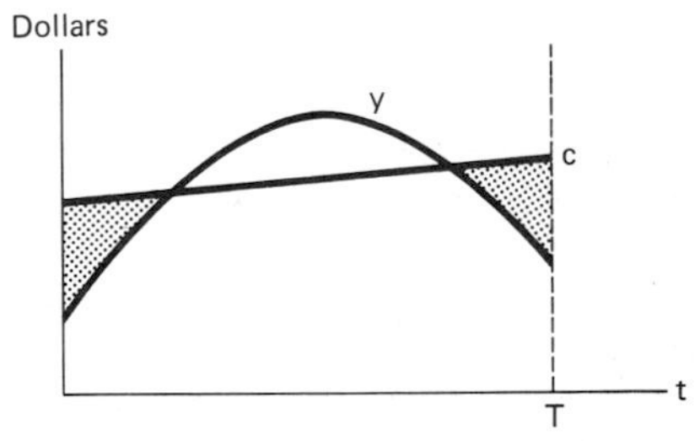

The kind of gradual changes in age and income distribution that we have seen in the United States since World War II certainly meet the Ando-Modigliani stability assumptions.

The next step in developing an operational consumption function from equation (9) is to relate the *PV* term to measurable economic variables. This is the crucial step in empirical investigations of the consumption function, as it is in almost any empirical study in economics. The theory involves consumption as a function of *expected* income, which of course cannot be measured. The problem is to link expected income back to measured variables by making further assumptions. Choosing the right assumptions and making the right linkage is the crucial art in empirical economics. The work of Ando and Modigliani provides an excellent example of the practice of this art. Ando and Modigliani begin to make the *PV* term operational by noting that income can be divided into income from *labor* y^L and income from assets or *property* y^P. Thus,

$$PV_0 = \sum_{0}^{T} \frac{y_t^{L}}{(1 + r)^t} + \sum_{0}^{T} \frac{y_t^{P}}{(1 + r)^t} \, ,$$

where time 0 is the current period, and t ranges from 0 to the remaining years of life, T. Now if capital markets are reasonably efficient, we can assume that the present value of the income from an asset is equal to the value of the asset itself, measured at the beginning of the current period. That is, the present value of the property income stream is equal to the current aggregate value of assets:

$$\sum_{0}^{T} \frac{y_t^{P}}{(1 + r)^t} = a_0,$$

where a_0 is real household net worth in period 0. Furthermore, we can separate out *known* current labor income from unknown, or expected, future labor income. This gives us for PV_0,

$$PV_0 = y_0^{L} + \sum_{1}^{T} \frac{y_t^{L}}{(1 + r)^t} + a_0.$$

The next step in this sequence is determining how expected labor income $y_1^{L}, \ldots, y_T^{L}$ might be related to current observable variables. First let us assume that there is an average expected labor income in time 0, y_0^{e}, such that

$$y_0^{e} = \frac{1}{T} \sum_{1}^{T} \frac{y_t^{L}}{(1 + r)^t} \, ,$$

where T is the average remaining life expectancy of the population, about 45 years, and the term $1/T$ averages the present value of future labor income over T years. Then the expected labor income term can be written as

$$\sum_{1}^{T} \frac{y_t^L}{(1 + r)^t} = Ty_0^e.$$

This gives us an expression for the present value of the income stream,

$$PV_0 = y_0^L + Ty_0^e + a_0, \tag{10}$$

which has only one remaining variable that is not yet measurable—average expected labor income y^e. We now need a final hypothesis linking average expected labor income to an observable variable—current labor income.

There are several assumptions that might be tested to see how they fit the data coming from observations of the real world. The simplest assumption would be that average expected labor income is just a multiple of present labor income:

$$y_0^e = \beta y_0^L,$$

with β some positive fraction. This assumes that if current income rises, people adjust their expectation of future incomes up so that y^e rises by the fraction β of the increase in y^L. We might note here that this assumption assigns great importance to movements in current income as a determinant of current consumption. If an increase in current income shifts the entire expected income stream substantially, it will have a much larger effect on current consumption than it would if the expected income stream did not shift, leaving the increment to current income to be allocated to consumption over the remaining years of life. This point is important for the effectiveness of stabilization policy, as we will see later.

Alternatively, we could assume that y^e is related to both present labor income and employment, on the theory that as employment goes up, people will expect their chances for future employment, and thus income, to rise too. This assumption can be formulated as

$$y_0^e = \beta y_0^L = f\left(\frac{N}{L}\right) \cdot y_0^L; \qquad f' > 0,$$

where N is employment and L is the size of the labor force.

Ando and Modigliani tried a number of similar assumptions, and found that the simplest assumption that $y^e = \beta y_L$ fits the data as well as any. Thus, substituting βy_0^L for y_0^e in equation (10) for PV, we obtain

$$PV_0 = (1 + \beta T)y_0^L + a_0, \tag{11}$$

as a final operational expression for PV, in that both y^L and a can be measured statistically. Substitution of this equation into the consumption function of equation (9) yields

$$c_0 = k(1 + \beta T)y_0^L + ka_0, \tag{12}$$

as a statistically measurable form of the Ando-Modigliani consumption function. The coefficients of y^L and a in this consumption function were estimated statistically by Ando and Modigliani using annual U.S. data. A typical result of this estimation is

$$c_t = 0.7\, y_t^L + 0.06\, a_t, \tag{13}$$

which says that an increase of $1 billion in real-labor income will raise real consumption by $0.7 billion—the marginal propensity to consume out of labor income is 0.7. Similarly, the marginal propensity to consume out of assets is 0.06.

Comparing the estimates of the coefficients in equation (13) with the derived coefficients in (12), we can see from the coefficient of a in equation (13) that k is 0.06. This suggests, from equation (9), that on aggregate, households consume about 6 percent of net worth in a year. Using this value for k and 45 years as a rough estimate of average remaining lifetime T, we can also obtain the value of β from equation (12) that is implicit in the estimate of the y^L coefficient in (13):

$$0.7 = k(1 + \beta T) = 0.06(1 + 45\beta),$$

so that β is about 0.25. This suggests that when current labor income goes up by $100, people's estimate of the average expected annual labor income rises by $25.

The Ando-Modigliani consumption function of equation (13) is shown in Figure 10.6, which graphs consumption against labor income. The intercept of the consumption-income function ka_t is set by the level of assets. The slope of the function—the marginal propensity to consume out of labor income—is the coefficient of y^L in the Ando-Modigliani consumption function. In short-run cyclical fluctuations with assets remaining fairly constant, consumption and income will vary along a single consumption-income function. Over the longer run, as saving causes assets to rise, the consumption-income function shifts up as ka_t increases.

Thus, over time we may observe a set of points such as those along the line OX in Figure 10.6, which shows a constant ratio of consumption to

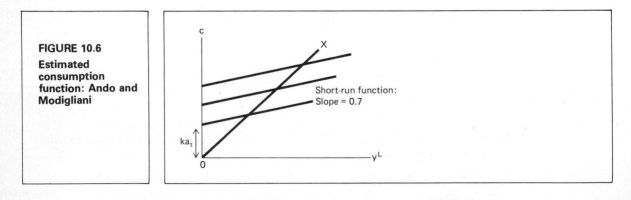

FIGURE 10.6

Estimated consumption function: Ando and Modigliani

labor income as the economy grows along trend. This ratio can be obtained by dividing all the terms in equation (13) by labor income y^L:

$$\frac{c_t}{y_t^L} = 0.7 + 0.06 \, \frac{a_t}{y_t^L} = 0.7 + 0.06 \, \left(\frac{a_t}{y_t} \cdot \frac{y_t}{y_t^L} \right).$$

If the c/y^L ratio given by this equation is constant as y^L grows along trend, then the line OX will go through the origin in Figure 10.6. This ratio will be constant if a/y, the ratio of assets to total income, and y^L/y, the share of labor in total income, are constant. The observed data for the United States confirm that both of these terms are fairly constant. Over time the labor share of income has remained around 75 percent with a slight tendency to drift up, and the ratio of assets to income has been roughly constant at about 3 with a slight tendency to drift downward over time.

Inserting these values into the expression for c/y^L we obtain

$$\frac{c}{y^L} = 0.7 + 0.06 \, \left(3 \cdot \frac{1}{0.75} \right) = 0.94.$$

Thus, the slope of the OX line in Figure 10.6 is approximately 0.94.

To obtain the trend ratio of consumption to *total* income, we can divide all the terms in equation (13) by total income y:

$$\frac{c_t}{y_t} = 0.7 \, \frac{y_t^L}{y_t} + 0.06 \, \frac{a_t}{y_t}.$$

Substitution of our values of the labor share and the asset-income ratio into this expression yields

$$\frac{c_t}{y_t} = (0.7)(0.75) + (0.06)(3) = 0.53 + 0.18 = 0.71.$$

Thus, the average propensity to consume out of *total* income is constant at about 0.7. A spot check of the data for 1979 shows that consumption expenditure was about \$1.5 trillion and national income was about \$1.9 trillion, giving a c/y ratio of 0.79.

Thus, the Ando-Modigliani model of consumption behavior explains all three of the observed consumption phenomena. It explains the $MPC < APC$ result of cross-sectional budget studies by the life-cycle hypothesis; it provides an explanation for the cyclical behavior of consumption with the consumption-income ratio inversely related to income along a short-run function in Figure 10.6; and it also explains the long-run constancy of the c/y ratio. In addition, it explicitly includes assets as an explanatory variable in the consumption function, a role which was observed in the post-World War II inflation.

There remains a question concerning the role of current income in explaining current consumption in the Ando-Modigliani model. The analysis of the relationship of current consumption to the present value of the entire future income stream suggested that a change in current income not accompanied by a change in expected future income would cause a relatively small change in current consumption. To a certain extent, the Ando-Modigliani analysis obscures this point by *assuming* that expected average income depends on current income, raising the leverage of current income on current consumption. Literal acceptance of the Ando-Modigliani results, typified by equation (13), would mean that all increases in labor income would tend to raise current consumption by 70 percent of the income change. But one can think of income changes that should have no effect on expected future income, for example, an explicitly temporary income tax surcharge, such as that enacted in July 1968. In this case, simple application of the Ando-Modigliani marginal propensity to consume to obtain the direct policy-induced consumption effect of the tax change would probably be (and in fact was) misleading; the consumption reduction should be far less than 70 percent of the disposable income cut. Thus, the econometric results should be used carefully with an eye on their underlying assumptions, which sometimes will not hold true.

The Friedman approach: Permanent income

Let us now turn to Friedman's model of consumption. Friedman also begins with the assumption of individual consumer utility maximization, which gives us the consumption function relation between an *individual's* consumption and present value, corresponding to equation (8) earlier,

$$c^i = f^i(PV^i); \qquad f' > 0. \tag{14}$$

Here the i *su*perscript index indicates that the function holds for a "representative individual," i, over time.

Friedman differs from Ando-Modigliani beginning with his treatment of the PV term in equation (14). The present value of the total income stream is the current asset value of that income stream. Multiplying this asset value by the rate of return r yields Friedman's *permanent income* from that asset value:

$$y_p{}^i = r \cdot PV^i.$$

Here PV includes the discounted values of the future streams of both labor and property income. The discounted value of future property income is the current value of net physical and financial assets, a_0 in the case of Ando-Modigliani. The discounted value of future labor income is known as *human capital*. The two are summed to obtain total PV. Friedman, along with Ando-Modigliani, assumes that the consumer wants to smooth his actual income stream into a more or less flat consumption pattern. This gives a level of *permanent consumption*, $c_p{}^i$, that is proportional to $y_p{}^i$,

$$c_p{}^i = k^i y_p{}^i.$$

The individual ratio of permanent consumption to permanent income k^i presumably depends on the interest rate—the return on saving—individual tastes shaping the indifference curve, and the variability of expected income. If there is no reason to expect these factors to change with the level of income, we can assume that the average k^i for all income classes will be the same, equal to the population average $\bar{k}$. Thus, if we classify a sample of the population by income strata, as is done in the cross-sectional budget studies, we would expect that the average permanent consumption in each income class i (using subscripts for income classes as opposed to superscripts to denote individuals) would be $\bar{k}$ times its average permanent income:

$$\bar{c}_{pi} = \bar{k} \, \bar{y}_{pi},$$

for each income class i.

Next we can observe that total income in a given period is made up of permanent income $y_p{}^i$ which the individual has imputed to himself plus a random transitory income component $y_t{}^i$ which can be positive, negative, or zero, and really represents current income deviations from permanent income. Notice here that the subscript t refers to "transitory," not "time," as in the previous section. This is the standard notation for transitory income in the literature. This gives us measured income as the sum of the permanent and transitory components:

$$y^i = y_p{}^i + y_t{}^i.$$

Similarly, total consumption in any period is permanent consumption $c_p{}^i$ plus a random transitory consumption component $c_t{}^i$, which represents positive, negative, or zero deviation from the "normal" or permanent level of consumption. Thus measured, consumption is the sum of permanent and transitory consumption:

$$c^i = c_p{}^i + c_t{}^i.$$

Next comes a series of assumptions concerning the relationships between permanent and transitory income, permanent and transitory consumption, and transitory income and consumption. The assumptions concerning these relationships give the explanation in the Friedman theory of the cross-sectional result that $MPC < APC$.

First, Friedman assumes that there is no correlation between transitory and permanent incomes; in other words, y_t is just a random fluctuation around y_p, so that the covariance of $y_p{}^i$ and $y_t{}^i$ across individuals is zero. This assumption has the following implication for cross-sectional budget study results. Suppose we take a sample of families from a roughly normal income distribution and then sort them out by income classes. Since y_p and y_t are not related, the income class that centers on the population average income will have an average transitory-income component $\bar{y}_t$ equal to zero, and for that income class $\bar{y} = \bar{y}_p$. As we go up from the average strata, more people will find themselves in any particular income group because they had unusually high incomes that year (implying $y_t{}^i$ positive) than because they had unusually low incomes that year ($y_t{}^i$ negative). This happens because in a normal distribution, for any income class above the average, there are more people with permanent incomes *below* that class who can come up into it because $y_t{}^i$ is positive in any one year than there are people *above* that class who can fall down due to $y_t{}^i$ being negative. Thus, for income classes above the population average, average transitory income y_t is positive, and observed average income $\bar{y}$ exceeds average permanent income $\bar{y}_p$.

Similarly, below the average income level, for any given income class, there are more people who can fall into it due to having a bad year so that $y_t{}^i$ is negative, than people who come up into it by having a good year so that $y_t{}^i$ is positive. Thus, for income classes below the population mean, average transitory income $\bar{y}_t$ is negative and average observed income $\bar{y}$ is less than average permanent income $\bar{y}_p$. This result—that when sorted by measured income, groups above the population mean have positive $\bar{y}_t$ and groups below the mean have negative $\bar{y}_t$—is important for Friedman's analysis, as we will see shortly.

Next, Friedman assumes that there is no relationship between permanent and transitory consumption, so that c_t is simply a random variation around c_p. Thus, the covariance of $c_p{}^i$ and $c_t{}^i$ is zero.

Finally, Friedman assumes that there is no relationship between transitory consumption and transitory income. In other words, a sudden increase in income, due to a transitory fluctuation, will not contribute immediately to an individual's consumption. This assumption is intuitively less obvious than the previous ones, but it seems fairly reasonable, because we are dealing with *consumption* as opposed to *consumer expenditure*. Consumption includes, in addition to purchases of nondurable goods and services, only the "use" of durables—measured by depreciation and interest cost—rather than expenditures on durables. This means that if transitory or windfall income is used to purchase a durable good, this would not appreciably affect current consumption. Thus, Friedman assumes that the covariance of c_t and y_t is also zero.

The last two assumptions, that transitory consumption is not correlated with either permanent consumption or transitory income, mean that when we sample the population and classify the sample by income levels, for each income class the transitory variations in consumption will cancel out so that for each income class $\bar{c}_{ti} = 0$, and

$$\bar{c}_i = \bar{c}_{pi}$$

for each income class i.

We can now bring this series of assumptions together into an explanation of the cross-sectional result that $MPC < APC$ even when the basic hypothesis of the theory is that the ratio of permanent consumption to permanent income is a constant $\bar{k}$. Consider a randomly selected sample of the population classified by income levels. A group i, with average observed income $\bar{y}_i$ *above* average population income will have a positive average transitory-income component $\bar{y}_{ti} > 0$. For this above-average group, then, observed average income will be greater than average permanent income, that is, $\bar{y}_i > \bar{y}_{pi}$.

All income groups will have average permanent consumption given by $\bar{c}_{pi} = \bar{k}\bar{y}_{pi}$. But since $\bar{c}_{ti}$ is not related to either $\bar{c}_{pi}$ or $\bar{y}_{ti}$, all groups, including the above-average income group, will have a zero average transitory-consumption component, so that $\bar{c}_i = \bar{c}_{pi}$. Linking these two consumption conditions gives us

$$\bar{c}_i = \bar{c}_{pi} = \bar{k}\bar{y}_{pi}. \tag{15}$$

Thus, the above-average income group will have average measured consumption equal to permanent consumption, but average measured income greater than permanent income, so that its measured $\bar{c}_i/\bar{y}_i$ ratio will be *less* than $\bar{k}$. Similarly, a below-average income group j will have a measured $\bar{c}_j/\bar{y}_j$ ratio greater than $\bar{k}$.

These results are illustrated in Figure 10.7. The solid line $\bar{k}$ represents the relationship between permanent consumption and income. The point $\bar{y}$ is the population average measured income, and if the sample is taken in a "normal" year when measured average income is on trend, average transitory income will be zero, so that $\bar{y} = \bar{y}_p$. The point $\bar{c}_p$ is the population's average measured and permanent consumption.

First, consider sample group i, with average income above population average, so that $\bar{y}_i > \bar{y}$. This group has a positive average transitory-income component $\bar{y}_{ti}$, so that its average permanent income $\bar{y}_{pi}$ is less than its average measured income $\bar{y}_i$; $\bar{y}_{pi} < \bar{y}_i$, as shown in Figure 10.7. To locate average consumption, both measured and permanent, for group i, we multiply $\bar{y}_{pi}$ by $\bar{k}$ to obtain $\bar{c}_i = \bar{c}_{pi}$ along the $\bar{k}$ line. Thus, for an above-average income group i, we observe $\bar{c}_i$ and $\bar{y}_i$ at the point A which lies below the permanent consumption line $\bar{k}$ in Figure 10.7.

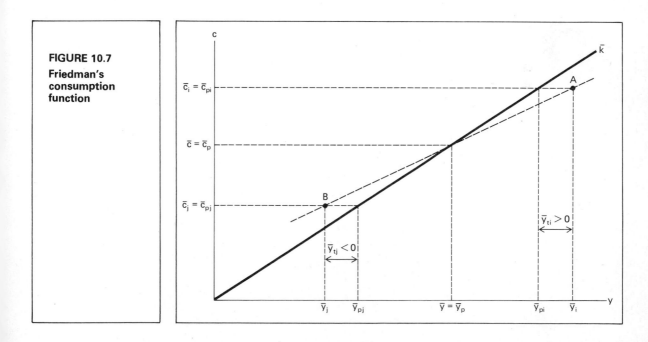

FIGURE 10.7
Friedman's consumption function

Next, observing lower-than-average income group j, we see that the average income of the group $\bar{y}_j$ is less than the national average income $\bar{y}$, so that the average transitory income of the sample group $\bar{y}_{tj}$, is less than zero. Furthermore, we observe $\bar{c}_j$ and know that $\bar{c}_j = \bar{c}_{pj} = \bar{k}\bar{y}_{pj}$ along the $\bar{k}$ line. The location of $\bar{c}_j$ and $\bar{y}_j$ gives us the point B lying above the $\bar{k}$ line for the below-average income group j. Connecting the points A and B, we obtain the cross-sectional consumption function that connects observed average income-consumption points. This function has a smaller slope than the underlying permanent function, so that in cross-sectional budget studies, we expect to see $MPC < APC$ if (but not only if) the Friedman permanent-income hypothesis is correct.

Over time, as the economy and the national average permanent income grow along trend, the cross-sectional consumption function of Figure 10.7 shifts up. What we observe in a long-run time series are movements of national average consumption and income along the line $\bar{k}$, giving a constant c/y ratio. As the economy cycles about its trend growth path, the average $\bar{c}/\bar{y}$ point will move above and below the long-run $\bar{k}$ line. In a boom year when $\bar{y}$ is above trend, the average transitory income of the population will be positive, so that $\bar{y} > \bar{y}_p$. But average transitory consumption will be zero, so that $\bar{c} = \bar{c}_p = \bar{k}\,\bar{y}_p$. Thus, when $\bar{y}$ is above trend, $\bar{c}/\bar{y}$ will be less than $\bar{c}_p/\bar{y}_p = \bar{k}$. Similarly, in a year when y is below trend, $\bar{y}_t$ will be negative, $\bar{y} < \bar{y}_p$, and the $\bar{c}/\bar{y}$ ratio will be greater than $\bar{k}$.

This cyclical movement is illustrated in Figure 10.8. In an average year, when $\bar{y}_t = 0$, the $\bar{c}_0$, $\bar{y}_0$ point falls on the long-run $\bar{k}$ line. In a year with above-trend income $\bar{y}_1$, transitory income is positive, so that average permanent income $\bar{y}_{p1} < \bar{y}_1$, and the $\bar{c}_1$, $\bar{y}_1$ point is below the $\bar{k}$ line of Figure 10.8. In a year with below-trend income $\bar{y}_2$, the $\bar{c}_2$, $\bar{y}_2$ point is above the $\bar{k}$ line, giving us the short-run function of Figure 10.8. The difference between Figures 10.7 and 10.8 is just that in Figure 10.7 the variation in income and consumption is in a cross section at any one time, while in Figure 10.8 the variation is in average c and y over the business cycle.

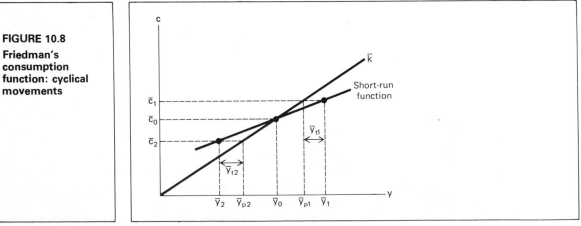

FIGURE 10.8

Friedman's consumption function: cyclical movements

Thus, Friedman's model also explains the cross-sectional budget studies and short-run cyclical observations that indicate $MPC < APC$, as well as the long-run observation that the c/y ratio is fairly constant, that is, $APC = MPC$. His model is somewhat less satisfactory than the Ando-Modigliani model in that assets are only implicitly taken into account as a determinant of permanent income, and it relies on less observable aspects of income—"permanent" income and "transitory" income—than the Ando-Modigliani model, which separates out the observable components—labor income and value of assets.

Nevertheless, the two models are closely related. Families with transitorily high income in Friedman's analysis could be families in the middle years in the Ando-Modigliani life cycle, and families with negative transitory income could be the ones at the ends of the life cycle. Thus, the life-cycle hypothesis could be one explanation of the distribution of Friedman's transitory incomes.

The two models are similar in the starting point of the analysis in the consumption–present-value relationship given in equation (14)

$$c^i = f^i(PV^i),$$

and in the explanation of cross-sectional results. The Ando-Modigliani model might be more useful to econometric model builders and forecasters since it explicitly includes measured current income and assets to explain consumption, but it may also need careful interpretation in cases where income changes are clearly temporary, and permanent income considerations are more relevant.

The Duesenberry approach: Relative income

The model developed by Duesenberry in 1949 differs considerably from the Ando-Modigliani and Friedman models in that it does not begin with the basic consumption–present-value relationship derived early in this chapter. Instead, Duesenberry's analysis is based on two relative-income hypotheses.

The first hypothesis is essentially that consumers are not so much concerned with their absolute level of consumption as they are with their consumption relative to the rest of the population. The Ando-Modigliani and Friedman models are based on the solution to the problem of consumer choice where the individual tries to maximize $U = U(c_o, \ldots, c_t, \ldots, c_T)$ subject to the equality of the present value of income and consumption. In that case only the absolute level of the individual's consumption enters the utility function. Duesenberry, however, writes the utility function as

$$U = U\left(\frac{c_0}{R_0}, \ldots, \frac{c_t}{R_t}, \ldots, \frac{c_T}{R_T}\right), \qquad [16]$$

where the R's are a weighted average of the rest of the population's consumption. This says that utility increases only if the individual's consumption rises relative to the average.

This assumption leads to the result that the individual's c/y ratio will depend on his position in the income distribution. A person with an income below the average will tend to have a high c/y ratio because, essentially, he is trying to keep up to a national average consumption standard with a below-average income. On the other hand, an individual with an above-average income will have a lower c/y ratio because it takes a smaller proportion of his income to buy the standard basket of consumer goods.

This provides the explanation of both the cross-sectional result that $MPC < APC$ and the long-run constancy of c/y. If, as income grows along trend, the relative distribution of income is stable, there will be no reason for c/y to change. As people earn more along trend they can increase their consumption proportionately to maintain the same ratio between their consumption and the national average.

Duesenberry's second hypothesis is that present consumption is not influenced merely by present levels of absolute and relative income, but also by levels of consumption attained in previous periods. It is much more difficult, he argues, for a family to reduce a level of consumption once attained than to reduce the portion of its income saved in any period. This assumption suggests that the aggregate ratio of saving to income depends on the level of present income relative to previous peak income, $\hat{y}$. Thus in Duesenberry's formulation the saving ratio is given by

$$\frac{s}{y} = a_0 + a_1 \frac{y}{\hat{y}}, \tag{17}$$

where y is real disposable income. As present income rises relative to its previous peak, s/y increases, and vice versa. We can convert this Duesenberry saving function into a consumption function by observing that if y is disposable income, $c/y = 1 - (s/y)$, so that from equation (17) we can obtain

$$\frac{c}{y} = (1 - a_0) - a_1 \frac{y}{\hat{y}} \tag{18}$$

as the Duesenberry consumption function.

As income grows along trend, previous peak income will always be last year's income, so that $y/\hat{y}$ would be equal to $1 + g_y$ where g_y is the growth rate of real income. If y grows at 3 percent along trend, $y/\hat{y}$ will be 1.03 and c/y will be constant, as required by the long-run data of Kuznets.

But as income fluctuates around trend, the c/y ratio will vary inversely with income, due to the negative coefficient of $y/\hat{y}$ in equation (18). To compute the MPC, we can multiply the c/y ratio of equation (18) by y to obtain

$$c = (1 - a_0)y - a_1 \frac{y^2}{\hat{y}}.$$

The MPC, the change in c as y changes, is then

$$MPC = \frac{\Delta c}{\Delta y} = (1 - a_0) - 2a_1 \frac{y}{\hat{y}}. \tag{19}$$

Comparison of equation (19) giving the MPC and equation (18) giving the APC shows that in the short run, with previous peak income fixed, the Duesenberry model implies $MPC < APC$.

This combination of short-run and long-run behavior of consumption gives us the *ratchet effect* shown in Figure 10.9. As income grows along trend, c and y move up along the long-run function of Figure 10.9, with a constant c/y ratio. But if, at some point like c_0, y_0, income falls off and the economy goes into a recession, c and y move down along a short-run function c_0c_0 with a slope given by the MPC in equation (19). Recovery of income back to its trend level, which is also the previous peak, will take c and y back up c_0c_0 to the initial c_0, y_0 point, where trend growth resumes along the long-run function. If another recession occurs at c_1, y_1, consumption and income will fall back along c_1c_1, and rise back to c_1, y_1 during the recovery. Thus, Duesenberry's model implies a ratchet effect in that when income falls off, consumption drops less than it rises as income grows along trend. We might note that this mechanism is formally the same as that suggested by wage rigidity in Chapter 8.

This completes our survey of the three principal theories of the consumption function. Each theory improves our understanding of the consumption-saving-income relationships. The theories of Ando-Modigliani and Friedman seem to be more successful than is Duesenberry's, in terms of its present acceptance among economists. The strength of Friedman's theory is related to the acceptance by many economists of the proposition that people base current consumption-saving decisions on more than just current and past values of income and assets. The notion, common to both Ando-Modigliani and Friedman, of a basic permanent consumption path that is tied to an expected income stream and is somewhat insensitive to temporary fluctuations in income, is persuasive. On the other hand, it is useful to know what *does* cause fluctuations in current consumption and the Ando-Modigliani model has a relative strength in its

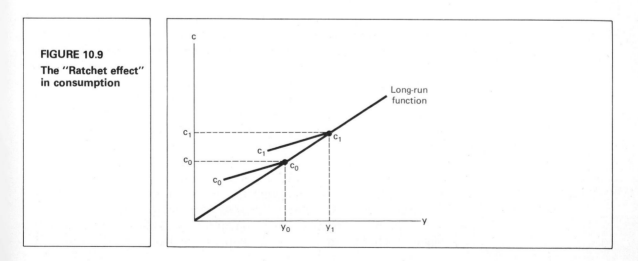

FIGURE 10.9

The "Ratchet effect" in consumption

10. CONSUMPTION AND CONSUMER EXPENDITURE

explicit inclusion of current income and assets in the explanation of consumption. Perhaps the best compromise is to explain consumption using the Ando-Modigliani model, but with reservations in cases of temporary income and asset fluctuations as suggested by the permanent-income hypothesis.

THE MIT-PENN-SSRC (MPS) MODEL

Beginning in 1967, a group of economists centered originally at the Federal Reserve Board in Washington and the Massachusetts Institute of Technology (MIT) in Cambridge, under the general direction of Ando and Modigliani, developed an econometric model of the economy.

This research project was largely supported by the Federal Reserve Board (the Fed) and the Social Science Research Council (SSRC). The model is used for policy analysis and forecasting by economists at the Fed and in major centers of economic research. With the leaders of the project coming from the University of Pennsylvania (Ando) and MIT (Modigliani), the model has become known as the MIT-Penn-SSRC, or MPS model.

Included in this model are consumption function estimates that are based on the original Ando-Modigliani work discussed earlier, and which introduce more clearly the difference between the concepts of *consumption* and *consumer expenditure* which are implicit in all of the other models. Furthermore, this model deals explicitly with the dynamic nature of the multiplier by predicting how long it takes for a one-time, or step, increase in income to achieve its full impact on consumption.

The term *consumption* as we have been using it in most of this chapter means the *use* of a good rather than the expenditure on it in any one period. Durable goods have a lifetime of service. The present value of the services rendered by the good is equal to the original price of the good. Consumption is the amount of services of a good which is used up in any one period, while *consumption expenditure* is the expenditure on consumer goods in a period. The two values are usually different, unless all purchases of the services of durable goods are in the form of rents, or the economy is in a stationary state where all durable purchases are for replacement.

Considering the distinction between consumption and consumer expenditure, it can be seen that an increase in income in period 0 will lead immediately to an increase in *desired consumption*, given by the *MPC*. But to increase consumption services from durables, a person has to buy the entire capitalized stream of services in the current period. Thus, the increase in consumer expenditure resulting from an increase in income could greatly exceed the original income change. (Consider a tax cut of $200/month which leads to an auto purchase of $8,000.)

The consumption function in the MPS model predicts the size of increases in both consumption and consumption expenditure following an exogenous change in income as well as the length of time needed

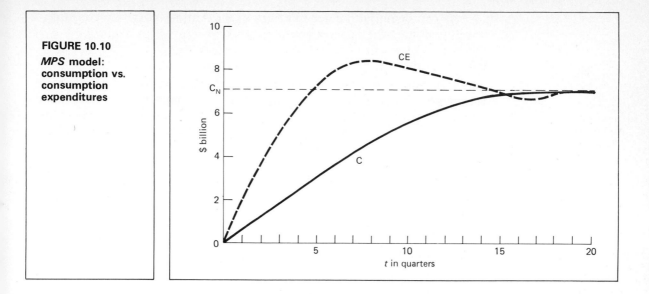

FIGURE 10.10

MPS model: consumption vs. consumption expenditures

before the new levels are fully reached, holding all other variables, for example, P and r, constant. This is illustrated in Figure 10.10, which shows the adjustment of both consumption and consumer expenditure to their new equilibrium levels following a one-time increase in income of $10 billion in period 0. This corresponds to the simplest multiplier effect of Chapter 3, where we are now looking at the *timing* of the effect. The solid line in Figure 10.10 represents the increased *consumption* resulting from the step increase in disposable income. It can be seen that it approaches the ultimate level c_N asymptomatically. The dashed line represents actual *expenditures* on consumption goods. This increment to expenditures rises above c_N after 5 quarters, and then declines to below that level after 15 quarters.

In the static model we have discussed, we have dealt only with the values for consumption and we have observed only the two equilibrium points c_0 and c_N. One virtue of the MPS model is that it permits us to see the time dimension of changes from c_0 to c_N and to relate changes in consumption to changes in consumer expenditure. The latter is the value which appears in the national income accounts whereas the former is the concept relevant to economic theory.

THE WEALTH EFFECT IN THE STATIC MODEL

We have now seen that the level of real household net worth—*wealth* or *assets*—has an effect on the level of consumption. In the original discussion of the effects of changes in consumption on the equilibrium of the money and product markets we did not allow assets to enter into consideration. Now we will examine the implications for the general equilibrium analysis of including real assets in the consumption function.

We can begin with a general form of the Ando-Modigliani consumption function:

$$c = \alpha_0 y^L + \alpha_1 a, \qquad [20]$$

where α_0 and α_1 are the positive coefficients that Ando and Modigliani estimated, shown in equation (13) earlier. An increase in either labor income or assets raises current consumption. The definition of assets at the beginning of the period that brought the a term into the function in the first place is

$$a_0 = \sum_0^T \frac{y_t^P}{(1+r)^t} = y_0^P + \sum_1^T \frac{y_t^P}{(1+r)^t}.$$

Thus, current property income y_0^P also enters the consumption function (20) positively through the assets term, and we can write the expanded consumption function in the general form

$$c = c(y - t(y), a). \qquad [21]$$

Real consumption increases with an increase either in disposable income or in real assets.

Now if, at a given level of disposable income, an increase in real assets raises consumption, it must reduce saving since $s + c = y - t(y)$. This is not in violation of commonsense notions of saving. People save in order to accumulate assets or wealth. If there should suddenly be an exogenous increase in one's wealth, such as an inheritance, there is less need to save, and the saving rate will diminish.

Changes in assets and the IS curve

The effect of adding real assets to the saving function in the basic static model is shown in the four-quadrant diagram of Figure 10.11. With an initial asset level a_0, the IS curve is positioned at $I_0 S_0$. In general, an increase in real assets to a_1 shifts the saving function in the southeast quadrant from $s(a_0)$ to $s(a_1)$; the exception to this is an increase in asset value that follows from a change in the interest rate, as explained below. Since $s + t$ is measured from the origin down on the vertical axis, this shift represents a decrease in saving at any given level of income.

The downward shift in the saving function shifts the IS curve out to $I_1 S_1$ in Figure 10.11. The increase in real assets reduces saving and increases consumption, raising equilibrium y in the product market at any given r. Thus, an increase in real assets shifts the IS curve to the right and tends to increase equilibrium income, output, and employment.

Real assets, the price level and the interest rate

Net assets of the private sector, in money terms, can be defined as

$$A = K + R + B, \qquad [22]$$

where

$K \equiv$ the value of capital stock measured, perhaps, by the total value of stockholder's equity, that is, stock market shares;

R = the value of reserves held at the central bank, that is, the part of the money supply which is a private sector claim on the government; and

B ≡ the money value of government bonds held by the public.

It should be noted that here only that part of the money supply held as reserves at the central bank is included in assets, because the rest of the money supply represents the claims in the form of deposits of the nonbank public on the commercial banks. If the latter are included in the "public," this part of the money supply is a net zero asset, since the asset of the nonbank public is balanced by the liability of the banks. On the other hand, reserves and government bonds are included because they are claims of the private sector on an "outsider"—the government. The validity of including the latter is open to question, because they could be seen as future tax liabilities of the private sector. For the present, however, we will ignore that possibility and treat bonds as private claims on the government.

Net real assets a is the money value of assets A divided by the price level P, so that

$$a = \frac{A}{P} = \frac{K + R + B}{P}.$$

If the average price of a stock share moves with the price level, we can write the value of the capital stock as $K = Pk$, so that the first term in the

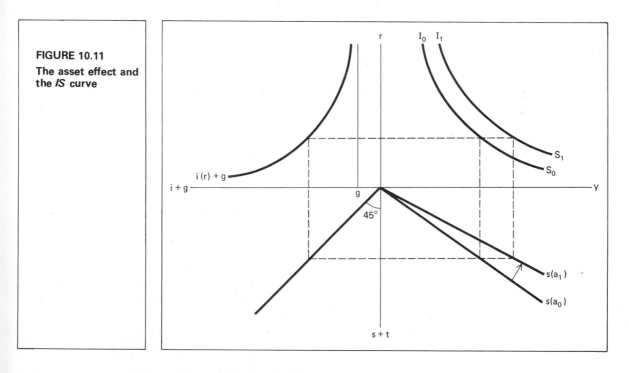

FIGURE 10.11

The asset effect and the *IS* curve

real-assets equation is Pk/P, or just k, the real capital stock. In the short-run analysis of the determination of income, we are holding the capital stock constant, so that k is fixed.

If we assume that all government bonds have a standard annual yield of \$1, then the total value of outstanding bonds is the number of bonds b divided by the interest rate. Thus, $B = b/r$. If, in fact, the standard yield is not \$1, but, say, \$100, this just moves the decimal point in our measurement of b and does not change the qualitative analysis at all.

Now the expression for real assets can be rewritten as

$$a = k + \frac{R}{P} + \frac{B}{P} = k + \frac{R}{P} + \frac{b}{rP}. \qquad [23]$$

We can combine this expression with the analysis of the effect of changes in a on the IS curve to see the *direct* effects of changes in R, b, P, and r on the IS curve through the asset effect. To begin with, it is clear that a price increase reduces real assets, shifting the IS curve to the left, and conversely a price decrease shifts the IS curve to the right.

An increase in b due to an increase in the government deficit, which has to be financed by selling more bonds, will increase a, shifting the IS curve to the right. Concerning R changes, the way the monetary authorities change the level of the money supply is by buying or selling bonds from the commercial banks so that when R goes up, B goes down by the same amount, and vice versa when R falls. This means that, as long as only the reserves part of the money supply is included in A in the first place, money supply changes do not affect a, and thus do not *directly* shift the IS curve.

Interest rate changes affect saving and consumption here through their effects on the real value of the stock of bonds, b, in equation (23) above. As the interest rate falls, bond prices rise, increasing the real value of the bond stock, and of total assets. This, in turn, tends to reduce saving and increase consumer spending, increasing demand and the level of income y. Since the IS curve is drawn in r, y space, inclusion of these interest rate effects flattens the IS curve. In the basic model of Chapter 9, the IS curve is downward sloping because a drop in the interest rate increases investment and thus raises equilibrium national income. Now we see that it also increases consumer spending, further raising national income y. So inclusion of the interest rate effects on real-asset values flattens the IS curve; other sources of variation in real-asset values shift it.

Price level changes and the Pigou effect

The principal importance of the introduction of real assets into the saving function lies in the first of the effects just discussed. A price increase reduces the real value of assets, shifting the IS curve to the left. In Part II the adjustment of demand-side equilibrium output to changes in the price level came only through the money market, shifting the LM curve. Now it is clear that price level changes also shift the IS curve, and in the same direction as the LM curve; a price increase shifts both to the

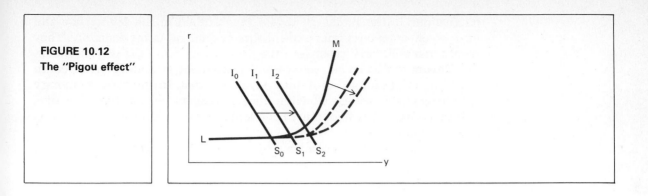

FIGURE 10.12
The "Pigou effect"

left. This makes demand-side equilibrium output more sensitive to price level changes, and flattens the economy's demand curve in the P, y space.

The main importance of the inclusion of real wealth in the consumption function from an historical point of view is that it eliminates the liquidity trap inconsistency in the classical model which Keynes used to attack that model. According to Keynes it was possible for interest rates to fall so low in the classical model that neither an expansionary monetary policy nor falling prices could ever increase the level of demand-side equilibrium output. Thus, with employment determined in the labor market and demand caught in the liquidity trap, the classical model had no solution. Professor Pigou, who responded to Keynes, pointed out that, in our terms, the price drop would shift the *IS* curve out. As prices fall the level of real assets rises, leading to downward shifts in the saving function.

These increases in real consumption that occur with falling prices would shift the *IS* curve out, raising the level of demand-side equilibrium output as shown in Figure 10.12. Thus, the *Pigou effect* refuted the suggestion by Keynes that the so-called classical model was inconsistent in the liquidity trap case.

CONCLUSION: SOME IMPLICATIONS FOR STABILIZATION POLICY

Our analysis of consumer behavior and the consumption function has two important implications for stabilization policy, which are briefly reviewed here. In Chapter 14 we take another thorough look at monetary and fiscal policy after we have further analyzed investment demand and the money market.

The first implication, mentioned several times already, is that the degree of reliance to be placed on temporary tax changes for stabilization policy depends on how correct the permanent income hypothesis of Friedman is. It is quite possible that if there were a variable income tax surcharge set, say, every year by the president, people would soon calculate an average expected value for the surcharge, and set their consumption pattern to fit disposable income with this average surcharge. Thus, fluctuations in the surcharge would be absorbed in the saving rate and have no effect on consumer expenditure or demand in the economy. They would just shift saving between the public sector and the private sector.

This might be an extreme case of permanent income behavior counteracting fiscal policy, but it does seem clear that, in any case, temporary tax changes will be less effective than permanent ones of the same size, and small, explicitly temporary tax changes may have little or no effect on aggregate demand.

The second point is that inclusion of real assets as a determinant of consumer demand probably increases the effectiveness of monetary policy relative to fiscal policy through the interest rate effect on assets. With a flatter IS curve, a given shift in the LM curve will yield a bigger increase in y than with the steeper IS curve of Chapter 9. Thus, the asset effect complements the effect of monetary policy and provides a link from monetary policy changes to consumer demand through the interest rate.

On the other hand, an expansionary fiscal policy tends to raise interest rates, reducing the real value of assets, which has a negative effect on consumer spending. In Figure 10.13, an increase in government purchases

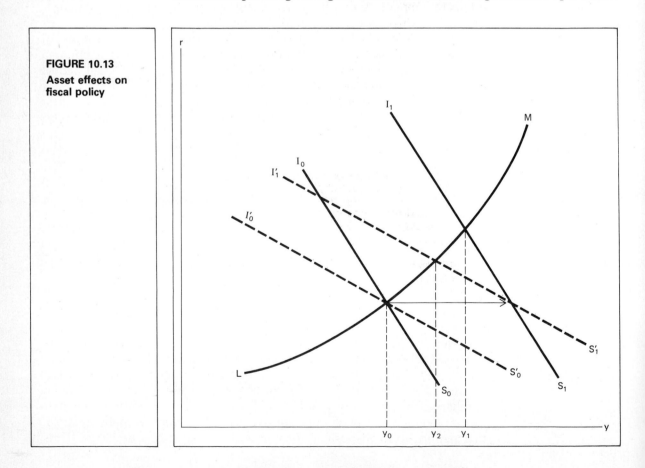

FIGURE 10.13

Asset effects on fiscal policy

will shift the IS curve out to the right, raising interest rates and income. The shift, shown by the horizontal arrow, would raise equilibrium output demanded from y_0 to y_1 with the steeper solid I_0S_0 and I_1S_1 curves. Introduction of the asset effect on consumption flattens the IS curve to the dashed $I_0'S_0'$. The same shift to $I_1'S_1'$ then increases equilibrium output demanded from y_0 only to y_2, as the interest rate increase cuts back consumer spending. Thus, through the interest rate, the asset effect creates a consumption demand change which complements the effects of monetary policy but tends to offset partially the effects of fiscal policy.

QUESTIONS FOR DISCUSSION AND REVIEW

1. Cross-section studies of spending behavior indicate the average propensity to consume is higher for low-income families than for high-income families. What does this imply for aggregate consumption if income is redistributed from high-income families to low-income families?

2. If there is a sudden surge in investment spending, the level of equilibrium income and output will grow. There is, of course, a tax surcharge that can be imposed by policy makers to offset immediately the increased investment spending with a reduction in consumer spending. If the increase in investment spending continues over time, would you expect the surcharge rate to remain constant?

3. How would you expect the average propensity to consume to be affected by an improvement in the level of social security benefits under the life-cycle hypothesis?

4. How does the introduction of wealth into the consumption function alter the slope of the aggregate demand schedule?

5. Assume you have established a consumption function of:

$c = .40\, y_t + .20\, y_{t-1} + .06\, a_t$

    a. What would you estimate the short-run marginal propensity to consume to be?
    b. What would you estimate the long-run marginal propensity to consume to be?
    c. What would you estimate the long-run average propensity to consume to be?

SELECTED READINGS

A. Ando and F. Modigliani, "The 'Life Cycle' Hypothesis of Saving: Aggregate Implications and Tests," *American Economic Review*, March 1963.

F. de Leeuw and E. Gramlich, "The Federal Reserve—MIT Econometric Model," *Federal Reserve Bulletin*, January 1968.

J. S. Duesenberry, "Income Consumption Relations and Their Implications," in M. G. Mueller, ed., *Readings in Macroeconomics* (New York: Holt, Rinehart and Winston, 1971).

R. Ferber, "Consumer Economics: A Survey," in P. G. Korliras and R. S. Thorn, eds., *Modern Macroeconomics* (New York: Harper & Row, 1979).

I. Fisher, *The Theory of Interest* (New York: Macmillan, 1930).

M. Friedman, *A Theory of the Consumption Function* (Princeton University Press, 1957), chaps. 1–3, 6, 9.

S. Kuznets, *National Product Since 1869* (New York: National Bureau of Economic Research, 1946).

A. M. Okun, "The Personal Tax Surcharge and Consumer Demand," *Brookings Papers on Economic Activity,* vol. 1, 1971.

J. Tobin, "Relative Income, Absolute Income and Saving," in *Money, Trade and Economic Growth: Essays in Honor of J. H. Williams* (New York: Macmillan, 1951).

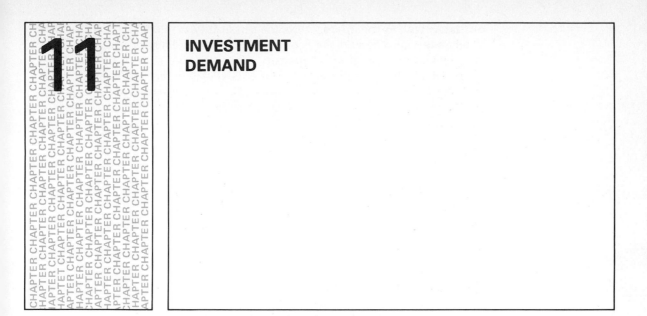

INVESTMENT DEMAND

In Chapter 4 we introduced investment demand as a simple function of the interest rate, offering as a rationale the present value (PV) criterion for investment decisions. This simple function was sufficient for the purposes of Part II—to expose and manipulate the basic interconnections between the product, money, and labor markets. But the $i = i(r)$ function is obviously not a good representation of the complex determinants of investment in the "real world." In fact, it is only since the middle of the 1960s that empirical investigators have been able to obtain even barely reasonable empirical explanations of investment demand.

This chapter first reviews the basis in microeconomic theory for a macroeconomic view of investment demand, developing along the way the rationale for the PV rule and a comparison of this criterion with the concept of the *marginal efficiency of investment.* We then develop an investment demand function that includes both replacement investment as a function of the *level* of output and the interest rate, and net investment as a function of *changes* in output—the accelerator principle—and the interest rate.

This framework includes the *user cost of capital* as a variable explaining equilibrium capital stock. Discussion of the user cost takes us into the role of profits and liquidity as partial determinants of investment demand through the interest rate and user cost.

After the theory of investment demand has been fairly fully developed, we summarize recent empirical results concerning the response of investment to changes in output and the cost of capital, in terms of both the size and time dimensions. Since the theory leads to an investment function in the static model in which investment depends on the level of output as well as the interest rate, the possibility is raised that the *IS* curve is positively sloped and the economy is unstable. The empirical findings suggest that the *marginal propensity to spend*—the sum of the marginal propensity to invest and the *MPC* out of GNP—is in fact less than unity so that the *IS* curve is negatively sloped. Finally, we end with some comments on monetary and fiscal policy, to be extended in Chapter 14. But the best place to begin is back with the present value criterion and the microeconomic theory of investment.

THE PRESENT VALUE CRITERION FOR INVESTMENT

In Chapter 4 we suggested that a firm should rank investment programs by the present discounted value of the projects' income streams,

$$PV_t = -C + R_t + \frac{R_{t+1}}{1 + r} + \frac{R_{t+2}}{(1 + r)^2} + \cdots + \frac{R_{t+n}}{(1 + r)^n},$$ [1]

where C is the cost of the project, and $R_t, \ldots, R_{t+n}$ is the stream of net returns. A natural starting point for a discussion of investment demand is the rationale of the PV criterion and its implications for the determinants of investment. To develop the rationale of the PV criterion, let us look at a simple firm owned by persons who want to maximize their utility as a function of a stream of real consumption as in Chapter 10,

$$U = U(c_0, c_1, \ldots, c_T),$$ [2]

where $c_0, \ldots, c_T$ is the consumption stream from time 0 to time T.

The firm has the following kind of sales and income possibilities. With a given amount of resources in period 0, the firm can produce net output for sale in all the periods 0 through T. Its net revenues in each period can then be either disbursed to the owners as income, $y_0, \ldots, y_T$, or invested to produce a greater amount of output at some future date. Thus, by reducing current income, the owners can increase future income by investing the firm's retained earnings. An increase in income in any one period, y_t, requires a decrease in some other period. This decrease can come before period t in order to generate more total revenue in t so that additional income can be withdrawn then without reducing income beyond period t. Or the decrease could come after t as a result of reduced investment in t.

From the point of view of the firm's owners, this situation can be expressed by an *income possibility curve*,

$$0 = \phi(y_0, y_1, \ldots, y_T).$$ [3]

If we hold all but two y's constant, then an increase in one y requires a decrease in the other. This must be true for any pair of y's. The problem, now, is for the firm to choose the set of y's, given its initial endowment of resources—cash or, in general, capital—that will permit the owners to maximize utility. In the two-period case, this income possibility curve is shown in Figure 11.1 as $0 = \phi(y_0, y_1)$. From a maximum income in time 0,

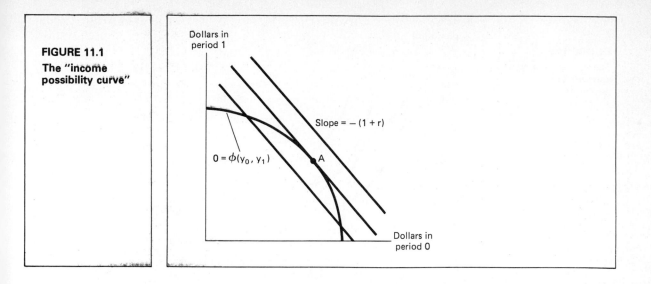

FIGURE 11.1

The "income possibility curve"

y_0^{max}, which is equal to the total initial resource endowment, the firm's owners can trade income in time 0 for income in time 1 through the investment process, with diminishing returns. The slope of the income possibility curve of Figure 11.1 is the *marginal rate of transformation* (MRT) of y_0 into y_1 given by

$$MRT = \frac{\Delta y_1}{\Delta y_0}. \qquad [4]$$

The firm can produce any income stream y_0, y_1 on the income possibility curve of Figure 11.1, given its initial resources.

Once the firm chooses an income stream, such as point A in Figure 11.1, the owners can then borrow or lend to a consumption point along a budget constraint with slope $-(1 + r)$ in exactly the same fashion as we showed in Chapter 10. A set of such budget lines is shown in Figure 11.1. The problem here is to choose an income stream y_0, y_1 along the income possibility curve that gets the owners to the highest possible budget line. As shown in Figure 11.1, the highest budget line that can be reached is the one just tangent to the income possibility curve, where $MRT = -(1 + r)$.

In Figure 11.2, we have added to the picture the owners' indifference curves from the utility function (2). These show rising levels of utility as one moves northeast, that is, $U_0 < U_1 < U_2$, as we saw in Chapter 10. The slope of an indifference curve is the *marginal rate of substitution* (MRS) of c_1 for c_0:

$$MRS = \frac{\Delta c_1}{\Delta c_0}, \qquad [5]$$

trading present for future composition.

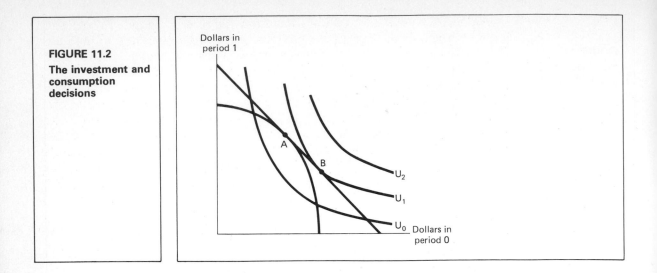

FIGURE 11.2

The investment and consumption decisions

From Figure 11.2 it should be clear that the owners reach their highest possible indifference curve by finding an indifference curve tangent to the *highest possible budget line*. So production is arranged by the firm to reach the highest budget line where $MRT = -(1 + r)$, for example, point A in Figure 11.2. The owners then transform this income stream into a utility-maximizing consumption stream by borrowing or lending to the highest possible indifference curve, where MRS is also equal to $-(1 + r)$. This gives, as the condition for utility maximization in this case that combines both production and consumption decisions,

$$MRT = -(1 + r) = MRS. \qquad [6]$$

Now the intercept of the budget line on the horizontal period-0 axis is given by the present value of the y_0, y_1 income stream,

$$PV_0 = y_0 + \frac{y_1}{1 + r},$$

as we also saw in Chapter 10. But this means that to reach the highest possible budget line, the firm should maximize present value—move to the budget line with the farthest-right time-0 intercept in Figures 11.1 and 11.2, given the location of the income possibility curve. Once this maximum PV line has been reached, the owners can worry about reaching the highest possible indifference curve independently of the production decision. Thus, the owners can insure that they can (but not will; this is a *necessary,* not *sufficient* condition) reach the maximum possible U level by giving the firm's manager the rule: Maximize present value!

The manager does not need any information on the shape of the owners' utility function and indifference curves; the production and consumption decisions are completely separate. Thus, the firm that is trying to maximize its owners' welfare will follow the rule: Maximize PV. And in the economy this will result in equating the MRT along the production function to MRS along indifference curves, a basic condition for economic efficiency.

Now if the economy is populated by firms that are trying to maximize their owners' welfare in a competitive capitalist economy or directly to maximize the social value of output in a socialist economy—note that the first case may also maximize the social value of output—they will order investment plans to maximize the present discounted value of the income stream coming from the sum of all investment projects, that is, the capital stock. Any investment rule which is not consistent with maximizing PV will not achieve these ends, and thus will not be consistent with profit (or welfare) maximization in a competitive economy.

This kind of reasoning led us, in Chapter 4, to the investment rule that the firm should maximize its present value by investing in any project with positive PV, where PV is defined as in equation (1):

$$PV_t = -C + R_t + \frac{R_{t+1}}{1 + r} + \frac{R_{t+2}}{(1 + r)^2} + \cdots + \frac{R_{t+n}}{(1 + r)^n}.$$

Under the present value criterion, the firm computes a present value for each possible project it might undertake, and then ranks the projects in order of their PV's. This ranking is represented in Figure 11.3. The vertical axis measures the present value of each investment relative to its cost, and the horizontal axis gives the real value of the sum of all investment projects. In order to maximize its present value, the firm should invest in all projects that have a $PV > 0$. This gives an equilibrium level of real investment for the firm of i_0, where the present value of the marginal project is zero.

As can be seen from the PV expression in equation (1), an increase in the market interest rate reduces the present value of each investment project. This causes a downward shift of the curve in Figure 11.3 and reduces the firm's equilibrium investment level to i_1. On the other hand, if the

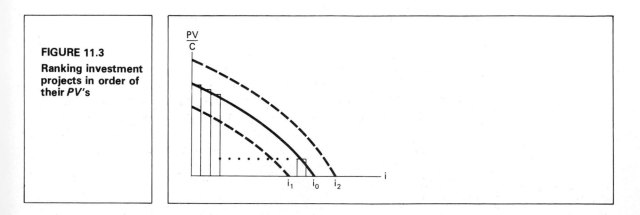

FIGURE 11.3

Ranking investment projects in order of their PV's

expected returns in each period were to increase, perhaps because of an increase in demand in the present period which is expected to be fairly permanent, the curve shifts up, and a higher level of investment, i_2, results. This is the basic theory behind the simple investment function of Part II.

THE MARGINAL EFFICIENCY OF INVESTMENT

A different criterion for investment decisions was suggested by Keynes and has been used in macroeconomics texts ever since. This is the *marginal efficiency of investment* criterion. This criterion is very convenient as a teaching device, but has its analytical weaknesses. The marginal efficiency of an investment project, m, is *defined* as the rate of interest that will discount the PV of the project to zero. Thus, m is defined by

$$0 = -C + R_t + \frac{R_{t+1}}{1+m} + \frac{R_{t+2}}{(1+m)^2} + \cdots + \frac{R_{t+n}}{(1+m)^n}.$$

If, with any given C and R stream, we solve this expression for m, we have the interest rate that would discount the project's net returns back to zero.

Investment programs can be ranked by m, much as they were by PV. It would seem that a project with a "high" returns stream would have a "high" PV and thus require a "high" m to discount the net returns stream to zero. Thus, m can be plotted against i, as shown in Figure 11.4, much as PV was in Figure 11.3. As the size of the total investment program is increased, we go to projects with lower and lower R streams, so that as i rises, m falls.

The supply of funds

This m function, representing investment demand, can now be confronted by a *supply-of-funds* schedule to determine the equilibrium level of investment, similar to i_0 in Figure 11.3. This supply schedule, r, is shown in Figure 11.4. It shows that up to a certain point the interest cost of financing investment is roughly constant. But as the size of the investment program goes beyond that point the cost of borrowing, or the opportunity

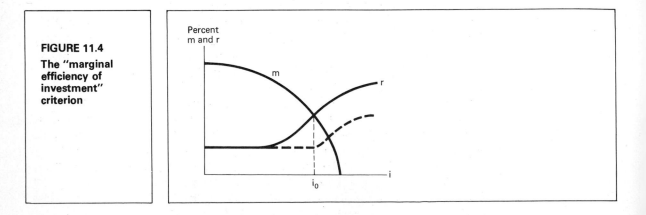

FIGURE 11.4

The "marginal efficiency of investment" criterion

cost of using retained earnings, begins to rise. Thus, the r curve in Figure 11.4 can be regarded as a supply-of-funds schedule. The m curve, which gives the interest rate at which each successive project could just break even, can be regarded as an investment demand schedule. The intersection of the m and r schedules determines i_0. To the left of i_0 all projects have positive PV's since m is greater than r.

As we will see in a moment, this model is not satisfactory as a general criterion for investment demand. However, it does have an advantage in that it points out the fact that there may be more than one *cost of capital* or interest rate facing a firm, depending on the extent to which it draws on various sources of investment funds; and these various cost-of-capital levels affect the firm's decision to invest. For example, firms tend to *impute* a lower interest rate to funds which are available from retained earnings. Higher interest rates are imputed to external sources of funding such as bond issues, because they represent a fixed liability that must be paid on time regardless of the financial position of the firm, or stocks, because they dilute the management's degree of control over the firm.

The possible sources of internal financing, of course, consist of depreciation and retained earnings, after-tax profits less dividends. Since internal financing is imputed at a lower interest rate, it can be visualized as the flat part of the r curve in Figure 11.4. As profits increase, the amount of internal funds which are available for investing increases, and the flat part of the r curve is extended, as is shown by the dashed line in Figure 11.4. Thus, an increase in profits will lead to an increase in investment by shifting out the supply-of-funds curve, r, in Figure 11.4. Conversely, a lower profit rate shifts the supply curve left, and reduces the level of investment.

The profit level, through the supply-of-funds schedule and the cost of capital, is undoubtedly an important determinant of investment demand, as we will see later in this chapter. But the marginal efficiency of investment is, nevertheless, not a very useful analytic device. The difficulty with the marginal efficiency of investment criterion is that it does not necessarily yield the same ranking of investment projects as the present value criterion. Intuitively, it should be clear that if we compare two projects, one of which has large returns in the distant future, the other with smaller returns coming sooner, the first will have a higher PV at some low interest rate, while the second project will have a higher PV at some higher rate that pushes down the PV of the distant returns of the first project.

Present value and marginal efficiency

The important point here is that the PV ranking depends on the *market* rate of interest—the rate at which earnings can be reinvested—while the marginal efficiency of investment is not related to the market rate. So the PV rankings can be different from m rankings.

The best way to see this is to look at an example which can be generalized easily. Suppose we have two investment projects, both with cost $C = 1$ ($1,000, perhaps). Both projects have zero return in period 1, when

TABLE 11.1 Marginal Efficiency and Present Value		Cost	Return in Period 2	Return in Period 3	m	PV $r = 0$	PV $r = 1$
Project I		1	0	4	1	3	0
Project II		1	2	1	1.414	2	0.25

they are being built. Project I returns 0 in period 2, and 4 in period 3; project II returns 2 in period 2, and 1 in period 3. This information is summarized in the left-hand part of Table 11.1.

Now let us calculate the m values for these two projects. For project I we have

$$0 = -1 + 0 + \frac{0}{1 + m} + \frac{4}{(1 + m)^2}.$$

Solving this equation for m, we have $(1 + m)^2 = 4$, and $m = 1$, as shown in Table 11.1. For project II the m equation is

$$0 = -1 + 0 + \frac{2}{1 + m} + \frac{1}{(1 + m)^2}.$$

Moving the -1 to the other side of the equation and multiplying both sides by $(1 + m)^2$ gives

$$(1 + m)^2 = 1 + 2m + m^2 = 2 + 2m + 1,$$

where the middle term is just $(1 + m)^2$ written out. Subtracting $(1 + 2m)$ from both sides of the right-hand equation gives us $m^2 = 2$, or $m = 1.414$ for project II, again shown in Table 11.1. As the table shows, both projects have the same costs, but one has a very low return in period 2 and a high return in period 3 while the other has a moderate return in period 2 and a low return in period 3. The marginal efficiency of investment criterion indicates that project II is unequivocally better than project I, since $m_2 > m_1$.

However, under the present value criterion there is no unequivocally correct answer because the PV ranking depends on the market interest rate. With r = 0, project I has a present discounted value given by

$$PV = -1 + 0 + \frac{0}{1} + \frac{4}{1} = 3,$$

while project II has a PV given by

$$PV = -1 + 0 + \frac{2}{1} + \frac{1}{1} = 2,$$

so that at the (very) low rate $r = 0$, project I, with its high, but delayed, returns, is superior. With $r = 1$, project I has a PV given by

$$PV = -1 + 0 + \frac{0}{2} + \frac{4}{4} = 0,$$

while project II's PV is

$$PV = -1 + 0 + \frac{2}{2} + \frac{1}{4} = 0.25$$

Thus, at a (very) high interest rate that discounts project I's returns heavily, project II is preferable. These PV results are shown in the last column of Table 11.1. They illustrate the deficiency of the marginal efficiency criterion for ranking investment projects. This criterion makes no reference to the market rate of interest, which measures the opportunity cost of investment.

The example we have just used can be generalized, as is shown in Figure 11.5, where the PV's of projects I and II are plotted as functions of the market interest rate. Table 11.1 shows that when $r = 0$, PV of project I is 3, and PV of project II is 2. The table also locates the PV's of the two projects where $r = 1$. Since at a low r, $PV(\text{I}) > PV(\text{II})$, while at a high r, $PV(\text{I}) < PV(\text{II})$, there must be some r in between where the PV's are equal. To find this value of r, we set $PV(\text{I}) = PV(\text{II})$:

$$0 - 1 + \frac{0}{1 + r} + \frac{4}{(1 + r)^2} = 0 - 1 + \frac{2}{1 + r} + \frac{1}{(1 + r)^2}.$$

Dropping $(0 - 1)$ from both sides and multiplying through by $(1 + r)^2$ gives us

$$4 = 2r + 2 + 1 \quad \text{and} \quad r = 0.5.$$

At $r = 0.5$, the PV of both projects is 0.78, locating the equal PV point in Figure 11.5. At interest rates below 0.5, project I will have the higher PV;

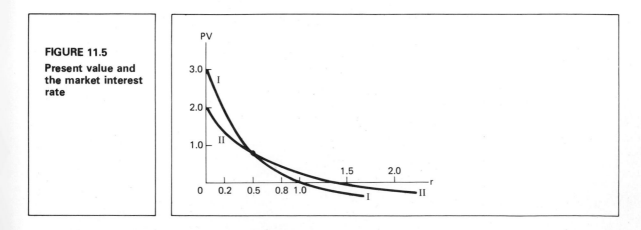

FIGURE 11.5

Present value and the market interest rate

above 0.5, project II wins. Thus, the way for a firm to obtain a true ranking of investment projects in terms of their opportunity costs is to compute PV for each project at the relevant market rate of interest.

In the discussion of the present value criterion at the beginning of this chapter, we assumed that the firm faces a competitive capital market, so that the interest rate at which it can borrow appears fixed. In that case, the firm invests until it reaches the marginal project with $PV = 0$, as shown in Figure 11.3. But then we saw that the firm might face a rising supply-of-funds schedule, shown in Figure 11.4. It was this likelihood that led to the use of the notion of the marginal efficiency of investment as a demand curve. Now that we have seen why the marginal efficiency rule is not satisfactory, we must ask, how should a firm facing a rising supply-of-funds schedule jointly choose the level of the interest rate and the total amount of investment it should undertake applying the PV rule? The answer is fairly simple.

The firm can build a PV function in the following way. First, choose an initial low level of total investment, i_0. From Figure 11.4's supply-of-funds schedule, the interest rate needed to finance i_0 can be determined. This interest rate can then be applied to all possible projects to calculate PV's, and the maximum PV obtainable within i_0, PV_0, can be plotted, as in Figure 11.6. As the firm then increases i, repeating this procedure, PV should first rise and then fall as the firm encounters a rising supply-of-funds schedule. The firm should then select the level of investment, i_1, that maximizes PV at PV_{max} in Figure 11.6. The interest rate needed to finance this PV-maximizing level of investment can be obtained from the supply-of-funds schedule.

This procedure will yield an equilibrium level of investment for any given supply-of-funds schedule. An upward shift in that schedule will then raise the interest rate needed to finance any given level of investment, reducing the total PV that can be obtained with each i level. Thus, an increase in interest rates will shift the PV function of Figure 11.6 to the left and down, reducing the equilibrium level of investment under the PV

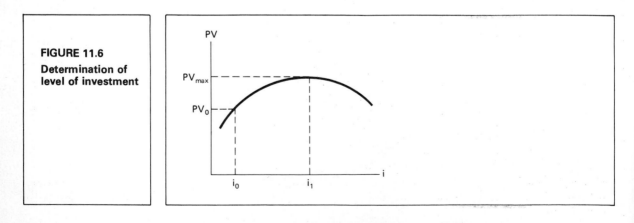

FIGURE 11.6

Determination of level of investment

rule. So with a rising supply-of-funds schedule, an upward shift in that schedule will increase the interest rate r and reduce equilibrium i. This gives us the $i = i(r)$ investment function of Part II.

What we now have developed is a static view of investment, in the following sense. Once the equilibrium level of investment has been reached, and if interest rates and expected returns do not change, there will be no net investment beyond the current period. Firms will have built the desired level of capital stock to produce the expected returns, or sales; all future investment will be to replace that part of the capital stock which wears out. There would be a further incentive to invest in future periods only if interest rates dropped or if there were an increase in expected sales. Either of these circumstances would raise to a level above zero the present value of projects which were rejected in previous calculations. Thus, the static PV model explains the amount of net investment that will bring the capital stock up to the optimum amount needed to produce a given level of output at a given interest rate. Once this desired capital stock is in place, there is no incentive for further net investment unless the level of output or the interest rate changes. It is the *growth* of output that induces continuing *net* investment. We can now turn to a more dynamic approach to the investment demand function that has been developed in the economics literature of the past 10 to 15 years.

INVESTMENT DEMAND AND OUTPUT GROWTH The relationship between the *growth rate* of output and the *level* of net investment implied in the previous section is called the *accelerator principle* since it suggests that an increase in the growth rate of output—an acceleration—is needed to increase the level of investment. The PV criterion suggests that this relationship between output growth and net investment is not a fixed one, however. An increase in the interest rate should reduce the level of net investment associated with a given growth rate of output. This variable relationship beween the growth rate of output and the level of net investment is frequently called the *flexible-accelerator* model, which we will develop in some detail in this section.

There are two distinct and virtually independent steps in the development of the flexible-accelerator model. The first involves the determination of the level of desired capital stock, K^E. We will approach this problem in much the same way as we did labor demand in Chapter 6. The second step is the translation of movements in desired, or equilibrium, capital *stock* into a *flow* of realized net investment. This involves an investment demand function that includes both net and replacement investment with the appropriate lags behind movements in equilibrium capital stock.

The second step here is really quite independent of the first. The investment demand function will show how movements in actual investment are related to changes in equilibrium capital stock ΔK^E. This makes no assumption about where K^E comes from, which is the subject of the first step—the production function approach to the determination of equilibrium capital stock K^E.

Equilibrium capital stock

We can begin with the general production function used in Part II,

$$y = y(N, K). \tag{7}$$

Here y is output per unit of time, N is man-hours input per unit of time, and K is the capital stock—plant and equipment. Output increases, but at a decreasing rate, as either input is increased holding the other constant. Implicitly we assume here a constant rate of utilization of capital stock so that there is a one-to-one relationship between capital stock and machine-hour input. This assumption will be relaxed later.

A firm will expand its plant size until the marginal product of capital (MPK) equals the real *user cost* of capital:

$$MPK = \frac{C}{P} \equiv c, \tag{8}$$

where C is the user cost of capital and c is the real user cost. We will discuss the concept of user cost in more detail later, but for the present we can define C as an implicit *rental value* assigned to the use of capital equipment, which includes both a depreciation charge and an interest cost. Equation (8) says that a firm will reach an equilibrium level of capital stock when the marginal product of capital equals the real user cost of capital.

This can be seen in another way. The increase in revenue that a competitive firm will obtain by adding another unit of capital, given its labor input, is given by the price of output times the increment to output produced by the increase in K:

$$\frac{\Delta R}{\Delta K} = P \cdot MPK.$$

The increased cost to the firm of adding another unit of capital is simply the *user cost* of that unit,

$$\frac{\Delta C}{\Delta K} = C.$$

As long as the increase in revenue is greater than the increase in cost from another unit of capital the profit-maximizing firm will add capital. Equilibrium will be reached when

$$\frac{\Delta R}{\Delta K} = \frac{\Delta C}{\Delta K} \quad \text{and} \quad P \cdot MPK = C,$$

which is the same condition as equation (8). This marginal condition determines the equilibrium capital stock of the firm.

Let us take for an example a particular form of the production function, known as the Cobb-Douglas function after Charles W. Cobb and (Senator) Paul H. Douglas:

$$y = aK^{\alpha}N^{1-\alpha}.$$

This production function has the property that the exponents of the inputs add up to one, which gives constant returns to scale. If capital and labor inputs are doubled, output will also double. The marginal product of capital in the Cobb-Douglas function is given by the expression

$$MPK \equiv \frac{\Delta y}{\Delta K} = \frac{\alpha a K^{\alpha}N^{1-\alpha}}{K} = \frac{\alpha y}{K},$$

substituting y back in for $aK^{\alpha}N^{1-\alpha}$. Thus, with the Cobb-Douglas function, in equilibrium

$$MPK = \frac{\alpha y}{K} = \frac{C}{P}.$$

The right-hand equation here can be solved for the equilibrium level of the capital stock in the Cobb-Douglas function,

$$K^E = \frac{\alpha P y}{C} = \frac{\alpha y}{\dfrac{C}{P}}.$$

The equilibrium capital stock rises with an increase in output demanded and falls with an increase in the real user cost of capital. This expression gives equilibrium capital stock K^E for one particular production function. We can generalize this by writing K^E as a function of y, C, and P,

$$K^E = K^E(y, C, P), \tag{9}$$

where K^E increases with increases in y and P, and decreases as C rises, holding the other variables constant. With equation (9) as a general expression for the determinants of K^E, we can now develop the investment demand function relating realized investment to K^E.

The investment demand function

Total investment, or gross investment, i_g, is the sum of net investment i_n and replacement investment i_r:

$$i_g \equiv i_n + i_r. \tag{10}$$

Replacement investment is that part of gross investment needed to keep the capital stock at a constant level, and it is equal to the economic depreciation of the stock in any one period. Net investment is that part of gross investment that increases the level of capital stock. Replacement investment will simply be the depreciation δK in each period of the capital stock,

$$i_r = \delta K,$$

where δ is the depreciation rate, a number like one-tenth per year. Net investment, in the absence of lags in the adjustment process of actual capital stock to desired capital stock, would be the change in the equilibrium capital stock,

$$i_n = \Delta K^E.$$

Thus, we can see that *net* investment depends on *changes* in the equilibrium level of the capital stock, whereas *replacement* investment depends on the *level* of the capital stock.

Let us look first at net investment. In the Cobb-Douglas production function,

$$i_n = \Delta K^E = \Delta\left(\frac{\alpha P y}{C}\right).$$

If we assume that the ratio of the user cost of capital to the price level, C/P, remains fairly constant over time, we can rewrite this net investment function as

$$i_n = \left(\frac{\alpha P}{C}\right)\Delta y.$$

This makes it clear that over the long run, with no trend in C/P, it is the *growth* of output, or demand, that gives us the *level* of net investment.

This relation between the *change* in output and the *level* of net investment is the *accelerator principle*. It introduces a basic dynamic relationship into the model of the economy. Thus, if net investment is related to Δy, and net investment is also some given fraction—the net saving ratio s—of y,

$$i_n = sy,$$

then we have the basic growth relationship

$$sy = \left(\frac{\alpha P}{C}\right)\Delta y,$$

and

$$\frac{\Delta y}{y} = \text{growth rate of } y = \frac{s}{\frac{\alpha P}{C}}. \qquad [11]$$

Since investment increases the *supply* of output by increasing the capital stock, but also is associated with the *level* of *demand* through the multiplier, equation (11) gives the rate of growth of output that would maintain supply = demand. Growth models are introduced in Part IV. Here we are just interested in exposing the link between investment and growth.

With the introduction of the accelerator, we have moved into the dynamics of the economy. We shall see shortly that the accelerator can create some difficult dynamic stabilization problems. But first let us look at total investment using the concepts of net and replacement investment we have developed. From the expressions for net and replacement investment, we have their sum for gross investment:

$$i_g = i_n + i_r = \Delta K^E + \delta K,$$ [12]

putting aside, for the time being, the problem of lagged adjustment of actual to desired investment. In the general case, we can write this gross investment equation as

$$i_g = \Delta K^E(y, C, P) + \delta K.$$ [13]

In the Cobb-Douglas example, i_g is given by

$$i_g = \Delta \left(\frac{\alpha P y}{C} \right) + \delta K,$$

and in the special case where the real user cost, c, is fairly constant we have

$$i_g = \frac{\alpha}{c} \cdot \Delta y + \delta K,$$

the accelerator relationship.

The accelerator and stabilization policy

The accelerator relationship in the gross investment function, equation (13), poses an interesting difficulty for short-run stabilization policy. The problem is illustrated in Figure 11.7, which shows, in essence, what happens to investment as output in the economy rises from one stable level to another. In Figure 11.7, we show two time periods, 0 to t_1, and t_2 on, and a transition period of unspecified length between the two. In the first period there is a given level of output y, which implies a given equilibrium capital stock K. Now suppose at time t_1, the government increases government purchases g to stimulate demand, and the monetary authority increases the money stock to hold the interest rate and the user cost of capital constant. This increases output, and equilibrium capital stock moves to a new, higher level in the second period, from t_2 on. Since

FIGURE 11.7

The "accelerator principle" of investment

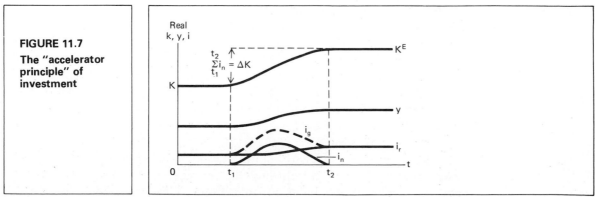

the capital stock is constant both before t_1 and after t_2, the level of net investment is zero in each period, and the level of i_r is positive in each.

In order for the capital stock to increase to its new higher level in the second period, there must be a positive level of net investment in the transition period. This is indicated by the bulge in i_n between t_1 and t_2. Since i_g is the sum of i_n and i_r, this means that, during the transition period, gross investment demand i_g also has this bulge, shown by the dashed line in Figure 11.7. Thus, total investment in each period is as follows:

from 0 to t_1, $i_g = i_r$
from t_1 to t_2, $i_g = i_r + i_n$
from t_2 on, $i_g = i_r$

From Figure 11.7 it is clear that in the first part of the transition period the growth rate of total investment i_g is greater than the growth rate of the economy as a whole given by the slope of y. Thus, if the economy is running at less than full employment, as it was in the early 1960s, a monetary or fiscal policy change designed to bring the economy up to the full-employment growth path runs the risk of temporarily overshooting the desired growth of demand. Initially demand will grow at an apparently excessive and unsustainable rate due to the i_n buildup needed to increase the capital stock. But after this initial period of rapid growth, net investment will fall off again to its normal level in a growing economy. The important point to recognize is that the accelerator effect will produce a *temporarily* rapid growth of demand which will subside.

Capacity utilization and the accelerator

It should be clear that the accelerator relationship may not hold if the economy is operating with substantial excess plant capacity, that is, at a low capacity-utilization rate. In this case, the actual capital stock is greater than equilibrium, so that an increase in output can raise the equilibrium capital stock up toward the actual existing stock with little effect on net investment. Thus, to the extent that substantial excess capacity exists, fiscal policy can stimulate demand without encountering the difficulty described in the last section.

This qualification of the accelerator principle should be interpreted with care, however. Much of what appears to be excess capacity at any one time may actually be an obsolete plant which embodies old, uneconomic technology, especially in a period of rapidly increasing energy prices. In this case, a major increase in demand could be temporarily met by bringing old plant back on the line, but after a while producers will replace this plant with a newer plant embodying up-to-date technology. Thus, the accelerator effect might appear with a delay as an upsurge in replacement investment.

THE USER COST AND LIQUIDITY EFFECTS

Let us return now to the concept of the real user cost of capital, c, which was introduced earlier. It is through the user cost that both the interest rate and the level of profits enter our investment demand function.

We have already tentatively defined C as the nominal value of the imputed rental of capital services used in each period. This is not a measurable input price such as a wage rate or total compensation per man-hour, since typically capital goods are bought in one period and then used over a length of time, not rented, as are labor services. This is the major difference between the market for capital goods and that for other inputs, including labor, that makes capital theory so complex and also makes measurement of capital inputs very difficult. In an economy free of slavery, firms do not buy labor, that is, workers themselves; firms rent labor services at a wage rate, a price stated as a payment per time unit of services rendered. On the other hand, since capital goods are generally bought at one point in time and then used by their owners over a long period, there is no direct measurement of the price of a machine-hour of service of a given quality. If all capital goods were owned by persons (or firms) that rented, or leased, the goods' services to other firms, and no firm used the capital goods it owned, we would have a satisfactory measure of the value of capital service—the user cost of capital—in the rental rate. But this is not the case, so we have to construct a measurement of the user cost C, using a large input of economic theory in the process.

Suppose that a machine is purchased at price P_I (I for investment). There are three components which make up the user cost of the good to its owner in each period of its life.

1. The first is the interest cost of the capital good, which is the opportunity cost incurred by tying up funds. This is the interest rate r times P_I. If the firm buys a machine for, say, $100,000, and the interest rate it could have lent that sum at was 10 percent per year, then the firm is giving up an opportunity cost of $10,000 that it could have earned in interest in the first year.
2. Next is the amount the good depreciates in each period, δP_I. If the economic depreciation rate δ is 10 percent, then the firm loses 10 percent of the value of the machine a year in depreciation—$10,000 in the first year on the $100,000 machine.
3. Any change in the market price of the good, once purchased, enters into user cost. If the market price of a new machine of the same model is rising through time, this will pull the price of used machines up above the price dictated by the original purchase price less depreciation. This price increases as a *capital gain*—a negative cost equal to $\Delta P_I/\Delta t$, the time rate of change of P_I.

Adding up these components, the imputed nominal user cost of a capital good to its owner is given by

$$C = rP_I + \delta P_I - \frac{\Delta P_I}{\Delta t},$$

or

$$C = P_I(r + \delta - \dot{P}_I), \tag{14}$$

where $\dot{P}_I$ is the proportional, or percentage, capital gain:

$$\dot{P}_I \equiv \frac{\dfrac{\Delta P_I}{\Delta t}}{P_I}.$$

Equation (14) can be rewritten as

$$C = P_I(r - \dot{P}_I + \delta),$$

to bring out the relationship of the user cost to the "real" rate of interest, $r - \dot{P}$. If lenders and borrowers are concerned about the real, or purchasing power, value of assets and liabilities, they will discount nominal interest rates r for the expected rate of inflation $\dot{P}$. If the annual interest rate on a loan is 10 percent and the rate of inflation is 5 percent, the real rate of return, in terms of purchasing power, is 5 percent. If both r and $\dot{P}$ go up by the same amount, the real rate will not change, and lending, borrowing, and investing decisions should not change. This will be the case if user cost is calculated as we show in equation (14), since an equal increase in r and $\dot{P}$ leaves C unchanged so that the equilibrium capital stock is unaffected.

The $\dot{P}$ term in equation (14) has been dealt with in several ways in the empirical studies. It might be assumed that investors either do not know or do not care what the anticipated capital gains will be when they consider purchasing a capital good, in which case the $\dot{P}_I$ term can be eliminated from equation (14), giving us

$$C = P_I(r + \delta).$$

This is the method used by Jorgenson and collaborators in several early (1963–1967) studies of postwar investment behavior. Since these studies used data that ended in the mid-1960s, before the inflation that began in 1966 or so, this was probably not a bad approximation. If there is little variance in the $\dot{P}_I$ term in the data, omitting it from a regression analysis will not harm the results much.

But in a period when the rate of inflation varies from 4–5 percent to 10–15 percent, the $\dot{P}$ term in the user cost expression is important. Therefore, more recent work by Jorgenson and by Bischoff and others connected with the MIT-Penn-SSRC (MPS) model group has approximated $\dot{P}_I$ in equation (14) with a lag distribution on past price changes. This is on the theory that people form expectations of future price changes essentially by extrapolating past changes. In addition, the MPS formulation allows the $\dot{P}_I$ term to enter equation (14) only if $\dot{P}$ has exceeded some threshold value in recent quarters, on the assumption that inflation must reach some minimum rate before people "notice" it. These adjustments provide a better explanation of investment behavior since the mid-1960s than does the use of the truncated user cost expression omitting the inflation $\dot{P}$ term.

The next important question to be answered about the user cost is what determines the value of r, the imputed interest, or opportunity, cost of capital in equation (14). As we mentioned briefly earlier, a firm can raise money for the purchase of new capital in three ways, by using internal funds, by selling bonds (debt), and by issuing stocks (equity). In a world of perfect competition and no tax biases, the imputed cost assigned to each of these means of raising money would be the same, allowing for risk differential.

In fact, however, because they assign extra costs to funds borrowed outside the firm due to the fixed liability associated with bond issue or to the dilution of control that comes from stock issue, firms are likely to impute a lower rate to funds raised inside the firm by retained earnings plus depreciation allowances than to the other two sources of funds. Thus, the interest rate, or opportunity cost, used to compute the user cost of capital may be a weighted average of the interest rates that apply to these three different sources of funds, where the weights are the fractions of total funds raised from these alternative sources:

$$r = r_I \left(\frac{\text{internal funds}}{\text{total investment}} \right) + r_D \left(\frac{\text{bond issue}}{\text{total investment}} \right)$$
$$+ r_E \left(\frac{\text{equity issue}}{\text{total investment}} \right), \quad [15]$$

where

$r_I \equiv$ the opportunity cost of lending the firm's retained earnings,
$r_D \equiv$ an established bond rate such as Moody's Aaa corporate bond rate, and
$r_E \equiv$ average earnings-price ratio on corporate equity.

Both r_D and r_E are assumed to be greater than r_I.

By breaking down r into these three components, we have introduced profits, or liquidity, into the investment function. As profits increase, the amount of internal funds available for investment increases. If the interest rate r_I imputed to internal funds is lower than the other rates, the increase in profits will reduce the weighted average of all interest rates, as is shown in equation (15), and this in turn will lower the user cost of capital as is shown in equation (14). A lower user cost means that more investment will be undertaken, so that we have established a link back from profits to the level of investment through the user cost.

In the data on investment, it is very difficult to see the effect of profits on investment because profits are highly correlated with changes in output. Yet surveys of business executives indicate that profits are important to their decision to invest, and therefore it seems reasonable that profits should be included as a determinant of investment demand.

At this point it may be useful to summarize the theory of investment demand we have developed. First we have the investment demand function for gross investment given earlier as equation (13),

$$i_g = i_n + i_r = \Delta K^E(y, C, P) + \delta K,$$

still ignoring lags between changes in K^E and movements of i_n, one of the subjects to be dealt with in this section. Next we have the definition of the user cost of capital, C,

$$C = P_I(r - \dot{P}_I + \delta),$$

which brings the interest rate into the picture. Finally, we have the expression for the interest rate as a weighted average of rates on the three principal sources of funds,

$$r = w_I r_I + w_D r_D + w_E r_E,$$

where the w's are the fractions of funds raised internally (I), by bond issue (D), and by stock issue (E), and $\Sigma w = 1$. Here the profit level enters the picture since r_I is presumably lower than r_E and r_D. Up to now we have been dealing with a static situation, with no notion of the time lags involved in changing the level of capital stock. We will now take a more dynamic view of the investment process, and look at some empirical results.

We can begin by regarding the demand for investment as a function of two things: the real user cost c of capital goods and the demand for the output y of capital goods. That is, if the cost of capital goes up relative to the cost of labor, for a given output we would expect a firm to use more labor and less capital in its production process, and we would also expect output to be reduced. On the other hand, for a given cost of capital, if the demand for output increases, we would expect a firm to increase its use of both capital and labor to produce more output.

Let us suppose that a firm decides to invest in a new plant. It will survey the various blueprints available for the new plant and choose the one which has a capital-labor ratio K/N that allows it to produce any given output at a minimum cost. Let us assume further that this new plant is a "putty-clay" investment. That is, the firm can choose between many blueprints with different K/N ratios, so that the K/N ratio is variable and K and N are substitutable *ex ante*; the capital stock is "putty" *ex ante*. But once the plant is built, capital and labor must be used in the fixed proportions to produce a given level of output as specified in the chosen blueprint; the capital stock turns into "clay" *ex post*. Thus, *ex ante* the firm's capital-output and capital-labor ratios are changeable; *ex post* they are fixed.

Now we want to see what effect changes in demand and changes in the cost of capital will have on the actual investment pattern of the firm, given the putty-clay production function. First we look at changes in demand. Since the output of the existing plant is fixed *ex post*, if the firm expects the new level of demand to be permanent and wants to respond to it, it will have to add to its plant immediately in the absence of excess capacity. This response is shown in Figure 11.8. The increment to output demanded eventually raises the equilibrium capital stock by ΔK^E, raising replacement investment gradually to $\Delta i_r = \delta(\Delta K^E)$. The increment to net investment along the i_n curve is added to the i_r curve to obtain the change in gross investment along the i_g curve in Figure 11.8. Within a short period the total capital stock is increased by an amount equal to the area under the i_n curve. Because there is now a higher equilibrium level of capital stock, there is an increase in the level of replacement investment by an amount Δi_r so that the path of total investment is shown by the i_g curve. The main point here is that these increases in i_n, i_r, and i_g all take place with a short lag due to the *ex post* fixity of output capacity and the need to expand plant to meet demand.

Now let us suppose that the firm has the same original "clay" plant, but instead of a change in the demand for its product it sees a reduction in the relative cost of capital. The principal effect of this change will be that the firm will want to increase the amount of capital it uses relative to labor, that is, raise the K/N ratio. The firm will gradually replace its old plant with a new *kind* of plant—a more capital-intensive plant with a higher capital-labor ratio. The result is that with a change in the user cost of capital there is a much longer process of change than with an increase in demand, that is, there is a longer lag until the change is completed, as is shown in Figure 11.9.

Simulations of the effects of changes in output and the cost of capital on investment expenditures on producers' durable equipment i_g are shown in Figures 11.10 and 11.11. These are taken from the MPS model; most of the investment equations there come from a study by Charles W. Bischoff. Figure 11.10 shows the effect of a sudden increase in output demanded by 10 percent ($71.9 billion at the level of 1964 initial condition). The effect on gross investment peaks at three quarters and levels off after five quarters. This is the empirical counterpart of the i_g path in Figure 11.8. Figure 11.11 shows the effect of a 10 percent decrease in the user

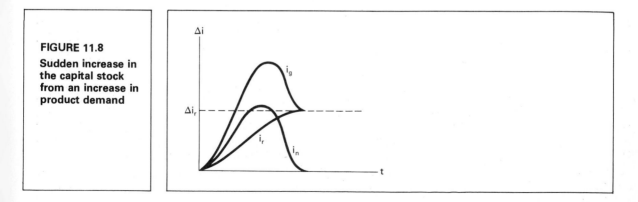

FIGURE 11.8

Sudden increase in the capital stock from an increase in product demand

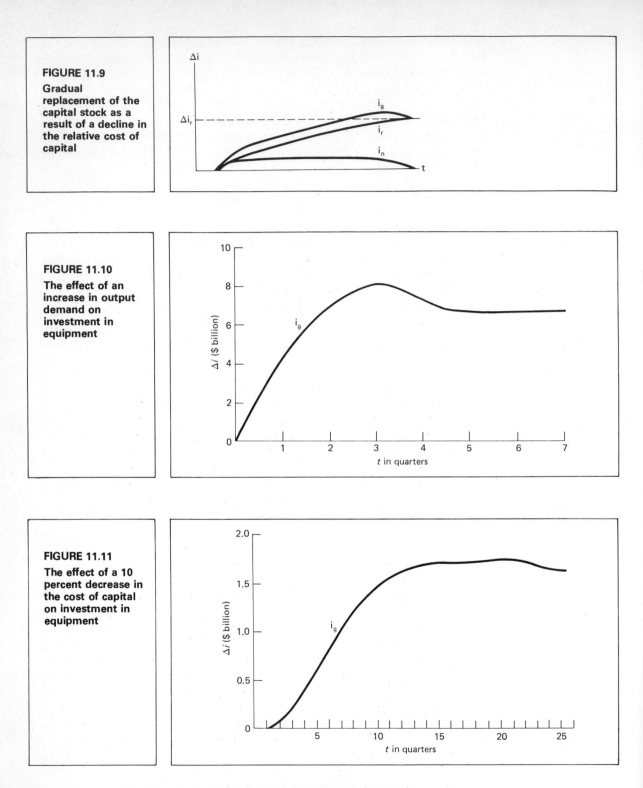

FIGURE 11.9
Gradual replacement of the capital stock as a result of a decline in the relative cost of capital

FIGURE 11.10
The effect of an increase in output demand on investment in equipment

FIGURE 11.11
The effect of a 10 percent decrease in the cost of capital on investment in equipment

cost. Gross investment peaks at 20 quarters and levels off at 26 quarters or so. This is comparable to the i_g path in Figure 11.9.

As far as the long-run, steady-state response of investment demand to changes in its principal determinants, r and y, is concerned, Bischoff found that the long-run elasticity of investment demand with respect to changes in output is about unity, with a short lag. This implies a fairly constant capital-output ratio over the long run since, with a lag, the capital stock would grow at the same rate as output. Bischoff also found that the long-run elasticity of investment demand with respect to changes in the interest rate is about -0.5. In other words, if the interest rate on corporate bonds increases from 10 to 11 percent, a change of 10 percent, we could expect a 5 percent drop in investment over the long run, for example from $200 billion to $190 billion, occurring gradually over a two- to three-year period. This is predicated, of course, on the assumption that investors see changes in the cost of capital as permanent, just as they assume that increases in demand now will continue into the future.

INVESTMENT IN THE STATIC MODEL

The investment demand function, equation (13), implicitly makes net investment a function of changes in both the interest rate and the level of output. We analyzed the implications of this accelerator mechanism for stabilization policy earlier. The level of replacement investment i_r depends on the preexisting level of the capital stock. If the economy is in equilibrium with a given r and y, the existing capital stock may be about equal to equilibrium capital stock K^E, which in turn depends on the level of y and r. Thus, in the static model which determines equilibrium values of the variables, the investment function is now

$$i = i(r, y), \qquad\qquad [16]$$

replacing the $i = i(r)$ function of Part II. Investment i increases as y increases or r decreases, each time holding the other independent variable constant. Here we are dealing with a *static* model, in which replacement investment is a function of the *level* of output and the interest rate. An increase in the interest rate reduces equilibrium capital stock K^E, reducing replacement investment, so that i falls as r increases. An increase in output raises K^E, so that i increases as y rises. We are not dealing with the accelerator discussed previously, since the accelerator depends on *rates of change* of income and we are dealing only with a change from one *level* of income to another.

By making i depend on y as well as r we change the slope of the IS curve considerably. This is shown in Figure 11.12, which displays the four-quadrant IS diagram with $i = i(r, y)$. For every value of y, there is a different investment demand curve in the northwest quadrant of Figure 11.12. Thus to trace the IS curve here, we must begin with a y value—y_0 or y_1 in Figure 11.12—and move around the diagram clockwise, locating the

FIGURE 11.12

Modification of the
IS curve: $i = i(r,y)$

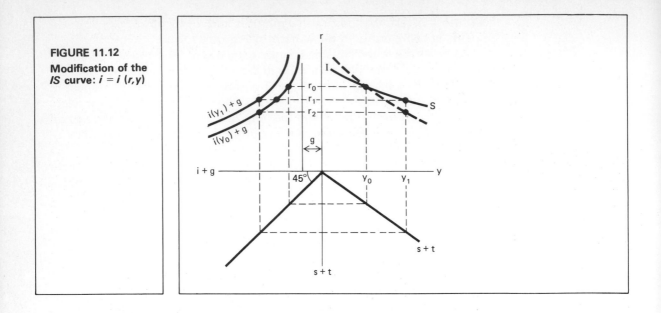

appropriate $i(y)$ curve to determine the corresponding product market equilibrium value of r.

In Figure 11.12, as income rises from y_0 to y_1, the investment demand curve shifts up from $i(y_0)$ to $i(y_1)$. This flattens the *IS* curve that gives r, y points that maintain product market equilibrium. If the investment function had remained at $i(y_0)$, the equilibrium interest rate corresponding to y_1 would have been r_2 in Figure 11.12.

With $i = i(r, y)$, a given interest rate drop will stimulate a greater increase in product market equilibrium output than with $i = i(r)$, because the initial y increase pulls i up, which further increases y. Thus with $i = i(r, y)$, starting from r_0, y_0 in Figure 11.12 an interest rate drop to r_1 moves product market equilibrium y to y_1 along the solid *IS* curve, with the i function shifting up to $i(y_1)$. With $i = i(r)$, it would have taken a drop from r_0 to r_2 to get an increase from y_0 to y_1 along the dashed *IS* curve.

A reduction in the interest rate now leads to an increase in investment, and that in turn leads to higher income which leads to yet higher investment because of the shift of the $i(y)$ function. We could even have an upward sloping *IS* curve if $i(r, y)$ were sufficiently responsive to increases in y. In Figure 11.12, if the increase from y_0 to y_1 caused the $i(y)$ curve in the northwest quadrant to shift much higher, it can be seen by tracing through the effects that the *IS* curve could be made to slope upward.

The slope of the *IS* curve
Fortunately, it seems from the empirical evidence that the *IS* curve in the United States does, in fact, have a negative slope, eliminating this source of instability in the economy. The *IS* curve would be positively sloped if the *MPC* out of GNP plus the marginal propensity to invest out of GNP—the effect of y on i in the investment function in equation (16)—

summed to more than unity. If this sum—the *marginal propensity for expenditure (MPE)*—were greater than unity, a given increase in income y would lead to an increase in spending, $c + i + g$, larger than the original y increase. This would require an *increase* in the interest rate to *reduce* investment and maintain equilibrium in the product market. As long as the *MPE* is less than unity, an increase in income stimulates a smaller increase in expenditure (a net increase in saving), requiring a drop in the interest rate to maintain equilibrium in the product market.

The empirical estimates discussed in Chapter 10 suggest that the long-run marginal propensity to consume is about 60–65 percent of GNP. Thus, *MPC* is between 0.60 and 0.65. The empirical estimates of investment demand functions suggest that the output elasticity of investment demand is about unity:

$$1 = \frac{\Delta i}{\Delta y} \cdot \frac{y}{i}.$$

This implies that the marginal propensity to invest, $\Delta i/\Delta y$, is about the same as the ratio of investment to GNP, i/y, which is about 0.15 in the United States. Thus, *MPE* is about 0.75–0.80, and the *IS* curve is negatively sloped.

Fiscal policy and investment

In Part II, under the assumption that investment was a function only of the interest rate, $i = i(r)$, we saw that while an increase in government purchases raises both y and r, it reduces the level of investment since i', or $\Delta i/\Delta r$, is negative. Now that we have expanded the investment function to $i = i(r, y)$, the effect of an increase in government purchases on investment is no longer unambiguous. What are the conditions under which an increase in government spending will lead to an *increase* in investment?

Graphically, we can locate in the r, y space the sets of r, y points lying on trade-off lines—iso-investment lines, conceptually similar to indifference curves—which hold investment at a constant level as r and y change. Two such lines are shown by $i_0 i_0$ and $i_1 i_1$ in Figure 11.13. The slope of the *ii* lines is positive since an increase in output tends to raise investment, requiring an increase in the interest rate to hold actual investment constant. Rising investment is indicated by a movement rightward across the *ii* map, since an increase in y with r held constant increases investment.

The rule which we can now state just by inspection of Figure 11.13 is that if at an initial equilibrium (y_0, r_0) the $i_0 i_0$ line is steeper than the *LM* curve, an upward shift of the *IS* curve due to an expansionary fiscal policy will lead to a higher level of investment. In Figure 11.13 the shift of *IS* from $I_0 S_0$ to $I_1 S_1$ due to an expansionary fiscal policy action moves demand-side equilibrium from r_0, y_0 to r_1, y_1. Since the *ii* curve was steeper at r_0, y_0 than the *LM* curve, the new equilibrium is on an *ii* curve, $i_1 i_1$, that gives a higher level of investment than at the original equilibrium. The reader should convince himself or herself that the reverse is true if the *ii* curve is *flatter* than *LM* at the initial equilibrium.

In general, if an expansionary fiscal policy step is taken when the

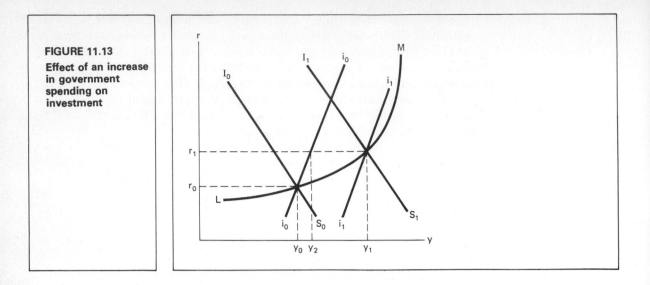

FIGURE 11.13

Effect of an increase in government spending on investment

economy is slack, and the initial equilibrium point lies along the relatively flat part of the LM curve, the movement from r_0, y_0 to r_1, y_1 will involve a large increase in y relative to r, and thus is likely to increase i. But if the expansion begins in the relatively steep part of the LM curve, the r increase will be large relative to the y increase, and investment is more likely to fall.

CONCLUSION: INVESTMENT DEMAND AND MONETARY AND FISCAL POLICY

In the last section we saw that whether replacement investment—and thus desired capital stock K^E—rises or falls with an expansionary fiscal policy action depends on the initial position of the economy. Thus, a fiscal policy stimulus in a period of relative slack in the economy, but reasonably high capacity utilization, such as the 1971–1972 period in the United States, will be complemented by an increase in investment. The effect of the r increase tending to decrease K^E will be offset by the effect of the y increase, so that K^E rises. This gives both a temporary accelerator effect boost to investment and a more permanent increase in replacement demand. On the other hand, when the economy is taut, changes in government purchases will tend to be partially offset by opposite changes in investment demand as the movements in r dominate the movements in y.

This reinforces our previous view that fiscal policy will be relatively more effective at changing equilibrium output and unemployment when the economy is slack and unemployment is high, while monetary policy will be more effective when unemployment is very low and interest rates are high. This also reinforces the corollary to the view that the size of the multipliers depends on the initial state of the economy—a search for multipliers with "stable," or constant numerical, values is likely to be fruitless.

1. The flexible-accelerator theory makes investment a function of both levels of expected output and interest rates. Since one can change interest rates more quickly than levels of output, would you expect monetary policy to be the best route to accomplish a rapid change in investment?

2. Despite very low rates of interest in the Great Depression of the 1930s, the volume of investment was very low. Is this in contradiction to the theory of investment?

3. What problems are created for the policy maker by the recognition of the accelerator effect on investment?

4. Why is investment likely to be positively correlated with the level of corporate retained earnings and depreciation allowances?

5. How does inclusion of income as one of the determinants of investment affect the relative strengths of monetary and fiscal policies?

SELECTED READINGS

A. Ando and F. Modigliani, "Econometric Analysis of Stabilization Policies," *American Economic Review*, May 1969.

C. W. Bischoff, "Business Investment in the 1970's: A Comparison of Models," *Brookings Papers on Economic Activity*, vol. 1, 1971.

R. Eisner, "A Permanent Income Theory for Investment," *American Economic Review*, June 1967.

R. Eisner, "Econometric Studies of Investment Behavior: A Comment," in P. G. Korliras and R. S. Thorn, eds., *Modern Macroeconomics* (New York: Harper & Row, 1979).

J. Hirscheifer, "On the Theory of Optimal Investment Decisions," *Journal of Political Economy*, August 1958.

D. W. Jorgenson, "Econometric Studies of Optimal Investment Decisions," *Journal of Economic Literature*, December, 1971; with comments by R. Eisner and L. R. Klein, *JEL*, March 1974; also in P. G. Korliras and R. J. Thorn, eds., *Modern Macroeconomics* (New York, Harper & Row, 1979).

D. W. Jorgenson and C. D. Siebert, "Theories of Corporate Investment Behavior," *American Economic Review*, September 1968.

M. I. Nadiri and S. Rosen, "Interrelated Factor Demands," *American Economic Review*, September 1969.

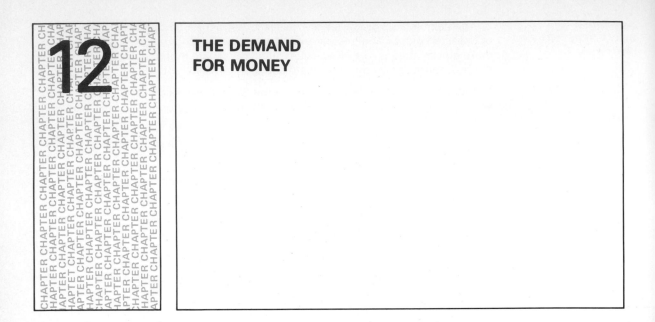

12

THE DEMAND FOR MONEY

The demand for money was introduced in Chapter 4 as the demand for real-money balances, $m = M/P$. There we suggested, in a fairly loose way, that the demand for real balances could be divided into a *speculative* demand component, inversely related to the interest rate, and a *transactions* demand component, positively related to income and inversely related to the interest rate. This gave us the demand-for-money function in Part II:

$$\frac{M}{P} = m = m(r, y), \qquad [1]$$

with the demand for real balances increasing as y rises and decreasing as r rises.

Since the 1930s, economists have developed the theory underlying the demand for money along several different lines, each of which provides a different answer to the basic question: If bonds earn interest and money does not, why should a person hold money? Although the way the various theories answer this question differs, in general they come down to a demand-for-money function similar to the one shown in equation (1).

In this chapter we will develop four prominent approaches to the demand for money. The first is the *regressive expectations* model attributed to Keynes and described by Tobin in his article on liquidity preference. This essentially says that people hold money when they expect bond prices to fall, that is, interest rates to rise, and thus expect that they would take a loss if they were to hold bonds. Since people's estimates of whether the interest rate is likely to rise or fall, and by how much, vary fairly widely, at any given interest rate there will be someone expecting it to rise, and thus someone holding money.

The obvious problem with this view is that it suggests that individuals should, at any given time, hold *all* their liquid assets either in money *or* in bonds, but not some of each. This is obviously not true in reality. Tobin's model of liquidity preference deals with this problem by showing that if the return on bonds is uncertain, that is, bonds are risky, then the investor worrying about both risk and return is likely to do best by holding both bonds and money. That is, his *optimum portfolio* of assets should include some risky assets *and* some of a risk-free asset.

A third approach to the demand for money is the inventory approach to transactions demand developed by both Baumol and Tobin. They show that there is a transactions need for money to smooth out the difference between income and expenditure streams, and that the higher the interest rate—the return on holding bonds instead of money—the smaller these transactions demand balances should be. Finally, we will look at Friedman's modern version of the quantity theory of money. Friedman analyzes the demand for money as an ordinary commodity. It can be viewed as a producer's good; businesses hold cash balances to improve efficiency in their financial transactions and are willing to pay, in terms of foregone interest income, for this efficiency. Money can also be viewed as a consumer's good; it yields utility to the consumer in terms of smoothing out timing differences between the expenditure and income streams and also in terms of reducing risk. This type of analysis brings Friedman to much the same demand-for-money function as that based on the other theories.

Our discussion of the demand for money initially focuses on the individual's decision concerning the composition of his liquid assets. We assume that he has a given amount of liquid wealth W which remains unchanged during the period under discussion. He must decide how much of that liquid wealth should be allocated to each of two kinds of assets: money (M), defined as currency plus demand deposits, which is riskless and does not earn interest; and bonds (B), which do earn interest and bear a liquidity risk. This is the risk that they might have to be sold at a capital loss if, when money is needed, bond prices are lower than they were when the bonds were purchased. "Bonds" here represent the whole range of risky assets that exist in reality. This simplification is made in order to focus on the basic analytics of the demand for money. Later in our analysis we will see how the individual's preferences can be generalized into a community liquidity preference. We can begin with the regressive expectations model of the demand for money.

THE REGRESSIVE EXPECTATIONS MODEL

Our development of the regressive expectations model follows Tobin's analysis in his article on liquidity preference. A bond holder has an expected return on the bond from two sources, the bond's yield—the interest payment he receives—and a potential capital gain—an increase in the price of the bond from the time he buys it to the time he sells it. The bond's yield Y is usually stated as a percentage yield equal to Y divided by the face value of the bond. For example, if a $100 bond has a yield of $5, the percentage yield is 5 percent. The market rate of return on the bond r is the ratio of the yield to the price of the bond P_b. If the price of the above bond were $125, the $5 yield would correspond to a market rate r of 4 percent—$5/$125. Thus,

$$r = \frac{Y}{P_b} . \qquad [2]$$

Since the yield Y is a fixed amount stated as a percentage of the bond's face value, the market price of a bond is given by the ratio of yield to market rate:

$$P_b = \frac{Y}{r} . \qquad [3]$$

The expected percentage capital gain g is the percentage increase in price from the purchase price P_b to the expected sale price P_b^e. This gives us an expression for the percentage capital gain, $g = (P_b^e - P_b)/P_b$. From equations (2) and (3), with a fixed Y on the bond, an expected price P_b^e corresponds to an expected interest rate, $r_e = Y/P_b^e$. Thus, in terms of expected and current interest rates, the capital gain can be written as

$$g = \frac{\dfrac{Y}{r^e} - \dfrac{Y}{r}}{\dfrac{Y}{r}} .$$

Canceling the Y terms and multiplying the numerator and denominator by r gives us

$$g = \frac{r}{r^e} - 1, \qquad [4]$$

as the expression for expected capital gain in terms of current and expected interest rates. For example, if the present market interest rate is 10 percent, and the purchaser of the bond expects the rate to drop to 8 percent, his expected capital gain would be

$$g = \frac{0.10}{0.08} - 1 = 1.25 - 1 = 0.25, \text{or} \, 25 \text{ percent.}$$

The total percentage return on a bond—e for earnings—will be the sum of the market rate of interest at the time of purchase and the capital gains term. Thus, $e = r + g$, and substituting for g from equation (4), we have an expression for the total percentage return as the sum of interest yield and capital gains:

$$e = r + \frac{r}{r^e} - 1. \qquad [5]$$

The individual's
demand-for-money
function

Now with an expected return on bonds given by e, and with a zero return on money, the asset holder can be expected to put his liquid wealth into bonds, if he expects the return e to be greater than zero. If the return on bonds is expected to be less than zero, he will put his liquid wealth into money.

In the regressive expectations model, each person is assumed to have an *expected* interest rate r^e corresponding to some *normal* long-run average rate. If rates rise above this long-run expectation, he expects them to fall, and vice versa. Thus, his expectations are *regressive*. Initially we will assume that his expected long-run rate does not change much with changes in current market conditions.

The asset holder's expected interest rate r^e, together with the observable market interest rate r, determines his expected percentage return e. Given this, we can compute the critical level of the market rate r, r_c, which would give him a net zero return on bonds, that is, the value of r that makes e = 0. When actual $r > r_c$, we would expect him to hold all of his liquid wealth in bonds. When $r < r_c$, he moves 100 percent into money. To find this critical value of r, r_c, we set the total return shown in equation (5) equal to zero:

$$0 = r + \frac{r}{r^e} - 1;$$
$$r(1 + r^e) = r^e;$$

and thus

$$r = \frac{r^e}{1 + r^e} = r_c. \tag{6}$$

Here r_c, the value of the market interest rate r that makes e = 0, is given by $r^e/(1 + r^e)$.

This relationship between the individual's demand for real balances and the interest rate is shown in Figure 12.1. Here we label the horizontal axis to show the demand for real balances, since later developments will

FIGURE 12.1

Individual's demand for money in the no-risk case

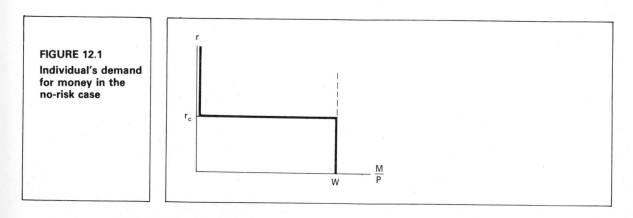

show, as suggested in Chapter 4, that it is the demand for real balances, $m = M/P$, that depends on the interest rate. Since we are implicitly holding the general price level constant throughout this section, changes in real balances M/P correspond to changes in M, so the picture in Figure 12.1 would be the same whether we label the axis M or M/P.

In Figure 12.1, when r is greater than r_c, the asset holder puts all of W into bonds, so that his demand for money is zero. As r drops below r_c so that expected capital losses on bonds outweigh the interest yield and e becomes negative, the asset holder moves his entire liquid wealth into money. This gives us a demand-for-money curve, for an individual, that looks like a step function. When r exactly equals r_c, $e = 0$ and the asset holder is indifferent between bonds and money. At any other value of r, the asset holder is either 100 percent in money or 100 percent in bonds.

The aggregate demand-for-money function with regressive expectations

The individual demand curves of Figure 12.1 can be aggregated for the entire money market as follows. Locate the individual with the highest critical interest rate, r_c^{max} in Figure 12.2. As the interest rate falls below that r_c^{max} he shifts all of his liquid wealth into money. As the interest rate drops, more individual r_c's are passed and more people shift from bonds to money. Eventually, r will drop far enough that no one will want to put liquid wealth into bonds, and the demand for money will equal total liquid wealth, ΣW.

Figure 12.3 shows the frequency distribution of the critical interest rates. The area under a frequency distribution equals 100 percent, and for any level of r_c, the area under the curve to the left of that r_c gives the proportion of people with r_c less than that r_c. The population average r_c is shown as $\bar{r}_c$ in Figure 12.3. If r_c's are distributed among the population as shown in Figure 12.3, that is, few people having extreme r_c's and more people bunched around a central r_c, $\bar{r}_c$, then the aggregate demand-for-

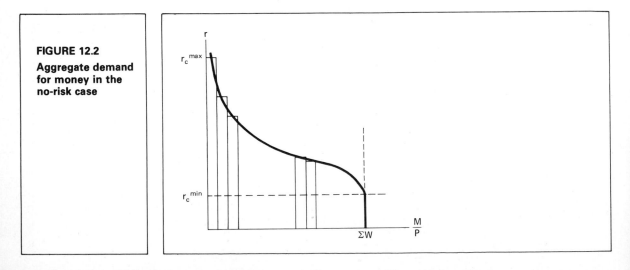

FIGURE 12.2

Aggregate demand for money in the no-risk case

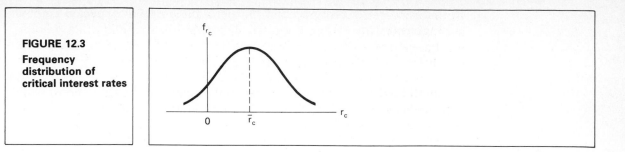

FIGURE 12.3
Frequency distribution of critical interest rates

money curve will have the shape shown in Figure 12.2—steep at the ends and flat in the middle, for a given aggregate liquid wealth, ΣW.

Thus, the regressive expectations model yields a demand-for-money function that looks much like the one we have been using so far in this book. As interest rates fall, the demand for money increases, and the demand curve is likely to be convex. That is, successive interest rate decreases of equal amounts will bring increasing increments in the demand for money.

There are two troublesome aspects of this analysis, however. In the first place, if the money market remained in equilibrium for a long enough period, people should begin to adjust their expected interest rates to correspond to the actual prevailing interest rate. They would all tend to adopt eventually the same critical interest rate as time passes, so that the aggregate demand curve for the entire money market would increasingly look like the flat curve of Figure 12.1, instead of the negatively sloped demand curve with a variety of critical rates shown in Figure 12.2. This implication of the regressive expectations model—that the elasticity of demand for money with respect to changes in the interest rate is increasing over time—is not supported by empirical studies.

Secondly, if we assume that people actually do have a critical interest rate as shown in Figure 12.1, then the clear implication of the model is that, in this two-asset world, individuals hold either all bonds or all money, never a mix of the two. The negative slope of the aggregate demand curve is due to the fact that people disagree about the value of r^e, and thus in their critical rates r_c. In fact, however, individuals do not hold portfolios consisting of just one asset. In general, portfolios hold a mixture of assets; they are *diversified*. An explanation of this result—that people hold both money and bonds at the same time—can be found in the portfolio balance approach to the demand for money developed by Tobin.

THE PORTFOLIO BALANCE APPROACH

The portfolio balance approach begins with the same expression for total percentage return e that we developed in the last section,

$$e = r + g. \tag{7}$$

In that section we assumed that the percentage rate of expected capital gain, given by

$$g = \frac{r}{r^e} - 1,$$

is determined with certainty by the individual; he (or she) chooses his expected r^e as a function of r, and no consideration of uncertainty, or risk, enters the problem. The basic contribution of the portfolio balance approach is to enter risk considerations explicitly into the determination of the demand for money.

The probability distribution of capital gains

Rather than some *fixed* expected capital gain, here we will assume that the asset holder has a whole spectrum of *expected* capital gains, each with a probability of its occurrence attached. Such a *probability*, or *frequency, distribution* of expected gains is shown in Figure 12.4. Each possible value of capital gain g has a probability f_g attached to it. If one asks the asset holder what the probability is of achieving a gain greater than g_1, say, 15 percent, the answer will be the area under the probability distribution to the right of g_1. Thus, the asset holder is not certain of the value of g he expects, but has an implicit distribution of these gains around some central value—the average, or *expected gain*, $\bar{g}$.

If the probabilities of capital gains are distributed "normally"—according to the familiar symmetrical bell-shaped distribution shown in Figure 12.4—then we have a natural measure of uncertainty, or risk. This measure is the *standard deviation*, σ_g, of the probability distribution of capital gains. To find the standard deviation of expected gains, σ_g, we can locate the two points symmetrically opposite each other on the normal probability distribution that have the following property: The area under the curve between these two points is two-thirds of the total area under the curve. Given the shape of the normal curve, these points are also the inflection points of the curve, where it turns from concave to convex. The standard deviation of the probability distribution, σ_g, is the distance between either of these two points and the mean of the distribution, $\bar{g}$. The statistical significance of σ_g is that, since two-thirds of the area under the curve is between the points $\bar{g} - \sigma_g$ and $\bar{g} + \sigma_g$, the asset holder has a 66.7

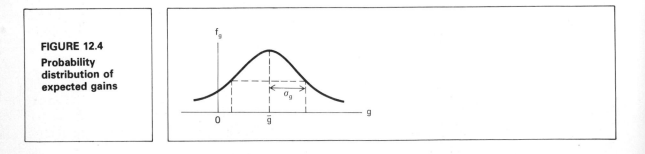

FIGURE 12.4

Probability distribution of expected gains

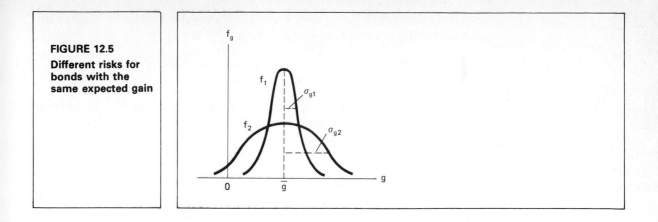

FIGURE 12.5

Different risks for bonds with the same expected gain

percent chance that the *actual* g will turn out between $\bar{g} \pm \sigma_g$. Thus, if $\bar{g} = 10$ percent, and $\sigma_g = 2$ percent, the investor has a two-thirds chance that actual g will be between 8 and 12 percent.

That the standard deviation is a natural measure of the riskiness of bonds can be seen by considering the two probability distributions, both with the same $\bar{g}$, shown in Figure 12.5. The narrow distribution, f_1, illustrates a case in which the asset holder is very *certain* of the gain—it has a small σ_g. The wider distribution f_2 shows a case in which with the same central expected gain $\bar{g}$, the investor has a very uncertain estimate of the gain; thus, σ_{g2} is greater than σ_{g1}. If we can identify riskiness with uncertainty, σ_g is a measure of the risk of holding liquid assets in bonds.

Now in place of a return expected with certainty, e, we have an *expected return*, $\bar{e}$, where

$$\bar{e} = r + \bar{g},$$

and $\bar{g}$ is the mean expected capital gain from the probability distribution of Figure 12.4. If the asset holder is putting B dollars of his liquid assets into bonds, his expected total return $\bar{R}_T$ is then

$$\bar{R}_T = B \cdot \bar{e} = B \cdot (r + \bar{g}). \qquad [8]$$

Similarly, if the standard deviation of return on a bond is σ_g, a number like 2 percent, and all bonds are alike, then the total standard deviation of bond holdings is given by

$$\sigma_T = B \cdot \sigma_g. \qquad [9]$$

The individual's portfolio decision

Equations (8) and (9) give us the technical situation facing the asset holder—the budget constraint along which he can trade increased risk σ_r for increased expected return $\bar{R}_T$. They also give the investor a formula for deciding how much funds to put into bonds to achieve a given risk-return mix along the budget line. From equation (9) we have

$$B = \frac{\sigma_T}{\sigma_g} = \frac{1}{\sigma_g} \, \sigma_T.$$

With σ_g fixed by the asset holder's probability distribution, this expression gives the total bond holdings B needed to attain any given level of risk σ_T. Using this expression to replace B in equation (8) gives us the *budget constraint*, facing the investor trading between return R_T and risk σ_T:

$$\bar{R}_T = \frac{\sigma_T}{\sigma_g} (r + \bar{g}) = \sigma_T \left(\frac{r + g}{\sigma_g} \right). \tag{10}$$

Here r is a known current value, fixed, at least to the individual, by the bond market. The investor knows $\bar{g}$ and σ_g, at least implicitly, from his probability distribution of g's in Figure 12.4. Thus, the expression in parentheses in the budget constraint in equation (10) is a given, determined number which gives the constant rate of trade-off between return $\bar{R}_T$ and risk. If r is, say, 5 percent, $\bar{g}$ is 10 percent, and σ_g is 5 percent, $(r + \bar{g})/\sigma_g$ is 3. In this case, an increase of one percentage point in the standard deviation in the total portfolio σ_T will buy a 3 percentage increase in expected total return $\bar{R}_T$.

The budget constraint in equation (10) for an individual asset holder is shown in the top half of Figure 12.6. The standard deviation of the total portfolio, σ_T, is shown on the horizontal axis. The vertical axis above the horizontal axis measures the expected rate of return on the portfolio, $\bar{R}_T$. The straight line in the top half shows the trade-off between risk and expected return which faces the individual: Its slope from equation (10) is $(r + \bar{g})/\sigma_g$. Each of these terms, and thus the slope of the budget line, is fixed for each individual.

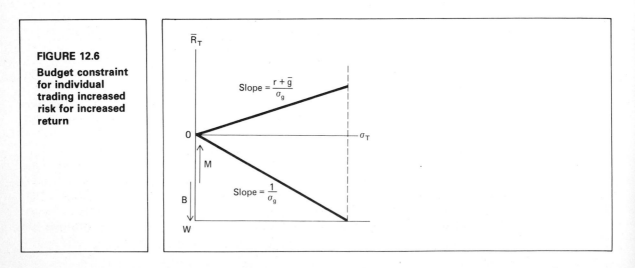

FIGURE 12.6

Budget constraint for individual trading increased risk for increased return

The length of the vertical axis below the horizontal axis in Figure 12.6 is given by the total liquid wealth W of the individual. The distance from the origin along this axis gives total bond holdings B; the distance from $W(= W - B)$ gives money holdings M. For any given value of σ_T, we can locate the value of B by multiplying by $1/\sigma_g$ from the equation $B = (1/\sigma_g)\sigma_T$, or projecting it from the line with slope $1/\sigma_g$ in the bottom half of Figure 12.6. Thus, once we locate an optimum return-risk point along the budget line in the top half of Figure 12.6, knowing σ_T we can determine the corresponding portfolio mix of B and M in the bottom half of the diagram.

In order to locate the individual's equilibrium risk σ_T and expected rate of return $\bar{R}_T$, we must confront the technical budget constraint of equation (10) and Figure 12.6 with the individual's utility function trade-off between risk and return. These preferences are represented by indifference curves such as those used in our analysis of consumption and investment. The shape of the curve depends on the nature of the investor's preferences between risk and return.

Tobin distinguished three kinds of preferences that an individual might have. Each of these is shown in Figure 12.7. Figures 12.7(a)–(c) represent *risk averters*. In these cases the indifference curves have positive slopes, indicating that the person demands more expected return in order to be willing to take more risk. Figure 12.7(d) shows the indifference curves of a person who might be called a *risk lover*. The slope of his indifference curves is negative, showing that the risk lover is willing to take less return in order to be able to assume more risk.

The indifference curves shown in Figure 12.7(a) are representative of a subclass of risk averters known as *diversifiers*. As risk increases by equal increments the diversifier demands increasing increments of return, so that his indifference curves are convex to his budget line. As usual in this kind of analysis, the diversifier will attempt to reach as high an indifference curve as possible, given his budget constraint. Thus, the expected return and risk of his portfolio $\bar{R}_T$, σ_T will be determined by the point of tangency of the budget line with the highest possible indifference curve. Given the convex shape of his indifference curves, the diversifier is likely to reach an *interior equilibrium* at $\sigma_T{}^0$ holding both bonds B_0 and money M_0. Only part of this person's total wealth is put into bonds. This is why he is called a *diversifier*. Thus, in the case of the diversifier, who demands increasing increments of return to induce him to take on constant increments of risk, the portfolio balance approach does away with the all-or-nothing version of the demand for money shown earlier in Figure 12.1.

Figures 12.7(b) and (c) show the indifference curves representative of a subclass of risk averters called *plungers*. The plunger will either not put his wealth into bonds at all, or will put all of his wealth into bonds. In Figure 12.7(b), the plunger's indifference curves are steep relative to the budget line, so that he holds all money and no bonds. If his indifference curves are flat relative to the budget line as in Figure 12.7(c), he will hold

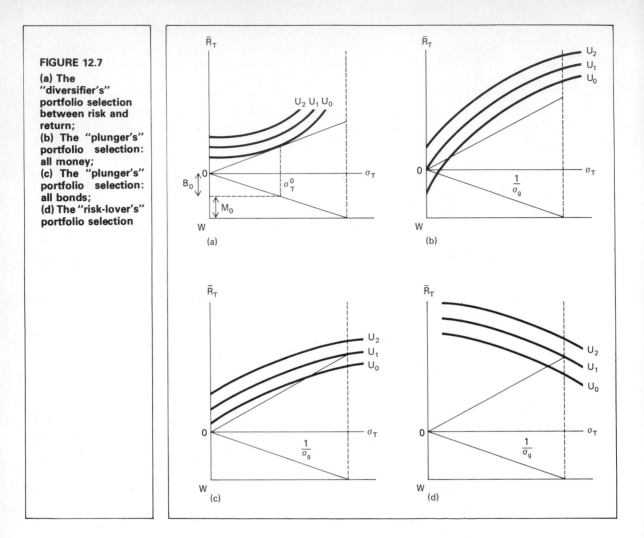

FIGURE 12.7

(a) The "diversifier's" portfolio selection between risk and return;
(b) The "plunger's" portfolio selection: all money;
(c) The "plunger's" portfolio selection: all bonds;
(d) The "risk-lover's" portfolio selection

(a)

(b)

(c)

(d)

all bonds, no money. This behavior would be consistent with the earlier regressive expectations model, but not with reality for most asset holders. Finally, Figure 12.7(d) shows the utility curve of the risk lover. He will attempt to maximize risk and thus he, too, will put his entire wealth into bonds.

Since we observe empirically that the world is characterized by diversification, we can conclude that, in terms of the portfolio balance model, most asset holders are *diversifiers*. Thus, the situation shown in Figure 12.7(a), with indifference curves representing *increasing risk aversion*, is the basis for the portfolio balance model of the demand for money.

The aggregate demand for money in the portfolio balance model

We can now derive a demand function for money by varying the interest rate in Figure 12.7(a) and following the changes in the allocation of liquid wealth to bonds and money, particularly the latter. What happens in this model when interest rates rise? The result is shown in Figure 12.8. Since the slope of the budget line is $(r + \bar{g})/\sigma_g$, as r increases from r_0 to r_1 to r_2 the slope increases, and the line rotates upward. At any given level of risk, return will be increased as r rises. As r increases, the budget line touches successively higher indifference curves. This traces out the *optimum portfolio curve* connecting the points of tangency, shown in Figure 12.8. As r increases from a very low value, the diversifiers' tangency points move up and to the right, increasing both the expected rate of return and risk.

The progressively smaller increases in optimum risk from σ_T^0 to σ_T^1 to σ_T^2 in Figure 12.8 that come from continuing equal increases in r give successively smaller increases in the amount of wealth put into bonds. This is shown as B rises from B_0 to B_1 to B_2 in Figure 12.8. If, as r rises by constant increments, B rises by decreasing increments, then the demand for money must *decrease* by progressively smaller amounts as r increases, since $B + M$ equals a fixed W. This relationship between M and r is shown

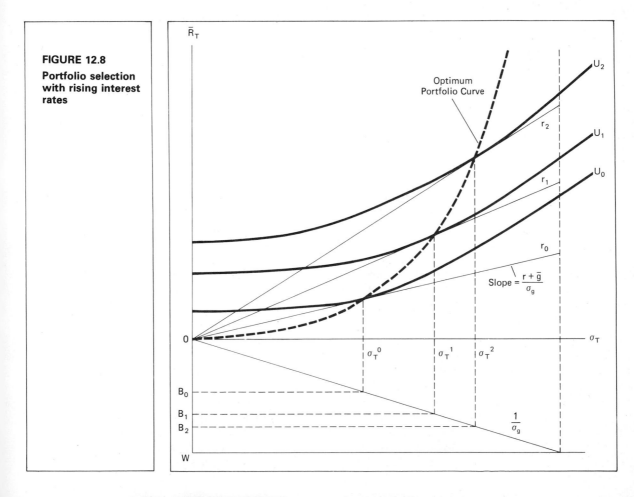

FIGURE 12.8

Portfolio selection with rising interest rates

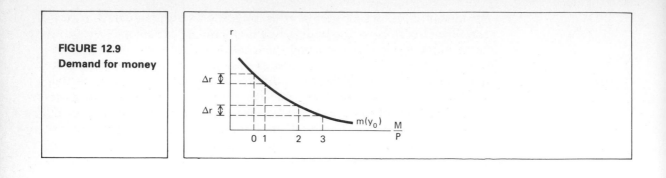

FIGURE 12.9
Demand for money

in Figure 12.9, which is simply the same demand-for-money curve that we derived in Chapter 4. Along this demand-for-money function, a given drop in r, measured by Δr in Figure 12.9, gives a bigger increase in the demand for money at a low interest rate—from point two to point three—than at a high interest rate—from point zero to point one.

The demand-for-money function of Figure 12.9 is drawn as $m(y_0)$, assuming a given level of real income. This is because the portfolio balance model is basically a theory of the speculative demand for money. It analyzes the allocation of a given amount of liquid wealth to bonds and money depending on interest rates and expectations concerning the return and risk on capital gains. No reference is made in the model to a transactions demand for money. Thus, the portfolio balance model gives us a more satisfactory theory of the speculative demand for money than does the regressive expectations model, particularly in its explanation of diversification. In the next section we will review briefly the inventory-of-money approach to transactions demand that has been developed by Baumol and Tobin. But first, let us look at the effects of changes in expected capital gains $\bar{g}$ and risk estimates σ_g in the portfolio balance model.

An increase in expected capital gains $\bar{g}$, holding the standard deviation σ_g constant, will have the same effect as an increase in the interest rate, rotating the budget line up and increasing the amount of liquid wealth held in bonds, decreasing the demand for money at any given interest rate. This would shift the demand curve in Figure 12.9 to the left; at any r, the demand for money is decreased.

What happens if estimates of risk change? The standard deviation σ_g of the probability distribution of Figure 12.4 may increase due to increasing uncertainty about future movements in bond prices and interest rates. This increase would rotate the budget line in the upper half of Figure 12.8 down (smaller slope) and also rotate the line in the lower half up by reducing $1/\sigma_g$. Since $\sigma_T = B \cdot \sigma_g$, an increase in σ_g means that the amount of bonds B yielding any given total risk falls. The increase in σ_g thus reduces bond holdings B in two ways. In the upper half of Figure 12.8, the downward rotation of the budget line reduces desired risk σ_T. Even with the original σ_g value, a reduction in σ_T would cause a drop in B. But the additional effect of the increase in σ_g, rotating upward the $1/\sigma_g$ line in the bottom half of Figure 12.8, would further increase the drop in B needed to reduce total risk σ_T while risk per bond σ_g is rising.

Tobin's model of portfolio balance provides a much firmer ground for the speculative demand for money by explaining why rational individual asset holders might hold their portfolios distributed among several assets of differing riskiness and expected return. It also explains why the speculative demand for money should be inversely related to the interest rate, in the way that was assumed in Chapter 4. We will now turn to the transactions demand to see that it, too, should be sensitive to interest rate changes.

THE TRANSACTIONS DEMAND FOR MONEY

In Chapter 4 we suggested that one principal motive for holding money is the need to smooth out the difference between income and expenditure streams. This *transactions motive* lies behind the the transactions demand for money which is related to the level of income. The alternative to holding money, which is the means of payment and earns no return, is bonds, which earn a return but also incur transactions costs—brokerage fees—as one moves from money (received as pay) to bonds and back to money to make expenditures. In Chapter 4 we suggested that the higher the interest rate bonds earn, the tighter transactions balances should be squeezed to hold bonds, giving the transactions demand some degree of sensitivity to interest rate changes. Here we can develop this point a bit more thoroughly.

Suppose an individual is paid monthly (in cash or by check) and spends the total amount c of his income in purchases spread evenly throughout the month. He has the option of holding transactions balances in money or in bonds which yield a given r, r_0, if held for a month, and proportionately less than r_0 if they are held for a shorter period. The individual would prefer to hold bonds since they yield a return but will have to convert bonds to cash during the month to meet expenditure plans. The first question we want to ask is how frequently should he convert bonds into cash? That is, how many bonds-to-cash transactions should he plan, where n is the number of these transactions?

The optimum number of transactions

To begin on the revenue side, if an individual plans no bonds-to-cash transactions, he buys no bonds in the first place. In this case, then he can hold no bonds during the period and would earn zero return. Next, suppose he plans one bonds-to-cash transaction, putting half of c into bonds which he holds half the month. In this case total revenue R from interest will be $r_0/2$ times $c/2$, or $(r_0 c)/4$, as shown in Table 12.1. Marginal revenue (MR) from the increase in transactions from zero to one is also $(r_0 c)/4$.

If two transactions are planned, two-thirds of c can be put into bonds initially. Ten days into the month, half the bonds—one-third of c—can be cashed. Each bond will have earned $r_0/3$, giving revenue on this third of c equal to $(r_0 c)/9$. Ten days later the other half can be cashed having earned

$2r_0/3$ per bond or $(2r_0c)/9$ revenue for this third of c. Total revenue in the two-transaction case will then be $(r_0c)/9 + (2r_0c)/9 = (r_0c)/3$. The increase in revenue, MR, over the one-transaction case is $(r_0c)/12$, as shown in Table 12.1.

In the three-transaction case, one-fourth of c will earn interest for one-fourth of the month, yielding $(r_0c)/16$, one-fourth will earn for half the month, yielding $(2r_0c)/16$, and the final fourth will earn interest for three-quarters of the month, yielding $(3r_0c)/16$. The total revenue in this case if $(6r_0c)/16$, or $(3r_0c)/8$. MR in the three-transaction case is $(r_0c)/24$.

This example is sufficient to establish that the marginal revenue from increasing the number of transactions is positive and decreasing as the number of transactions n increases. Furthermore, looking at the *differences* in the MR column in Table 12.1, we can see that as n increases the drop in MR decreases. This gives us the $MR(r_0)$ curve in Figure 12.10, which shows MR as a function of the number of transactions n for the given initial interest rate r_0.

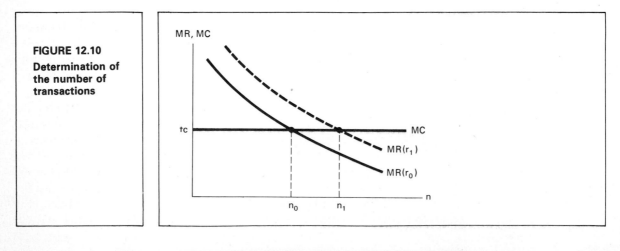

TABLE 12.1

Marginal Return from Increasing Transactions from Bonds to Cash

Number of Transactions (n)	Total Revenue (R)	Marginal Revenue (MR)
0	0	
1	$\dfrac{r_0c}{4}$	$\dfrac{r_0c}{4}$
2	$\dfrac{r_0c}{3}$	$\dfrac{r_0c}{12}$
3	$\dfrac{3r_0c}{8}$	$\dfrac{r_0c}{24}$
.	.	.
.	.	.
.	.	.

FIGURE 12.10

Determination of the number of transactions

On the cost side, we will assume each transaction has a given cost tc, perhaps a broker's fee or the implicit cost of time spent transacting business. Then we can add a (marginal cost) $MC = tc$ schedule to Figure 12.10. Combined with the initial $MR(r_0)$ curve, this gives a profit-maximizing number of transactions n_0 where $MR = MC$.

For any given number of transactions, such as n_0 in Figure 12.10, an increase in the expenditure stream c will increase average holdings of both money and bonds during the month. If the expenditure stream is smooth, so that total transactions balances of $B + M$ equal c at the beginning of the month and zero at the end, then the average total holding is $c/2$. The number of transactions tells us how that $c/2$ is split between money and bonds. Thus, an increase in expenditure, or in general an increase in the flow of real income and output y, will raise the transactions demand for money.

The interest elasticity of the transactions demand

From the example in Table 12.1, it should be fairly clear that an increase in the number of transactions increases the average bond holding during the month and decreases the average money balance. At one extreme, with zero transactions, no bonds are held and the average money balance equals $c/2$. With a very large number of transactions, very little money is held, and average bond holdings approach $c/2$.

Now the MR curve in Figure 12.10 is positioned by a given interest rate r_0. The MR entries in Table 12.1 all have r in their numerators, so an increase in r from r_0 to r_1 will increase MR for any given number of transactions, shifting the MR curve up to $MR(r_1)$ in Figure 12.10. With no change in the cost per transaction, this increases the optimum number of transactions to n_1. The increase from n_0 to n_1 is made in order to increase average bond holdings to take advantage of the higher r.

Thus, an increase in the interest rate should reduce the transactions demand for money for any given level of the income-expenditure stream. This takes us back to the demand-for-money function of Chapter 4,

$$\frac{M}{P} = m(r, y).$$

The transactions demand for money should respond to a change in the interest rate through a change in the number of bonds-to-money transactions. The speculative demand should respond to a change in r due to portfolio-balancing considerations. Both effects are combined here in the negative effect of an increase in r on the demand for real balances M/P.

We will now turn to another major perspective on the demand for money—Friedman's view of money as a consumer's and producer's good. This will lead us back again to the original demand-for-money equation.

MONEY AS A CONSUMER'S AND PRODUCER'S GOOD

The money demand models discussed so far, due mainly to Keynes and Tobin, draw an important distinction between transactions and speculative demands for money. These are basically portfolio-balancing models of financial market behavior. Friedman, however, develops the demand for money within the context of the traditional microeconomic theories of consumer behavior and of the producer's demand for inputs. Consumers hold money because it yields a utility—the convenience of holding the means of payment rather than making frequent trips to the broker and risking losses on bonds. Their demand for money should be a demand for real balances, just as any consumer demand should be a demand for real consumer goods, as opposed to their money value, in the absence of money illusion. This demand for real balances should depend on the level of real income. It should also depend on the returns to other ways of holding assets such as bonds or consumer durables, much as the demand for one kind of fruit should depend on the prices of other kinds.

Producers hold money as a productive asset which smooths payments and expenditure streams. Just as their demand for real capital services depends on the level of real output and the relative price of capital, as shown in Chapter 11, their demand for real balances should depend on real output (or income), and the relative returns on other ways of holding wealth.

The approach gives us a demand function for real balances,

$$\frac{M}{P} = m(y, r_1, \ldots, r_j, \ldots, r_J), \qquad [11]$$

where $r_1, \ldots, r_J$ are the rates of return on all assets which are alternatives to money. If the ratio between the demand for real balances and real income is relatively trendless through time, and depends at any given point in time on the returns to alternative assets, we have Friedman's modern quantity theory version of the demand for money:

$$\frac{M}{P} = k(r_1, \ldots, r_J) \cdot y, \qquad [12a]$$

or

$$\frac{m}{y} = k(r_1, \ldots, r_J). \qquad [12b]$$

In fact, as we shall see shortly, the elasticity of m with respect to changes in y may well be about unity, so that the ratio between m and y is roughly constant along trend, and equation (12) is a good approximation to equation (11).

To fill out the demand function, we can include the rates of return on bonds and on durable goods as examples of the more complete list of alternative assets that might be relevant substitutes for money.

As we have already shown at some length in this chapter, as the rate of return on bonds rises, the demand for money falls. Rather than distinguish between transactions demand and speculative demand, we can simply note that as the expected total return on bonds rises, the demand for bonds should rise and the demand for money should fall. Earlier we developed an expression for the expected return on bonds, equation (5):

$$e = r + \frac{r}{r^e} - 1.$$

Since bonds are a relevant substitute for money, we would insert r and r^e into the demand function in equation (12). If r^e depends on r, as discussed earlier, we can condense this expression of the dependency on the bond rate by simply including r in equation (12).

The effect of the rate of inflation

Another asset that serves as an alternative to money is consumer durables. As the price level rises, the value, or purchasing power, of a stock of durable goods remains roughly constant as durable goods prices rise along with the general price index. On the other hand, the purchasing power of money falls with an increase in prices, so that an increase in the *expected rate of inflation* should cause a shift out of money and bonds and into consumer durables. This should be interpreted carefully in two different respects. First, in equation (12), a one-time increase in the price level will cause an increase in the nominal demand for money to keep M/P constant with y and all the r's in the k function unchanged. But an increase in the expected *continuing* rate of inflation will reduce the demand for real balances m. Second, the shift from financial assets to durable goods tends to raise the (nominal) interest rate. The reduction in the demand for money shifts the LM curve down. But the increase in the demand for durable goods shifts the IS up even more since in addition to shifting out of money, asset holders are moving out of *all* financial assets.

Thus, compared with money, the rate of return on speculative holdings of consumer durables is the rate of inflation, $\dot{P} = (\Delta P/\Delta t)/P$, where as usual $\dot{P}$ stands for the proportional rate of change of prices. On the assumption that expected rates of inflation are positively related to the current rate, we can include $\dot{P}$ among the rates of return in equation (12).

With the rates of return of the two principal alternatives to money included, we now have the demand-for-money function,

$$\frac{M}{P} = m = m(y, r, \dot{P}). \tag{13}$$

The demand for real balances increases with an increase in y, and falls with an increase in r or $\dot{P}$. In the modern quantity theory version of equation (13), we would have

$$\frac{M}{P} = k(r, \dot{P}) \cdot y, \tag{14}$$

so that the ratio of m to y varies with changes in r and $\dot{P}$. The desired ratio of real balances to income, k, falls as either r or $\dot{P}$ increases.

This function is very close to the one we developed in Chapter 4. The only important difference is the inclusion of the rate of inflation, $\dot{P}$, in the demand function. It should be noted that equation (14) suggests that the *level* of the demand for real balances depends on the expected *rate* of inflation. Thus, if the economy shifts from a 6 percent rate of inflation to an 8 percent rate, the demand for money in the static model will shift down to a new level, and the demand for consumer goods will shift up. But once the demand function has shifted, the economy will reach a new static equilibrium unless there is another change in the *rate* of inflation. Thus, adding $\dot{P}$ to the demand function will not greatly affect the qualitative nature of the static model unless substantial *variations* in $\dot{P}$ are expected.

The velocity of money
 From the demand-for-money equation (14), we can conveniently develop an expression for the income velocity of money, $v = y/m$. Replacing M/P in (14) by m and rearranging terms, we have the expression for the *income velocity* of money, the ratio of income to the money stock:

$$v = \frac{y}{m} = \frac{1}{k(r, \dot{P})} = v(r, \dot{P}). \qquad [15]$$

Since k falls with an increase in either r or $\dot{P}$, desired velocity v rises with an increase in r or $\dot{P}$. An increase in either the interest rate or the rate of inflation should cause people to economize on money holdings since these are the rates of return on the alternative assets, bonds and durable goods. This would result in an increase in velocity as money demand falls relative to GNP.

In the long-run U.S. data, the velocity of money seemed, on balance, to decline along trend up to World War II. Since then it has risen, along with interest rates, fairly steadily. This suggests that, over the long run, the ratio of y to m is rather stable, as is the ratio of consumption to income, c/y. The question of the relative stability of the y/m ratio v and the $c–y$ relationship is, as we will see in Chapter 14, one of the points at the heart of the *Keynesian-monetarist* controversy.

If the short-run elasticity of v with respect to changes in interest rates were very low, we could approximate $v(r,\dot{P})$ in equation (15) by a constant $\bar{v}$, giving a direct relationship between movements in m and y: $y = \bar{v}m$. However, there is substantial empirical evidence that the interest elasticity of the demand for money is not insignificant in the short run. This suggests, through equation (15), that the interest elasticity of velocity is not insignificant so that, in fact, both the product and money market equations are needed to predict movements in nominal and real GNP. We will return to this point in some detail in the discussion of monetary and fiscal policy in Chapter 14.

EMPIRICAL ESTIMATES OF INCOME AND INTEREST ELASTICITIES
 In the absence of substantial shifts in expected rates of inflation, which are not fully compatible with a static model of income determination which deals with movements from one equilibrium price *level* to another, the demand-for-money function that emerges from the analysis of this chapter is the familiar

$$\frac{M}{P} = m(r,y) \qquad\qquad [16]$$

of Chapter 4.

The y term in the demand function represents transactions demand or, in Friedman's terms, the increasing demand for money as a producer's, and consumer's good, through an income effect, as income rises. The r term represents the interest elasticity of both the transactions demand for money and the speculative demand through Tobin's portfolio balance model. It also represents a potential substitutability against bonds in production and consumption decisions.

There have been many investigations into the values of the elasticities of the demand for *real money*—currency plus demand deposits, M_1, or M_1 plus time deposits, M_2, deflated by the price level P as in equation (16)—with respect to interest rate and income changes. And there are many continuing controversies concerning the values of these elasticities and the proper form of the demand-for-money function. However, representative elasticities of the demand for real balances from Goldfeld's 1973 article are about 0.7 with respect to changes in real income, and −0.25 with respect to changes in r. Here r is a short-term interest rate—a three-month commercial paper rate, a three-month treasury bill rate, or a time-deposit rate. With the money stock M_1 at about \$400 billion in 1979, GNP at about \$2.4 trillion, and the short-term interest rate at about 10 percent, these elasticities imply that a \$25 billion GNP increase—1.1 percent—would raise the demand for money by about \$3.1 billion, and a 2-point drop in short-term interest rates—20 percent—would increase the demand for money by about \$20 billion.

Most demand-for-money estimates suggest that demand changes lag slightly behind interest rate changes. Thus, if interest rates fell from 10 to 8 percent, causing an increase of \$20 billion in the desired holdings of money, the estimates suggest that about 30 percent of a discrepancy between actual and desired money holdings would be eliminated in one quarter, 50 percent in two quarters, and 75 percent in a year. This means that if an increase in y or decrease in r increases the level of desired equilibrium real balances from $(M/P)_0$ to $(M/P)^*$ at time t_0 in Figure 12.11, the path of actual holdings of $M/P = m$ would tend to follow the dashed adjustment path toward the final desired level of real balances, $(M/P)^*$.

This partial adjustment pattern leads to the same kind of overreaction of interest rates to changes in the money supply that we see in traditional microeconomic analysis, in which demand changes yield larger short-run than long-run changes in prices, and vice versa for output. In Figure 12.12 the demand-for-money curve $M(y_0)$ is the long-run curve reflecting the long-run interest elasticity mentioned above as about −0.25. The intersection of $M(y_0)$ with the given initial money supply, $(M/P)_0$, at point E_0, gives an initial equilibrium interest rate r_0. Through E_0 we can also draw a short-run demand function $m(y_0)$ that reflects the partial short-run adjust-

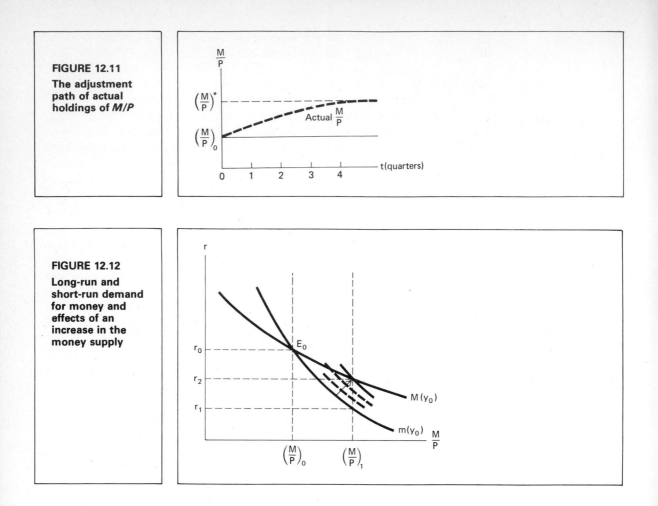

FIGURE 12.11

The adjustment path of actual holdings of M/P

FIGURE 12.12

Long-run and short-run demand for money and effects of an increase in the money supply

ment mechanism of Figure 12.11. This shows the one-period reaction of demand to interest rate changes, while the $M(y_0)$ curve shows the long-run relationship between M/P and r.

Now if the money supply is increased to $(M/P)_1$ the interest rate will initially fall to r_1 along the short-run $m(y_0)$ function, holding y constant throughout this partial analysis, that is, assuming a vertical IS curve. As time passes, and the actual demand shifts up toward equilibrium along the dashed path of Figure 12.11, the interest rate will rise toward r_2, with the short-run demand function shifting up, shown as the dashed short-run functions of Figure 12.12. Eventually, holding y constant at y_0, the interest rate will settle at r_2, rising from the short-run level of r_1, but below the initial equilibrium r_0.

If the level of income has also risen during the process as the LM curve shifts along an actual nonvertical IS curve, the interest rate will end up higher than r_2, on a higher $M(y_1)$ function, but lower than the initial r_0.

Thus, since the demand for money is less elastic in the short run than in the long run, due to the partial adjustment process of Figure 12.11, we can expect an increase in the money supply to push interest rates down somewhat more in the short run, one quarter, than in the slightly longer run, one year.

Since this chapter's review of the several approaches to the demand for money has not altered substantially the demand function we began with in Chapter 4, there is no need to return to the static model of income determination here. This chapter has illustrated another kind of channel that economic research follows. In this chapter, the emphasis has been on developing theoretical explanations—or, put more simply, ways to understand common empirical observations, such as people holding some of two assets with different rates of return at the same time (diversification), and the interest elasticity of transactions balances. After we briefly discuss in Chapter 13 the supply of money—a quantity taken as given up to now—we will return to some of the important points in the analysis of the demand for money in Chapter 14.

QUESTIONS FOR DISCUSSION AND REVIEW

1. Assume that your savings account pays interest at a rate of 6% per year and that you earn $900 per month payable at the beginning of the month. You spend $900 per month evenly over the month. What percent of your monthly income will you hold in cash balances on average if:

    a. you pay bills only on the 30th of the month?
    b. you pay bills on the 15th and 30th of the month?
    c. you pay bills daily?

2. How would your answers to problem 1 change if you discovered it cost $1 to withdraw funds from your savings account? How would they change if the transactions fee rose to $20?

3. A consol is a government security which yields a fixed-interest premium in perpetuity. Assume you have the opportunity to buy such instruments when the market rate of interest is 10%. What would your total percentage return be for one year if interest rates fell to 8%? At what expected rate of interest would you prefer to remain in cash?

4. Contrast the effect of a one-time increase in the price level on the demand for nominal money balances with the effect of continued expected inflation. How would the demand for real balances be affected by these two phenomena? How would you expect income velocity to respond to each?

5. Assume the real income elasticity of the demand for real balances is less than unity, say .7, and the interest elasticity of the demand for real balances is significantly below zero at .25. From 1960 to 1975, GNP grew from $506 billion to $1,529 billion or about 202% while prices rose about 85% and interest rates approximately doubled. What would you predict to be the change in income velocity of money? Given the changes that have taken place in the banking industry, would you expect an estimate based only on income and interest elasticities to be high or low?

SELECTED READINGS

F. De Leeuw and E. Gramlich, "The Federal Reserve–MIT Econometric Model," *Federal Reserve Bulletin,* January 1968.

M. Friedman, "The Quantity Theory of Money—A Restatement," in M. G. Mueller, ed., *Readings in Macroeconomics* (New York: Holt, Rinehart and Winston, 1971).

S. M. Goldfield, "The Demand for Money Revisited," *Brookings Papers on Economic Activity,* vol. 3, 1973.

S. M. Goldfield, "The Case of the Missing Money," *Brookings Papers on Economic Activity,* vol. 3, 1976.

F. Modigliani, R. A. Rasche, and J. P. Cooper, "Central Bank Policy, Money Supply, and the Short-term Rate of Interest," *Journal of Money, Credit, and Banking,* May 1968.

R. L. Teigen, "The Demand for and Supply of Money," in R. L. Teigen, ed., *Readings in Money, National Income and Stabilization Policy,* 4th ed. (Homewood, Ill.: Irwin, 1978).

J. Tobin, "The Interest-Elasticity of the Transaction Demand for Cash," *Review of Economics and Statistics,* September 1956.

J. Tobin, "Liquidity Preference as Behavior Toward Risk," *Review of Economic Studies,* February 1958, also in M. G. Mueller, ed., *Readings in Macroeconomics* (New York: Holt, Rinehart and Winston, 1971).

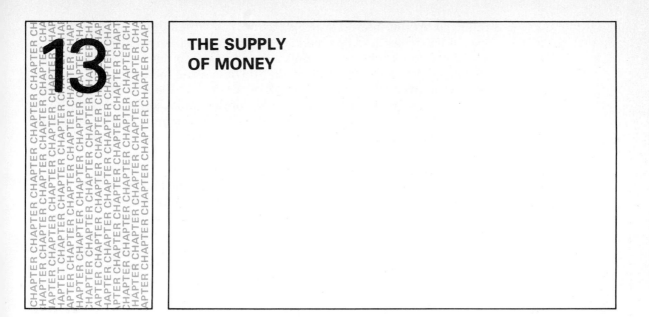

13

THE SUPPLY
OF MONEY

The money supply that will be discussed in this chapter consists of currency—paper money and coins—in the hands of the nonbank public plus demand deposits—checking account balances—in commercial banks. These particular liquid assets have two characteristics in common that separate them from other liquid assets: They are the generally accepted means of exchange in the economy and they earn no interest. This definition of money as currency plus demand deposits is known in the economics literature as M_1, perhaps the first definition of money supply. This is the most widely used money supply concept, although some economists prefer to add time deposits—savings deposits at commercial banks, savings and loan associations, and mutual savings banks—to M_1 to obtain a broader definition of money called M_2. Time deposits are not, however, a commonly used means of exchange. In general, banks and savings and loan associations can limit the frequency with which withdrawals can be made from a savings account—normally to one a month. While this rule is not frequently enforced, persons who attempt to use a savings account like a checking account, making several transactions a week, will run into difficulty at the bank. In addition, time deposits are differentiated from demand deposits in that the latter pay no interest, while time deposits do. Thus, there is a natural separation in the spectrum of assets between demand and time deposits, and between M_1—the money supply *narrowly defined*—and M_2. Choice between the two concepts will not make much difference for the money supply analysis presented in this chapter, so we will focus on the usual measure of the money supply, M_1.

In the late 1970s, the neat distinction between demand deposits and time deposits became blurred if not entirely erased as savings banks were allowed to offer interest bearing accounts on which drafts, that is, checks, could be written and commercial banks provided automatic transfer services between checking accounts and savings accounts. In addition, other financial intermediaries such as Credit Unions and money market mutual funds allowed shareholders to write drafts on their accounts. These changes have required new definitions of the money supply. We will use the simple M_1 definition to develop the basics of money supply analysis. The new alternative definitions of the money supply are presented in the appendix to this chapter.

In the following sections we first describe the instruments of monetary policy available to the Federal Reserve System—the Fed—and a bit of the institutional apparatus of money supply determination. Next we review the process of money supply expansion. This is followed by the development of a money supply model that makes clear the roles of the Federal Reserve, the public, and the banks in determining the actual money supply, and then we review some empirical estimates of the interest elasticity of the money supply. We then work this new money supply function into the static model by altering the LM curve to account for the sensitivity of the supply of money to the interest rate.

THE INSTRUMENTS OF MONETARY POLICY

Up to this point we have just assumed that the Federal Reserve System can change the level of the money supply when it chooses. The Fed controls the level of the money supply first by setting reserve requirements against demand deposits, and then by changing the amount of reserves it supplies, both on its own initiative and on the initiative of the banks. The reserve requirements state that commercial banks must hold as reserves some fraction z, say 20 percent, of their total demand-deposit liabilities, that is, of their customers' total checking account balances. These reserves are held in the form of commercial bank deposits at Federal Reserve Banks. Thus, if the reserve requirement z is 0.2, and the commercial banks hold a total of $40 billion in deposits at the Federal Reserve Banks, demand deposits cannot total more than $200 billion.

The Fed has three ways of changing the money supply, all operating through the reserve mechanism. First, it can increase reserves by open market operations. The Fed can buy, say, $100 million in federal government bonds in the market in New York, paying with checks drawn on itself. The sellers of the bonds will then deposit the checks drawn on the Fed in their banks. These checks then become the banks' claims on the Fed, or reserves from the banks' point of view. The banking system can then expand its demand-deposit liabilities by $500 million = ($100/0.2) by a technique that we describe in the next section. Open market operations of this sort—buying and selling in the bond market on the Fed's account—are handled by the Federal Reserve System's open market manager, usually a vice-president of the Federal Reserve Bank of New York, under supervision of the system's Open Market Committee, made up of the seven members of the system's Board of Governors in Washington and five of the Federal Reserve Bank presidents. These open market operations are the Fed's normal policy tool for making day-to-day changes in the money supply.

Banks can obtain additional reserves by borrowing from the Fed at the *discount rate* r_d, usually set somewhat below short-term market rates such as the rate on three-month Treasury bills. When a bank borrows at the Fed's *discount window,* a deposit at the Fed, in the amount of the borrowed reserves, is created in the bank's name. This is essentially the same procedure that a bank follows in making a loan to a private person; it credits his or her checking account with the amount of the loan. It should be noted here that, where reserve creation by open market operations comes at the Fed's initiative, an increase in borrowed reserves at the discount window comes at the banks' initiative. This distinction will be important in the money supply model we develop later in this chapter.

Open market and discount window operations both affect the money supply by changing the level of reserves with a given reserve ratio z. The Fed's third way to operate on the money supply is through changes in the reserve ratio itself. With z at 0.2, $40 billion in reserves will support a $200 billion money supply ($200 = 40/0.2). An increase in the reserve ratio z to 0.25 would reduce the money supply supported by the $40 billion reserve base to $160 billion = ($40/0.25). Thus reserve ratio increases amount to what is called *effective reserve* changes, changing the money supply that can be supported by a given amount of reserves.

The Fed tends to use its three policy instruments—open market operations, the discount window, and the reserve ratio—for somewhat different purposes. Open market operations are the technique used for day-to-day control of the money supply, or, more generally, credit conditions. If interest rates are rising faster or higher than the Open Market Committee desires, given the position of the economy, the manager of the open market account can buy bonds, shoring up bond prices and keeping interest rates down. This operation increases the money supply. Or, focusing on the money supply, if it is growing less rapidly than the Open Market Committee wishes, the manager can also buy bonds. These operations are conducted every day by the manager, and provide the Fed with a continuing, relatively unpublicized, way of controlling the money supply.

Discount window operations provide banks with the opportunity to acquire reserves in a pinch, within the context of overall credit conditions set by the Fed. Discount operations thus contribute to the degree of control over the money supply exercised by the banks.

Finally, reserve ratio changes are used by the Fed as an overt, well-publicized move to change effective reserves in a major way, as opposed to the normal, more continuous changes generated by open market operations. Thus, changes in the reserve ratio signal a major shift in the Fed's monetary policy, and serve as a warning of the change to the financial community.

In general, banks create deposits on which no interest is paid, in order to make loans on which interest is earned. The deposits are created in the process of making the loans; a loan is credited to the borrower's account. Thus, the incentive to increase deposits lies in the possibility of making profitable loans. When loan demand by potential borrowers falls off, banks may not create deposits up to the full limit that reserves would support. Thus, they may, from time to time, have on hand *excess reserves*. On the other hand, when loan demand is particularly strong, banks may borrow reserves at the discount window to support the additional deposit creation that accompanies the increase in loans. This degree of freedom that the banks have to hold excess reserves or to borrow reserves makes the money supply responsive, to a certain extent, to loan demand and the interest rate. When loan demand is strong and interest rates are high, the banks will squeeze excess reserves and increase borrowing at the discount window, increasing the money supply supported by a given amount of *unborrowed reserves* supplied by the Fed. Thus, the money supply itself will have a positive elasticity with respect to the interest rate, reducing the slope of the *LM* curve—that is, flattening it. Before we develop a simple model showing the relationships between *free reserves* (*excess reserves less borrowed reserves*), the interest rate, and the money supply, we will briefly review the mechanism of money expansion in a fractional reserve system.

THE MECHANISM OF MONETARY EXPANSION

As we have defined it, the money supply consists of currency and demand deposits which are supplied by commercial banks. These banks have balance sheets made up of liabilities, including demand deposits, and assets, including loans and reserves. The Federal Reserve requires that commercial banks retain a certain percent z of their liabilities as reserves, mainly as deposits in the Federal Reserve Banks.

Suppose that a decision is made by the Open Market Committee to expand the money supply. The manager of the Fed's open market account buys, in the bond market in New York, a certain amount of Treasury bonds, say, $100,000 worth, and issues a check, drawn on the Federal Reserve System, for $100,000 to the seller. The seller then deposits the check in his or her checking account in bank A, creating $100,000 in liabilities for the bank, the claim on the bank by the depositor, and also $100,000 in assets for the bank, the claim on the Federal Reserve System. If there is a 20 percent reserve requirement, bank A can loan $80,000 of its increase in assets and must retain $20,000 as reserves, as shown in Table 13.1.

The borrower of the $80,000 presumably spends it, transferring the $80,000 to the seller's bank, bank B, which can in turn loan out $64,000. This amount is transferred to bank C and the process continues. As a

TABLE 13.1

Balance sheet effects of a $100,000 increase in reserves

Bank A		Bank B		Bank C	
Assets	Liabilities	Assets	Liabilities	Assets	Liabilities
$100	$100	$80	$80	$64	$64
(20 reserves		(16 reserves		(12.8 reserves	
80 loans)		64 loans)		51.2 loans)	

result, the total increase in the money supply from the $100,000 reserve increase is given by

$$\Delta M = \$100,000 + 80,000 + 64,000 + \cdots,$$

or

$$\Delta M = \$100,000[1 + 0.8 + (0.8)^2 + \cdots]$$
$$= \$100,000 \; \frac{1}{1 - 0.8} = \$500,000.$$

Thus, in this simple example the change in the money supply is given by

$$\Delta M = \frac{1}{z} \Delta R, \qquad [1]$$

where ΔR is the initial reserve increase and z is the reserve ratio. This is a *reserve multiplier* giving the effect of reserve changes on the money supply M, exactly analogous to the simple investment or government spending multipliers that we developed in Chapter 3, which give the effects of changes in these variables on output.

The multiple increase in M came from each bank holding as reserves only a fraction, z, of its increased deposits—that is, liabilities—and lending out $1 - z$ percent of the increased deposits. Thus, from the point of view of each bank, it is simply lending out a fraction, $1 - z$, of its increased deposit inflow, but the system as a whole is increasing deposits by $1/z$ times the reserves increase.

This example includes two important oversimplifications. First, since the banks stay *loaned up,* excess reserves do not enter the picture so that the dependence of the money supply on the interest rate is obscured. Second, no place is provided for leakage into increased public holdings of currency, which would reduce the value of the reserves multiplier. We will now look at a more realistic model that incorporates these effects.

THE DETERMINANTS OF THE MONEY SUPPLY

The relationship between the money supply—currency in the hands of the public outside the banking system plus demand deposits—and unborrowed reserves provided by the Fed's open market operations depends on the public's preference between currency and demand deposits, and on the banks' holding of excess reserves or borrowing of reserves at the discount window. The latter activity will make the money supply a function of the interest rate and change somewhat our view of the *LM* curve. In this section we will develop a money supply model that follows fairly closely work done by Teigen. Then we will review some empirical results on the interest elasticity of the money supply obtained by Teigen, more recently by Modigliani, Rasche, and Cooper in the MPS model, and by Hendershott and De Leeuw.

The money supply M is currency held by the public C_p plus demand deposits held by the public in the commercial banking system D_p:

$$M = C_p + D_p. \tag{2}$$

The public holds h percent of its money in currency and $1 - h$ percent in checking account deposits, so that the currency component C_p is given by

$$C_p = hM, \tag{3}$$

and the demand-deposit component D_p is

$$D_p = (1 - h)M. \tag{4}$$

Earlier we introduced the required reserve ratio z, which gives the fraction of demand deposits D_p that must be held as required reserves RR:

$$RR = z \cdot D_p = z(1 - h)M. \tag{5}$$

Total reserves can be divided on the one hand into the *sources* of reserves, and on the other hand into the *uses* of reserves. The Fed provides unborrowed reserves, RU, mainly by buying U.S. government securities in the bond market. It also supplies borrowed reserves, RB, by lending to the commercial banks through the discount mechanism. These reserves are allocated to three uses. The banks can allocate their reserves to required reserves RR or to excess reserves RE, which is defined as total bank reserves less RR. In addition, some of the reserves provided by the Fed through open market purchases of bonds will end up as currency in the hands of the public C_p. Since both sources and uses must sum to total reserves R, this gives us the basic reserves identity.

$$RU + RB \equiv R \equiv RR + RE + C_p. \tag{6}$$

The reserve identity also gives us an expression for the policy instrument that the Fed directly controls through open market operations, unborrowed reserves:

$$RU = RR + RE - RB + C_p = RR + RF + C_p, \tag{7}$$

where *net free reserves*, RF, is defined as $RE - RB$. Free reserves should be sensitive to movements in the interest rate, as we will see shortly.

Equations (3) for C_p and (5) for RR can be combined with equation (7) for unborrowed reserves to yield an equation giving the money supply as a function of unborrowed reserves, controlled by the Fed, and free reserves, controlled by the commercial banks. Substituting from equations (3) and (5) for C_p and RR, respectively, into the right-hand side of (7), we have

$$RU = z(1 - h)M + RF + hM.$$

Solving this equation for M gives us the money supply equation,

$$M = \frac{RU - RF}{h + z(1 - h)} = \frac{RU - RF}{z + h(1 - z)}.$$ [8]

It should be apparent from equation (8) that the money supply M rises with an increase in RU, and falls with an increase in RF, z or h, holding the other variables constant. In other words, the money supply rises as the Fed provides more unborrowed reserves, and falls as free reserves increase, the public's preference for currency rises, or the Fed increases the reserve ratio. The banks, through decisions on excess reserves and borrowing at the discount window, determine RF, the Fed determines z directly and RU by open market operations, and the public's tastes between currency and checking deposits determine h. These variables taken together determine the money supply M.

Next we can separate the right-hand term of the money supply equation (8) into two pieces:

$$M = \frac{RU}{h + z(1 - h)} - \frac{RF}{h + z(1 - h)}.$$ [9]

The RU term in equation (9) gives the portion of the money supply determined mainly at the initiative of the Fed, which might be considered the exogenous or policy-determined portion of the money supply. Unborrowed reserves grew from about $19 billion in 1960 to $42 billion in 1979.

The RF term in equation (9) gives the portion of the money supply, which is mainly endogenously determined by the banking system in response to loan opportunities and interest rates. In tight credit conditions, when loan demand is high relative to the supply of unborrowed reserves from the Fed, we would expect free reserves to be negative, with banks squeezing excess reserves as tightly as possible and borrowing substantially at the discount window. When credit conditions are easier, RF will be positive. In the early 1960s, as GNP grew up to potential from 1960 to 1965, and then excess demand developed after 1965, free reserves fell steadily from $0.7 billion at the end of 1960 to zero at the end of 1965, and then more erratically to −$0.8 billion at the end of 1969. Since 1969 free reserves have typically been negative, fluctuating between zero and −$2.4 billion. As credit demand increased during the 1960s, the banking system added perhaps $1.5 billion to reserves by squeezing excess reserves and increasing borrowings at the discount window. During the 1970s, free-reserve fluctuations have accounted for up to $2.5 billion of changes in total reserves. In the depression days of the 1930s, free reserves were

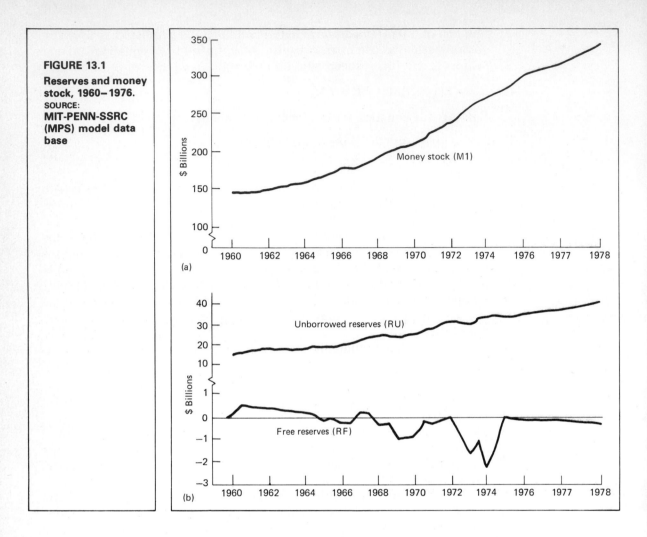

FIGURE 13.1

Reserves and money stock, 1960–1976.

SOURCE:

MIT-PENN-SSRC (MPS) model data base

positive, standing at $3 billion at the end of 1935 and $2 billion at the end of 1936. Movements in M_1, RU, and RF are shown in Figure 13.1.

This response of free reserves to changes in credit conditions, which might be measured by interest rates, gives the money supply a positive elasticity with respect to the interest rate.

EMPIRICAL ESTIMATES OF INTEREST ELASTICITY

Commercial banks lend at market interest rates, represented by r, and borrow reserves at the Fed's discount window at the discount rate r_d. As the market rate rises relative to the discount rate, banks will reduce excess reserves and increase their borrowing at the discount window to take advantage of the widening $r - r_d$ differential. Since free reserves RF equal excess reserves RE less borrowed reserves RB, both of these effects tend to reduce free reserves as the differential increases. Thus, we can write RF as a function of the $r - r_d$ differential,

$$RF = f(r - r_d),$$ [10]

with RF falling as $r - r_d$ increases.

With unborrowed reserves RU and the reserve ratio z determined exogenously by the Fed, and with h a parameter depending on the public's preferences between currency and demand deposits, the free-reserve function in equation (10) makes the money supply also a function of $r - r_d$, given RU, z, and h:

$$M = \frac{RU - f(r - r_d)}{h + z(1 - h)} = M(r - r_d),$$ [11]

and M' is positive.

The most direct way to estimate the interest elasticity of the money supply is to estimate a version of the free-reserve equation (10), and then calculate the effect of an r change on the money supply M through the money supply equation (11). Studies by Modigliani, Rasche, and Cooper, in developing the money market sector of the MPS model, and by Hendershott and De Leeuw, have estimated essentially linear versions of (10):

$$RF = a_0 - a_1(r - r_d).$$

Both studies estimate the coefficient a_1 of the interest differential to be about $500 million. Thus, an increase in the market interest rate r of one percentage point—from 15 to 16 percent, for example—will reduce free reserves by $500 million. With unborrowed reserves held constant, this gives an increase in $RU - RF$ of $500 million. Since $RU - RF(= RU + RB - RE$ by the definition of RF) was about $43 billion in 1979, an increase in $RU - RF$ of $500 million is a 1.2 percent ($= 0.5/43.0$) change. With short-term rates at about 15 percent during the same period, a one-point change in the market rate is a 6.7 percent ($= \frac{1}{15}$) change. Hence, during 1979, the elasticity of reserves to changes in the interest rate was about 0.18 ($=1.2/6.7$), a 1 percent increase in the interest rate will increase $RU - RF$ by about 0.18 percent.

We can convert this interest rate elasticity of reserves into an interest elasticity of the money supply by observing that the money supply function, equation (8), can be written as

$$M = \frac{1}{h - z(1 - h)} (RU - RF).$$ [12]

with the denominator held constant, a 1 percent change in $(RU - RF)$ will yield a 1 percent change in M. Thus, if a 1 percent increase in the interest rate r raises reserves, $RU - RF$, by 0.18 percent, it also raises the money supply by 0.18 percent, so that the elasticity of the money supply with respect to changes in r is about 0.18 percent on the Modigliani-Rasche-Cooper and Hendershott-De Leeuwe estimates.

A different approach to measurement of the interest elasticity was taken earlier by Teigen. He observed that in equation (9), repeated here,

$$M = \frac{RU}{h + z(1 - h)} - \frac{RF}{h + z(1 - h)},$$

the term with RU in the numerator is the portion of the money supply determined mainly by the Fed, while the term in RF is determined mainly by the banks. If the term in RU is defined as an exogenously determined M^*:

$$M^* \equiv \frac{RU}{h + z(1 - h)}, \qquad [13]$$

then the ratio of actual M to exogenous M^* is a function of the $r - r_d$ spread. Dividing all the terms in equation (12) by M^*, as defined in equation (13), we have

$$\frac{M}{M^*} = 1 - \frac{\dfrac{RF(r - r_d)}{h + z(1 - h)}}{M^*} = g(r - r_d), \qquad [14]$$

where the ratio M/M^* increases as $r - r_d$ increases since RF is a decreasing function of $r - r_d$, so that $g' > 0$.

Using the actual values of z and RU, and an average value of h, M^* can be constructed, on a quarterly basis, from equation (13). Then the ratio of actual M to constructed M^* can be related to $r - r_d$ in a linear regression,

$$\frac{M}{M^*} = b_0 + b_1(r - r_d),$$

to obtain an estimate of the interest sensitivity of M/M^*. Using this procedure, Teigen obtained estimates of the elasticity of the money supply with respect to changes in r ranging from 0.12 to 0.17, depending on the estimating technique used. For our purposes, this estimate is not at all different from the estimates coming from the direct relation of RF to $r - r_d$, discussed earlier. Thus, for a *typical* estimate of the interest elasticity of the money supply, culled from a small but rapidly growing literature on the subject, we can use 0.15. An increase of 1 percent (not percentage point) in the short-term interest rate will increase the money supply by about 0.15 percent.

THE MONEY SUPPLY IN THE STATIC MODEL

The interest sensitivity of the money supply can be worked into the static model in several ways. Figure 13.2 shows the supply and demand curves for real balances $m = M/P$. With an initial income level y_0, the demand-for-money curve is $m(y_0)$. With an initial real-money supply $m_0 (= M_0/P$; we hold P constant throughout this analysis), the interest rate is r_0. Now suppose income rises, due perhaps to an upward shift of the *IS* curve. Then the demand curve in Figure 13.2 shifts up to $m(y_1)$, and with a money supply fixed at m_0, as in Part II, the interest rate would rise to r_1.

But if the money supply is sensitive to changes in the interest rate, the money supply function through the initial equilibrium point r_0, y_0, m_0 looks like the positively sloped supply function $M(r - r_d)/P$ in Figure 13.2. In this case, the increased demand for money calls forth an increase in supply equal to $m_1 - m_0$ as the interest rate rises to r_2 instead of r_1. Thus, the interest elasticity of the money supply reduces the increase in r—from $r_1 - r_0$ to $r_2 - r_0$—needed to maintain money market equilibrium with a given increase in y, from y_0 to y_1, in Figure 13.2.

The last sentence says that with an interest-sensitive money supply, the slope of the *LM* curve is smaller than otherwise. This is shown in the four-quadrant *LM* diagram of Figure 13.3. At the initial interest rate r_0, the real-money supply is equal to $M(r_0)/P$ in the southwest quadrant. If the interest rate rises to r_1, with the money supply fixed at $M(r_0)/P$, as we assumed in Part II, the level of income must rise to y_1 to maintain money market equilibrium. The interest rate increase reduces the speculative *and* transactions demands for money, as we saw in Chapter 12, freeing money to support an increase in y within the constraint of a given m.

But now we have seen that the money supply is not fixed, but is an increasing function of the interest rate r:

$$M = M(r); \qquad M' > 0. \qquad [15]$$

Now an increase in the interest rate from r_0 to r_1 shifts the money supply out from $M(r_0)/P$ to $M(r_1)/P$ in Figure 13.3. This increase in money supply will support an increase in income to y_2, as opposed to y_1. Thus, the *LM*

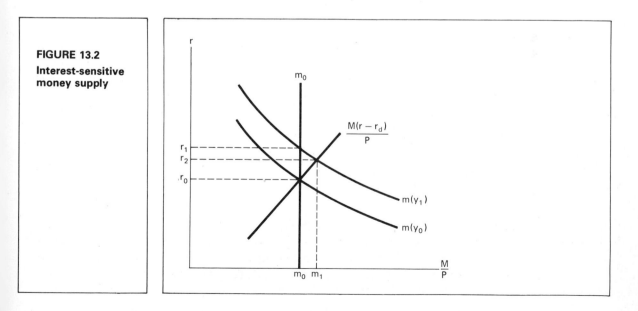

FIGURE 13.2

Interest-sensitive money supply

FIGURE 13.3

LM Curve with
interest-sensitive
money supply

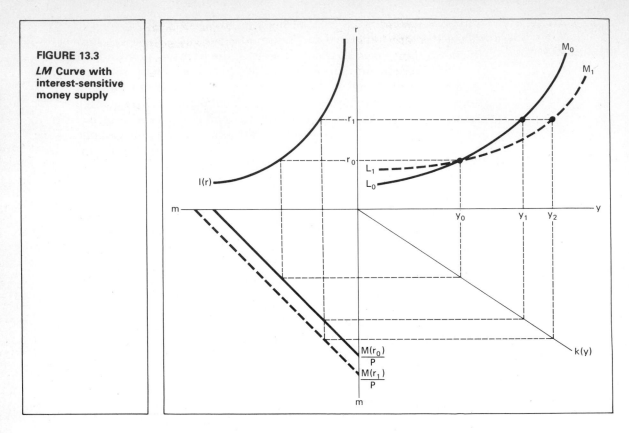

curve with an interest-sensitive money supply looks like L_1M_1 in Figure 13.3—flatter than L_0M_0 which assumes a fixed money supply.

The slope of *LM* is important for the derivation of multipliers in the extended model. A change in y of Δy will increase money demand by $k \cdot \Delta y$. A change in r of Δr will lead to a change in money demand of $l'(r) \cdot \Delta r$ as well as change in money supply of $M' \cdot \Delta r$ from equation (15). The change in money demand must equal the change in money supply if r and y are to remain on the *LM* curve:

$$k \cdot \Delta y + l'(r) \cdot \Delta r = M' \cdot \Delta r$$

or

$$k \cdot \Delta y = [M' - l'(r)] \cdot \Delta r.$$

Thus,

$$\frac{\Delta y}{\Delta r} = \frac{M' - l'(r)}{k} = \text{slope of } LM.$$

Since k and M' are positive and $l'(r)$ is negative, the slope of *LM* is positive. The larger the response of money supply to interest rates M', the flatter is the *LM* curve.

CONCLUSION: THE RELEVANCE OF INTEREST SENSITIVITY OF THE MONEY SUPPLY

In Chapter 12 we noted that if the interest elasticity of *demand* for money is small, the velocity of money may be taken as a constant. In this special case the *LM* equation can be reduced to

$$y = \hat{v}m, \qquad\qquad\qquad [16]$$

where $\bar{v}$ is the fixed velocity of money. Equation (16) is, then, one equation with one exogenous unknown, m. A monetarist could use it to predict real GNP (y) changes without reference to any other part of our multimarket system.

If the money *supply* is sensitive to interest rate changes, then this position does not hold up even in the face of an interest elasticity of the *demand* for money equal to zero. Suppose the demand for real balances is given by

$$m^d = \frac{1}{\bar{v}}y,$$

with zero interest elasticity. If the money supply function, at a given price level, can be written as

$$m^s = m(r),$$

then the equilibrium condition in the money market, in this world of interest-insensitive demand for money, is

$$m(r) = \frac{1}{\bar{v}}y.$$

Thus, if the money *supply* is sensitive to the interest rate, the money market equilibrium condition contains *both* y and r, regardless of the degree of interest elasticity of money demand. This means that both the *IS* and *LM* equations must play a role in the determination of equilibrium GNP, even in the extreme case where the demand for money is unrelated to interest rate changes. We now move on to a fuller discussion of the debate between monetarists and Keynesians that has been alluded to in these last two chapters.

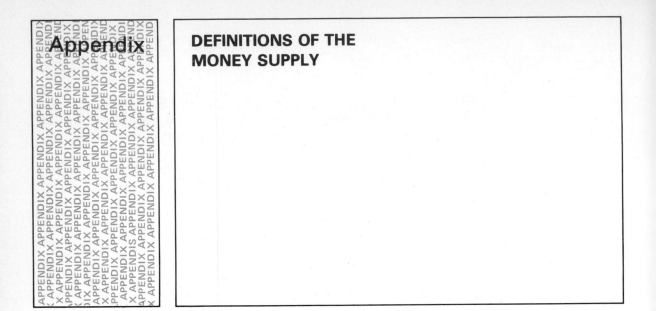

DEFINITIONS OF THE MONEY SUPPLY

As indicated in the text, in the late 1970s a number of changes took place in the ways people could allocate their liquid wealth in the United States. New types of accounts were permitted for existing institutions, and new institutions assumed more significant positions. Traditional savings banks permitted funds deposited with them to be transferred directly to others by the simple act of writing a check (for example, NOW accounts). Commercial banks developed automatic transfer systems (ATS) that kept an individual's checking account balance at zero: funds were transferred from savings to cover checks that were drawn and to savings when funds were deposited. Mutual funds that invested primarily in short-term debt instruments were developed to allow investors of modest means access to the high yields on assets previously available only to large investors. Shareholders in these funds were permitted, within limits, to "sell" their shares by the simple act of writing a draft against them.

For our purposes, the primary impact of these developments was to call into question the usefulness of the traditional measures of the money supply. For example, currency plus demand deposits at the commercial banks, the old M_1, no longer measured the funds available to the public that could easily be transferred for transactions purposes. In response to this, the Federal Reserve has developed a series of monetary definitions that have replaced M_1 and M_2. These changes, and changes in the reserve requirements applicable to financial institutions, do not alter the basics of money supply we have developed in Chapter 13. The complexities and refinements on the basics are within the domain of Money and Banking courses and texts.

TABLE 13A.1
 	
Definitions of the money supply
	M-1A: Demand deposits owned by the nonbank public at commercial banks
	+ Currency outside the Treasury, Federal Reserve, and the vaults of commercial banks
	
	M-1B: *M*-1A
	+ NOW accounts and ATS accounts at banks and thrift institutions
	+ Credit union share draft accounts
	+ Demand deposits at mutual savings banks
	
	M-2: *M*-1B
	+ Savings and small-denomination time deposits at all depository institutions
	+ Overnight repurchase agreements at commercial banks
	+ Certain overnight Eurodollars held by US residents
	
	M-3: *M*-2
	+ Large-denomination time deposits
	+ Term repurchase agreements
	
	L: *M*-3
	+ Other liquid assets:
	    Term Eurodollars held by US residents
	    Bankers acceptances
	    Commercial paper
	    Treasury bills and other liquid Treasury securities
	    US Savings bonds

In Table 13A.1 we describe the new measures as we believe such knowledge is required as part of basic, economic literacy. M-1A is very similar to the old M_1. M-1B is a broader measure including most other "checkable" deposits. M-2 is a broad measure of the very liquid assets in the hands of the public: those funds that are not in a readily transferable form will be very quickly. M-3 and L are very broad measures of the liquid wealth in the hands of the public.

QUESTIONS FOR DISCUSSION AND REVIEW

1. Assume that banks are required to hold reserves equal to $1/6$ of their demand deposits. No bank chooses to hold excess reserves and people hold all of their money balances in demand deposits.

    a. By how much will the money supply change if the Fed purchases $1 billion in bonds from the public?
    b. By how much will the money supply change if the Fed induces the banks to borrow $1 billion at the discount window?
    c. By how much will the money supply change if a very rich miser decides to hold $1 billion in cash?

How will your answers to the above change in qualitative terms if people choose to hold some percent of their money balances in the form of cash? What if banks choose to hold excess reserves?

2. In what way would you expect the money supply to change as people transfer money from checking accounts to savings accounts?

3. What will the *LM* curve look like if the Federal Reserve expands the money supply whenever interest rates are below 8% and contracts when rates exceed 8%? If the Federal Reserve expects that *on average* the *IS* curve is such that the desired income level, y_0, is consistent with an interest rate of 8%, would you recommend the above policy as the *IS* curve shifts about its position or would you recommend that the Fed attempt to keep the money supply at that level which equals $M(.08, y_0)$?

4. Explain how interest sensitivity in the supply of money alters the effectiveness of fiscal policy.

5. Prior to Chapter 13, expansionary or contractionary monetary policy could be indicated by simple reference to the stock of money. Recognizing that the stock of money is itself a variable, what indicator would you watch to see if monetary policy had eased or tightened?

SELECTED READINGS

J. G. Gurley and E. S. Shaw, "Financial Intermediaries and the Savings Investment Process," in R. L. Teigen, ed., *Readings in Money, National Income and Stabilization Policy*, 4th ed. (Homewood, Ill.: Irwin, 1978).

P. H. Hendershott and F. De Leeuw, "Free Reserves, Interest Rates, and Deposits: A Synthesis," *Journal of Finance*, June 1970.

F. Modigliani, R. Rasche, and J. P. Cooper, "Central Bank Policy, Money Supply, and the Short-term Rate of Interest," *Journal of Money, Credit, and Banking*, May 1970.

W. L. Smith, "The Instruments of General Monetary Control," in R. L. Teigen, ed., *Readings in Money, National Income and Stabilization Policy*, 4th ed. (Homewood, Ill.: Irwin, 1978).

R. L. Teigen, "The Demand for and Supply of Money," in R. L. Teigen, ed., *Readings in Money, National Income and Stabilization Policy*, 4th ed. (Homewood, Ill.: Irwin, 1978).

J. Tobin, "Commercial Banks as Creators of 'Money'," in R. L. Teigen, ed., *Readings in Money, National Income and Stabilization Policy*, 4th ed. (Homewood, Ill.: Irwin, 1978).

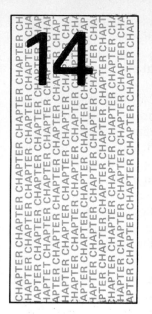

14

MONETARY AND FISCAL POLICY IN THE EXTENDED MODEL

Chapters 10 through 13 have reviewed, in some detail, both the theoretical underpinnings and empirical results concerning the four important functions on the demand side of the economy—consumer demand, investment demand, the demand for money, and the supply of money. Wherever it seemed appropriate in these chapters, we briefly discussed the effect of the analysis on our view of monetary and fiscal policy. Here, we pull together the results of Chapters 10 through 13 to obtain a more comprehensive view of how monetary and fiscal policies affect the economy, and of some important current policy issues concerning the use of monetary and fiscal policy. In considering the effects of policy, we focus on the timing relationships discussed in Chapters 10–13—for example, the lags of consumer expenditure changes behind income changes and of investment demand behind changes in output and interest rates. Thus, here we add the timing elements to the analysis of monetary and fiscal policy of Part II, which dealt mainly with changes from one equilibrium position to the next, with little discussion of the time path of the economy between equilibria.

In the first section of this chapter we summarize the basic static model as modified or extended by Chapters 10–13. Then we look at the general effects of fiscal and monetary policy changes in this extended model, focusing partly on timing effects and partly on the relationship between the labor market and supply curve assumptions and the effects of policy changes. This discussion leads naturally, in the third section, to a consideration of two significant challenges to the general Keynesian model. The first was raised by the monetarists and led to the heated *monetarist-Keynesian* debate of the 1960s. The second has been raised by those we would label the "new classical" economists. This dispute began in the

275

1970s and continues to be the focus of a good deal of economic research. Both of these attacks challenge the fundamental conclusion that the government can alter the output and employment levels existent in the economy through its use of stabilization policy in general and fiscal policy in particular.

In the final section we deal with the question of debt management from the point of view of stabilization policy. Here we will see what difference it makes, in stabilization terms, *how* a deficit of a given size is financed. Roughly speaking, an increase in the deficit will shift out the *IS* curve; however, the behavior of the *LM* curve will depend on to whom the Treasury sells its debt. The *LM* curve may remain fixed or shift out. Thus, the size of the *y* increase and whether the interest rate rises or falls for a given increase in the deficit depend partially on how it is financed. If wealth is a factor in the demand for money, it is even possible for the *LM* curve to shift inwards. This discussion will allow us to treat explicitly the issue of "crowding out."

THE STATIC MODEL EXTENDED

In Chapter 10 we saw that the consumption function of Part II must be extended at least to include the real value of assets a ($=A/P$). In addition, we saw that consumer expenditure will probably react quickly to a change in disposable income that seems permanent to consumers—as opposed to the effect of a temporary tax rate change. Further, the increase in consumer expenditure might exceed the increase in disposable income, at least in the short run, since the increase in *desired consumption* that follows the increase in income will reflect a disproportionate increase in purchases of consumer durables. The consumption function that emerged from Chapter 10 is repeated here:

$$c = c(y - t(y), a),$$
[1]

where real consumer net worth (assets) $a = A/P$. *Consumption c* increases as disposable income or real net-worth increases.

The second modification of the components of the *IS* product market equilibrium condition came in Chapter 11, where we saw that investment should be a function of the level of output, as well as the interest rate. Here it should be noticed that, in a model of static equilibrium *replacement investment* should depend on the *level* of output; *net investment*, due to changes in interest rates or output, does not appear in the static model, but is an important factor in determining the path of the economy between equilibria.

Thus, in the static model we have a function for replacement investment, given the equilibrium level of capital stock:

$$i = i(r, y).$$
[2]

Replacement investment increases as y rises and falls as r rises. In addition, to move from one equilibrium level of capital stock to another, net investment will appear as a function of the *change* in r or y. Thus, a drop in the interest rate r will increase the equilibrium capital stock. This will bring a transitory positive level of net investment as the capital stock is increased to its new equilibrium level. At that level, the static investment function of equation (2) will show a higher level of replacement investment as a function of the lower interest rate.

The *IS* curve

These modifications of the consumption and investment functions give us a revised form of the product market equilibrium condition,

$$y = c(y - t(y), a) + i(r, y) + g, \tag{3a}$$

or

$$s(y - t(y), a) + t(y) = i(r, y) + g, \tag{3b}$$

shown as the *IS* curve in Figure 14.1.

In Figure 14.1, the position of the curve showing saving plus tax revenue—gross social saving—as a function of the level of real income is determined by the level of real consumer net worth a_0. For a given level of income, reduction in real net worth, normally due to a price increase in the short run, would reduce consumer expenditure, and thus increase saving. This would rotate the $s + t$ curve in the southeast quadrant of

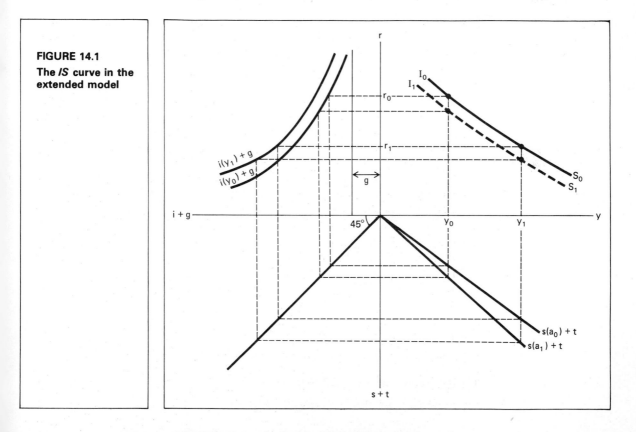

FIGURE 14.1

The *IS* curve in the extended model

Figure 14.1 down, or clockwise, increasing the level of saving corresponding to any given level of income y.

The investment function $i = i(r, y)$, gives us a family of curves in the northwest quadrant of Figure 14.1. As income rises from y_0 to y_1, the level of (replacement) investment associated with any given interest rate rises, so that the demand curve shifts from $i(y_0) + g$ to $i(y_1) + g$ in Figure 14.1.

At an initial real-asset level a_0, which fixes an $s + t$ function in Figure 14.1, the IS curve giving the r, y points that maintain equilibrium in the product market can be traced using the appropriate $i(y)$ curves. As we saw in Chapter 11, introduction of the sensitivity of investment demand to the level of real output flattens the IS curve. For a_0, the IS curve I_0S_0 is traced out as an illustration in Figure 14.1.

Now if the real value of consumer net worth falls to a_1, due perhaps to a price increase, the IS curve will shift down to I_1S_1 in Figure 14.1. At any given level of income there is a greater desire to save (*ex ante* saving is higher). Thus, at any given level of the interest rate, the equilibrium level of output in the product market will fall as the price level rises due to the falling level of consumer demand as the real value of assets is reduced. Recognition of the important role that real net worth plays in the determination of consumer expenditure and saving introduces real assets as a factor that shifts the IS curve in the r, y space of Figure 14.1.

The *LM* curve   In Chapter 12 we developed four different views of the demand for money, all of which came to the same function that we used in Part II. For a given stock of liquid assets, the speculative demand for real balances is negatively related to the interest rate; the transactions demand is positively related to the level of transactions, or income, and negatively related to the interest rate. Thus the demand-for-money function can be written as the demand for real balances:

$$\frac{M}{P} = m(r, y) \quad \text{or} \quad M = P \cdot m(r, y).$$

As we saw in Chapter 13, for a given amount of unborrowed reserves supplied by the Fed, and given the public's preferences between money and currency, the supply of money is an increasing function of the interest rate,

$$M = M(r); \qquad M' > 0.$$

Equating money supplied to money demanded gives us the equilibrium condition for the money market,

$$M(r) = P \cdot m(r, y) \quad \text{or} \quad \frac{M(r)}{P} = m(r, y). \tag{4}$$

With the demand for real balances M/P approximated by

$$m(r, y) \approx l(r) + k(y); \qquad l' < 0 \quad \text{and} \quad k' > 0,$$

we can construct the LM curve of Figure 14.2.

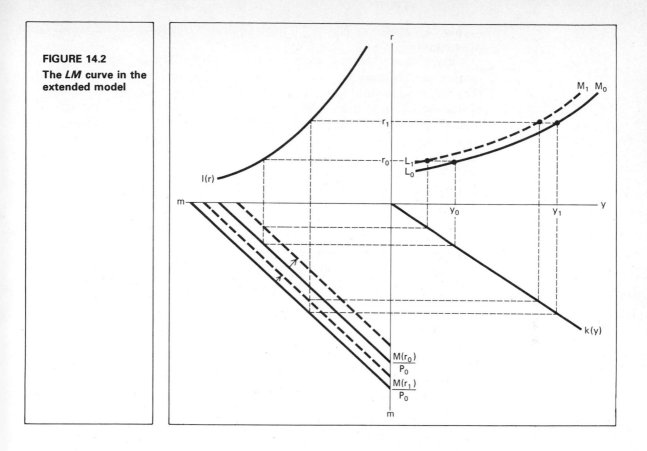

FIGURE 14.2
The *LM* curve in the extended model

The $k(y)$ curve in the southeast quadrant gives the movement in the demand for real balances as y changes. The $l(r)$ curve in the northwest quadrant gives changes in demand—both speculative and transactions—as the interest rate changes. The 45° line in the southwest quadrant constrains the two components of demand to add to total supply of real balances, $M(r)/P_0$. Here P_0 is the given initial price level. As the interest rate changes, this supply of real balances changes.

To trace out the LM curve in Figure 14.2, we can begin with an initial interest rate r_0, which fixes the supply of real balances at $M(r_0)/P_0$. At r_0, the liquidity preference schedule $l(r)$ shows an interest-sensitive demand for money at $l(r_0)$ in Figure 14.2. With $M(r_0)/P_0$ fixed by r_0, this leaves $M(r_0)/P_0 - l(r_0) = k(y_0)$ for transactions balances, an amount that will support income level y_0. This establishes the r_0, y_0 point on the LM curve in the northeast quadrant in Figure 14.2.

At interest rate r_1, greater than r_0, the supply of real balances expands to $M(r_1)/P_0$ due to shrinkage of free reserves in the banking system. Tracing counterclockwise around the four-quadrant diagram from r_1 to $M(r_1)/P_0$ to y_1, we can establish another money market equilibrium point r_1,

y_1. The L_0M_0 curve of Figure 14.2 can be drawn through the two points r_0, y_0 and r_1, y_1.

If the money supply were fixed at the level $M(r_0)$, then the money market equilibrium y level corresponding to r_1 would be less than y_1, since the trace from r_1 would bounce off the $M(r_0)/P_0$ money supply line instead of the $M(r_1)/P_0$ line. In this fixed money supply case the LM curve would then be steeper than that shown in Figure 14.2. Since an increase in r would not increase the money supply, for any given increase in r the increase in money market equilibrium y would be smaller than in the flexible money supply case where $M = M(r)$.

The L_0M_0 curve of Figure 14.2 is drawn on the assumption of a given initial price level P_0. An increase in the price level will reduce the supply of real balances—or what amounts to the same thing, increase the demand for nominal balances at any given r and y—and shift the LM curve up and to the left. In Figure 14.2 a price level increase shifts each M/P line in to the right, as shown by the dashed lines in the southwest quadrant. This represents a reduction in M/P and a drop in the money market equilibrium y associated with any given r. Thus, a price increase shifts the LM curve up toward the L_1M_1 curve in Figure 14.2.

The aggregate demand curve

Given the money value of assets and the price level, the IS equation (3) and the LM equation (4) are two equations in two unknowns, r and y. These can be solved for equilibrium demand-side r and y, given P; the solution is shown graphically as the intersection of the I_0S_0 and the L_0M_0 curves in Figure 14.3, which are the I_0S_0 and L_0M_0 curves from Figures 14.1 and 14.2, based on the initial price level P_0.

As in Part II, we can derive the economy's aggregate demand curve by varying the price level and observing the movement of equilibrium demand-side y in Figure 14.3. An increase in the price level, we have seen,

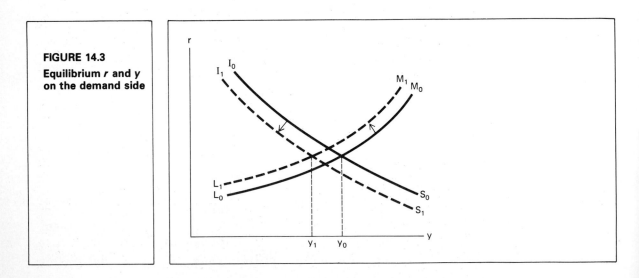

FIGURE 14.3
Equilibrium _r_ and y on the demand side

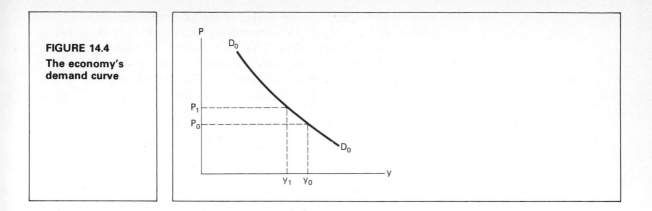

FIGURE 14.4

The economy's demand curve

reduces real household net worth, increasing desired saving at any income level and rotating the $s + t$ line in Figure 14.1 downward. This reduction in consumption demand shifts the IS curve to the left, toward I_1S_1 in Figure 14.3. As we saw in the previous section, a price level increase also shifts the LM curve left toward L_1M_1 in Figure 14.3 by reducing the supply of real balances. Thus, as prices rise, both the IS and LM curves shift left in Figure 14.3, reducing the equilibrium level of output.

This relationship between equilibrium demand-side output and the price level is shown as the economy's demand curve D_0D_0 in Figure 14.4. As the price level rises from P_0 to P_1 consumption demand is reduced directly due to the reduction in the real value of assets—our analog to the Pigou effect. As should be apparent from Figure 14.3, the drop in the real-money supply, shifting LM left, tends to raise interest rates. On the other hand, the drop in income that follows the drop in consumer demand, shifting the IS curve left, reduces the demand for money, tending to reduce interest rates. Thus, the price increase may raise or lower interest rates, depending on the relative sensitivity of both the supply of and the demand for money to the interest rates, on the one hand, and of consumer demand to real assets, on the other.

With investment demand a function of both real output and the interest rates, $i = i(r, y)$, the leftward movement of the IS and LM curves virtually assures a decrease in investment demand from one static equilibrium to the next with the price level rising. The interest rate may rise or fall as P rises from P_0 to P_1, but with the drop in income and output, the equilibrium capital stock will drop, reducing replacement investment in the new static equilibrium. There will also be a transitory negative net investment to reduce the capital stock between equilibria.

The drop in consumption demand and investment demand following an increase in the price level from P_0 to P_1 moves equilibrium demand-side output from y_0 to y_1 in Figures 14.3 and 14.4. The reduction in consumption demand will come fairly quickly, probably within two to three quarters, certainly within a year, after the price increase. The speed of reaction of *consumer expenditure* will probably be more rapid than this, since, as we saw in Chapter 10, expenditure must overadjust to bring consumption of durables into line. The reduction in investment demand may come fairly rapidly as firms react to excess capacity by cutting net investment to reduce capital stock. After this transitory reduction of net investment, which reduces equilibrium capital stock, is completed over the period of perhaps one to two years, gross investment will rise to its new replacement investment level $i_1 = i(r_1, y_1)$, lower than the initial $i_0 = i(r_0, y_0)$ level but higher than gross investment during the transitory period of negative net investment.

Thus, the demand curve of Figure 14.4 reflects changes in equilibrium demand-side output due to the effect of price level changes on both consumption and investment demand. An increase in the price level from P_0 to P_1 will bring a reduction in equilibrium demand-side output from y_0 to y_1 over a period of a year or two. Due to the transitory drop in net-investment demand, income may temporarily fall below y_1; as gross investment revives, equilibrium demand-side output will then rise to y_1.

Labor market equilibrium   The supply-side equilibrium conditions are the same as those developed in Chapter 9, so we do not have to discuss them in detail here. Output y is linked to employment by the production function

$$y = y(N, \bar{K}).$$ [5]

The demand for labor by an individual firm sets employment at the level at which the real-wage rate the employer pays equals the marginal product of labor. In the aggregate, this gives us a demand-for-labor function that can be written as the wage employers will offer as a function of the price level and the level of employment,

$$W^d = P \cdot f(N).$$ [6]

The wage offered along the labor demand function decreases for an increase in employment; $f' < 0$. Here $f(N)$ can be thought of as the aggregate marginal product of labor (*MPL*), so that equation (6) equates the *MPL* to the real wage $w = W/P$. The labor demand function (6) is shown in Figure 14.5, given the initial price level P_0.

On the supply side of the labor market, we have the supply function written as an equation giving the money wage

$$W^s = h(P, N).$$ [7]

This is a more general formulation—and somewhat easier to write—than the labor-supply function of Chapters 6–9. Workers require an increase in the nominal wage W to provide additional labor at a given price level. Thus the supply functions in Figure 14.5 are positively sloped. And here an increase in the price level raises wage demands, that is, shifts the labor supply curve up in the W, N space. A decrease in the price level leads to a reduction in the money wage necessary to call forth a given supply of labor. In the general Keynesian model, the vertical shift in the supply

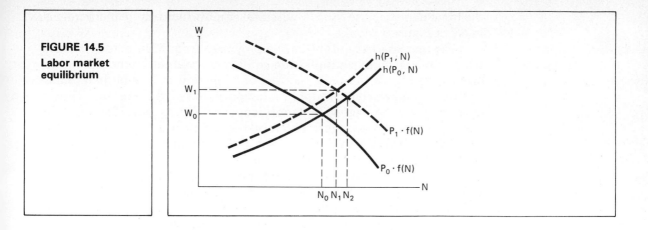

FIGURE 14.5

Labor market equilibrium

curve will be less than the price change leading to the shift. This results either from the incomplete adjustments in price perceptions or expectations by labor, as discussed in Chapter 6, or from nominal-wage rigidities as described in Chapter 8. In the classical case where labor supply depends only on the real wage, the price level would enter multiplicatively, and equation (7) could be written as $W = P \cdot g(N)$.

Equating the demand wage to the supply wage gives us the labor market equilibrium condition

$$P \cdot f(N) = h(P, N). \tag{8}$$

For a given price level P_0, equation (8) can be solved for the equilibrium level of employment N_0. Since equilibrium employment is *defined* as that level of N that equates W^d and W^s, the equilibrium N_0, along with P_0, can be inserted into either equation (6) or (7) to obtain the equilibrium money wage rate. This solution of the labor market equilibrium equation is shown graphically in Figure 14.5, where the intersection of the supply and demand functions, at the initial price P_0, gives equilibrium employment N_0 and wage rate W_0.

The aggregate supply curve

We can derive the aggregate supply curve by changing the price level in the labor market, Figure 14.5, and observing how supply-side equilibrium output changes. With our general labor supply function $W = h(P, N)$, an increase in the price level from P_0 to P_1 shifts both the labor demand and labor supply curves up in Figure 14.5.

The price increase raises marginal revenue products for all firms, so they all want to expand employment and will offer a higher wage to attract workers. On the other hand, the price increase reduces the purchasing power of money wages, and thus should raise wage demands, shifting the labor supply curve up. If labor supply is less sensitive to price changes than it is to wage changes, the upward shift of the labor supply function to $h(P_1, N)$ will be smaller than the demand function shift to $P_1 \cdot f(N)$, so that the price increase from P_0 to P_1 will raise equilibrium employment from N_0 to N_1 in Figure 14.5.

The increase in equilibrium employment from Figure 14.5 is translated into a change in supply-side equilibrium output by the production function in Figure 14.6. The increase of employment from N_0 to N_1 raises equilibrium output on the supply side from y_0 to y_1 in Figure 14.6. This, in turn, gives us the aggregate supply curve of Figure 14.7. The price increase from P_0 to P_1 in Figure 14.5 raised equilibrium employment from N_0 to N_1. This increase in employment yields an increase in supply-side equilibrium output from y_0 to y_1 in Figure 14.6, so that we have the supply curve relationship between the price level and equilibrium output on the supply side shown as S_0S_0 in Figure 14.7. As P rises from P_0 to P_1, supply-side output rises from y_0 to y_1.

In the polar real-wage labor supply model, where $W^s = P \cdot g(N)$, a price level increase would shift the labor supply and demand functions up by the same amount in Figure 14.5, so that equilibrium employment remain unchanged. In this case the supply curve of Figure 14.7 would be vertical. In the polar money wage model, the price increase would not shift the labor supply function at all, so that the price increase from P_0 to P_1

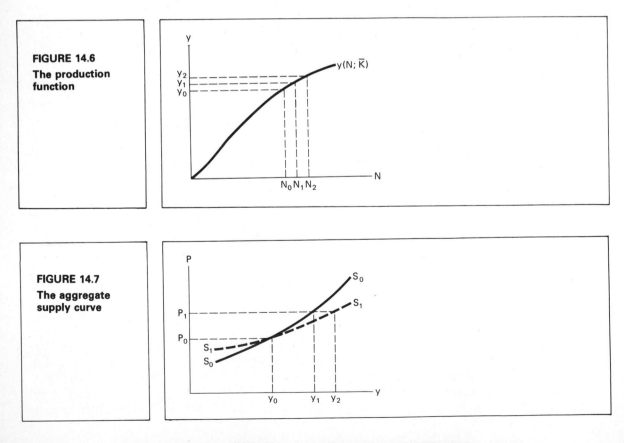

FIGURE 14.6
The production function

FIGURE 14.7
The aggregate supply curve

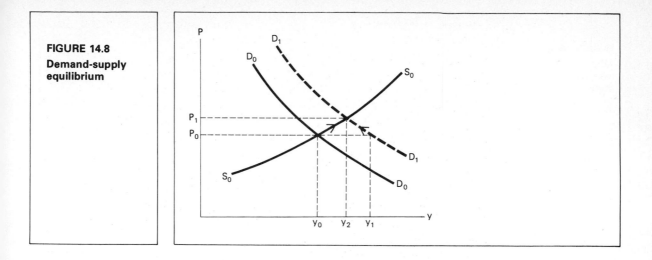

FIGURE 14.8
Demand-supply equilibrium

would raise employment to N_2 in Figure 14.5, raising equilibrium output on the supply side to y_2 in Figures 14.6 and 14.7. Thus, in the polar money wage case the supply function would be the flatter S_1S_1 curve in Figure 14.7.

Equilibrium in the extended model

In Figure 14.8 we bring together the demand curve of Figure 14.4 and the supply curve of Figure 14.7 to determine equilibrium price and output, P_0, y_0. Given equilibrium P_0 and y_0 we can trace back through the system to determine the equilibrium values of the other variables.

On the supply side, y_0 gives us equilibrium employment N_0 through the production function of Figure 14.6. With N_0 and P_0, we can determine W_0 in Figure 14.5. Going back on the demand side, the equilibrium price level P_0 gives us the position of the I_0S_0 curve in Figures 14.1 and 14.3. Combining equilibrium y_0 and the position of the IS curve gives us equilibrium r_0 in Figure 14.3. With r_0 we can determine the level of the money supply $M(r_0)$, which, combined with P_0, fixes the position of the LM curve at L_0M_0 in Figure 14.3. Thus, the four-equation system of the IS equation (3), the LM equation (4), the production function (5), and the labor market equation (8) give us the equilibrium values of the key variables y, r, P, and N. Given r we can determine the value of M, and given N we can determine the value of W. Next we can briefly follow through the effects of a fiscal policy change in this system, focusing on the likely timing effects suggested by the empirical work reviewed in Part III.

THE EFFECTS OF FISCAL POLICY CHANGES

As usual, a fiscal policy increase in government purchases g shifts the IS curve in Figure 14.9 out to I_1S_1 and shifts the economy's demand curve in Figure 14.8 out to D_1D_1. The demand increase raises equilibrium output demanded at the initial price level to y_1 in Figures 14.8 and 14.9 creating excess demand measured by $y_1 - y_0$, which pulls the price level up.

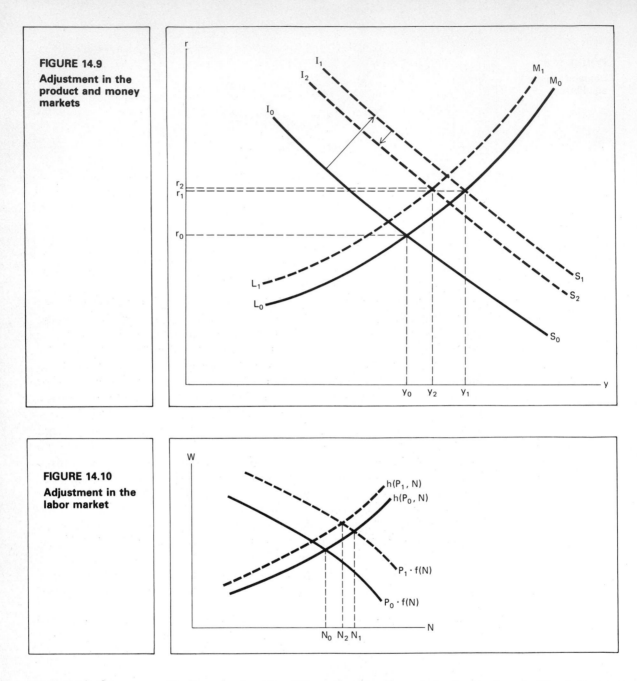

FIGURE 14.9
Adjustment in the product and money markets

FIGURE 14.10
Adjustment in the labor market

Adjustment in the labor market

On the supply side of the economy, the excess demand and price increase will shift the demand-for-labor curve up fairly rapidly, toward $P_1 \cdot f(N)$ in Figure 14.10, so that employment and output respond quickly to the increase in demand. The upward shift in the labor supply curve toward $h(P_1, N)$—due to the workers perceiving a cut in purchasing power and, as a result, raising wage demands—will come more slowly and with a lag. Thus, there is a possibility of an overadjustment of employment on the supply side, with the price increase initially raising employment along the original $h(P_0, N)$ labor supply curve to N_1. Then, once adjustment seems complete, the labor supply will begin shifting up toward $h(P_1, N)$ tending to reduce employment toward N_2 in Figure 14.10.

The effect on consumer demand

The increase in income, on the demand side, should be reflected fairly quickly in a rise in consumer demand. This is true especially for consumer durables, as consumers increase purchases to adjust their future stream of consumption of services from the durables upward. The increase in consumer expenditure on nondurable goods and on services should rise more gradually, over a period of two quarters to a year. Thus, the increase in consumer demand in response to the increase in income generated by the initial g change should come fairly rapidly and be initially weighted toward an increase in purchases of consumer durables.

The price rise generated by the excess demand shown in Figure 14.8 will reduce the real value of household net worth, tending to increase saving and reduce consumption somewhat. The price increase thus shifts the IS curve back from I_1S_1 toward I_2S_2 in Figure 14.9, partially offsetting the effects of the initial g increase.

The effect on investment demand

If the increase in demand comes at a time when the economy is operating near full capacity, perhaps above 85 percent on the Federal Reserve index, investment demand should respond within two or three quarters through the accelerator mechanism. This will bring a spurt of net investment to increase the capital stock to a new equilibrium level. Once this is completed, after a year or so, investment demand should taper off toward the continuing replacement requirements of the larger capital stock. This level of investment demand is represented in the static $i = i(r, y)$ investment function, and is reflected in the slope of the IS curves of Figure 14.9.

But the accelerator mechanism creates the likelihood of overadjustment on the demand side. The g increase raises output. This increase generates a spurt of net investment which further raises output. This spurt of net investment could be represented by a further temporary shift in the IS curve out beyond I_1S_1 in Figure 14.9. Then after a period of perhaps two years, investment demand will fall off to replacement level, shifting the IS curve back down to I_1S_1, or to I_2S_2 if the asset effect on consumer demand has taken hold.

Adjustment in the money market

The price rise generated by the excess demand shown in Figure 14.8, and the increase in income as y and N rise, both increase the demand for money, pulling interest rates up. The interest rate increase works to eliminate the excess demand in the money market both by reducing the demand for money and by increasing the money supply.

The rise in interest rates due to the increase in transactions demand following the increase in income and output, and the money supply response to the interest rate increase, are both built into the slope of the LM curve, as is shown in Figure 14.2. Thus, these money market adjustments are represented in Figure 14.9 by the rise in r from r_0 along the initial LM curve L_0M_0.

The effect of the price increase, raising the demand for nominal balances or reducing the supply of real balances, is reflected in a leftward shift of the LM curve toward L_1M_1 in Figure 14.9. Thus, at the *initial* price level P_0, equilibrium demand-side output rises to y_1 as a result of the g increase. The subsequent price increase shifts both IS and LM left, reducing equilibrium demand-side output toward y_2 in Figure 14.9.

Demand and supply in the new equilibrium

The movement of demand-side equilibrium output back toward y_2 as the price level rises is shown as a movement along the new demand curve D_1D_1 in Figure 14.8. At the same time, equilibrium supply-side output is increasing with the increase in employment toward N_2 in Figure 14.10. This is represented by a movement along the initial supply curve from y_0 to y_2 in Figure 14.8. The price level continues to rise until excess demand is eliminated at P_1, y_2.

For a significant increase in g, movement from P_0, y_0 to P_1, y_2 might take two or three years in the U.S. economy. As we have seen, it is quite possible that the economy will overshoot the final y_2 level, both because of the net-investment spurt that shifts IS temporarily beyond I_1S_1 in Figure 14.9, and because of the lag in the shift of the labor supply curve up toward $h(P_1, N)$. Thus, in reality we are likely to see a cyclical movement from the initial y_0 to the final y_2, with real output first rising above y_2, then falling back to the final equilibrium. This would be the case regardless of which policy instrument is used to stimulate the economy.

KEYNESIANS, MONETARISTS, AND THE "NEW CLASSICAL" ECONOMICS

The model we have just described is the "Keynesian" or "neo-Keynesian" model of the current macroeconomic literature. It has important distinguishing features both on the demand side and on the supply side. On the demand side, in the general Keynesian model, *both monetary and fiscal policy shift the aggregate demand curve*, putting pressure on both P and y. On the supply side, *the aggregate supply curve has a positive slope in the short run, and tends to become vertical only in the long run*. The short-run nonverticality of the aggregate supply curve could come either from slowly adjusting price perceptions or expectations on the part of labor as described in Chapter 6, or from nominal wage rigidities in the short run, as described in Chapter 8. Either of these will result in a positively-sloped short-run aggregate supply curve. If we combine the Keynesian assumptions on demand and supply, we obtain the standard result from the basic static model that *both expansionary monetary and fiscal policy will pull up both P and y in the short run*.

There are two schools of macroeconomic theory that disagree with this basic Keynesian proposition. One is the "demand-side monetarist" school, associated with the popular writings of Milton Friedman. Taken to an extreme, the monetarists position seems to be that *as between aggregate fiscal and monetary policies, only monetary policy can shift the aggregate demand curve.* The basic assumption of the monetarists is that the interest elasticities of both the demand for and the supply of money are zero, so that the *LM* curve is vertical. In this case fiscal policy changes do not shift the aggregate demand curve. Fiscal policy alters the composition, but not the level, of national output. But monetary policy, shifting a vertical *LM* curve, does shift the aggregate demand curve, moving *P* and *y* in proportions that depend on the slope of the aggregate supply curve. Thus in the monetarist world, interest elasticities in the money market are essentially zero, giving the result that only monetary policy can shift aggregate demand.

The other dissenting school is the "New Classical" macroeconomics, associated with Robert E. Lucas of Chicago and Thomas J. Sargent of Minnesota. Their position is that with "rational expectations" on the part of both workers and employers, *the aggregate supply curve is vertical even in the short run.* In terms of our general basic static model, the new classical macroeconomics assumes that workers, on average, know that prices will rise after a fiscal or monetary expansion, and by roughly how much. Consequently, they immediately shift the labor supply curve of Figure 14.10 up by the full amount of the expected price increase. And that increase is, on average, the actual price increase. In terms of the supply-side analysis of Chapter 6, in the new classical model $P^* = P$. *Thus the new classical economics assumes full and immediate nominal wage adjustment to the actual price change, making the aggregate supply curve vertical in the short run.* This is the power of the assumption of rational expectations. *In the new classical economics, aggregate demand measures can only move the price level, with employment and output determined on the supply side.*

In the next two subsections we develop these models a bit more thoroughly. These two positions are analytically different—Milton Friedman is not a new classical economist. There is a tendency in the economic literature and in journalistic writing to merge them into one position.

The monetarist model

The basic monetarist model makes a crucial simplifying assumption about money supply and demand: both have zero interest-elasticity. This assumption makes the *LM* curve vertical, and carries the implication that fiscal policy does not shift the aggregate demand curve. Let's work through the analysis.

The demand-for-money function of Chapter 11 can be written as

$$M^d = P \cdot m(r, y).$$

If the elasticity of demand for real balances with respect to real income is about unity, we can rewrite the demand for money in Friedman's quantity theory form,

$$M^d = P \cdot y \cdot k(r). \qquad [9]$$

Frequently this demand-for-money equation is written in terms of the income velocity of money, $v(r)$, which is the inverse of $k(r)$ in equation (9),

$$M^d = P \cdot y \cdot \frac{1}{v(r)} \cdot$$

The monetarist model assumes that the demand for money is insensitive to changes in the interest rate. This means that $k(r)$ in equation (9) and the income velocity v, are not really functions of r, so that the demand function for money can be written as

$$M^d = P \cdot y \cdot \frac{1}{v} = \frac{P}{v} \cdot y,$$

with a fixed income velocity v. With the money supply given exogenously as $M^s = \bar{M}$, the money market equilibrium condition in the monetarist model can be written as

$$\bar{M} = \frac{P}{v} \cdot y. \tag{10}$$

To translate equation (10) into an LM curve in r, y space, note that, given $\bar{M}$ and P_0, equilibrium y is determined in the money market independently of the interest rate. At $P = P_0$, equation (10) fixes y at $y_0 = \bar{M}v/P_0$. The LM curve then is vertical at y_0, which is determined independently of the interest rate, as shown in Figure 14.11. To complete the demand side of the monetarist model, we can add the usual I_0S_0 curve with initial price level P_0. In this case, the IS curve serves to determine the interest rate r_0, with y_0 fixed in the money market.

A price level increase from P_0 to P_1 reduces money market equilibrium y to y_1 shifting the vertical LM curve to L_1M_1 in Figure 14.11. This relationship between P and y gives us the normal negatively sloped de-

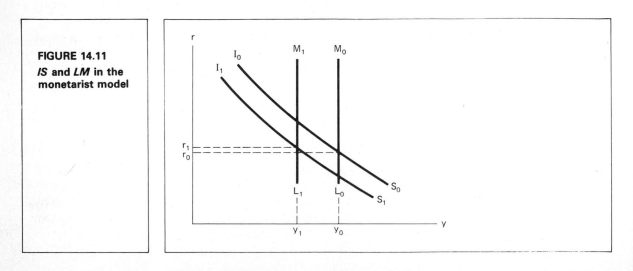

FIGURE 14.11

IS and *LM* in the monetarist model

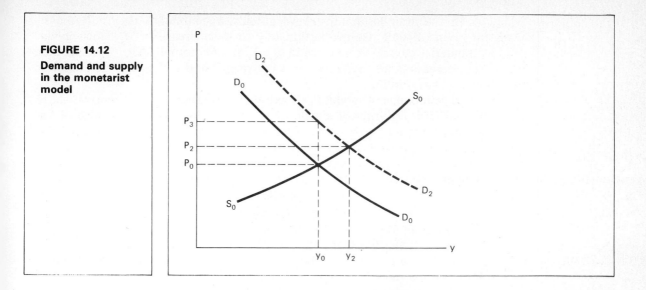

FIGURE 14.12

Demand and supply in the monetarist model

mand curve of Figure 14.12, D_0D_0. The price increase, of course, also shifts the *IS* curve left to I_1S_1 in Figure 14.11. This affects the interest rate, but not the level of income, in the monetarist model.

The demand curve D_0D_0 in Figure 14.12 can be paired with either a positively-sloped supply curve or the vertical supply curve of the classical case. The monetarist assumption about the *LM* curve is a demand-side assumption. It does not restrict possibilities on the supply side. Here we see the difference between the monetarist school and the new classical school. In the short run, the monetarists do not assume that the aggregate supply curve is vertical. In Figure 14.12 we include a positively-sloped supply curve S_0S_0. The intersection of the demand and supply curves determines equilibrium P_0, y_0, and y_0 can be traced back to the $IS - LM$ diagram of Figure 14.11 to determine r_0.

In this monetarist model, an increase in g or a cut in t will shift the IS curve up in Figure 14.11, but leave the vertical L_0M_0 curve unchanged. There is no change in equilibrium demand-side y, so there is no shift of the demand curve in Figure 14.12. The upward shift of the IS curve in Figure 14.11 raises interest rates, reducing investment enough to just offset the g increase or the policy-induced consumer expenditure increase. This is a full "crowding out" effect on investment by fiscal policy. Thus, in the monetarist model, a fiscal policy change alters the composition of final output but leaves both equilibrium P_0 and y_0 unchanged. This result occurs regardless of whether the economy's supply curve is positively sloped or vertical.

An increase in the money supply $\bar{M}$ will shift the vertical LM curve of Figure 14.11 out in the monetarist model. This will shift the demand curve of Figure 14.12 out to D_2D_2. If the labor supply follows our general model $W = h(P, N)$, the price level and output will rise along the S_0S_0 curve to P_2,

y_2. On the other hand, if the classical real-wage model holds, y will remain at y_0 and P will rise proportionately to the increase in M. Thus, in the monetarist model, an increase in $\bar{M}$ will raise nominal GNP, $P \cdot y$. Whether the increase is all in P or is split between P and y depends on the labor market assumption.

The monetarist model is an extreme special case of our general static model with the interest elasticity of demand for money, and also of the supply of money, for that matter, set at zero. Empirical studies of the money supply and demand functions suggest that this assumption is not generally correct. At very high interest rates where almost the entire money stock is used for transactions purposes—and velocity is near a technical maximum—the monetarist model would be relevant as a special case. But in general the interest elasticity of the excess demand for money, demand less supply, may be around -0.65 measured over three quarters, so that the strict monetarist model will not generally hold.

The new classical model   As the name suggests, the new classical model is a modern version of the classical model, which we analyzed in Chapters 6 and 7. The difference between the new classical school and the general Keynesian model is on the supply side. In the Keynesian model the aggregate supply curve is positively sloped in the short run, and tends to become vertical only in the long run. For the "new classicists," the aggregate supply curve is vertical in the short run as well. What are the basic assumptions that take us from the Keynesian supply side to the new classical version?

The new classical economists begin with the assumption of no wage or price rigidities. This eliminates one reason why the aggregate supply curve would be nonvertical in the short run. Next, they assume that in the long run there is no price misperception or money illusion. This is in agreement with the supply side view of the general Keynesian model of Chapter 6, where in the long run P^* approaches P. This, in turn, implies that the long-run aggregate supply curve of the economy is roughly vertical.

Next comes the assumption that is crucial to the new classical view. All actors, or "agents," in the economy—workers, firms, consumers—are assumed to know approximately what the structure of the economy is. They have seen that in the past, on average, monetary and fiscal policy shifts have, *in the long run*, moved only the price level. Thus they understand that the long-run supply curve is roughly vertical. This is the key assumption of the new classical school. Economic agents can see through to the long run because they know the structure of the economy. This knowledge could come from economic analysis and econometrics, or simply by careful (*very* careful, indeed!) observation of the consequences of past disturbances.

If the people (agents) in the economy understand that the long-run aggregate supply curve is vertical, *then* they will see that the result of *any* demand shift will be to move the long-run value of P, but not y. In Figure 14.13, anything moving DD will influence only P in the long run. But if

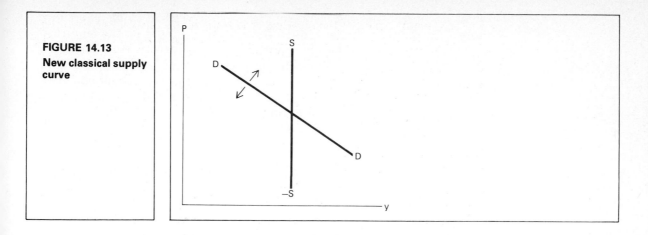

FIGURE 14.13
New classical supply curve

agents know the long-run movement of P after a disturbance, they will move the price level there immediately. If they did not, profits would be lost unnecessarily in the movement from the short run to the long run. This is the key implication of the crucial assumption that agents know the economy's reaction to disturbances. This knowledge telescopes long-run reactions into the short run.

A specific example may be useful. Suppose workers know that in the long run a 10 percent increase in the money supply will lend to a 10 percent increase in all wages and prices. This would restore the initial equilibrium at the original values of y, r, M/P, and W/P. Then workers will *immediately* increase wage demands by 10 percent. The result is an immediate jump of W and P in response to the M increase. This telescoping of the long-run result into the short run is the fundamental implication of the set of "rational expectation" assumptions of the new classical economics. In terms of Chapter 6, in the new classical school $P^* = P$ always. Agents know the structure of the economy and act immediately on that knowledge. This gives us a vertical aggregate supply curve even in the short run.

The implications of the new classical model for the effectiveness of monetary and fiscal policy should be clear from Chapter 7. If $P^* = P$ in the short run, we are in the extreme classical case of Chapter 6. With a vertical supply curve, shifts in monetary or fiscal policy move the price level but not real output y. They influence the composition of output, but not its total.

The new classical view is a powerful application of the notion of rational expectations at the macroeconomic level. It is a view that has radical implications for thinking about policy. If all wages and prices are flexible, and all agents understand the structure of the economy and the disturbances hitting it, then systematic policy will have no effect on real output. The relevance of the model, and of its underlying assumptions, is currently under fire from several directions. On the essential question of whether, in fact, the aggregate supply curve is vertical in the short run, Robert Gordon has challenged the new classical model on the empirical data. (1) Gordon finds that the aggregate supply curve is very flat in the short run. (2) The underlying assumption of wage flexibility has been questioned by John Taylor and others. With long-period (about one year) wage contracts, the economy has substantial wage rigidity in the short run. (3) The assumption that agents know the structure of the economy depends on the assumption of knowledge being passed along from one generation to the next. If each entering agent has to learn, and takes his or her knowledge away when leaving the economy, then we are in a perpetual state of learning and imperfect understanding. (4) Finally, the difficulty in understanding the long-run, and therefore by implication the short-run, effects of disturbances has been illustrated by Harris and Purvis. If agents do not know whether demand shifts are temporary or permanent, they should be cautious in moving directly to the long-run equilibrium. This response would yield a positively-sloped short-run aggregate supply curve. If the Fed increases M, agents do not know initially whether the shift is permanent or temporary. So they move prices only a fraction of the long-run change which would be rational if the shift is permanent. This gives the movement from P_0 to P_1 in Figure 14.14. Since agents are uncertain about the permanence of the shift, they move up a short-run supply curve S_sS_s. If the monetary increase persists, they become convinced of its permanence and P moves to P_2 as the supply curve rotates from S_sS_s to S_1S_1. But if the increase is reversed, the price level falls back to P_0. Thus as long as agents are uncertain about the temporariness or permanence of disturbances, we again see the Keynesian distinction between short-run and long-run supply slopes.

The new classical economics with its emphasis on rational expectations has required a serious reevaluation of the classical model. That reevaluation is underway in the macroeconomics literature now. The use-

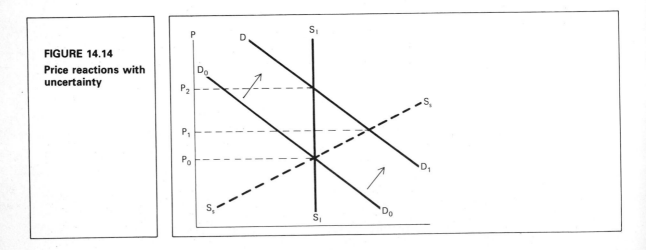

FIGURE 14.14
Price reactions with uncertainty

fulness of the new classical model to date has been to make more explicit the necessary assumptions under which the short-run supply curve will be nonvertical and it has provided us with a better analytical basis for the long-run tendency of the model. But as a short-run model of the supply side, it still stands as an extreme case—an illustrative polar example rather than a real alternative.

THE EFFECTS OF FINANCING A BUDGET DEFICIT

The equilibrium value of real income, y, along with the level of government purchases, g, and the net tax structure, $t(y)$, will give us an equilibrium value for the budget deficit, d, in real terms,

$$d = g - t(y) \tag{11}$$

The deficit may be positive or negative, that is, deficit or surplus. In a closed economy, it is equal to the excess of private saving over investment, since the equilibrium in the IS curve:

$$d = g - t(y) = s - i. \tag{12}$$

Thus a deficit increases net private-sector financial assets, and real wealth. The deficit can be financed either by effectively printing money or by borrowing from the public. From the public's point of view, this is an increase in wealth or real assets a. In general, the result is an upward shift of the IS curve with a continuing deficit, or a downward shift with a surplus. The LM curve also will generally move with a deficit, but the *direction* of its movement depends on *how* the deficit is financed. In this section we will analyze just how the short-term equilibrium will be affected by a continuing surplus or deficit. We begin with methods of financing the deficit and movement of the LM curve.

Deficit financing and the LM curve

In the basic money-market model of Chapters 11 and 12, the effect of financing a deficit on the LM curve depends on whether the *way* the deficit is financed changes commercial bank reserves. With an LM curve given by equation (4) above,

$$M(r) = P \cdot m(r, y),$$

the question is: Does financing the deficit shift the money supply function $M(r)$? If the financing technique does not increase reserves provided to the commercial banking system by the Fed, it does not increase the money supply and the LM curve does not shift. If additional reserves are created, the money supply increases and LM shifts right.

The Treasury has essentially four ways to finance an increase in the deficit. As we saw earlier, each of these ways must end up increasing net financial assets in the private sector by the amount of the deficit.

First, the Treasury can draw down its demand deposits—checking account balances—at the commercial banks. This directly transfers ownership of part of the money supply to the public, increasing the public's net financial assets, but does not change reserves, and leaves LM at $L_0 M_0$.

Second, the Treasury can sell bonds to the nonbank public. This does not affect reserves and thus leaves the *LM* curve unshifted. When the Treasury spends the proceeds of the bond issue, it restores the public's holdings of money, which results in an increase in the public's net financial assets by the amount of the bond sale.

Third, the Treasury can sell bonds to the commercial banks. This operation, in itself, does not change reserves and thus leaves the *LM* curve unshifted. To make room in their asset portfolios for the additional government securities, the banks will have to reduce lending to the private sector.

These three financing techniques all involve no change in reserves and thus leave the *LM* curve unshifted. The fourth way the Treasury could finance the deficit is by selling bonds to the Federal Reserve System in exchange for deposits at the Fed. The Treasury then would spend these funds by transferring ownership of the deposits to the public, who would then transfer them to their banks in exchange for a demand deposit at the bank. Thus, the ownership of the deposits at the Fed would find its way to the commercial banks. These deposits would then become additional reserves to the banks, and the money supply could expand by a multiple of the reserve increase.

This fourth case, then, increases the reserve base and the money supply by transferring ownership of deposits at the Fed from the Treasury to the commercial banking system. The procedure of financing a deficit by selling bonds to the monetary authority is frequently referred to as *monetization of the debt*. If we view the Treasury and the Fed as one unit, it is apparent in this case that the Treasury is financing the deficit by creating deposits for the commercial banking system at the central bank, that is, by *printing money*. The deficit in this case is financed by additional money creation.

Wealth in the *LM* curve

This analysis of the effects of how the deficit is financed concludes that, with a continuing deficit, the *LM* curve may stay put or shift out, but not shift left. This result depends importantly on the absence of asset, or wealth, effects on the *demand* for money in the *LM* equation (4). If there were wealth effects in the demand for money, the *LM* curve could shift up with a continuing deficit. Let's look at this possibility carefully.

The Tobin portfolio balance model of Chapter 12 analyzed the problem of a risk averse investor splitting his portfolio between bonds and money. If these were the *only* assets available, we saw in Figure 12.8 that there would be an equilibrium *proportion* of wealth held in money. In this case, the money demand function would be

$$\frac{M}{P} = m(r, y) \cdot a. \qquad [13]$$

The *fraction* of real assets a held as real money balances M/P would be given by $m(r, y)$. Then an increase in real wealth would shift the demand for money up.

If there were only two assets, risky bonds and risk-free money, and the money demand function (13) were the result, financing a deficit by *printing money* would shift *LM* out, but financing by selling bonds would shift *LM* left. The key to understanding this is remembering that in this case $m(r, y)$ in equation (13) is a *fraction*, giving the proportion of real wealth held in money. Financing the deficit by selling bonds increases a but not M. With the proceeds of the bond sale, the government buys goods or makes transfer payments, so the money goes back to the public, which ends up with more a and the original M. This increases demand for money relative to supply and shifts *LM* up.

Financing the deficit by printing money increases M/P and a by the same amount. But since $m(r, y)$ is less than unity, demand increases less than supply. With some of the increased money stock people want to buy bonds, to rebalance their portfolios. Thus the supply of money goes up more than demand, and *LM* shifts down. This was the case when assets did not enter the demand for money.

Thus it appears that *LM* might shift left with a continuing budget deficit. This would reduce equilibrium income y and tax revenue $t(y)$ and increase the deficit. This would be destabilizing in that an initial deficit would tend to increase with *LM* shifting up and y falling. This unstable result is unlikely to appear for two reasons. First, in the real world there are many assets, rather than two, and there is good reason to think that there is no wealth effect in the demand for money. Second, if there were a wealth effect, the authorities would move toward money finance of a deficit if expansion were desirable, and toward bond finance if the economy were overheated.

Regarding the actual existence of a wealth effect in the demand for money, consider a financial system that includes assets that are virtually riskless but yield a return such as savings account deposits or Treasury bills. In the case of savings account deposits there may be limitations in the frequency of withdrawal; for Treasury bills there are small fluctuations in market prices. But these risk elements are very small compared to long-term debt or equities. In a system with a riskless asset earning a return, money is "dominated" by the other riskless assets. There is no portfolio-balancing demand for money since the other asset plays money's risk-reducing role *and* yields a higher overall rate of return.

In this situation, the demand for money is reduced to a pure-transactions basis. As shown in Chapter 12, the transactions demand is responsive to the interest rate on the dominating riskless asset, which is the opportunity cost of holding money. The portfolio decision is split into two: money demand as a function of the rate of return on the other riskless asset, and demands for other assets each dependent on the set of rates of return for all assets and total wealth less money. As wealth increases in this case, all of the increased demand goes to nonmonetary assets since money is dominated for portfolio-balancing purposes.

In this pure-transactions model of money demand, with P and y given from the "real" sector and M fixed by the Fed, our standard money market equilibrium condition,

$$\frac{M}{P} = m(r, y)$$

determines r. Movements in wealth do not shift the LM curve in this pure-transactions model.

To summarize, in a model with a strict-transactions basis for the demand for money, there are no wealth effects on the LM curve. But if we go to the portfolio balance model, wealth effects enter the LM curve. In this case, an increase in the money stock shifts LM down (or right), and an increase in government debt shifts LM up (or left).

The empirical evidence, as summarized by Goldfeld, favors the transactions demand model. Once income is included in the money demand function, it is hard empirically to detect an independent role for wealth. This result is in sharp contrast with the empirical evidence on wealth effects on the IS curve. Through the consumption function, it is clear that an increase in real assets a shifts IS out. For our purposes here, the results of this balance of empirical evidence are two: (1) in the extended model we include wealth effects in IS but not LM, and (2) with bond finance of a deficit in the following analysis we assume the IS shift dominates the LM shift, so that a deficit tends to increase y.

Deficit spending and income

The effect of the existence of a deficit in equilibrium on the equilibrium position itself is shown in Figure 14.15. The IS curve shifts out as the wealth of the public increases. The LM curve will also shift to the right if part of the deficit is monetized. Pure bond financing is most likely to leave the LM curve at $L_0 M_0$. Thus the existence of a deficit tends to increase equilibrium income y.

With income increasing, tax revenues rise and the deficit shrinks. How long will dynamic adjustment process last? It will continue until tax

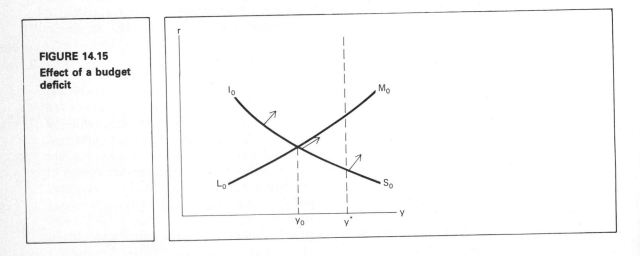

FIGURE 14.15
Effect of a budget deficit

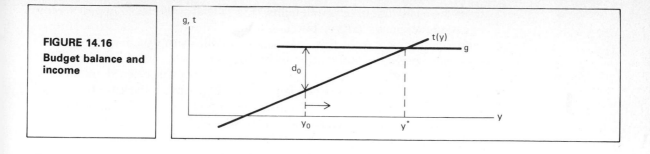

FIGURE 14.16
Budget balance and income

revenue rises enough to eliminate the initial deficit. From our definition of the real deficit in equation (13) above,

$$d = g - t(y),$$

we can find the level of income where tax revenue just equals the exogenously given level of government spending g. This is illustrated in Figure 14.16. There at the budget-balancing level of income y^* the deficit is eliminated. Thus in Figures 14.15 and 14.16 the initial equilibrium y_0 that gave a deficit $d_0 = g - t(y_0)$ moves gradually toward y^* where the budget is balanced. The budget deficit tends to be self-eliminating in the long run, because tax revenues increase with income.

CROWDING OUT OF INVESTMENT BY DEFICIT SPENDING

We have just noted that, in theory at least, a bond-financed budget deficit could shift the LM curve up. This effect would tend to reduce equilibrium income. This potentially negative effect on equilibrium income of a bond-financed budget deficit is one version of a phenomenon labeled "crowding out" in the recent literature. In general, the term "crowding out" refers to the tendency for an increase in government spending, or a tax cut, to reduce private investment. This tends to offset the effects of the original increase in g, or cut in t, on y. The potentially destabilizing effects of bond finance are one type of dynamic crowding out. Here we summarize the various aspects of crowding out which we have seen in this text, following the taxonomy set by Buiter.

At the simplest level, crowding out appears on the demand side of the static model of Chapter 5; an increase in g raises r, reducing investment. We saw in Chapter 5 that the multiplier for g is smaller when we endogenize the interest rate than when it is held exogenous. Earlier in this chapter, the *monetarist* model provides an example of full crowding out on the demand side. With a vertical LM curve, an increase in g pulls up the interest rate enough to provide an offsetting decrease in investment. This is a first stage of crowding out, which determines how far the aggregate demand curve shifts for a given increase in g or tax cut.

The second level of crowding out involves the aggregate supply curve and the price reaction to the shift in demand. Suppose the economy follows the basic model on the demand side so that an increase in g shifts the aggregate demand curve, but combine this with the classical supply model of Chapter 6. In this case, the aggregate supply curve is vertical, and the increase in demand simply pulls the price level up enough to restore the original equilibrium value of y. With the basic demand-side model and a vertical aggregate supply curve, the price increase following the shift in aggregate demand raises the interest rate enough that again investment falls by as much as g increased, and the fiscal policy increase is fully crowded out.

Here we have introduced the possibility of a third level of crowding out. If an initial increase in government spending or a tax cut led to a budget deficit, and this was bond-financed, in theory the LM curve could begin to shift up, raising interest rates and causing a further reduction in investment. As Buiter noted, this is balanced by a "crowding-in" effect on consumption. As wealth increases, the IS curve shifts up, tending to increase income. Only if the investment effect were to outweigh the consumption effect would we see a dynamically unstable net crowding out. The empirical evidence says that this is not likely to be the case in the U.S. economy.

CONCLUSION TO PART III

Part II focused on the basic structure of the economy and studied *how* the parts of the economy are interconnected. In Part III, we have examined in more detail the parts of the economy. We have expanded the basic behavioral relationships and attempted to provide empirical estimates of the equations including appropriate lags. This has provided a better grasp of the extent to which policy may affect the economy, how long it will take, and the sequence it will follow. With this in hand, in Part IV we consider the specific issues of inflation, balance-of-payments equilibrium, and economic growth.

QUESTIONS FOR DISCUSSION AND REVIEW

1. Describe the effects of a price increase on the *IS* and *LM* curves in the extended model. What implications do these changes have for the aggregate demand curve?

2. Fiscal policy has no impact on equilibrium income if either the *LM* curve is vertical or the aggregate supply curve is vertical. Is monetary policy rendered ineffective as well under either of these assumptions?

3. The text has demonstrated that, in the long run, a given expenditure and tax policy will yield a level of income at which there is no budget deficit. Will this proposition hold when the aggregate supply curve is vertical and, consequently, the long-run level of real income is not altered by fiscal policy?

4. A government with a budget initially in balance which decides to spend less must then decide to tax less, retire existing debt, or reduce the public's holding of money. How will choice among these acts affect the final effect on aggregate demand? Which component of aggregate demand is the major source of the differences in final demand?

5. Lincoln, were he to have read Keynes, might have commented, "Policy will have an effect all of the time only if you can fool some of the people all of the time." Discuss this propostion.

SELECTED READINGS

A. S. Blinder, *Fiscal Policy in Theory and Practice* (New York: General Learning Press, 1973).

A. S. Blinder and R. M. Solow, "Measuring Fiscal Influence," in R. L. Teigen, ed., *Readings in Money, National Income and Stabilization Policy,* 4th ed. (Homewood, Ill.: Irwin, 1978).

A. S. Blinder and R. M. Solow, "Lags and Overestimates in Fiscal Policy: General Considerations and the 1968–1970 Experience," in R. L. Teigen, ed., *Readings in Money, National Income and Stabilization Policy,* 4th ed. (Homewood, Ill.: Irwin, 1978).

W. H. Buiter, "Crowding Out and the Effectiveness of Fiscal Policy," *Journal of Public Economics,* 7, 1977.

R. Eisner, "What Went Wrong," *Journal of Political Economy,* May/June, 1971.

M. Friedman, "A Monetary and Fiscal Framework for Economic Stability," in M. G. Mueller, ed., *Readings in Macroeconomics* (New York: Holt, Rinehart and Winston, 1971).

M. Friedman, "The Role of Monetary Policy," *American Economic Review,* March 1968, also in R. L. Teigen, ed., Readings in *Money, National Income and Stabilization Policy,* 4th ed. (Homewood, Ill.: Irwin, 1978).

Robert J. Gordon, "New Evidence That Fully Anticipated Monetary Changes Influence Real Output After All," National Bureau of Economic Research Working Paper No. 361, July 1979, Cambridge, Mass.

Richard G. Harris and Douglas D. Purvis, "Equilibrium Theories of the Forward Exchange Rate," Mimeo, Queens University, Kingston, Ontario, March 1979.

F. Modigliani, "The Monetarist Controversy, or Should We Forsake Stabilization Policies?" in P. Korliras and R. S. Thorn, eds., *Modern Macroeconomics* (New York, Harper & Row, 1979).

R. Rasche and H. Shapiro, "The FRB-MIT Econometric Model," *American Economic Review,* May 1968.

T. J. Sargent and N. Wallace, "Rational Expectations and the Theory of Economic Policy," in P. G. Korliras and R. S. Thorn, eds., *Modern Macroeconomics* (New York, Harper & Row, 1979).

John B. Taylor, "Staggered Wage Setting in a Macro Model," *American Economic Review* 69, May 1979.

R. L. Teigen, "A Critical Look at Monetarist Economics," *Federal Reserve Bank of St. Louis Review,* January 1972, also in R. L. Teigen, ed., Readings in *Money, National Income and Stabilization Policy,* 4th ed. (Homewood, Ill.: Irwin, 1978).

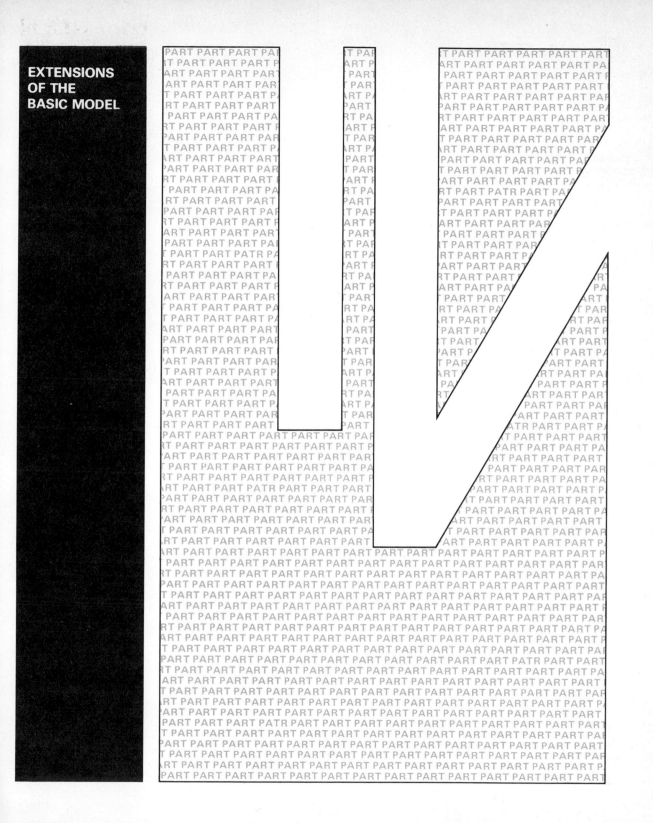

EXTENSIONS OF THE BASIC MODEL

INFLATION

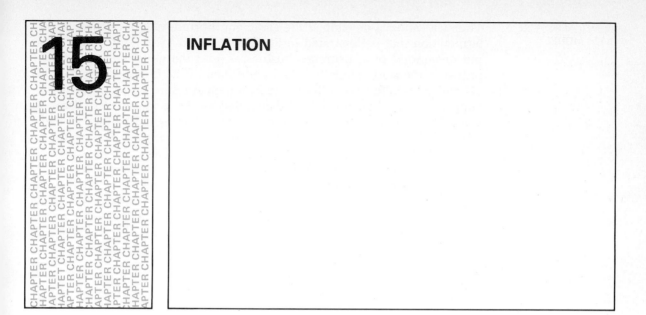

Up to now, we have been dealing with a static model and the movement from one equilibrium level to another. In dealing with inflation, we begin a transition to a model with dynamic elements. The transition is continued in the following chapters where we look at the relationships between the various sectors and between key variables in the economy as it grows along trend in static equilibrium.

The following sections begin with a discussion of the nature of inflation—a general increase in the price level—in the static model. A distinction is drawn between demand-pull inflation, which is due to a shift in the economy's demand curve, and cost-push inflation, which has its impetus in an upward shift of the supply curve. Next we develop the relationship between wage rate and productivity increases that leave the economy's supply curve undisturbed. This gives us the basic rule for noninflationary wage increases: Wage rates can rise at the same rate as labor productivity without generating a cost-push inflation. Development of this *wage-price-productivity* arithmetic then takes us into a discussion of the Council of Economic Advisers' wage-price guideposts, which were based on that arithmetic.

In the last two sections of this chapter we turn to the question: What determines the rate at which the labor supply function *actually* shifts up? The brief answer is the Phillips curve—the relationship between the rate of wage increase and the level of unemployment. First we develop the theoretical rationale for the Phillips curve and then review some empirical estimates of the U.S. Phillips curve.

Thus far we have developed the static equilibrium model of income determination that is illustrated in Figures 15.1 and 15.2. Equilibrium output *demanded* by consumers, businesses, and the government is determined in the static model by the intersection of the *IS* and *LM* curves of Figure 15.1(a). To derive the economy's demand curve we can ask what happens to equilibrium output demanded as the price level P rises. A price increase shifts the *LM* curve left by reducing the supply of real-money balances. It shifts the *IS* curve left by reducing the real value of household net worth and, in an open economy, reducing real net exports. Thus a price increase will shift both the *IS* and *LM* curves left, so that on the demand side equilibrium real output y falls as P rises, due to the drop in consumption and investment demand. This inverse relationship between y and P gives us the demand curve D_0D_0 of Figure 15.2.

The equilibrium output *supplied* by producers in the static model is given by the economy's production function, $y = y(N; \bar{K})$, combined with

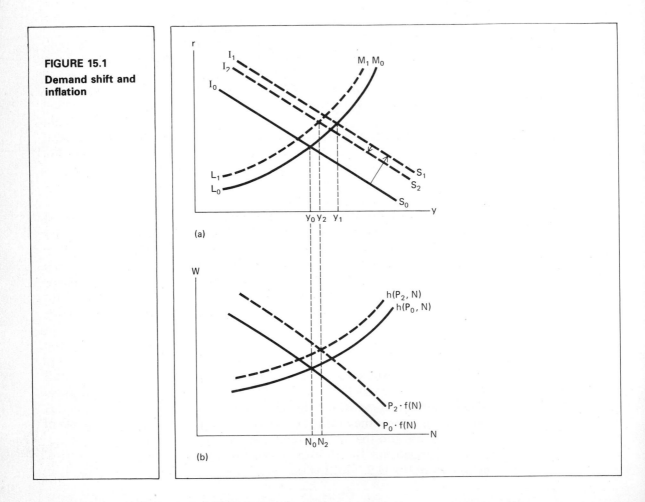

FIGURE 15.1

Demand shift and inflation

(a)

(b)

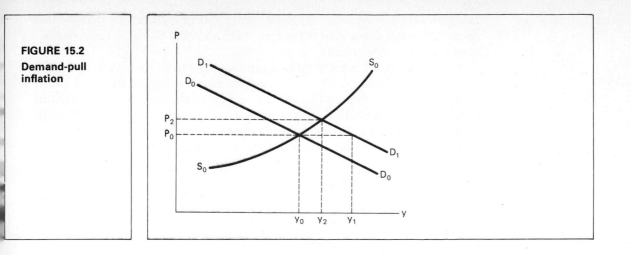

FIGURE 15.2
Demand-pull
inflation

the equilibrium intersection in the labor market of Figure 15.1 (b), which determines employment N_0. To derive the economy's aggregate supply curve we can ask what happens to equilibrium employment as the price level rises. A price increase from P_0 to P_2 shifts the labor demand curve of Figure 15.1(b) up from $P_0 \cdot f(N)$ to $P_2 \cdot f(N)$. It also shifts the supply curve up from $h(P_0, N)$ to $h(P_2, N)$. If the labor market reflects the workers' inability to fully perceive the change in prices, the shift in the demand curve will be larger than the supply curve shift, increasing equilibrium employment from N_0 to N_2 in Figure 15.1(b). This action increases equilibrium output on the supply side from $y_0 = y(N_0; \bar{K})$ to $y_2 = y(N_2; \bar{K})$ along the production function. This positive relationship between P and y on the supply side is shown as the $S_0 S_0$ supply curve in Figure 15.2.

The effect of a demand increase: demand-pull inflation

In the previous chapters we analyzed the operation of the static model in terms of a shifting demand curve. Any shift in a demand or supply function underlying the IS or LM curve will, in general, result in a shift in the demand curve of Figure 15.2. For example, if the saving function shifts down—reflecting less saving at any given income level—so that there is an exogenous increase in consumer demand, the IS curve in Figure 15.1(a) will shift up toward $I_1 S_1$, and the demand curve of Figure 15.2 will shift up to $D_1 D_1$.

In this case, at the initial price level, P_0, the equilibrium output on the demand side of the economy rises to y_1 in Figures 15.1(a) and 15.2. This creates excess demand measured by $y_1 - y_0$, and prices begin to rise. The price increase shifts both the IS and LM curves left, reducing output demanded toward y_2 along the new demand curve $D_1 D_1$.

The reduction of demand due to the price increase comes from three factors. First, the price increase reduces the supply of real balances, raising interest rates and eventually reducing investment demand. Second, the price increase reduces the real value of assets, shifting the saving function up and reducing consumer demand. Third, the price increase reduces real net exports. All these effects tend to reduce excess demand from the demand side of the economy.

While demand is falling from y_1 toward y_2 in Figure 15.2, the price increase also raises equilibrium output on the supply side from y_0 toward y_2. With the labor demand curve shifting more than the supply curve in Figure 15.1(b), employment and output rise, reducing excess demand from the supply side. When the price level has risen to P_2 in Figure 15.1(b) and Figure 15.2, excess demand is eliminated and the economy is at a new equilibrium level of output, y_2, and of employment, N_2.

The price increase generated by an upward shift in the economy's demand curve is frequently called *demand-pull inflation*. A general price increase is an inflation, and one caused by a demand shift is identified as demand-pull inflation. This is in contrast with a *cost-push inflation* which has its impetus on the supply side of the economy.

The effect of a supply shift: cost-push inflation

Inflation can also result from an upward, or inward, shift of the supply curve, as illustrated in Figures 15.3 and 15.4. The upward shift of the supply curve creates excess demand at the initial price level, P_0, raising prices but bringing a *reduction* in equilibrium output, as opposed to the demand-pull case where the price increase *raises* output.

In Figure 15.3(b) we show an exogenous upward shift in the labor supply curve from $h^0(P_0, N)$ to $h^1(P_0, N)$. This may result from an increase in wage demands in a highly unionized economy, due perhaps to past or expected price increases, or from a shift in tastes toward leisure. The upward shift in the labor supply function reduces equilibrium employment at the initial price level. In other words, the economy's supply curve shifts back to S_1S_1 in Figure 15.4.

The shift of the supply curve creates excess demand measured by $y_0 - y_1$ in Figure 15.4. At the initial price level, P_0, producers want to supply y_1, but consumers, business, and government want to buy y_0. As usual, excess demand raises the price level.

On the demand side of the economy, the price increase reduces equilibrium output from y_0 toward y_2 along the original demand curve D_0D_0. This movement is shown in Figure 15.3(a) by the leftward shifts of the IS and LM curves. At the same time, the price increase raises equilibrium output on the supply side from y_1 toward y_2 along the new supply curve S_1S_1 in Figure 15.4. In Figure 15.3(b) the labor demand curve shifts up toward $P_2 \cdot f(N)$ while the price increase induces a further upward shift in the supply function toward $h^1(P_2, N)$.

The price increase thus reduces the excess demand gap by reducing demand along the D_0D_0 curve and increasing supply along the S_1S_1 curve in Figure 15.4. Equilibrium is restored at P_2 in Figures 15.3(b) and 15.4, where the excess demand is eliminated and output has fallen to y_2. Inflation due to an upward shift of the supply curve is generally called *cost-push inflation*. The increase in wage demands, represented as an upward

FIGURE 15.3
Supply shift and
inflation

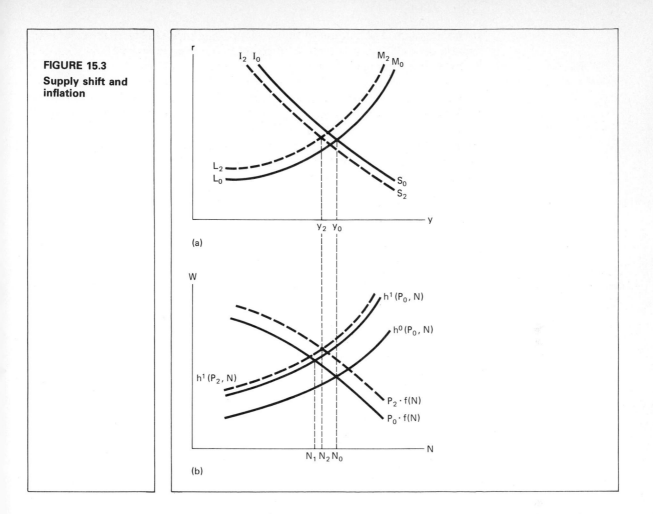

(a)

(b)

shift in the labor-supply curve of Figure 15-3(b), raises costs and causes producers to cut back output and raise prices.

The aggregate supply curve can also shift up due to a reduction of supply of other inputs into production such as agricultural raw materials or oil. In such cases, a given level of employment leads to a reduced level of real output or value added. This may be the result of reduced output possibilities, the weather conditions reducing crop yields, or relative price changes which require that a larger amount of real resources be exchanged for a given factor of production—as has been occurring in the case of oil.

The self-liquidating nature of inflation

In the static model, inflation is caused by excess demand in the product market. Excess demand can, however, come from an upward shift in the demand curve which generates demand-pull inflation or from an up-

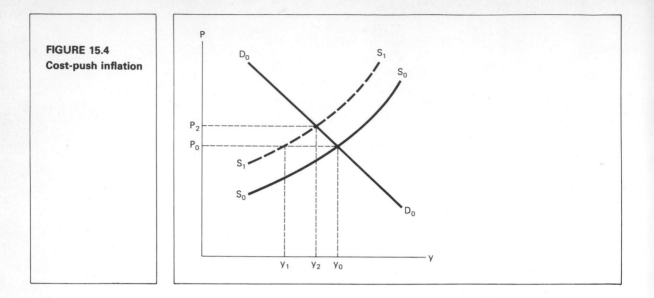

FIGURE 15.4
Cost-push inflation

ward shift in the supply curve which generates cost-push inflation. Both types of inflation are characterized by excess demand.

With either demand-pull or cost-push inflation, the excess demand means that at the initial price level and interest rate level, aggregate demand exceeds supply in the economy. The ensuing price increase from P_0 to P_2 in both the demand-shift and supply-shift cases works on both the demand and supply sides of the economy to eliminate excess demand.

As we have seen, the price increase reduces investment demand through the money market effect on r; it reduces consumer demand by reducing real household net worth; and it reduces real net exports by making U.S. goods more expensive relative to foreign goods. On the supply side, the price increase raises equilibrium output and employment in our general model, while in the classical real-wage model all the adjustment comes on the demand side. In either case, inflation is a self-liquidating phenomenon in the static model. Price increases are caused by the appearance of excess demand and tend to eliminate that excess demand as long as the IS and LM curves are not shifted by the government to counter the effects of the price increase in changing employment and real output.

If the government is committed to maintain full employment, a cost-push inflation can become more or less continuous, due to a policy reaction known as *validation*. In Figure 15.3(b) the upward shift in the labor supply curve reduces the equilibrium level of employment to N_2 from N_0, presumably increasing measured unemployment. In Figure 15.4 this is represented by the output drop to y_2. A full-employment policy, rigorously pursued, would lead the government to shift the demand curve in

Figure 15.4 out by monetary or fiscal policy measures, in order to restore the full-employment level of output y_0.

The price increase associated with this demand increase could, in turn, bring another upward shift of the labor supply curve, followed by another *validating* increase in demand, and so on. This kind of mechanism could produce a continuing upward pressure on prices through the reaction of government policy to cost-push inflation. Thus, while inflation is self-liquidating in the static model, it may be fairly continuous if there is a tendency for the labor supply curve to shift up faster than productivity at full employment, with aggregate demand policy validating the cost-push.

Identification of demand-pull and cost-push inflation

In practice, it is extremely difficult to separate demand-pull from cost-push inflation. All that the price and wage data show is an unending sequence of price and wage increases. If we choose a wage increase as the initial departure from equilibrium, then the subsequent inflation may be labeled *cost-push*. But if a price increase is taken as the initial departure, the inflation is *demand-pull*.

In addition, with labor union bargaining the picture is more complicated. With a union contract period of three years, an initial burst of demand-pull inflation can leave the union asking for a wage increase to compensate not only for the past lag of wages behind prices, but also for the *expected* price increase. In this case the labor supply function may shift up in *anticipation* of an *expected* demand-pull price rise.

WAGES, PRICES, AND PRODUCTIVITY

It was pointed out earlier that while an upward shift in the labor supply curve will tend to shift the economy's supply curve up, creating cost-push inflation, an upward shift in the labor demand curve due to an increase in the marginal productivity of labor will tend to shift the economy's supply curve down, so that the two movements—in wages and in productivity— tend to cancel each other out. A case in which the two effects just balance each other is shown in Figure 15.5(a). There at the initial price level, P_0, equilibrium supply-side employment remains at N_0 as $h(P_0, N)$ and $f(N)$ both shift up. This shows a noninflationary wage increase with wages rising as fast as productivity, leaving equilibrium employment at N_0 and the equilibrium price level undisturbed.

In Figure 15.5(b), we see that the increase in productivity represented by the upward shift of $f(N)$ in Figure 15.5(a) shifts the production function up. At any employment level N, output y is greater along $y^1(N; \bar{K})$ than on $y^0(N; \bar{K})$, and the slope of the production function is also steeper, that is, greater. This is equivalent to saying that at an employment level of N_0, the real-wage rate is higher.

Thus the increase in productivity represented by the shift from $f^0(N)$ to $f^1(N)$ in Figure 15.5(a) raises equilibrium output supplied at any given level of employment. At the initial equilibrium P_0, N_0 level, equilibrium output on the supply side rises from y_0 to y_1 in Figure 15.5(b); with wages and marginal productivity of labor growing at the same rate, the econ-

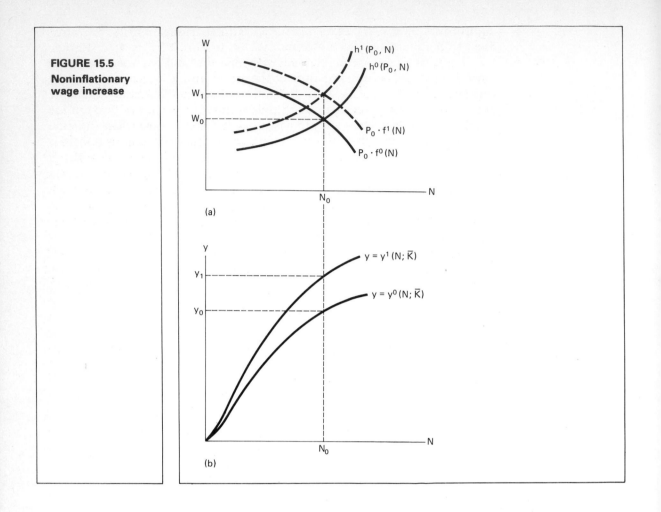

FIGURE 15.5
Noninflationary wage increase

(a)

(b)

omy's supply curve in the P, N space is undisturbed, while the supply curve in the P, y space shifts out.

This relationship between the two supply curves is shown in the four-quadrant diagram of Figure 15.6. In the northeast quadrant of Figure 15.6 is the supply curve in the P, N space, as derived, for example, from the labor market diagram of Figure 15.1(b). The production function in the southeast quadrant of Figure 15.6 translates employment into output supplied; $y^0(N, \bar{K})$ is the production function of Figure 15.5(b) turned upside down. The 45° line in Figure 15.6 transfers y to the horizontal axis. Starting with equilibrium P_0, N_0 in the northeast quadrant of Figure 15.6, the same P_0 and N_0 as in Figure 15.5, we can obtain y_0 from the production function and P_0, y_0 in the northwest quadrant of Figure 15.6 is a point on the aggregate supply curve in the P, y space, $S_0 S_0$.

If labor productivity and the wage rate now rise by an equal amount, equilibrium P_0 and N_0 will be retained with W rising from W_0 to W_1 in Figure 15.5(a). Equilibrium output will rise to y_1 in Figure 15.6, shifting the aggregate supply curve in the P, y space to $S_1 S_1$. The initial level of employment and price level are now consistent with a higher wage rate W_1 and level of output y_1, due to the productivity increase. Thus, to maintain equilibrium in the economy at P_0, N_0, y_1, demand-side equilibrium output must also be expanding, with the economy's demand curve shifting out. This requires the *IS-LM* intersection to shift out, as shown in Figure 15.7, to maintain supply-demand balance at the equilibrium price level P_0. If the labor supply curve shifts up as shown in Figure 15.5(a), raising wages along with productivity, the initial employment level, N_0, will remain the equilibrium employment level at price level P_0 so that the economy will remain in equilibrium with output, productivity, and the wage rate rising, and employment and the price level constant.

The basic wage-price-productivity relationship can be derived from a version of the labor market equilibrium condition,

$$W = P \cdot f(N). \qquad [1]$$

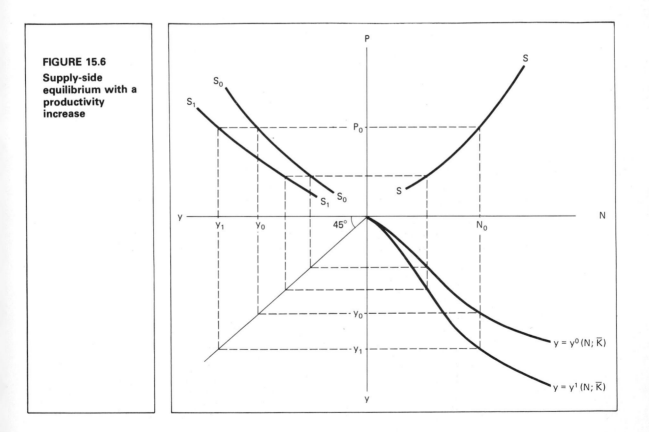

FIGURE 15.6

Supply-side equilibrium with a productivity increase

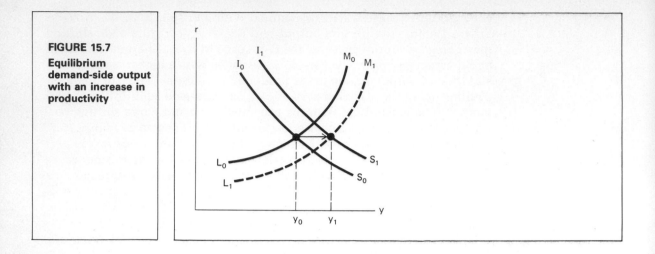

FIGURE 15.7

Equilibrium demand-side output with an increase in productivity

For any given N, the price level is given by

$$P = \frac{W}{f(N)} \cdot \qquad [2]$$

If the money wage W and the marginal productivity of labor $f(N)$ grow at the same rate, there will be no change in equilibrium P. For example, starting from

$$P_0 = \frac{W_0}{[f(N)]_0},$$

assume that both W and $f(N)$ grow at 10 percent per year, so that $W_1 = W_0(1.10)$ and $[f(N)]_1 = [f(N)]_0 \cdot (1.10)$. Then for P_1 we have

$$P_1 = \frac{W_1}{[f(N)]_1} = \frac{W_0(1.10)}{[f(N)]_0(1.10)} = \frac{W_0}{[f(N)]_0} = P_0.$$

In general, if the numerator and denominator of a ratio grow at the same rate, the value of the ratio does not change.

The percentage rate of growth of a ratio is approximately equal to the growth rate of the numerator less the growth rate of the denominator. In the following discussion we will denote the percentage growth rate of a variable by a dot over it. Thus, we define

$$\dot{X} \equiv \frac{\Delta X}{X} \cdot$$

If X is the ratio of two variables, that is,

$$X = \frac{Y}{Z},$$

then the growth rate of X is given by the difference in growth rates of Y and Z:

$$\frac{\Delta X}{X} = \frac{\Delta Y}{Y} - \frac{\Delta Z}{Z}, \quad \text{or} \quad \dot{X} = \dot{Y} - \dot{Z}.$$

From this, it also follows that the growth rate of a product is the sum of the growth rates. If $Y = XZ$, then

$$\frac{\Delta Y}{Y} = \frac{\Delta X}{X} + \frac{\Delta Z}{Z}, \quad \text{or} \quad \dot{Y} = \dot{X} + \dot{Z}.$$

Applying these results to equation (2) we have

$$\dot{P} = \dot{W} - f(N). \tag{3}$$

Thus, if W and $f(N)$ in equation (3) grow at the same rate so that $\dot{W} = f(N)$, $\dot{P}$ will be 0, that is, the equilibrium price level will remain unchanged.

Another way to look at equation (3) is to note that since the real wage w is just W/P, the growth rate of the real wage is given by

$$\dot{w} = \dot{W} - \dot{P}. \tag{4}$$

If money wages grow as fast as productivity, and P remains unchanged so that $\dot{P} = 0$, equation (4) combined with equation (3) gives us

$$\dot{w} = \dot{W} - \dot{P} = f(N). \tag{5}$$

Unit labor cost and the labor share

This line of analysis can be carried further. We can define the unit labor cost (ULC)—the labor cost per unit of real output—as

$$ULC = \frac{WN}{y} = \frac{W}{\dfrac{y}{N}}, \tag{6}$$

where N is the total labor force employed. Thus,

$$\dot{ULC} = \dot{W} - (y/N). \tag{7}$$

This tells us that if the money wage rate and productivity increase at the same rate, $\dot{W} = (y/N)$, then unit labor cost remains constant.

The labor share of total output S_L can be written as

$$S_L = \frac{WN}{Py} = \frac{w}{\dfrac{y}{N}}. \tag{8}$$

We have seen that if the real wage w and productivity y/N grow at the same rate, the equilibrium price level can remain unchanged. Using our rule for percentage growth rates,

$$\dot{S}_L = \dot{w} - (y/N). \tag{9}$$

Thus, if w and y/N grow at the same rate, the labor share of output remains constant: $\dot{S}_L = 0$. If the capital share of output is just $1 - S_L$, then this implies that if w and y/N grow at the same rate, so that W can grow as fast as y/N with P constant, the capital share of output will also remain constant.

THE WAGE-PRICE GUIDEPOSTS

The wage-price-productivity arithmetic we have just reviewed says that if money wage rates W grow as fast as average labor productivity, (y/N), and the average price level P remains constant, then the relative shares of capital and labor—the distribution of output to the factors of production—will remain constant and unit labor costs will also remain constant. This is the fundamental arithmetic behind the Council of Economic Advisers' wage-price guideposts, first published in the *Economic Report of the President* in January 1962.

The CEA's general guidepost for wages was that the rate of increase of wage rates including fringe benefits in all industries should equal the economy-wide trend rate of productivity increase. Adherence to this guidepost would maintain a constant average unit labor cost in the economy. The general guidepost for prices was that in industries where productivity rose faster than average, prices should fall, and in industries where productivity rose slower than average, prices should rise, maintaining average price stability.

This formulation of the guideposts would have all wages growing at about the same rate. If we put bars over variables to indicate economy-wide averages, the wage guidepost says

$$\dot{W}_i = (\overline{\dot{y/N}}). \tag{10}$$

Wages in each industry i grow as fast as *average* labor productivity. If this is the case, unit labor costs in any given industry i will grow at the rate:

$$\dot{ULC}_i = \dot{W}_i - (\dot{y/N})_i = (\overline{\dot{y/N}}) - (\dot{y/N})_i. \tag{11}$$

So, if industry i has productivity growing faster than average, its unit labor costs will be falling and the price guidepost says that it should reduce prices at the rate of ULC decrease to preserve constant relative shares. Conversely, if the industry's productivity is growing slower than average, ULC_i will be rising, and prices must rise to preserve relative shares. On average, adherence to the price guidepost will maintain a constant price level.

Political difficulties with the guideposts

The CEA's guideposts came under fairly heavy political fire from the beginning, aimed both at the substance of the guideposts and at the way they were enforced. The guideposts, if followed, would maintain constant relative shares of output going to capital and labor, so that labor's aggregate share of total output would grow as fast as capital's share along trend growth in y. While this may seem to be the best neutral prescription for a functional income distribution policy, it is not satisfactory to either management or labor, both of which want to raise their relative shares. Thus the guideposts were not accepted by either business or labor as an income distribution prescription.

The guideposts, in addition, had no legal standing, so that enforcement in cases of price or wage increases by individual companies, unions, or industries was left to public exposure by the CEA or the president, followed by public pressure generated by the president to roll back the price or wage increase in question. Business naturally resented this kind of selective political pressure. Also, to some this seemed to be an arbitrary exercise of power in an extralegal fashion by the White House, although it was clear that the price increases that were subjected to scrutiny represented the exercise of monopoly power by industry.

Economic difficulties with the guideposts
From 1962 to 1965 wages and prices, by and large, followed the guidepost prescription. Whether this wage and price behavior was due to the guideposts, or whether it was due to the slackness of the economy and unusually rapid productivity increases which permitted substantial wage increases without disturbing unit labor costs, is another matter. In the next section we will note some empirical evidence that the guideposts did, in fact, make a difference for wages.

However, beginning in 1965, the guideposts broke down due to their two major economic weaknesses. First, the guideposts can be effective only in the monopolistic sectors of the economy. The guideposts prescribe how people should *set* prices and wages; firms and individuals in competitive markets have no control over their prices and so cannot observe the guideposts. Thus, as excess demand appeared and increased beginning in 1965, prices rose in competitive sectors of the economy, making it more and more difficult to require the monopolistic sectors to hold the line.

The second major problem is that the guideposts do not prescribe behavior for wages when prices violate their guidepost, and vice versa. With productivity rising at about 3 percent per year, the wage guidepost prescribes wage increases of 3 percent per year. If prices are rising, violating their guidepost, then real wages are rising slower than productivity and the labor share is falling relative to the profit share. If prices rise faster than 3 percent per year, as they did from 1966 to 1971, real wages would fall, as they did in manufacturing from 1966 to 1971. Thus, as prices rise it becomes unreasonable to ask labor to follow the wage guidepost, so wages begin to rise, making it hard to hold prices to the price guidepost in turn.

As a result of excess-demand pressure, combined with the lack of a remedy for bad price behavior, the guideposts broke down in the late 1960s. In its *Annual Report* of January 1969 the CEA, while repeating the indisputable correctness of the wage-price-productivity arithmetic underlying the guideposts, recognized that excess-demand pressures had made them unenforceable, at least for the time being, and did not publish a set of numerical wage and price guides for the coming year.

Although the guideposts broke down under excess-demand pressure, it is quite possible, even likely, that they are useful in holding down cost-push inflation in a situation where there is no general excess demand

and prices have been fairly stable so that wages can reasonably follow the wage guidepost. The U.S. economy experienced such conditions from 1961 to 1965. The first four years of the 1970s showed that in a period of rapid price increases, government pressure, including mandated controls, can keep wages from rising too rapidly at least for a short while. Continued price increases, however, soon lead to wage increase demands far in excess of any productivity increases. These wage increases then become a major source of continued inflation.

Alternatives to the guideposts

The continuing problems with inflation in the second half of the 1970s gave rise to a number of proposed solutions based, like the initial guideposts, on the relationship between productivity, wages, and prices. Foremost among these were the tax-based incomes policies that would introduce benefits for behavior that limited upward pressures on prices or penalties for behavior that contributed to inflationary pressures.

President Carter suggested a real-wage insurance plan that would—should inflation exceed the predicted rate—compensate, although only partially, those workers who agreed to wage increases below a stated rate. Others proposed plans to reduce taxes on firms whose price increases were moderate or to increase taxes on those firms whose price increases were deemed excessive. President Carter's plan was ignored by Congress, and the other plans gained insufficient support to influence policy makers. As with the guideposts, unions and business saw themselves receiving a lower share of real output than might be possible without restrictions. These plans had the seeming disadvantage of offering reduced inflation to a public that was unwilling to believe them.

THE RELATION OF WAGE CHANGES TO UNEMPLOYMENT: THE PHILLIPS CURVE

The wage-price-productivity arithmetic has shown us that if money wage rates rise as fast as productivity, in general there is no reason for the equilibrium price level to rise. This whole discussion *assumed* that the labor supply curve—the workers' money wage demands—shifts up through time, and focused on conditions for noninflationary wage increases. The question remains: What determines the rate at which the labor supply curve shifts upward? That is, what moves the money wage rate? The answer to this will lead us into a discussion of the Phillips curve—the relationship between the rate of increase of money wages W and the unemployment rate u.

The theoretial basis for the Phillips curve

From the labor market diagram of Figure 15.1(b), we can see that an increase in the demand for labor—an outward shift in the $P \cdot f(N)$ curve—will bring an increase in the money wage rate, due to the appearance of excess demand in the labor market. In Figure 15.8, at wage rate W_0 there is excess demand for labor measured by $N_0^d - N_0^s$. This excess demand bids the wage rate up from W_0. The assumption here is that the percentage rate of increase of the wage rate, $\dot{W}$, depends on the *magnitude* of the excess demand for labor, $N^d - N^s$. That is,

$$\dot{W} = f(N^d - N^s), \tag{12}$$

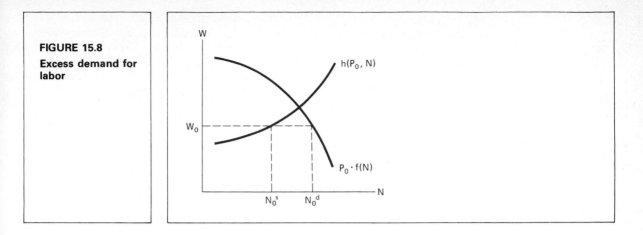

FIGURE 15.8

Excess demand for labor

with $\dot{W}$ rising with excess demand. Figure 15.8 shows that both the demand for and the supply of labor depend, in turn, on the level of the wage rate.

A complete model of the labor market would include empirical estimates of the labor demand curve, the labor supply curve, and the wage adjustment function, equation (12). Empirical estimates of labor demand and supply functions are very difficult to obtain, but the wage adjustment equation is more manageable and can be estimated independently of the demand and supply functions. Obtaining this estimate involves transforming the excess-demand expression in equation (12) into the unemployment rate. This was shown by the Australian economist A. W. Phillips who introduced the inverse relationship between the rate of wage increase and unemployment into the economic literature in 1958.

To begin with, we can note that excess supply in the labor market, $N^s - N^d$, is just the negative of excess demand, that is,

$$\text{Excess supply} = N^s - N^d = -(N^d - N^s). \tag{13}$$

Using this relationship, we can rewrite the wage adjustment equation (12) as

$$\dot{W} = -f(N^s - N^d). \tag{14}$$

The next step is to introduce the unemployment rate $u = U/L$ as a proxy for excess supply. As excess supply rises, the unemployment rate rises, as shown in Figure 15.9. From the discussion of unemployment in Chapter 8, we recall that there generally is positive unemployment even when the labor market is in equilibrium, that is, when excess supply is zero. Thus the excess-supply–unemployment rate function of Figure 15.9 crosses the horizontal axis at a positive value of unemployment.

Substituting the unemployment rate for excess supply in quation (14) gives us the wage adjustment equation,

$$\dot{W} = f(u). \tag{15}$$

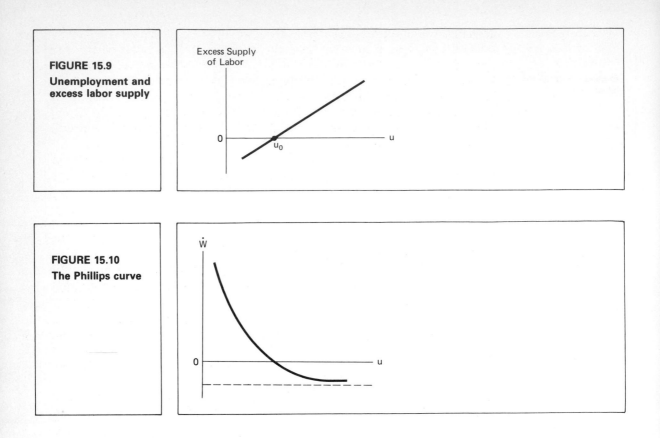

FIGURE 15.9

Unemployment and excess labor supply

FIGURE 15.10

The Phillips curve

Since $\dot{W}$ falls with an increase in excess supply, it also falls with an increase in u. Thus as unemployment rises, the rate of increase of wages falls, and vice versa as unemployment falls. Equation (15) is the basic Phillips curve equation relating $\dot{W}$ to u.

Figure 15.10 shows the basic Phillips curve, equation (15). We expect that the $f(u)$ function should have the convex shape shown in Figure 15.10 for the following reasons. As unemployment is reduced by constant amounts, the wage rate will rise at an increasing rate, with $\dot{W}$ approaching infinity as u approaches 0. In other words, a negative unemployment rate is not observable. On the other hand, there must be some institutional lower boundary below which $\dot{W}$ cannot fall. It takes time to change wage rates, especially to reduce them, so that $\dot{W}$ cannot approach $-\infty$ as the unemployment rate grows larger and larger, but rather reaches some stable rate of decrease of wages. Thus as u approaches 100 percent, $\dot{W}$ approaches the lower bound shown in Figure 15.10. These features give the curve its convex shape. Although these arguments are not really compelling, the empirical estimate we will review shortly support the convexity proposition.

The convex shape of the Phillips curve suggests that, on average, the economy will have less inflation if the level of unemployment has narrow fluctuations about some average ū than if the fluctuations are wider with the same mean u. If unemployment is fluctuating symmetrically about the 5 percent level, for example, the average pressure on prices goes up more below the 5 percent level than it goes down above 5 percent, because of the convex nature of the curve. Thus, the broader the fluctuation in unemployment levels at any given average unemployment rate, the greater will be the cost-push inflationary pressure on the economy.

Unemployment and the rate of price increase

If we assume that the distribution of income to labor and capital is constant over time, that is, relative shares are constant, the percentage rate of change of prices should equal $\dot{W} - (y/N)$, that is,

$$\dot{P} = \dot{W} - (y/N). \tag{16}$$

If this behavior is observed in fact—as we see it is in Chapter 17—then there is a link between wages and prices, so that the Phillips curve can be stated in terms of prices as well as wages. The Phillips curve relationship between the rate of price increase and unemployment is shown in Figure 15.11. If productivity grows at about 3 percent per year, roughly the U.S. average growth rate in the period 1950–74, then, with constant shares, a zero rate of price increase corresponds to a 3 percent rate of wage increase. Thus for any given level of unemployment we could read off the rate of increase of wages on the vertical axis to the left of Figure 15.11 and the rate of price increase on the vertical axis to the right.

In 1960 Samuelson and Solow suggested that the levels of unemployment and rate-of-wage increase that would maintain price stability were about 4.5 percent and 3 percent, respectively. The experience since

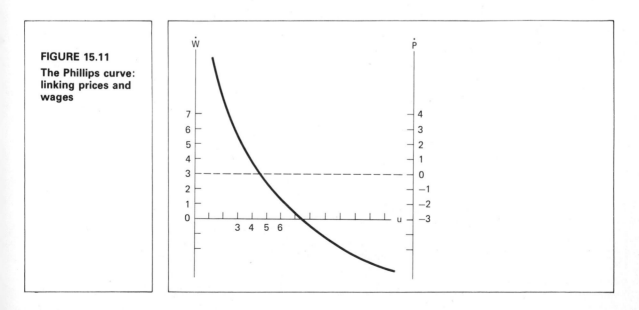

FIGURE 15.11

The Phillips curve: linking prices and wages

1965 has raised most experts' estimate of the noninflationary unemployment rate to 6 percent or so, and reduced estimates of the long-run productivity growth rate to around 1 percent.

The price-wage spiral The principal mechanism spreading inflation through the economy, once an initial impulse appears, is the price-wage spiral. Here the initial price increase leads to an increase in wage demands. This shifts the aggregate supply curve, generating another price increase, and so on. It is important to notice that this *endogenous* price-wage spiral spreads the effects of *both* cost-push and demand-pull initial impulses. Observation of the price-wage spiral at work cannot tell us whether the initial impulse was cost-push or demand-pull, because both trigger the spiral.

The price-wage mechanism can be shown with simplified versions of the wage and price equations we have just developed. The presentation here is adapted from the models of Robert J. Gordon and Warren L. Smith.

The Phillips curve can be written as

$$\dot{W} = f(u) + \alpha \dot{P}. \qquad [17]$$

Here $f' < 0$; as the unemployment rate rises, the rate of nominal-wage increase, $\dot{W}$ falls. The coefficient α measures the sensitivity of nominal-wage demands to price increases. In the classical model of Chapter 6, $\alpha = 1$; in the extreme Keynesian, $\alpha = 0$. Here we assume that α lies between these extreme values.

The Phillips curve of equation (17) is shown in Figure 15.12. There we see that as $\dot{P}$ rises from $\dot{P}_0$ to $\dot{P}_1$ ($\dot{P}_1 > \dot{P}_0$), the entire curve shifts up. Each individual Phillips curve for a given $\dot{P}$ is a "short-run" Phillips curve. Below in Figure 15.13 we will draw a "long-run" curve in Figure 15.12 by combining the price equation determining $\dot{P}$ with equation (17).

A reduction in labor supply due to an increase in demand for leisure would shift each short-run Phillips curve up; $f(u)$ would rise. Employers would have to offer larger wage increases to obtain the same amount of labor as before the change in tastes. Similarly, if the composition of the labor force changes with an increase in the proportion of workers with

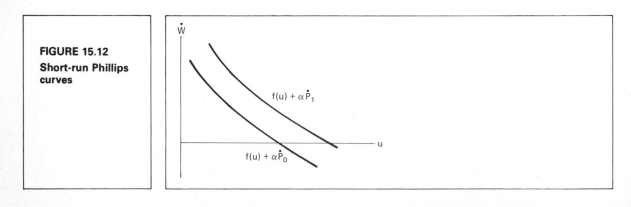

FIGURE 15.12
Short-run Phillips curves

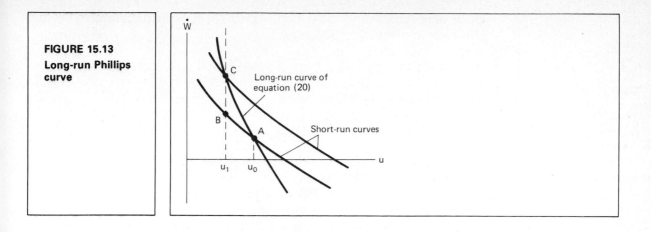

FIGURE 15.13
Long-run Phillips curve

less-than-average attachment to the labor market and higher-than-average unemployment—second earners in a family for example—the short-run $f(u)$ Phillips curve would shift up. For a given movement of wages, unemployment would rise because the composition shifted toward people with generally higher unemployment rates. As we see below, this factor has been at work in the United States since the mid-1960s.

The price equation that preserves constant-income shares is

$$\dot{P} = \dot{W} - (y/N) + \epsilon, \tag{18}$$

where the additional term ϵ represents cost-push disturbances. Normally we expect $\epsilon = 0$. When there is a major crop shortfall or drop in oil supply, ϵ becomes positive for a time. For example, Joel Popkin has estimated that in 1973 these two elements increased the U.S. consumer price index (CPI) by 4.5 percent. In that case, for 1973, $\epsilon = 0.045$.

Combining equations (17) and (18) we can see how the price-wage spiral works. An initial cost-push disturbance, $\epsilon > 0$, pushes the price level up, so $\dot{P} > 0$. This increases wage demands: $\dot{W}$ becomes positive. This in turn feeds back on $\dot{P}$ through equation (18), and so on. If the initial impulse were demand-pull, we would first see a drop in the unemployment rate u in equation (17) raising $\dot{W}$. This would push up $\dot{P}$ in equation (18), giving a further increase in wage demands in equation (17) and so on.

The effect of a change in the unemployment rate or a continuing cost-push pressure with $\epsilon > 0$ can be obtained by combining equations (17) and (18). Substitution of equation (17) for $\dot{W}$ into equation (18) gives us

$$\dot{P} = f(u) + \alpha\dot{P} - (y/N) + \epsilon,$$

and solving this for $\dot{P}$ yields

$$\dot{P} = \frac{1}{1 - \alpha}[f(u) - (y/N) + \epsilon] \tag{19}$$

as the long-run Phillips curve for the price level. Substitution of equation (19) back into equation (17) gives us

$$\dot{W} = f(u) + \frac{\alpha}{1-\alpha}\left[f(u) - \left(\frac{\dot{y}}{N}\right) + \epsilon\right],$$

and rearranging, we have

$$\dot{W} = \left(\frac{1}{1-\alpha}\right)\cdot f(u) - \frac{\alpha}{1-\alpha}\left[\left(\frac{\dot{y}}{N}\right) + \epsilon\right], \qquad [20]$$

as the long-run Phillips curve for the wage rate. In Figure 15.12, we saw a family of short-run Phillips curves with slopes given by f'. In the long-run Phillips curve of equation (20), the slope is $[1/(1-\alpha)]\cdot f'$, so the long-run curve is steeper than the short-run curves, since $0 < \alpha \le 1$.

The short-run curves of Figure 15.12, with the long-run curve given by equation (20), are shown in Figure 15.13. Suppose the economy is initially on the long-run curve at point A, and the government decides to reduce the unemployment rate from u_0 to u_1. The demand-pull stimulus would initially move the economy to point B along the short-run curve. But the $\dot{P}$ increase feeds through the wage equation and the rate of wage increase moves up toward point C. Where $\dot{W}$ and $\dot{P}$ only rise by $f'(u)$ in short run, they rise by $[1/(1-\alpha)]\cdot f'(u)$ in the long run. Thus the existence of the endogenous price-wage spiral gives us a long-run Phillips curve trade-off that is steeper than the short-run curve.

Validation of inflation

In terms of our aggregate supply and demand curves, the price-wage spiral is a continuing upward shift of the supply curve, once the initial cost-push or demand-pull impulse has passed through the system. Regardless of the *source* of the inflation, whether demand-pull or cost-push, the price-wage spiral shifts the supply curve of Figure 15.14 up further. In the absence of a shift in the demand curve (beyond any initial demand-pull impulse), this will tend to reduce output and employment and raise the unemployment rate. In the example of Figure 15.13, if monetary or

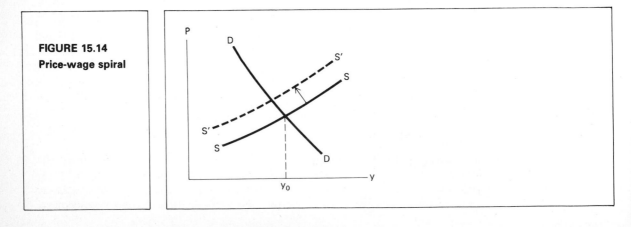

FIGURE 15.14
Price-wage spiral

fiscal policy shifted the aggregate demand curve enough to move from point A to point B initially, the price-wage spiral would shift the aggregate supply curve up as $\dot{W}$ moves toward point C. But unless further demand stimulus is provided, the supply shift will raise the unemployment rate, u, moving the economy not directly up from B to C, but rather out from B to some point on the long-run Phillips curve between A and C.

If the government wanted to hold the unemployment rate at u_1, as $\dot{W}$ and $\dot{P}$ rise from point B toward point C in Figure 15.13, it would have to stimulate demand more than the original boost that took the economy from A to B. As the price-wage spiral shifts the supply curve of Figure 15.14 up, the government would have to shift the demand curve up by equal amounts to hold output and employment constant at the desired y_0 level. A demand policy that does this is called *validation* of the inflation.

Given the initial demand-pull or cost-push stimulus, and its effect on output and employment (positive or negative), a validation policy eliminates the effect of the subsequent price-wage spiral on output and employment. If the initial impulse came from a policy decision to reduce the unemployment rate by expansionary monetary or fiscal policy, validation simply means sticking by the new unemployment target. If the policy decision was made with the knowledge that the economy would eventually move up along the long-run Phillips curve (from A to C in Figure 15.13), rather than the short-run curve (from A to B), the validation would make sense.

If the initial impulse were a cost-push from reduced oil supplies, for example, validation would eliminate the subsequent effects of the price-wage spiral further reducing output. In the 1973–1975 period, the administration in the United States chose *not* to validate, resulting in a fairly severe recession with unemployment rising to about 9 percent. A similar episode developed in 1980.

Once the initial inflationary stimulus has appeared, the choice between validating or not validating the subsequent price-wage spiral is essentially a choice of a preferred point on the long-run Phillips curve. Validation results in a lower unemployment rate and higher rate of inflation, in the long run, than does a policy of no validation.

INFLATION SINCE THE MID-1960s

The period 1965–1980 in the United States can be separated into three distinct inflation cycles. The first cycle was a classic case of a demand-pull inflation, touched off by the jump in defense spending in early 1966. This cycle moved into the price-wage spiral phase around 1968 and was coming to an end in 1971 when the administration resorted to price and wage controls.

The second cycle combined demand-pull and cost-push impulses. There was a rapid expansion of demand, worldwide, in 1972–1973. This coincided with a shortfall in world agricultural output in 1972, which provided a cost-push element. On top of this came the reduction of oil output by OPEC and the subsequent increase in energy prices beginning in early 1974. By mid-1975, the administration's policy of no (or even negative) validation had reduced demand enough that the rate of inflation showed substantially.

The third cycle began with demand-pull, as the United States recovered quickly from the 1974–75 recession. As U.S. recovery ran ahead of Europe and Japan, the U.S. current account balance ran into large deficits, and the dollar depreciated. The combination of a rapid expansion and dollar devaluation began a new burst of inflation and led to the administration's attempt to impose "voluntary" wage and price controls in November 1978. In 1979 OPEC added another oil price increase onto the inflation rate, and the administration and Federal Reserve began to squeeze demand to slow it. This resulted in the steep recession that began in January 1980. Policy makers will be fortunate indeed if this returns the United States to the noninflationary initial conditions of 1965.

Thus while the period 1965–1980 may appear to the untrained observer as one continuous inflation, in fact there were three separate cycles, with different causes, during the period. Before we look at these a bit more closely, we should see what was happening to the underlying Phillips curve during the period.

The shifting Phillips curve

Since the mid-1960s the long-run U.S. Phillips curve relating the rate of wage increase to unemployment has shifted up for two reasons, according to the research of Robert J. Gordon and George L. Perry. The first is the changing composition of the labor force toward secondary workers. The second is an increase in workers' sensitivity to inflation, an increase in the value of the α coefficient in equation (17) above. In addition, a slowdown in productivity growth has raised the rate of price increase consistent with any given rate-of-wage increase.

The labor force can be separated into *primary* and *secondary* workers. Primary workers are usually defined as the first, or major wage-earner in a family unit; other wage-earners are defined as *secondary* labor force participants. Thus heads of families and single individuals would generally be identified as primary workers. Given the working habits of American families, the proportion of primary workers among males over age 20 is higher than it is among females or males under age 20.

Primary workers tend to be more skilled and earn higher wages and tend to be more committed to the labor force than secondary workers. Unemployment rates are higher among secondary workers. In 1978, when the overall unemployment rate was 6 percent, it was 4.2 percent for men over age 20, 6 percent for women over age 20, and 16.3 percent for persons 16–19 years old. Since primary workers are more committed to the labor force, a given amount of unemployment among primary workers, say 100,000 persons, is likely to put more downward pressure on the wage rate than the same amount of unemployment among secondary workers. So a shift in the composition of the labor force that increases the number of secondary workers relative to primary workers will tend to raise the rate of wage increase associated with any given level of unemployment. A shift in composition toward secondary workers shifts up the $f(u)$ function in equation (17) and the Phillips curve of Figure 15.13.

Since the mid-1960s the composition of the U.S. labor force has shifted toward secondary workers. Two factors account for this shift. First, the ratio of population aged 16–19 years to the total population rose from 6.9 percent in 1965 to 7.7 percent by 1979. This increased the weight of young people in the labor force. Second, the labor force *participation rate* of women (the ratio of women in the labor force to total female population aged 16 and up) rose from 39.3 percent in 1965 to 51 percent by 1979. This increased the weight of women in the labor force.

The combination of these two factors shifted the Phillips curve up by more than one percentage point, according to Perry's estimates. In Figure 15.15 we show Perry's original estimate of the Phillips curve and his revised curve allowing for the change in labor force composition. The bottom curve is Perry's estimate of the curve in the mid-1950s. The center curve is his 1970 estimate, with the change in labor force composition. At

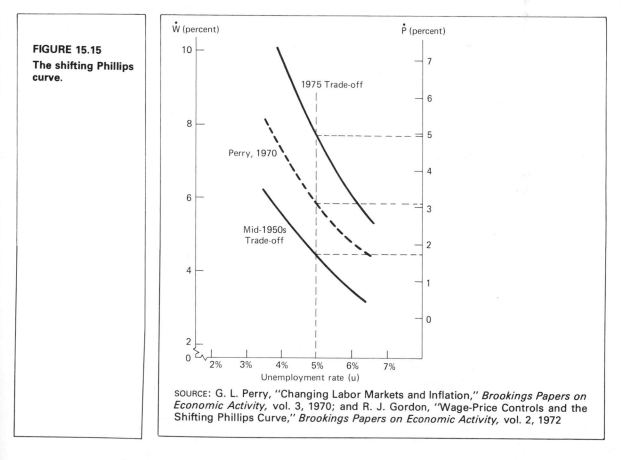

FIGURE 15.15

The shifting Phillips curve.

SOURCE: G. L. Perry, ''Changing Labor Markets and Inflation,'' *Brookings Papers on Economic Activity,* vol. 3, 1970; and R. J. Gordon, ''Wage-Price Controls and the Shifting Phillips Curve,'' *Brookings Papers on Economic Activity,* vol. 2, 1972

a 5 percent unemployment rate, the change in composition raises the long-run rate of inflation from about 1.5 to 3.0 percent.

The second factor shifting the Phillips curve up is increasing sensitivity of wage demands to inflation, the α parameter of equation (17). Perry's estimate of this parameter was a little under 0.4; for a 1 percent increase in the price level, wages rose 0.4 percent directly through the wage equation. This is the value of α in the bottom and middle Phillips curves of Figure 15.15.

As the rate of inflation increases, we would expect wage demands to become more sensitive to price changes, as more workers try to take account of inflation in setting nominal wages. Thus we would expect α to rise in inflationary periods. Gordon's results for the early 1970s confirmed this expectation. In his Phillips curve regression equations, the value of α rose during the 1970s. An estimate of 0.6 seemed best around 1975. The long-run Phillips curve of equations (19) and (20) has the factor $1/(1 - \alpha)$ in it. An increase in α from 0.4 to 0.6 raises this multiplicative factor from 1.7 to 2.5. This increase in α shifted the long-run Phillips curve up to the top curve in Figure 15.15 for 1975. At 5 percent unemployment, the mid-1970s Phillips curve gave us a 5 percent rate of inflation.

Since 1975, the Phillips curve has continued its upward drift, both because of a rising value of α and because of a slowdown in productivity growth. In recent work by Perry and Gordon, the estimate of α has risen to 0.8 or so. This gives us the further shift of the Phillips curve shown in Figure 15.16. There the 1975 trade-off is the same as in Figure 15.15, measured against the $\dot{W}$ axis. With α rising from 0.6 to 0.8, the long-run inflation rate for any given unemployment rate doubles. In Gordon's recent work, the α-value reaches unity, giving a vertical long-run Phillips curve in the neighborhood of 6% unemployment. This is the long-run classical result.

The rate of growth of labor productivity slowed markedly in the mid-1970s. This accounts for the other difference between Figures 15.15 and 15.16. In the 1960s, the trend rate of growth of productivity was a robust 3.2 percent per year. In the 1970s, this fell to at most 2 percent, with some estimates as low as 1 percent. Thus the $\dot{P}$ axis of Figure 15.16 shows a rate of price inflation of 10 percent corresponding to a 6 percent unemployment rate.

The upward shift of the Phillips curve lies beneath the inflation cycles since 1965. If the estimates of Gordon and Perry are correct, there has been an underlying trend toward a higher long-run inflation rate for any given unemployment rate. The long-run inflation rate seemed to have risen from 1.5 percent at a 5 percent unemployment rate in 1965 to 10 percent at a 6 percent unemployment rate in 1980. The major problem for macroeconomic policy over this period became controlling inflation.

The 1965–1971 inflation cycle

The first of the three inflation cycles began in 1966 when Federal purchases for defense spending jumped by $10 billion. At the end of 1965 the unemployment rate was 4 percent. The rate of inflation, measured by

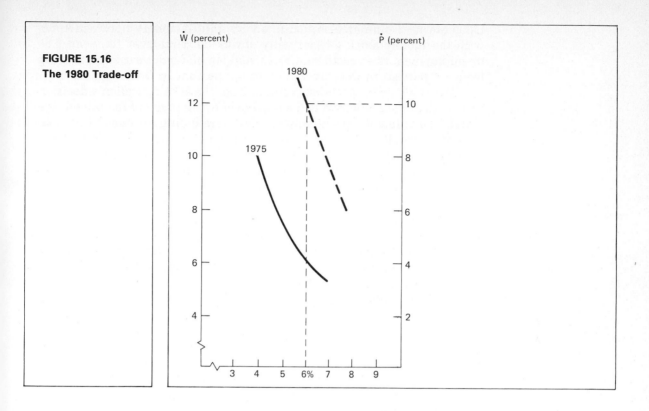

FIGURE 15.16
The 1980 Trade-off

the implicit deflator for GNP, was about 2 percent. Then, on top of a fully employed, essentially noninflationary economy, defense spending rose from $52.5 billion (annual rate) in the fourth quarter of 1965 to $65.5 billion in the fourth quarter of 1966, as the war in Vietnam was escalated. This stimulus, in the absence of a tax increase or substantial monetary restraint, quickly accelerated the rate of inflation. Year over year, the GNP deflator rose 1.8 percent in 1965 over 1964; it increased by 2.9 percent in 1967 over 1966, and by the last quarter of 1967 it was rising faster than 4 percent, annual rate.

Defense spending continued to rise in 1967 and 1968, reaching $80 billion at the end of 1968, an increase of more than 50 percent in three years. The output increase induced by the jump in defense spending tightened capacity utilization in the economy, stimulating a minor investment boom, which added further to demand. By the end of 1969, the GNP deflator was rising faster than 6 percent, annual rate. This was about the end of the demand-pull phase of the cycle, with the price-wage spiral pushing up prices against an aggregate demand curve that was more or less stationary.

The new administration, in early 1969, put the brakes on the economy, refusing to validate any further inflation. Federal purchases flattened out in 1969 and fell in 1970, shifting the IS curve left. The Federal Reserve's

Open Market Committee shifted to a very tight monetary policy in 1969, with the money stock (M_1) actually shrinking a bit over the year. The unemployment rate reacted with its usual lag of a half year or so, moving from 3.5 percent in December 1969 to 6.0 percent in December 1970.

The 1969–1970 recession resulted from the administration's decision to slow the inflation which had passed over to the phase of the price-wage spiral. The policy did eventually succeed in reducing the rate of inflation. Year over year, the GNP deflator rose 4.6 percent from 1970 to 1971, after a peak rate of inflation higher than 6 percent. In the third quarter of 1971, when the administration panicked and established wage and price controls, the inflation rate was actually down to 2.5 percent, annual rate.

Demand-pull and cost-push: 1972–1975

While the 1965–1971 cycle stemmed almost completely from excessive demand due to Vietnam War spending, the cycle beginning in 1972 had sources on both the demand-pull and cost-push sides. During 1972–1973, total demand grew unusually fast in the major industrial countries, as many of them moved out of shallow recessions around 1970. The average annual rate of growth of total real demand in the seven biggest OECD countries—Canada, United States, Japan, France, Germany, Italy, and the United Kingdom—was 4.8 percent from 1960 to 1971. In 1972 total demand in these countries grew by 5.8 percent, and in 1973 it grew by 6.8 percent. This demand growth pressed world and U.S. capacity to the limit, as was indicated by the 95 percent utilization rate as measured on the Wharton Economic Forecasting Associates index in late 1973. A concerted boom of this magnitude was bound to pull prices up fairly rapidly, even without shifts on the cost side.

The two major shifts on the supply side in 1972–1973 were in agricultural products and in fuel. The fuel situation is well known. The price of oil was rising throughout the period as the OPEC countries increased their exploitation of latent monopoly power. In late 1973 and early 1974, the OPEC countries engineered a jump in the price of oil by sharply reducing their total output. Viewed as an economic event, the oil price jump from the vicinity of $3–4 per barrel to $9–11 was a shift in monopoly power. Once this jump worked itself through the price-wage spiral, it left the U.S. price *level* higher, but it did not have a continuing effect on the *rate* of inflation.

The food situation was a bit more complicated. Estimates of annual production and consumption of total wheat and coarse grains, along with beginning-of-the-year stocks since 1968, are shown in Table 15.1. The ratio of stocks to the following year's consumption in 1968–1970 was a bit below the average for the 1960s, but not much. But consumption in excess of production in 1969 and 1970 drew stocks down from the 19–20 percent level to the 14–15 percent level. The small build-up in 1971 left stocks at the beginning of 1972 at 15.8 percent of the following year's consumption, well below the experience of the 1960s.

The biggest drop in world grain production since 1960 came in 1972,

	Production	Consumption	Beginning stock	
Year	(tons)	(tons)	(tons)	(percent of consumption)
1968	814	787	149	18.9
1969	818	832	176	21.2
1970	817	852	161	18.8
1971	902	886	128	14.5
1972	880	923	145	15.8
1973	964	953	101	10.6

TABLE 15.1

Production, consumption, and stocks of grain (millions of metric tons)

Source: D. E. Hathaway, *Brookings Papers on Economic Activity,* vol. 1, 1974

and it came at a point where stocks were already low. The combination of the shortfall in annual production below consumption (itself spurred by the world demand boom) and the low level of preexisting stocks resulted in the explosion of food prices that raised the retail food component of the CPI by 14.5 percent and the food component of the WPI by 20.3 percent in 1973 over 1972. This accounted for an estimated 3.7 percentage point increase in the overall CPI.

These cost-push shifts in food and fuel, working through the cost structure of the economy *before* any wage feedback occurred, account for an estimated 45 percent of the 1973 CPI increase, according to the estimates of Joel Popkin. Thus the second cycle of inflation might be divided about 50–50 between the demand-shift and cost-push origins.

Again in 1974, the administration acted to reduce aggregate demand to slow down the rate of inflation. Year over year, the GNP deflator rose 5.6 percent in 1973 over 1972, and 10.3 percent in 1974 as the price-wage spiral passed along the effects of the oil price increase. To slow down the rate of inflation, the administration tightened fiscal policy. In real terms (1958 dollars), federal purchases fell from a plateau of about $61 billion in 1971–1972 to $57 billion in 1973 and $56 billion in 1974. With a 10 percent rate of inflation, nominal federal purchases went up, but the drop in real g shifted the IS curve left. The Federal Reserve also pursued a tight money policy in 1973–1974. With inflation reaching 10 percent, the nominal-money stock grew only 4.7 percent from December 1973 to December 1974. This reduction of the real-money stock was a leftward shift of the LM curve. As a result, interest rates reached record highs in late 1974.

The result of the antivalidation policy was the deepest recession in the United States since the 1930s. Real GNP fell from the first quarter of 1974 to the middle of 1975, with the unemployment rate rising to over 9 percent. The result of this policy for the rate of inflation became apparent in mid-1975, with the rate of increase of the GNP deflator falling to around 5 percent. The stage was set by late 1975 for another demand expansion.

The expansion that began in late 1975 was spurred by fiscal stimulus and monetary accommodation. While real government purchases at the federal level remained essentially flat around $95–100 billion in 1972 dollars ($56–58 billion in 1958 dollars) from 1975 to 1980, small tax cuts and transfer payment increases shifted the high employment budget from a surplus of $9.3 billion in 1974 to a deficit of $18 billion in 1975. The high employment budget deficit remained in the $12–19 billion range until 1979, when fiscal policy tightened again.

The outward shift of the *IS* curve in 1975–76 was accompanied by monetary accommodation, shifting *LM* out. The money stock grew at an annual rate of 6.1 percent from 1974 to 1978, and short-term interest rates remained in the 5–7% range.

As a result of expansionary monetary and fiscal policy, the economy grew rapidly during 1975–78. Annual growth rates of real GNP were 5.9 percent in 1976, 5.3 percent in 1977, and 4.4 percent in 1978. The unemployment rate fell from 8.5 percent in 1975 to 5.8 percent by the end of 1978.

The rapid expansion led, unfortunately, to an increase in the rate of inflation and a depreciation of the dollar exchange rate. The GNP deflator rose by 5.2 percent in 1976; by 1979 the inflation rate was nearly 9 percent. The rapid expansion brought an increasing deficit in current account as imports grew and a dollar crisis in the fall of 1978. Following a pair of speeches on inflation and the dollar in November 1978, policy shifted to tightness. The high employment surplus shifted from a $12 billion deficit in 1978 to a $10 billion surplus in 1979. Money growth slowed and interest rates rose.

During 1979 the growth rate of real GNP slowed to 2.3 percent. OPEC again demonstrated its monopoly power by making use of reduced output in Iran to engineer even sharper rates of increase in oil prices than in 1973–1974. The inflation rate, spurred by the increase of the price of oil, rose above 10 percent. In October, 1979, the Fed tightened monetary policy another notch, and short-term interest rates rose above 10 percent. In January 1980 the economy moved once again into recession, with the unemployment rate jumping to 8 percent by May, 1980. The effects of the policy-induced recession on the inflation rate were just beginning to appear by then. The stage was set by mid-1980 for another expansion. The experience since 1965 has shown that it should be slow and gradual if another round of inflation is to be avoided.

Summary

The period since 1965 has seen three cycles of inflation in the United States. The first was a classic demand-pull, which was spread through the price-wage spiral as the administration hit the monetary and fiscal policy brakes in 1969. The second and third combined demand-pull and cost-push impulses, and was slowed by policy-induced recessions in 1974–1975 and 1980. These three inflation cycles were superimposed on an underlying Phillips curve that was shifting up through the period, converting a steady-state trade-off of 5 percent unemployment with a 1.5

percent rate of inflation to a 5 percent unemployment–5 percent inflation pair, as shown in Figure 15.15.

The three inflation cycles, and the shifting Phillips curve, are easily understood in the macro framework developed in Parts I–II of this book. As long as we recognize that inflationary impulses can come from the supply side, as well as from shifts in aggregate demand, we can see that rising inflation can accompany rising or falling unemployment. But although it is not too difficult to understand the causes of inflation, it is not easy to prescribe policy to deal with it.

Appendix

THE EFFECT OF INFLATION ON OUTPUT AND EMPLOYMENT

As indicated in Chapter 15, the sources of inflation can be separated into factors that shift either the aggregate demand curve or the aggregate supply curve. As shown in Figure 15A.1, these are defined as *demand-pull* and *cost-push* sources of inflation, respectively. Demand-pull—perhaps the most frequent source and the best understood—is the result of an exogenous shift up of the demand curve. The other source of inflation, which many economists feel was the major source of inflation in the 1970s, is an exogenous event which shifts up the supply curve. These may reflect increased wage demands—a shift in the labor supply curve—or a reduction in the supply of other factors of production, such as food or oil, as frequently occurred in the 1970s.

The behavior of output and employment will depend on the source of the inflation. We examine the impact on each of these important variables in the first two sections of this appendix. In the final section, we discuss the trade-off between employment and inflation that faces the policy maker.

THE IMPACT OF INFLATION ON OUTPUT

Inflation is always the result of excess demand. When aggregate demand exceeds aggregate supply, the price level will rise until supply and demand are balanced in the market. The impact on output, at least in the short run, will depend on the source of the excess demand. Has the gap been created by an increase in aggregate demand or is it the result of a decrease in aggregate supply?

A demand-pull impulse will shift the demand curve out and to the right as indicated in Figure 15A.2. At the initial price level, P_0, demand

334

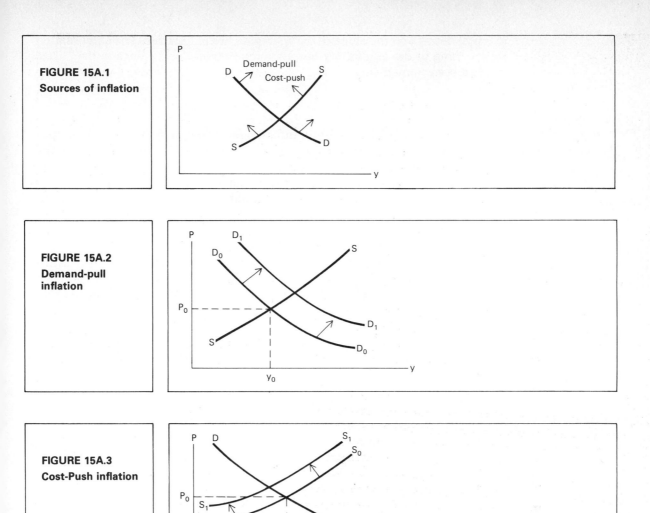

FIGURE 15A.1
Sources of inflation

FIGURE 15A.2
Demand-pull inflation

FIGURE 15A.3
Cost-Push inflation

exceeds supply and prices rise. Output increases as well as we move along the upward sloping aggregate supply curve. The extent to which the increase in demand is divided between increased output and increased prices depends on the slope of the aggregate supply curve.

The effect of a cost-push impulse is demonstrated by a shift to the left of the aggregate supply curve as depicted in Figure 15A.3. At the initial price level P_0 excess demand exists because a reduced quantity of output is being supplied. Once again, prices rise to eliminate the excess demand. With cost-push generated inflation, however, aggregate output falls. Whether the change leads largely to increased prices or reduced output will depend on the slope of the aggregate demand curve. The combination of rising prices and falling output, a too frequent occurrence in the 1970s, has been named stagflation.

THE IMPACT OF INFLATION ON EMPLOYMENT

The effect of demand-pull inflation on employment is clear. As output expands, employment must increase. The rise in the price level shifts the demand for labor out in Figure 15A.4, and employment increases.

The effect of cost-push inflation on employment is less clear. As above, the increase in prices will shift out the demand for labor; however, the cost-push impulse may have begun with a shift in the demand or supply of labor. The net impact on employment will depend on the magnitude and nature of these initial shifts.

In Figure 15A.5 we show an extreme case in which the shift in the production function does not shift the demand-for-labor curve, which is derived from the marginal product of labor (MPL)—the slope of the production function. If the production function shifts down horizontally, so that the slope is the same at each level of N, this will be the case. An example would be a production function in which raw materials M entered additively with capital and labor, which in turn produce value added:

$$y = F(K, N) + bM.$$

Here b is a fixed materials-output coefficient, and the MPL does not depend on M.

In this unusual case, the price increase that follows the aggregate supply curve shift will increase employment! In Figures 15A.5 and 15A.6 we see that the price rise increases employment from N_0 to N_2, partly cushioning the reduction in output. Essentially, as the supply of raw materials is reduced, employers substitute labor for materials in production, so production does not fall as much as it would if the labor input were fixed. Equilibrium output y_2 must lie between y_0 and y_1.

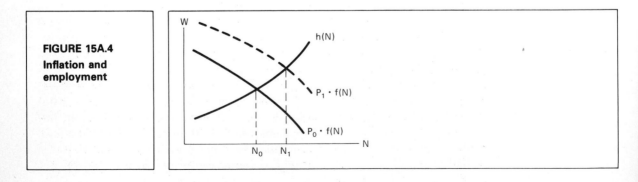

FIGURE 15A.4
Inflation and employment

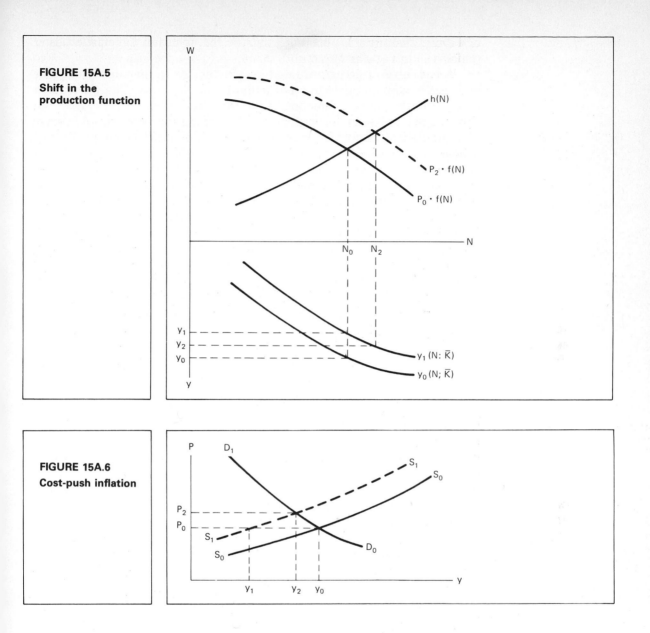

FIGURE 15A.5
Shift in the production function

FIGURE 15A.6
Cost-push inflation

Normally, we would expect a decrease in the supply of a cooperating factor of production to reduce the marginal product of labor as well as the average product. If this is the case, the $f(N)$ function in Figure 15A.5 would shift down along with the $y(N; K)$ function. The initial equilibrium level of employment would then drop along the labor supply curve. The subsequent price increase would restore some of the drop in employment. Whether the induced rise in employment could bring employment back to or beyond the initial N_0 level depends on the values of the elasticities of the curves in Figures 15A.5 and 15A.6.

A cost-push inflation initiated by a reduction in the supply of labor will lead unambiguously to a reduction in employment. The percentage increase in the vertical direction of the labor supply curve will equal the percentage increase in the vertical direction of the aggregate supply curve. The process of restoring equilibrium involves moving along an unchanged aggregate demand curve so that the equilibrium price level will not rise by the amount of the shift in aggregate supply. Thus, the increase in the demand for labor induced by a price rise will not fully offset the shift in labor supply, and employment will be reduced.

The effects of inflation on *output* are fairly clear: Demand-pull tends to increase it and cost-push reduces it. The effects on *employment* are less clear: Demand-pull tends to increase employment, but cost-push may not, in itself, reduce it and, in unusual cases, may increase it.

THE TRADE-OFF FOR POLICY MAKERS

The task facing the policy makers seems relatively easy in the case of a demand-pull inflationary impulse. If an increase in aggregate demand leads to undesired price increases, monetary and fiscal policies are available to offset the shifts in aggregate demand. Returning the aggregate demand curve to its initial level will remove the pressure for prices to rise and output will remain at its initial level.

In the case of a cost-push inflation the choices are more difficult. If the tools available can only operate on the demand curve, the initial combination of price level and output is no longer possible. The aggregate supply curve has shifted and no longer passes through the initial equilibrium. Should the policy makers shift aggregate demand to preclude prices from rising, they will pay a heavy price in terms of output and, in most cases, employment. If policy makers decide to prevent output from falling, a very large price change will result. If policy makers do nothing, the result will be stagflation with prices rising and output falling.

This unhappy choice results from the attempt to use demand policy to offset supply shifts. Clearly, what the policy maker needs to resolve this dilemma is a set of tools, such as have been discussed in Chapter 15, designed to operate on the aggregate supply curve.

The existence of stagflationary periods, in which both prices and unemployment rise, has been used to deny the existence of a Phillips curve and to support the claim that policy makers do not face a choice between unemployment and inflation. This claim appears to be misleading. As a result of a cost-push impulse, the economy may face more unemployment and more inflation. The policy maker, armed only with tools which operate on aggregate demand, still faces a choice as to how much of the change will be felt in prices and how much in output and employment. For this decision, the policy maker must continue to trade-off varying amounts of inflation with varying amounts of unemployment.

1. In the latter part of 1978 and the first half of 1979, the Federal Reserve policy makers set policy with reference to interest rates. Although the target rate did not appear to be particularly low, the high rates of actual inflation and increasing level of inflationary expectations meant the real rate of interest was, in fact, quite low. If the Federal Reserve continues in its attempt to pursue the given nominal rate of interest, or even if it raises the target rate moderately over time, what would you estimate would happen to the money stock and the price level? If the Fed abandons its interest rate target and pursues a steady growth rate in the money stock, what would you predict for the behavior of interest rates and prices?

2. Economists were widely praised in the 1960s for their use of demand management policies to deal with the problems facing the economy. In the 1970s, praise was replaced with questions as to whether the theories applied in the 1960s were still valid. Do you feel the high rates of inflation or unemployment or both, which characterized much of the 1970s, resulted from improper applications of demand management policies? Do they indicate an inability adequately to manage demand?

3. As an alternative theory to that described in equation (17), our Phillips curve discussion suggests replacing the price-change term with an inflation-expectation term. That is,

$$\dot{W} = f(u) + \dot{P}^e,$$

or, the rate of wage increase depends on the level of unemployment and the expected level of inflation.

What would the existence of a nonvertical Phillips curve in the long run imply about the manner in which price expectations relate to actual price behavior? If the rate of inflation expected always equals the rate of inflation experienced in the previous period, what will the short-run and long-run trade-offs between unemployment and inflation look like?

4. How are wage-price controls expected to cure inflation? Would the source of the inflation affect how well wage-price controls would be expected to work?

5. Estimates of the degree of unemployment required to have any significant impact on inflation were higher at end of the 1970s than at the beginning. Explain why!

SELECTED READINGS

M. Bronfenbrenner and F. D. Holzman, "Survey of Inflation Theory," *American Economic Review*, October 1963.

M. Friedman, "A Monetary and Fiscal Framework for Economic Stability," *American Economic Review*, June 1948; also in M. G. Mueller, ed., *Readings in Macroeconomics* (New York: Holt, Rinehart and Winston, 1971).

R. J. Gordon, "Wage-Price Controls and the Shifting Phillips Curve," *Brookings Papers on Economic Activity*, vol. 2, 1972.

R. J. Gordon, "Can the Inflation of the 1970s be Explained?" *Brookings Papers on Economic Activity*, vol. 1, 1977.

R. J. Gordon, "Recent Developments in the Theory of Inflation and Unemployment," in P. G. Korliras and R. S. Thorn, eds., *Modern Macroeconomics* (New York: Harper & Row, 1979).

D. E. Hathaway, "Food Prices and Inflation," *Brookings Papers on Economic Activity*, vol. 1, 1974.

J. M. Humphrey, "Some Current Controversies in the Theory of Inflation," in R. L. Teigen, ed., *Readings in Money, National Income and Stabilization Policy*, 4th ed. (Homewood, Ill.: Irwin, 1978).

D. Laidler and M. Parkin, "Inflation: A Survey," in P. G. Korliras and R. S. Thorn, eds., *Modern Macroeconomics* (New York: Harper & Row, 1979).

R. G. Lipsey, "The Relation Between Unemployment and the Rate of Change of Money Wages Rates in the United Kingdom, 1862–1957: A Further Analysis," *Economica*, February 1960.

W. Nordhaus and J. Shoven, "Inflation 1973: The Year of Infamy," *Challenge*, May/June 1974.

OECD, *Economic Outlook* (Paris/ December 1973).

G. L. Perry, "Changing Labor Markets and Inflation," *Brookings Papers on Economic Activity*, vol. 3, 1970.

G. L. Perry, "Slowing the Wage-Price Spiral: The Macroeconomic View," *Brookings Papers on Economic Activity*, vol. 2, 1978.

E. S. Phelps et al., *Microeconomic Foundations of Employment and Inflation Theory* (New York: Norton, 1970).

J. Popkin, "Commodity Prices and the U.S. Price Level," *Brookings Papers on Economic Activity*, vol. 1, 1974.

P. A. Samuelson and R. M. Solow, "Analytical Aspects of Anti-Inflation Policy," *American Economic Review*, May 1960.

J. A. Schnittker, "The 1972–1973 Food Price Spiral," *Brookings Papers on Economic Activity*, vol. 2, 1973.

C. L. Schultze, "Recent Inflation in the United States," Study Paper No. 1, Joint Economic Committee, 86th Congress, September 1959.

J. Tobin, "Inflation and Unemployment," in R. L. Teigen, ed., *Readings in Money, National Income and Stabilization Policy*, 4th ed. (Homewood, Ill.: Irwin, 1978).

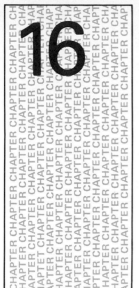

THE BALANCE OF PAYMENTS AND THE EXCHANGE RATE

In Parts I–III we ignored the foreign sector of the economy, essentially developing the theory of income determination in a closed economy. In this chapter we briefly sketch the relationship between the foreign sector and the domestic economy, beginning with a discussion of how domestic developments affect the balance of payments, and then shifting the focus to the feedback of the foreign sector onto determination of the equilibrium level of income, the price level, and the interest rate. While the U.S. economy is not particularly sensitive to foreign economic developments due to the small size of its foreign sector—gross exports of goods and services were $248 billion in a GNP of $2.4 trillion in 1979—many smaller and more open industrial economies such as those of the United Kingdom and the Netherlands are very sensitive to external developments. Thus, there is an obvious benefit to be gained by extending our discussion of income determination to include the foreign sector in terms of understanding macroeconomic developments in most of the industrialized world outside the United States. The cost of such an extension is low, since the foreign sector can be fitted into the *IS-LM* apparatus very conveniently.

The international balance of payments is divided into two major accounts. The *current account* records income from the sale of currently produced goods and of services, such as shipping, insurance, transportation of foreign tourists on U.S. airlines, and the use of U.S. technology and capital abroad. Income from provision of these capital services comes in the form of royalties and investment income. Total receipts for these sales of currently produced goods and services appear as exports, X, in the National Income and Product Accounts. The current account also records payments for the import of similar goods and services from abroad. These appear as imports, M, in the National Income and Product Accounts. Thus, the net exports term $X - M$ in the GNP identity,

$$\text{GNP} \equiv Y = C + I + G + (X - M),$$

from Chapter 2 is the current account balance in the balance of payments. It measures net receipts from the sale of currently produced U.S. goods and services abroad less payments for U.S. purchases of foreign-produced goods and services.

The second major account in the balance of payments is the *capital account*. This account measures the flow of funds from the United States to purchase assets from foreigners—U.S. firms' purchases of plant and equipment in Europe, U.S. investors purchasing stocks and bonds from foreigners, and so on—and the flow of funds into the United States as foreigners purchase assets here. The balance on capital account measures the net outflow of funds to purchase assets abroad. This has no direct relation to GNP, since the capital account involves asset transfers, not current production.

There is a minor third account in the balance of payments—net transfer payments to foreigners. This includes transfers by the private sector, R_f in Chapter 2, and government transfers such as AID grants and government pension payments to foreign citizens. These government transfers are in the T component of the GNP identity,

$$C + I + G + (X - M) \equiv \text{GNP} \equiv C + S + T + R_f.$$

The reader will recall from Chapter 2 that in computing T, we subtracted transfer, interest, and subsidy payments to U.S. citizens from gross tax receipts. Thus, government transfers to foreigners are included in T as taxes collected but are neither spent on purchases of currently produced goods and services, G, nor returned to the U.S. income stream as transfer, interest, or subsidy payments. So, R_f here includes only transfer payments to foreigners by the private sector.

The balance-of-payments surplus B is, then, net exports less the net private capital outflow F, less net transfers to foreigners R,

$$B = (X - M) - F - R, \tag{1}$$

where R is total government transfers plus private transfers, R_f above. Equation (1) defines roughly what is called officially the *Balance on Official Reserve Transactions Basis* in the U.S. balance-of-payments statistics. This is the net change in the country's official reserve position as a result of the transactions on the right-hand side of equation (1).

The interaction between the foreign and domestic sectors of the economy, as described in this chapter, goes roughly as follows. Exports enter the product market equilibrium condition, the *IS* equation, in about the same way as government purchases G—as exogenous expenditures for U.S. output. One difference is that exports should depend on the U.S. price level. As U.S. prices go up—holding foreign prices constant—U.S. exports should fall. Imports enter the *IS* equation in about the same way as saving or tax receipts—as withdrawals from the domestic income stream. Imports should rise with income and with an increase in U.S. prices relative to foreign prices. In the first section of this chaper we will build these relationships into the *IS* equation.

The capital account net outflow, *F*, depends on the level of U.S. interest rates, given foreign interest rates. As U.S. interest rates rise, the net outflow of capital decreases. In the second section of this chapter, we will combine these current and capital account relationships to identify the set of interest rate–income combinations for which the balance of payments surplus is zero. This will yield a line in the *r*, *y* space similar to the *IS* and *LM* curves. The position of the internal equilibrium *r*, *y* point relative to the balance-of-payments equilibrium line will tell us whether at that point the economy is running a balance-of-payments surplus or deficit.

In the third section we will develop the feedback of the surplus or deficit with fixed exchange rates on the domestic economy through the money supply. A balance-of-payments surplus, for instance, adds reserves to the banking system, increasing the money supply and shifting the *LM* curve right. The system will not really be in equilibrium until the *LM* curve stops shifting and the internal equilibrium position is consistent with external equilibrium.

In the fourth section we will look at the actual techniques used to maintain balance-of-payments equilibrium in recent years. Countries have used at times monetary and fiscal policy to maintain balance-of-payments equilibrium. This means, in our terms, moving the *IS-LM* intersection onto the balance-of-payments equilibrium line. On the other hand, if this involves reducing real output or raising interest rates beyond politically acceptable limits, countries have shifted the balance-of-payments equilibrium line by various means—import taxes, capital outflow taxes, import quotas, and so on—and also occasionally changed exchange rates to change the price relationship between foreign and domestic goods.

In the fifth section of this chapter we will look further into this obvious way to maintain balance-of-payments equilibrium by frequently—or even continually—changing the exchange rate to move the balance-of-payments equilibrium line to the *IS-LM* intersection. Here the balance-of-payments equation (1) can be reinterpreted as a fourth equilibrium condition—supply equals demand in the foreign exchange market—in our multimarket static equilibrium model.

In the sixth section we introduce a model of the domestic economy as a *price taker* in the world market. This model is relevant for most small countries, and for the United States in markets for raw materials, such as oil, or agricultural goods, such as wheat. Here we see the direct effect of movements on the exchange rate or the price level.

Finally we will conclude with some comments on likely developments of the balance-of-payments adjustment process in the 1980s. We can begin by introducing the foreign sector into the product market equilibrium condition, the IS equation.

THE CURRENT
ACCOUNT AND
PRODUCT MARKET
EQUILIBRIUM
Exports enter the product market equilibrium condition in a way analogous to government purchases; imports enter in a way similar to saving. For a given level of aggregate foreign demand and prices, real exports x depend on the U.S. price level P and the exchange rate p, which is measured in units of foreign currency per dollar. The foreign price of U.S. goods is given by $P^f = P \cdot p$. If the price of U.S. \$1 is 5 French francs so that $p = 5$, a good that sells for \$10 will sell for 50 F. Thus, for a given level of foreign demand and prices, our export function can be written as

$$x = x(P, p).$$

An increase in either the U.S. price P or the exchange rate p will raise the foreign price of U.S. goods and reduce exports.

Imports m depend on the U.S. level of income y, the exchange rate p which translates foreign prices into U.S. prices, and the price of competing U.S. goods P. An increase in the exchange rate p will reduce the U.S. price of foreign goods at a given foreign price level, tending to increase imports. An increase in the U.S. price level P will raise the price of U.S. goods that compete with imports, also tending to raise m. Thus, the import function is

$$m = m(y, P, p).$$

**Product market
equilibrium**
We can now expand the product market equilibrium condition, the IS equation, to include the foreign sector:

$$c + i + g + x - m = c + s + t + r_f,$$

or

$$i + g + x = s + t + m + r_f.$$

Since we might expect private transfer payments to foreigners r_f to rise with income, we can merge the r_f term into the import term to write the IS equilibrium equation as

$$i(r) + g + x(P, p) = s \left(y - t(y), \frac{A}{P} \right) + t(y) + m(y, P, p). \qquad [2]$$

Here foreign purchases of U.S. goods x inject income into the income stream, and U.S. imports m withdraw income. To keep the analysis as uncomplicated as possible and still get the basic qualitative points across, we will leave y out of the investment function. Inclusion of it would just flatten the IS curve somewhat.

The product market equilibrium condition (2) is shown for a given

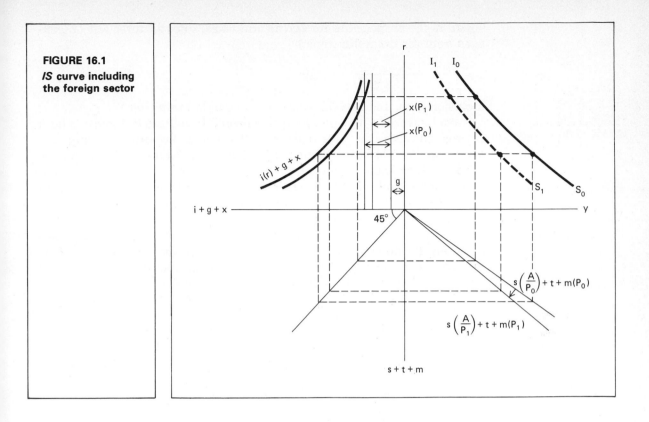

exchange rate and initial price level P_0 as the $I_0 S_0$ curve in the four-quadrant diagram of Figure 16.1. In the southeast quadrant $m(P_0)$ has been added to the $s + t$ function; in the northwest quadrant $x(P_0)$ has been added to the $i + g$ function.

An exogenous increase in exports due, say, to a general increase in foreign demand, will increase $x(P_0)$ and shift the *IS* curve out to the right in Figure 16.1. An exogenous upward shift in the import function due, say, to a change in consumer tastes between U.S. and European autos, will rotate the $s + t + m$ function downward and shift the *IS* curve left in Figure 16.1.

The *IS* curve becomes steeper with the inclusion of the demand for imports which depends on income. A drop in the interest rate r will stimulate investment and raise y through the multiplier process but the increase in y will be smaller in an open economy than in a closed economy due to the import leakage. Some of the increased spending is for foreign goods which generate no increase in domestic output and no increase in domestic incomes to induce further demand. In terms of the earlier simple multiplier of Chapter 3, the marginal propensity to import, m', is simply added to the propensities for saving and taxes, since all three reflect leakages from the domestic stream:

$$\Delta y = \frac{1}{s' \cdot (1 - t') + t' + m'} \, \Delta g.$$

Inclusion of m' reduces the value of the simple multiplier.

The effect of a price change on the *IS* curve

An increase in the domestic price level P from P_0 to P_1 increases both saving—through the real balance effect—and imports, rotating the $s + t + m$ line down in Figure 16.1. The price increase also shifts the $i + g + x$ function in Figure 16.1 to the right as exports are reduced. All of these effects work to shift the *IS* curve to the left toward I_1S_1 in Figure 16.1. The price increase reduces domestic income-related spending both by increasing saving to restore real assets and by redirecting expenditures to imports, which become relatively cheaper. It also reduces exports—spending on domestic output by foreigners—by making foreign goods relatively cheaper. This reduces the equilibrium income that goes with any given $i(r) + g$, shifting *IS* left.

An increase in the exchange rate will have the same effect on exports and imports as a P increase, but will not directly affect saving. Thus, a 10 percent exchange rate increase will shift the *IS* curve to the left a little less than a 10 percent increase in domestic prices relative to foreign prices.

The modified *IS* curve of Figure 16.1 can be combined with our usual *LM* curve representing the money market equilibrium condition

$$\frac{M(r)}{P} = m(r, y), \qquad\qquad [3]$$

to determine internal equilibrium r and y on the demand side of the economy. To see whether that r, y combination will yield a balance-of-payments surplus or deficit we can develop the line in the r, y space that traces out points where the balance-of-payments surplus $B = 0$, thus introducing the capital account into the analysis.

THE CAPITAL ACCOUNT AND BALANCE-OF-PAYMENTS EQUILIBRIUM

International capital *flows* result from the international purchase and sale of assets. In Chapter 12 we reviewed Tobin's portfolio distribution view of the demand for money in which persons with a given amount of liquid assets split their holdings between money and bonds as a function of the level of the interest rate. By completely analogous reasoning, we can see that a person will divide his holdings of assets between foreign and domestic assets depending on the level of interest rates at home and abroad. For a given set of interest rates he will reach an equilibrium distribution of his portfolio of assets between domestic and foreign assets. At any given asset level, a change in interest rates will produce a redistribution of assets, creating capital flows.

As total assets grow, the allocation of additions to portfolios among foreign and domestic assets will depend on interest rate levels. Thus, as

U.S. wealth grows and U.S. citizens will put a bigger fraction of additions to their portfolios into foreign assets, the higher the level of foreign interest rates relative to U.S. rates. And as foreign wealth grows and foreign investors will put a smaller fraction of increments to their portfolios into U.S. assets, the higher are foreign rates relative to U.S. rates. Thus, at given levels of foreign interest rates, the net outflow of capital F—net U.S. purchases of foreign assets less net foreign purchases of U.S. assets—will be a decreasing function of the U.S. interest rate,

$$F = F(r); \qquad F' < 0.$$

As the U.S. rate rises, the equilibrium net outflow from additions of foreign assets to portfolios falls.

The balance-of-payments equation

We can now complete the balance-of-payments equation by subtracting the net capital outflow F from net exports less transfer payments, measured in current U.S. dollars. Exports are measured at the U.S. price level; the dollar value of imports is given by the foreign price P^f divided by the exchange rate p. Thus, the balance on current account, in money terms, is given by

$$X - M = P \cdot x(P, p) - \frac{P^f}{p} \cdot m(y, P, p), \qquad [4]$$

and the balance-of-payments surplus B is

$$B = P \cdot x(P, p) - \frac{P^f}{p} \cdot m(y, P, p) - F(r). \qquad [5]$$

Here again we have merged transfers to foreigners into the import function. For the balance-of-payments surplus to be zero, net exports must equal the net capital outflow.

An increase in y reduces net exports, mainly by increasing imports, requiring an increase in r to reduce F if a zero surplus is to be maintained. Thus, the slope of the BP line in r, y space, along which $B = 0$, is positive.

Internal equilibrium and the balance-of-payments

We can derive the BP line from equation (4) by setting net exports equal to the net capital outflow, as is shown in Figure 16.2. At a given foreign price level and exchange rate, and a given initial U.S. price level P_0, net exports are shown as a decreasing function of y in the southeast quadrant of Figure 16.2. The net capital outflow is shown as a decreasing function of r in the northwest quadrant. The 45° construction line in the southwest quadrant represents the constraint that $B = 0$; net exports equal net capital outflow.

Starting with an initial income level y_0, we can trace around the four-quadrant diagram to find the interest rate r_0 that equates the net capital outflow to net exports. This gives us an r_0, y_0 point where $B = 0$. The line connecting all such r_0, y_0 points which maintain $B = 0$ is shown as the $B_0 P_0$ line in Figure 16.2. This is the balance-of-payments equilibrium line in the r, y space. Any r, y point below the line will yield a balance-of-payments deficit. At point A, for example, the interest rate

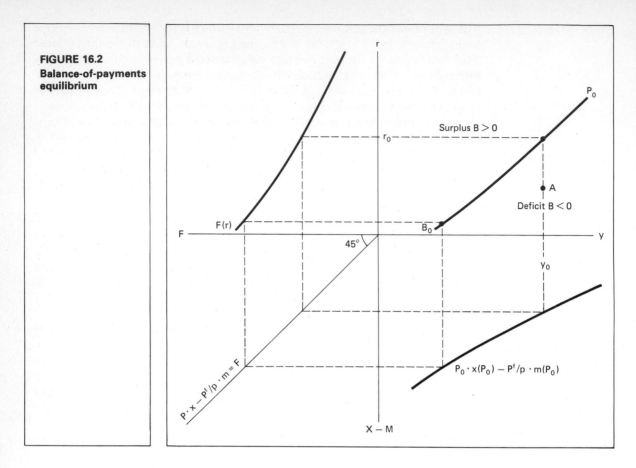

FIGURE 16.2
Balance-of-payments equilibrium

below r_0 yields a capital outflow in excess of the net exports level corresponding to y_0. Conversely, any r, y point above the B_0P_0 line will yield a balance-of-payments surplus.

To determine whether any given internal equilibrium r, y point determined by the intersection of the IS and LM curves will yield a balance-of-payments surplus or deficit, we can simply superimpose the BP line on the IS-LM diagram, as shown in Figure 16.3. There the equilibrium r_0, y_0 point lies below the B_0P_0 line, so that at the existing price level P_0, which maintains equilibrium between demand and supply in the demestic economy, the balance of payments is in deficit. At income level y_0, the interest rate would have to be raised to r_1 to reduce the net capital outflow enough to eliminate the deficit. We will turn to questions of balance-of-payments adjustment after analyzing the effect of a domestic price change on the position of the BP line.

Price changes and balance-of-payments equilibrium

The current account in the balance of payments, in money terms, is given by

$$CA = X - M = P \cdot x(P, p) - \frac{P^f}{p} \cdot m(y, P, p).$$

This expression is shown in the southeast quadrant of Figure 16.2 for a given exchange rate, foreign price level, and initial domestic price level P_0. An increase in the domestic price level will increase real imports as foreign goods are substituted for domestic goods. With a given foreign price level and exchange rate, this will also increase the U.S. dollar value of imports, M.

Similarly, an increase in P will reduce real exports. But whether the money value of exports X rises or falls depends on whether the decrease in real exports outweighs the increase in price—that is, on the elasticity of foreign demand for exports. If the demand for exports has an elasticity greater than unity in absolute value, that is, $E_x < -1$, $\Delta X/\Delta P$ will be negative and a price increase will reduce the money value of exports. In this case, a price increase reduces X and increases M, clearly reducing net exports at any given y level. Thus, a price increase will shift the net export line in the southeast quadrant of Figure 16.4 up, shifting the BP line up toward B_1P_1. If a price increase reduces net exports at the initial income level y_0, an increase in the interest rate from r_0 to r_1 is required to reduce the net capital outflow enough to eliminate the balance-of-payments deficit.

Even if the absolute value of the price elasticity of export demand is less than unity so that a price rise *increases* export revenue X, the increase in X would have to be large enough to offset the increase in M if the price increase is to shift the BP curve down instead of up in Figure 16.4. Thus, export price elasticity greater than one in absolute value is a sufficient, but not a necessary, condition for a domestic price increase to reduce net exports and shift the BP line up in Figure 16.4.

Empirically, it seems fairly clear that the price elasticities of both export and import demand are at least one in absolute value. For exam-

FIGURE 16.3
Balance-of-payments deficit

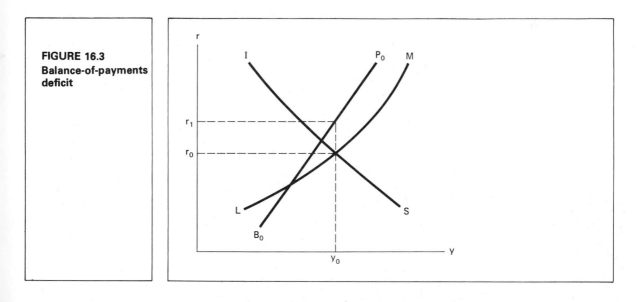

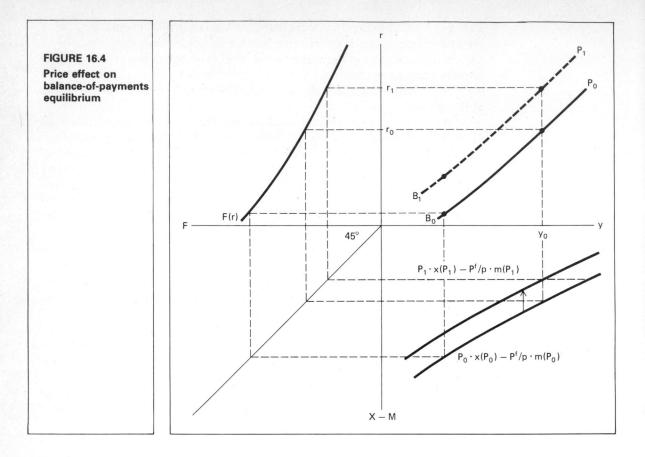

FIGURE 16.4

Price effect on balance-of-payments equilibrium

ple, Houthakker and Magee found that the overall price elasticity of demand for U.S. exports is about −1.5, and that U.S. import demand has a price elasticity of about −0.9. Thus while it is theoretically possible for a price increase to increase net exports $X − M$, the empirical studies suggest that, in fact, this is not the case.

The effect of a change in the exchange rate

Returning to the expression for net exports

$$X - M = P \cdot x(P, p) - \frac{P^f}{p} \cdot m(y, P, p),$$

we can see that an increase in the exchange rate—that is, an up-valuation of the dollar—will reduce real exports, and increase real imports. The real-export drop will reduce X at a given U.S. price level. But for a given foreign price level P^f, the p increase reduces the dollar price of imports, P^f/p. Thus, an increase in p reduces the dollar price of imports and increases real imports m. Again, whether M rises or falls with a p increase depends on the U.S. price elasticity of demand for imports in a way exactly analogous to the previous case concerning the effect on X of a change in P.

If the import elasticity E_m has an absolute value greater than one, the p increase will reduce net exports $X - M$, and shift the BP curve up in Figure 16.4. And even if the import price elasticity is less than one, so that a price increase reduces M, the p increase may reduce $X - M$ due to the reduction in export earnings. Since the empirical studies generally suggest that the price elasticity of import demand is substantially greater than one in absolute value, it seems clear that, in fact, an "up-valuation"—an increase in p—will reduce net exports and shift BP up. Conversely, a devaluation—a decrease in p—will shift BP down in Figure 16.4. This, of course, suggests the obvious way to handle the deficit situation in Figure 16.3 if the r_0, y_0 combination is right from the point of view of internal domestic needs. This takes us to the important question of the balance-of-payments adjustment process.

BALANCE-OF-PAYMENTS ADJUSTMENT AND THE *LM* CURVE

A balance-of-payments surplus situation is shown in Figure 16.5. The internal equilibrium interest rate and real-income point corresponding to the *IS-LM* intersection r_0, y_0 lies above the BP line. This means that at y_0 the interest rate r_0 is so high that net exports exceed the net capital outflow. It would take a reduction of the interest rate from r_0 to r_1 to reduce the surplus to zero.

The balance-of-payments surplus means that both the commercial banks and the central bank—the Federal Reserve System—are adding to reserves. With a surplus, the business sector's receipts from foreigners exceed payments. This means, essentially, that on balance the commercial banks in the United States are receiving for deposit checks denominated in foreign currencies. Either U.S. citizens are, on balance, receiving foreign currency checks and depositing them, or foreigners are buying U.S. currency from the banks, paying in foreign currency checks, and then paying their bills in dollars.

In either case, the commercial banks are in net receipt of foreign

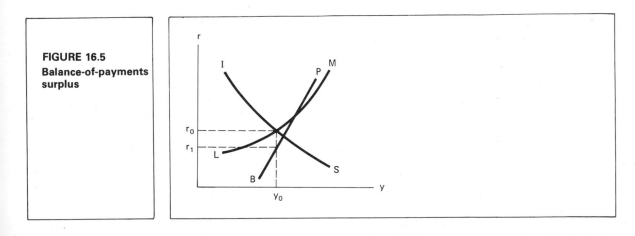

FIGURE 16.5
Balance-of-payments surplus

currency deposits, which they then deposit at the Fed, which credits them with the appropriate amount in dollars. At that point the Fed has an increase in foreign exchange reserves, and the commercial bank has an increase in unborrowed reserves, deposits at the Fed.

The Fed can essentially do two things with its increment to foreign exchange assets. First, it can lend them to the foreign country by buying, say, a Treasury bill of the foreign government. The bill is then held as an increase in U.S. official reserves. Or, the Fed can buy gold from the foreign central bank. The gold then becomes an addition to reserves.

Surpluses and the money supply

The more interesting result of the surplus, from the balance-of-payments adjustment point of view, is the effect on commercial bank reserves. When the commercial banks deposit foreign exchange at the Fed, their reserves go up by the amount of the surplus B. This represents an increase in unborrowed reserves, and, all other things equal, expands the money supply by

$$\Delta M = \frac{B}{h + z(1 - h)},$$

where h is the fraction of the money supply the public holds as currency, and z is the reserve ratio, as developed in Chapter 13.

Thus, the situation shown in Figure 16.5 cannot be a full equilibrium situation because the surplus is increasing the money supply, shifting the LM curve to the right. As long as the IS-LM intersection is not on the BP line the surplus or deficit tends to shift the LM curve toward the intersection of the IS and BP lines.

Adjustment through shifts of the LM curve

In the absence of central bank open market operations to counter the external reserve increase, the LM curve thus shifts right with a balance-of-payments surplus and left with a deficit as the money supply changes. Figure 16.6 shows the area around r_0, y_0 in Figure 16.5 blown up so we can follow the adjustment process.

As the money supply increases, the LM curve shifts right from L_0M_0. As usual, the LM shift increases demand in the economy, creating excess demand and raising prices. The price level increase moderates the LM shift, since with P rising the real-money supply $m = M/P$ increases less rapidly than the nominal-money supply M. The price level increase also shifts the IS curve left from I_0S_0 due to both the asset effect in the consumption function and the reduction in real net exports.

If the price increase is raising equilibrium output and employment on the supply side of the economy, then the internal equilibrium point A in Figure 16.6 is moving down and to the right, as indicated by the arrow from A. The point here is that since the price increase, resulting from excess demand, is raising supply-side output, the internal equilibrium point must move to the right in Figure 16.6; the IS and LM shifts resulting from the price increase cannot overbalance the LM shift due to the initial M increase and shift the internal equilibrium point A to the left.

At the same time that the surplus is raising output and the price level internally by increasing M, the price level increase is also shifting BP up from $B_0 P_0$, as we saw in the previous section. With the IS curve shifting left, this moves the IS-BP intersection at point B up and to the left, as shown in Figure 16.6.

With the internal equilibrium point A sliding *down* the shifting IS curve, and B moving *up* it, eventually equilibrium will be reached both internally and externally at r_1, y_1 in Figure 16.6, where all three lines cross. Since the A point is moving to the right, the final equilibrium y_1 exceeds the initial internal equilibrium y_0. The balance-of-payments surplus eliminates itself by increasing the money supply and the price level in the economy, which increases y and reduces r, both of which act to reduce the surplus.

Thus, in a fixed exchange rate system, balance-of-payments surpluses and deficits tend to be self-liquidating through the monetary mechanism. A surplus increases the money supply, expanding demand, output, and

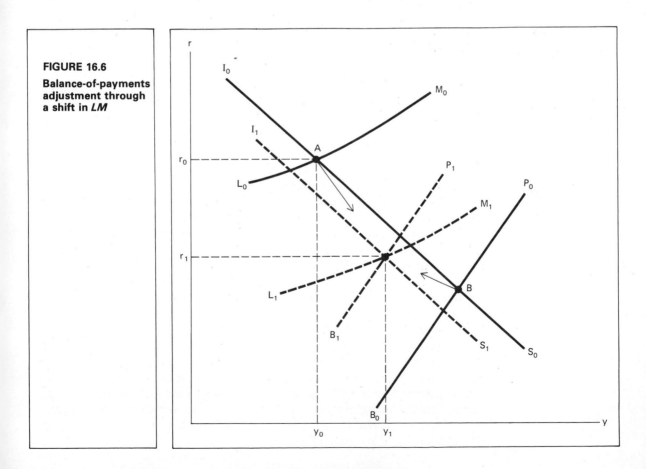

FIGURE 16.6

Balance-of-payments adjustment through a shift in LM

imports and reducing r, which increases the net capital outflow. A deficit reduces the money supply with just the opposite results.

The central bank can prevent this kind of adjustment, at least temporarily, in one of two ways. In the case of a surplus, the central bank can simply refuse to credit foreign exchange deposits as reserves. The commercial banks can obtain domestic deposits or currency for foreign exchange, but these may not be counted as reserves. This is sometimes called *sterilization of the surplus*—insulating the domestic economy from its effects.

The other way to counter the effect of a surplus on reserves is through open market operations, selling bonds to the banks to absorb reserves. This procedure will also work in the reverse situation of a deficit. The central bank can then sell reserves, buying bonds, to the commercial banks to replace their losses as they convert deposits at the central bank into foreign exchange to send abroad.

Both of these techniques are essentially stopgap measures taken to insulate the economy from the effects of the deficit or surplus while other policies work to bring the economy into full external and internal equilibrium. For example, if in the deficit situation of Figure 16.3 the r_0, y_0 point was considered the optimum from a domestic point of view—full employment and interest rates low enough to meet an investment target—the government would not wish to let the adjustment process work to raise r and reduce y. Or in the surplus situation of Figures 16.5 and 16.6 the government may feel threatened politically by the prospect of a price level increase—an inflation. In these cases the monetary authorities would counter the effects of the surplus or deficit while policies to shift the BP line to the desired position were undertaken.

BALANCE OF PAYMENTS ADJUSTMENT POLICY WITH FIXED EXCHANGE RATES

Suppose the policy maker finds the economy at the internal equilibrium r_0, y_0 point A in Figure 16.7, running a payments deficit since point A is below the B_0P_0 curve. The monetary adjustment process would normally involve some reduction in y and increase in r in the direction of the arrows from points A and B in Figure 16.7. But suppose further that the policy maker wants to establish full equilibrium at point E, with only a slight drop in y, but a larger increase in interest rates than would be attained by the normal adjustment process.

The problem, then, is to shift B_0P_0 to B_1P_1 and then use monetary and fiscal policy to shift L_0M_0 to L_1M_1 and I_0S_0 to I_1S_1. Thus, we can divide the policy problem into two parts. First, some direct action specific to the balance of payments must be taken to move BP to B_1P_1. Then the normal monetary and fiscal policy tools can be used to move the IS and LM curves to an intersection at E in Figure 16.7. The last part of this process—the change in the monetary-fiscal policy mix to move internal equilibrium from point A to point E—is already familiar. It is the policy that shifts the BP line that is of interest here.

Exchange rate adjustment

The most obvious way to shift the *BP* line and eliminate a deficit or surplus without much disturbing internal equilibrium is to change the exchange rate *p*. An increase in *p*—an up-valuation of the domestic currency—will raise the foreign price of exports and reduce the domestic price of imports, reducing net exports and the balance-of-payments surplus at any given interest rate and income combination. In graphical terms a *p* increase will shift the *BP* line up so that a country in the surplus position illustrated in Figures 16.5 and 16.6 can eliminate its surplus and restore full equilibrium by up-valuing its currency. Up-valuations were used repeatedly in the early 1970s by countries such as West Germany, Japan, and Switzerland to reduce or eliminate persistent balance-of-payment surpluses.

A decrease in *p*—a devaluation of the domestic currency—will increase the current account balance and reduce a balance-of-payments deficit. A country in the deficit position illustrated in Figures 16.3 and 16.7 could thus restore full equilibrium by devaluing, shifting the *BP* line down. This action was taken, for example, by the United Kingdom in 1968 when the pound sterling was devalued from $2.80 to $2.40 for £1, as well as by the United States in 1971 when the dollar was devalued by an average of 6 to 7 percent against the other major currencies.

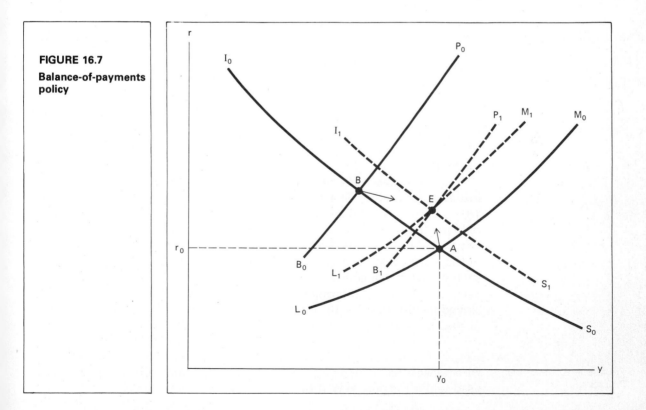

FIGURE 16.7
Balance-of-payments policy

Instead of changing the exchange rate, the government can change the current account surplus by manipulating tariffs, import quotas, taxes, or subsidies. For example, an increase in an import tariff will reduce the dollar value of imports if the price elasticity of demand is greater than one in absolute value. This would shift the *BP* line down and reduce a deficit. Similarly, an import quota will reduce imports to the quota level, again shifting *BP* down. Both of these techniques of adjustment run counter to the General Agreement on Tariffs and Trade (GATT), to which most nations are parties. The GATT basically rules out unilateral tariff changes and allows quota impositions only in extreme cases. This is because all countries realize that both tariffs and quotas reduce the gains in efficiency and welfare that are obtained by free trade. In addition, most countries understand that if one country violates the rules of the game established under GATT and erects import barriers, other countries will retaliate, cutting off the first country's exports and leaving everyone worse off.

A more politically acceptable direct current account measure is the use of taxes and rebates to influence trade flows. For example, several European countries rebate, to producers and sellers, taxes they pay on production of items shipped abroad, and apply to imports taxes equivalent to those paid in domestic manufacture of the item. Changes in the degree to which these subsidies and taxes are applied will shift the *BP* curve. Frequent manipulation of these taxes and subsidies is generally considered to be bad international behavior, since such action really is just a way around the GATT prohibition on tariff manipulation. Thus, countries tend to justify the institution of such schemes as long-run structural tax changes and to leave them in place once they are established.

The balance-of-payments surplus can be affected, and the *BP* line shifted, by direct measures affecting the net capital outflow, as well as the current account. The most prominent use of these measures in the 1960s was the interest equalization tax (IET) and the foreign credit restraint (FCR) program instituted by the United States to stem its capital outflow in the mid-1960s.

The IET was a tax on U.S. purchases of foreign stocks and bonds, initially imposed in 1964 and eliminated under floating exchange rates in 1974. The tax reduced the return on foreign portfolio investment, and thus reduced the fraction of additions to U.S. assets that go abroad. The FCR program, begun in 1965, and also eliminated in 1974, first limited the outflow of capital through lending by banks and nonfinancial institutions such as insurance companies. By 1970, corporate financing of direct investment abroad was brought under this program. These techniques all served to shift the U.S. *BP* line down during a period of chronic balance-of-payments deficit.

FLEXIBLE EXCHANGE RATES

Direct measures influencing the current and capital accounts were usually used under the post-WW II Bretton Woods system to avoid exchange rate adjustment in the case of a balance-of-payments disequilibrium. There are several reasons for this reluctance to change exchange rates.

First, at the International Monetary Conference held at Bretton Woods, New Hampshire, in 1944, which set up the International Monetary Fund (IMF), the industrial countries agreed that changes in exchange rates should be made only in cases of *fundamental disequilibrium*. This fixity of exchange rates was considered necessary to minimize uncertainty in order to encourage international trade. The fundamental disequilibrium notion was generally interpreted as ruling out frequent exchange rate changes, leading countries to resort to direct measures.

The second and closely related reason is that the international monetary system under Bretton Woods was biased toward devaluation. A country running a surplus—suitably sterilized—and accumulating reserves had no incentive, other than international disapproval of its behavior, to eliminate its surplus. But on the other side of the coin, the country running the corresponding deficit had to take some action before it ran out of reserves. The natural step was devaluation, which is politically unpopular for two kinds of reasons. First, in a country dependent on imports for basic staples of living, like the United Kingdom, a devaluation will be unpopular because it raises the price of imported foodstuffs. And the bigger and more obvious the devaluation, the more unpopular it will be. Second, there seems to be a loss of national "face" when the currency is devalued. Since most voters do not understand the issues involved very well, it is easy for an opposition politician to score points by decrying the "cheapening of our money."

Thus, in the Bretton Woods system, exchange rate changes tended to be infrequent. Since they came late they generally had to be large, and this exposed the government that devalued to severe political problems. As a result, exchange rate changes were used as a last resort after all the other ways of manipulating the *BP* line to restore equilibrium had been tried under Bretton Woods.

The shift to flexible exchange rates

During the period 1971–1973 the Bretton Woods system broke down under the pressure of enormous U.S. balance-of-payments deficits. By the end of the 1960s the U.S. trade balance had shrunk to zero under the pressure of excess demand and an overvalued dollar. The current account balance became negative in 1968, and was −$3.9 billion in 1971. With monetary policy easing in 1970–1971, following the recession of 1969–1970, the U.S. Official Settlements Balance was −$9.8 billion in 1970 and −$29.8 billion in 1971.

To keep exchange rates fixed, foreign central banks had to buy this outflow of dollars; this caused them sterilization difficulties, and they felt that their domestic money supplies were running out of control. In the face of the huge deficit in 1971, and the shrinkage of the U.S. gold stock from $15 billion in the mid-1960s to $10 billion in 1971, as foreign central banks exchanged dollars for gold, the Nixon administration ended gold sales in August 1971. This cut the Bretton Woods tie of the dollar to gold and clearly put the choice to the European countries and Japan: absorb the dollars flowing out through the U.S. payments deficit or permit exchange rates to float.

A new set of rates was negotiated at the Smithsonian Institute in Washington on December 1971, with the dollar devalued by about 7 percent on average. These rates held, more or less, through 1972, with another $10.4 billion flowing to foreign central banks through the U.S. deficit. As this deficit continued into early 1973, foreign central banks, especially the Deutsche Bundesbank and the Bank of Japan, gave up on holding the new parities and floated their exchange rates against the dollar. The monetary system has seen the major currencies floating, with frequent central bank intervention, since 1973. The smaller countries have been pegging their currencies to one of the major currencies, the Special Drawing Rights (SDR's) issued by the IMF, or an average of the major currencies.

Determination of the exchange rate

The polar opposite case from the Bretton Woods system is a completely free exchange rate system, with rates determined by supply and demand on the foreign exchange market. This provides continuous exchange rate changes, always maintaining the *BP* line passing through the intersection of the *IS* and *LM* curves and eliminating the balance-of-payments problem.

The foreign exchange market can be understood by viewing the *BP* equation,

$$B = P \cdot x(P, p) - \frac{P^f}{p} \cdot m(y, P, p) - F(r),$$

as the foreign exchange market equilibrium condition with $B = 0$.

Demand in the foreign exchange market is generated by U.S. exports $P \cdot x(P, p)$. These earn foreign exchange receipts, which exporters then take to the foreign exchange market to obtain dollars. The greater the total value of exports, the greater the demand for dollars. At the same time, foreigners are receiving dollars due to U.S. imports and net capital outflow. They supply these dollars to the foreign exchange market. The greater the value of imports and capital outflow, the greater the supply of dollars.

This gives us the supply of dollars to the foreign exchange market,

$$S = \frac{P^f}{p} \cdot m(y, P, p) + F(r),$$

where S rises with an increase in p. An increase in the exchange rate increases import earnings if import demand has a price elasticity greater than unity. The demand for dollars is given by

$$D = P \cdot x(P, p),$$

with D falling as p rises. The equilibrium price of the dollar—the exchange rate—is established where demand equals supply, at p_0 in Figure

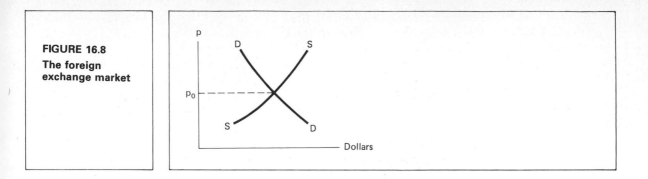

FIGURE 16.8
The foreign exchange market

p

D   S

p_0 ----

S   D

Dollars

16.8. Equating demand and supply gives us the foreign exchange market equilibrium condition,

$$P \cdot x(P, p) = \frac{P^f}{p} \cdot m(y, P, p) + F(r),$$ [6]

which is the same as equation (5) with B set at zero.

Internal and external equilibrium

With a given foreign price level P^f, the foreign exchange market equilibrium condition (6) can be combined with our usual equilibrium equations for the product, money, and labor markets and the production function to yield simultaneous equations in five key variables, y, N, P, r, and p, the exchange rate.

The foreign exchange market equilibrium condition (6) is represented by the BP line in the r, y space for any given p. A change in p, as we have seen, shifts the BP line. If p continually changes to clear the foreign exchange market so that the supply and demand of dollars in Figure 16.8 are always equal given the internal equilibrium r and y, then the p changes continually shifting the BP line to pass through the IS-LM intersection.

In Figure 16.9 the effect of monetary policy on the exchange rate is illustrated. Beginning with an initial equilibrium at point A, suppose the money stock is increased, so the LM curve shifts out to L_1M_1. The internal equilibrium point moves to B. What happens to the exchange rate p? It must change to shift the BP curve to B_1P_1, which passes through the new internal IS-LM equilibrium B. This implies an immediate drop in p to shift the BP curve down. The force behind the drop in p can be understood in Figure 16.8. As the interest rate falls, there is an increased capital flow $F(r)$, increasing the supply of dollars to the foreign exchange market. This shifts the supply curve out in Figure 16.8, reducing the equilibrium value of p. This movement is reinforced by the increase in y in Figure 16.9, which also shifts the supply curve in Figure 16.8 by increasing imports. Thus, an expansionary monetary policy will lead quickly to a devaluation in the floating exchange rate p, and a contractionary monetary policy will lead to an up-valuation.

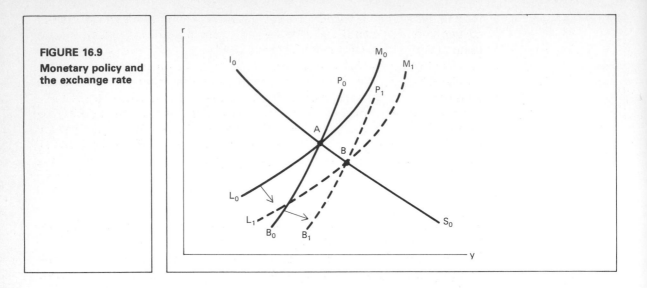

FIGURE 16.9

Monetary policy and the exchange rate

The effect of fiscal policy on the exchange rate is unclear, however. An increase in government purchases pulls up interest rates, reducing the capital outflow, but also increases real income y, increasing imports. The direction of the supply curve of shift in Figure 16.8 then depends on the relative strength of these two effects. In Figure 16.9, with B_0P_0 steeper than L_0M_0, an expansionary fiscal policy move, shifting IS up, would require a downward shift in BP, and thus a devaluation of e, to restore external equilibrium. But if BP were flatter than LM at the start, the opposite results would hold. Empirical results for the United States and Canada suggest that the BP line is fairly steep. Helliwell's stimulations for Canada show that the slope of the BP line is about the same as that of the LM curve; fiscal policy in Canada is approximately neutral with respect to the exchange rate. Branson's calculations for the United States, reported in a comment on Kwack and Schink, show a BP line steeper than the LM curve; an expansionary fiscal move will result in devaluation.

Comparing monetary and fiscal policy effects on the exchange rate, we see that a shift in monetary policy has a clear and probably quick effect on the exchange rate, while the sign of the effect of fiscal policy is unclear. Thus, in designing policies to maintain internal and external balance, it would make sense to assign fiscal policy to the internal output or employment target, with monetary policy eliminating the effects of any on the exchange rate. Or, if an active exchange rate policy is to be pursued, this should be done mainly through monetary policy, which has a comparative advantage in influencing the exchange rate.

THE DOMESTIC ECONOMY AS A PRICE TAKER

Up to now, we have taken the price relationship $P^f = p \cdot P$ as translating a domestically determined price level P into foreign terms. This implicitly assumes that the economy is large in terms of world markets, so that the foreign exchange, or world, prices of its goods are determined by internal cost and demand conditions. For the U.S. economy, this is probably a good assumption, at least for manufactured goods.

However, for smaller industrial economies, or for raw materials such as oil or wheat, the causation probably runs the other way. The small country is usually considered, in the literature on international trade, to be a *price taker* on world markets. If we consider the extreme simplifying example of a small industrial country that produces only goods that are traded on the world market, it faces given world prices P^f for these goods. The exchange rate p then translates the world price index P^f into home prices as

$$P = P^f/p.$$

In the extreme small-country case with all goods traded, the world price is fixed at P^f and the domestic price level is just P^f/p.

This gives us a horizontal aggregate supply curve at $P = P^f/p$ for the small country, as shown in Figure 16.10. The point of intersection with the usual downward-sloping aggregate demand curve gives the equilibrium level of output y_0 and the domestic price level $P_0 = (P^f/p)_0$. In the small-country case the usual *IS-LM* analysis fixes the demand curve. But the price level is determined in the world market, and the intersection of the normal demand curve with the world market supply price determines output.

Effects of an increase in P^f

The small-country model gives us a good interpretation of the effects of an exogenous increase in world prices. An example is the oil price increase in 1979–1980. We previously analyzed this case in terms of domestic supply in Chapters 6 and 7. Here we short cut that analysis with a small-country assumption.

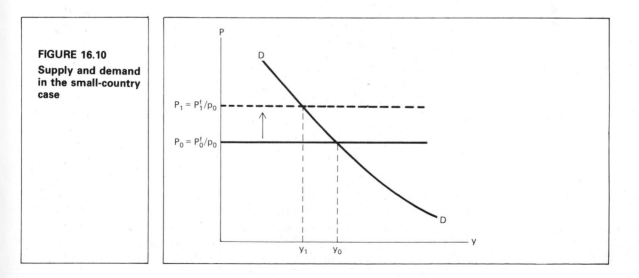

FIGURE 16.10

Supply and demand in the small-country case

As P^f rises, to take a pertinent recent example, the domestic price level (supply curve) rises to $P_1 = P_1^f/p_0$ in Figure 16.10. With the demand curve unshifted, output falls to y_1. In the *IS-LM* diagram implicit in the background, the price increase from P_0 to P_1 has reduced equilibrium output demanded from y_0 to y_1. The exogenous increase in the world price level both raises the internal price level and reduces output in the smaller industrial countries. This is a good illustration of the effects of the oil price increase in most European economies in 1979–1980.

The results of an increase in P^f on the current account are unclear. If the increase were on all goods, strictly speaking the price-taking small country would see no current account effects. Prices of imports and exports would rise by the same amount. But if the price increase were only on a specific import, such as energy, then the effect depends on the price elasticity of demand E_m. If it is less than -1 in absolute value $(0 > E_m > -1)$, then import payments will rise. This was clearly the case with the oil price increase, where substitution possibilities were severely limited in the short run. In that case the inflation and falling output in the European economies and Japan were accompanied by increased current account deficits. This analysis can be easily extended to changes in export prices and to tariffs on exports or imports, as well.

Movements in exchange rates give results that are symmetrically opposed to those due to changes in P^f. This should be apparent in Figure 16.10. The upward movement in the domestic price level from P_0 to P_1 could follow from a reduction in p, as well as from an increase in P^f. Thus, a devaluation with p falling can raise the internal price level of a small country, and reduce the level of output. An up-valuation would have the opposite effect.

This feedback from the exchange rate to the domestic price level, coupled with the effects of monetary policy on the exchange rate, discussed above, makes management of monetary policy a difficult task in the small open economy. Figure 16.11 shows the effects of an expansionary monetary policy action in this context. A monetary expansion shifts the demand curve out from D_0D_0 to D_1D_1. In the closed economy analysis of Chapters 1–14 this is clearly expansionary. But we saw in Figures 16.8 and 16.9 that a monetary expansion reduces the exchange rate p. This shifts the internal price level in Figure 16.11 up to $P_1 = P_0^f/p_1$. The result for the price level is clear; the exchange rate effect raises it. The result for real output is unclear. Whether the new value for real output at point B exceeds y_0 at point A depends on the entire structure of the economy. Thus, in the small open economy, monetary policy can influence the price level directly through the exchange rate, while the effects on real output may be unclear. Empirical evidence supporting these results has been presented by Dornbusch and Krugman.

This ambiguity does not exist for fiscal policy. As we saw earlier, a shift in *DD* in Figure 16.11 following a fiscal policy expansion is accompanied by an indeterminate movement in p. In the Helliwell study for

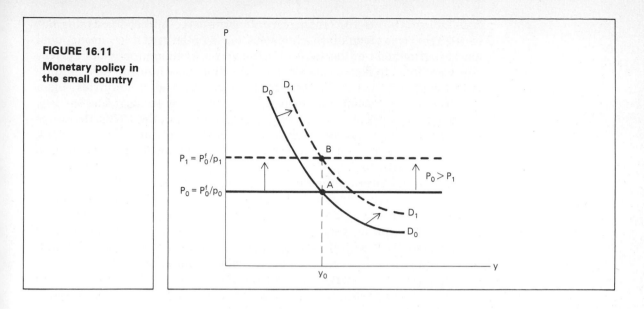

FIGURE 16.11
Monetary policy in the small country

Canada, there was approximately no effect on p, so the DD curve would shift out along the given P_0 supply schedule.

Thus, the small-country results reinforce our earlier conclusions in the use of monetary and fiscal policy. The comparative advantage of fiscal policy lies in influencing domestic output. Monetary policy has the comparative advantage in moving the exchange rate. In the small country, this gives monetary policy a clear target of the price level or the rate of inflation, with fiscal policy aimed at output.

Small countries and large countries

The small-country analysis above shows us a direct link from monetary policy to inflation. This link exists to some degree in large countries, even in the United States. So the message for management of the policy mix with flexible exchange rates is to look for the short-run effects of monetary policy on the exchange rate and the price level. With a flexible instead of a fixed exchange rate system, fiscal policy is likely to have a more predictable effect on output and less predictable effect on the price level.

As we move across the spectrum from large to small industrial countries, the separation between monetary policy as an instrument moving P via p and fiscal policy moving y becomes greater. But even for U.S. policy, an increased awareness on exchange rate effects of monetary policy would be a good idea.

LIKELY DEVELOPMENTS IN THE 1980s

The first half of the 1970s saw the end of the Bretton Woods system and a shift to a system of floating exchange rates among major countries. It also saw a tripling of international reserves as foreign central banks absorbed dollars in unsuccessful attempts to hold their exchange rates against the dollar. From 1971 to 1973 there were attempts to reestablish fixed rates, but in 1973 this was given up as a hopeless cause in the unstable international macroenvironment of the 1970s. Exchange rates among the major currencies were freed to float to their market equilibrium values in 1973, and by 1975 the system was fairly near an equilibrium. Smaller countries began to peg their currencies to the major currencies, or to *currency baskets*, defined as averages of them. During the second half of the 1970s, there was increasing management of the floating system by coordinated central bank intervention, as the system evolved toward a *managed float*. There was also a movement toward development of currency areas, with the European countries forming the *European Monetary System*.

The enormous increase in international reserves has pushed issues involving reserve creation through *SDRs* into the background. Instead the focus for the coming years is likely to be (a) financing of surpluses and deficits associated with the energy price increases through official institutions such as the IMF, and (b) coordinated management of floating exchange rates to meet targets of macroeconomic policy. The discussion of the connection between the exchange rate and monetary and fiscal policy in this chapter provides an initial analytical basis for policy thinking on exchange rate management.

QUESTIONS FOR DISCUSSION AND REVIEW

1. In a system of fixed exchange rates, would you expect fiscal and monetary policy to be able to stimulate insufficient aggregate demand and eliminate a balance-of-payments deficit? Could they be employed to restrain excessive aggregate demand and eliminate a balance-of-payments deficit?

2. Even if imports and exports are relatively price elastic, there is probably a fairly long lag between price changes and quantity responses. In a system of floating exchange rates, how would an increase in the desirability of foreign goods alter the domestic price of foreign currency in the short run? How would the long run response differ?

3. Imbalance in international accounts can be eliminated by adjusting the domestic economy. Would a low marginal propensity to import imply the internal adjustment costs would be high or low?

4. Would a country whose economy is thriving when the rest of world's economies are in recession expect a rise or a fall in the price of its currency?

5. How is the efficacy of monetary and fiscal policy to stabilize the domestic economy altered by the type of exchange rate regime adopted?

SELECTED READINGS

W. H. Branson, "The Trade Effects of the 1971 Currency Realignments," *Brookings Papers on Economic Activity*, vol. 1, 1972.

W. H. Branson, "Asset Market Equilibrium, the Exchange Rate, and the Balance of Payments," in R. L. Teigen, ed., *Readings in Money, National Income and Stabilization Policy*, 4th ed. (Homewood, Ill.: Irwin, 1978).

H. S. Houthakker and S. P. Magee, "Income and Price Elasticities in World Trade," *Review of Economics and Statistics,* May 1969.

R. A. Mundell, "The Appropriate Use of Monetary and Fiscal Policy for External and Internal Balance," *IMF Staff Papers,* March 1962.

E. Sohmen, *Flexible Exchange Rates,* 2nd ed. (The University of Chicago Press, 1969), chaps. 4–5.

R. M. Stern: "The Presentation of the Balance of Payments," in R. L. Teigen, ed., *Readings in Money, National Income and Stabilization Policy,* 4th ed. (Homewood, Ill.: Irwin, 1978).

M. V. N. Whitman, "Global Monetarism and the Monetary Approach to the Balance of Payments," in R. L. Teigen, ed., *Readings in Money, National Income and Stabilization Policy,* 4th ed. (Homewood, Ill.: Irwin, 1978).

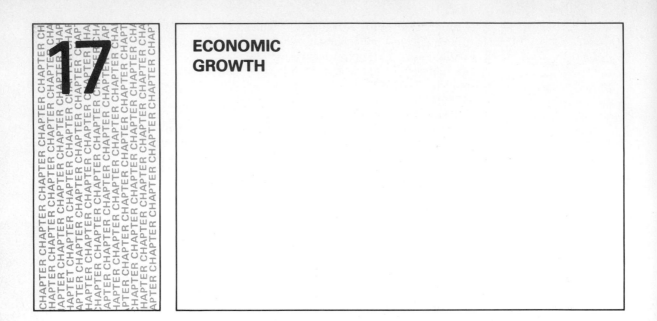

17

CHAPTER CHAPTER CHAPTER CHAPTER CH
CHAPTER CHAPTER CHAPTER CHAPTER CHA
CHAPTER CHAPTER CHAPTER CHAPTER CHA
CHAPTER CHAPTER CHAPTER CHAPTER CH
CHAPTER CHAPTER CHAPTER CHAPTER C
CHAPTER CHAPTER CHAPTER CHAPTER CHA
CHAPTER CHAPTER CHAPTER CHAPTER CHA
CHAPTER CHAPTER CHAPTER CHAPTER CHAPTER
CHAPTER CHAPTER CHAPTER CHAPTER CHAPTER
CHAPTER CHAPTER CHAPTER CHAPTER CHAP
CHAPTER CHAPTER CHAPTER CHAPTER CHAPTER
CHAPTER CHAPTER CHAPTER CHAPTER CHAP
HAPTER CHAPTER CHAPTER CHAPTER CHA
PTER CHAPTER CHAPTER CHAPTER CHA
HAPTER CHAPTER CHAPTER CHAPTER CHA
APTER CHAPTER CHAPTER CHAPTER CHAP

ECONOMIC
GROWTH

By introducing such factors as inflation, wage increases, and growth in labor productivity into the static model of income determination, in Chapter 15 we took the first steps away from a purely static model of the economy toward a more dynamic view. In this chapter we move on to a brief survey of dynamic models of economic growth—the growth of potential, or full-employment, output.

The relationship between actual and potential output is shown in Figure 17.1, which reproduces Figure 1.1(a). The potential line in Figure 17.1 shows the economy's potential output path, which is fairly smooth given the trend growth of labor force and productivity. This is also the *trend path* of full-employment output. It gives the level of output that could be attained at any given time with the unemployment rate at its full-employment level and labor productivity at its trend value.

The actual output line in Figure 17.1 shows actual measured real GNP. When actual output is below potential, real output is being lost. When actual output is above potential, as in 1968–1969 when the unemployment rate fell below 3.5 percent, additional output is gained, but only at the cost of a rate of inflation that is widely thought to be unacceptable. In the presidential campaign of 1968, all parties agreed that the 5 to 6 percent rate of inflation, which came along with the under-3.5 percent unemployment rate, was too high. In the 1980s, after the supply-side inflation of 1979, a *drop* of the inflation rate to 5 percent would be welcomed!

The potential output path in Figure 17.1, then, does not represent an absolute physical maximum level of output. Rather, it gives the level of output associated with a positive level of unemployment computed to

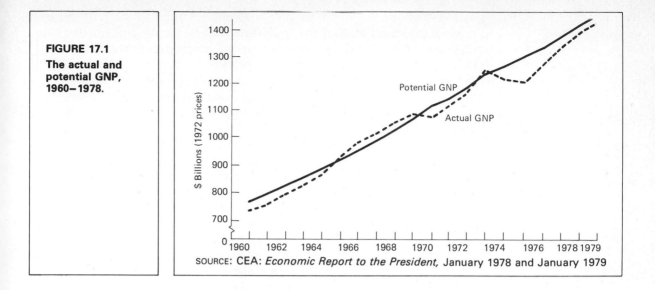

FIGURE 17.1

The actual and potential GNP, 1960–1978.

SOURCE: CEA: *Economic Report to the President,* January 1978 and January 1979

reflect both *frictional unemployment,* the unemployment resulting from the normal operation of the labor market in which some people are temporarily between jobs, and *structural unemployment,* the unemployment of those with no marketable skills or those whose skills are no longer in demand. In 1970, the Council of Economic Adviser's *Annual Report* estimated the full-employment level of unemployment to be just under 4 percent. This was the level that the long-run U.S. Phillips curve suggested might be compatible with "reasonable" price stability—a rate of inflation near 4 to 5 percent a year. More recent estimates have increased to 6.0 percent or more the full employment level of unemployment. Thus, the potential output path of Figure 17.1 can also be considered as a *feasible* trend path for actual output; monetary and fiscal policy should be set to maintain actual output as close to potential output as possible.

The stabilization policy measures discussed in Parts II and III are steps that can be taken to close the gap between the potential and actual output paths and maintain actual output near its potential level. Of course, when we considered time lags in Part III we recognized that once an output gap appears, movement toward the trend line cannot be instantaneous and complete. But the static model has shown how manipulation of such variables as government purchases, tax rates, or the money supply can close the gap between actual and potential output. Thus, if investment or consumer expenditure falls below its trend level associated with potential output and income, the government can take fiscal or monetary policy steps to counterbalance the effects of that exogenous drop in investment or consumer expenditure to keep the level of output up to its potential.

In this chapter we assume that the government is doing its stabilization job well. That is, it is reasonably successful in keeping the economy growing close to the trend, or potential output, line. There will be, of course, fluctuations around the trend line. Consumption and investment will fluctuate around their trend levels, and fiscal and monetary policy will react only with a lag. But when private demand deviates from its trend level, we assume that the government responds well enough to correct the deviations within a reasonable period, say, a year. Thus, *on average*, the actual growth path of the economy is represented by the trend line.

Assuming this, our interest is focused on what determines the nature of the trend line: How are its slope and height determined? In other words, what determines the potential rate and level of growth of the economy?

Before taking up these questions, we summarize the *long-run trend* nature of fiscal and monetary policy that will keep the economy growing along the trend path. To repeat, in the short run there will always be fluctuations in private demand—higher or lower levels of investment or consumption—which require higher or lower levels of government spending, tax rates, or money supply to maintain actual output close to potential. But *on average*, over the long run, monetary and fiscal policy will exhibit certain *trend* characteristics as the economy grows along its trend path.

ASSUMPTIONS UNDERLYING TREND GROWTH

As the economy grows along its full-employment trend path, the government's monetary and fiscal policy variables will be moving to counteract changes in private demand. To find the required trends in these policy variables we assume the economy grows along a path with the unemployment rate at some given average level, perhaps 6 percent, which we define as *full employment*.

To describe the trends in monetary and fiscal policy variables along the full-employment path, we make some further assumptions, each of which, as we shall see, is roughly consistent with the historical facts.

1. Interest rates are trendless; that is, they fluctuate around some mean level.
2. The rates of labor force growth, $\dot{L}$, and of average labor-productivity growth, y/L are fairly steady.
3. The capital-output ratio, K/y, is roughly constant.
4. The relative shares of labor and capital in output are roughly constant.

Here we are switching from a focus on employment N, to the labor force L. If the unemployment rate u is constant, both N and L will grow at the same rate. The unemployment rate u is defined as

$$u = \frac{U}{L} = \frac{L - N}{L} = 1 - \frac{N}{L},$$ [1]

where U is the number of persons unemployed. Thus if u is constant, the employment rate, N/L, is constant, and N and L both grow at the same rate $\dot{L}$.

To draw the implications of balanced growth for static equilibrium, we examine first the labor market to find the implied rate of growth of output, wages, and prices on average along trend. Then we find the average growth rate of the money supply that will keep the money market in equilibrium with real income growing and the price level rising, and interest rates remaining constant along trend. Finally, we see what full-employment product market equilibrium implies for the average level of the government deficit and debt.

TREND GROWTH OF OUTPUT AND PRICES

Our assumptions concerning the growth rates of the labor force and productivity can be combined to give the growth rate of potential output. We can define potential output as average labor force productivity y/L times the total labor force L:

$$y = \frac{y}{L} \cdot L. \qquad [2]$$

As we showed in Chapter 15, p. 314, the percentage rate of growth of the product of two variables can be approximated by the sum of the percentage rates of growth of the two variables if neither is very large. Thus the growth rate of output is the sum of the growth rates of productivity and the labor force:

$$\dot{y} = y/l + \dot{L}. \qquad [3]$$

Thus, the two assumptions give us the rate of growth of potential output. In the United States, with total productivity growing along trend at about 1.0 percent per year and available man-hours in the labor force growing at 1.5 percent, the growth rate of potential output y is at most 2.5 percent.

As we saw in Chapter 15, the assumption that relative shares remain constant along trend implies that the rate of growth of the price level is equal to the rate of growth of the money wage rate less that of productivity,

$$\dot{P} = \dot{W} - y/L. \qquad [4]$$

The rate of growth of productivity is given by assumption 2 above, and the rate of growth of wages, $\dot{W}$, comes from the long-run Phillips curve of Chapter 15 combined with the unemployment rate assumption. With the unemployment rate at about 6 percent, recent estimates of the Phillips curve suggest that $\dot{W}$ would be about 9 to 10 percent. Thus, with productivity growing at about 1.0 percent, we could expect $\dot{P}$ to be about 8 to 9 percent along trend, with relative shares remaining constant.

If the Phillips curve could be shifted to the left by an incomes policy such as the guideposts, and $\dot{W}$ held down to around 1 percent a year, then a zero rate of price increase, maintaining relative shares constant with real wages growing as fast as productivity, could be achieved. In fact, this has not been possible in the United States, so that to maintain constant relative shares with real wages growing as fast as productivity, $\dot{P}$ will probably have to be at least 8 percent.

Nominal GNP growth

Adding the growth rate of real output y and the growth rate of prices P, we can obtain the trend growth rate of money GNP, Y. Since $Y = y \cdot P$, we have

$$\dot{Y} = \dot{y} + \dot{P}. \tag{5}$$

Substituting the equation (3) expression for trend $\dot{y}$ and equation (4) for trend $\dot{P}$ gives us

$$\dot{Y} = \dot{y}/L + \dot{L} + \dot{W} - \dot{y}/L = \dot{L} + \dot{W}. \tag{6}$$

Along trend, with relative shares constant, the growth rate of nominal GNP will be the sum of the rates of growth of the labor force, $\dot{L}$, and of the money wage rate, $\dot{W}$. From equation (4) the money wage growth rate that maintains constancy of relative shares is

$$\dot{W} = \dot{P} + \dot{y}/L, \tag{7}$$

so that the $\dot{W}$ term in equation (6) simply represents productivity growth plus the rate of increase of prices, and the $\dot{L}$ term adds in the rate of growth of the labor force.

If the guideposts were followed, $\dot{P}$ would be zero, so that $\dot{Y} = \dot{y}$, and the rate of growth of money wages would simply represent productivity growth. Thus, under the guideposts,

$$\dot{Y} = \dot{L} + \dot{y}/l = \dot{y}. \tag{8}$$

Equilibrium growth on the supply side

Equations (3) and (4), which give the growth rates of output and the price level along the potential GNP path, can be conveniently interpreted as the conditions for equilibrium growth on the supply side. Given the growth rates of the labor force and productivity, equation (3) shows the growth rate of output that will maintain constant employment and unemployment rates. The assumed unemployment rate then fixes the rate at which wage rates increase—the rate at which the labor supply curve shifts up.

With the *rate of growth of output* which will maintain a given rate of unemployment and the *rate at which the labor supply curve shifts up* both fixed, equation (4) gives the rate of increase of the price level, P, that will keep the supply side of the economy in equilibrium. The next step in the analysis of trend growth in the static model is to determine the monetary and fiscal policies that will shift the economy's demand curve out along trend at just the rate that will maintain both demand and supply equilib-

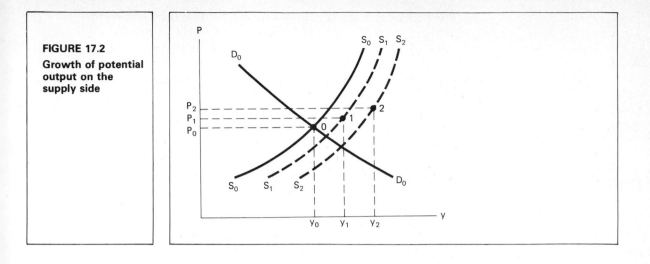

FIGURE 17.2

Growth of potential output on the supply side

rium along the growth path of y and P described by equations (3) and (4).

The problem is illustrated in Figure 17.2. Starting from an initial equilibrium P_0, y_0 point, where y_0 is potential output at time 0, the growth of the labor force and productivity raise y to y_1 and y_2 in time periods 1 and 2, following equation (3). With unemployment maintained at 4 percent as y moves to y_1 and y_2, the labor supply curve shifts up faster than productivity growth, so that the price level must rise from P_0 to P_1 to P_2 to maintain equilibrium on the supply side.

This analysis fixes points 0, 1, and 2 in Figure 17.2 as the equilibrium P, y points on the supply side as y and P grow according to equations (3) and (4). This means that the economy's supply curve is shifting out from $S_0 S_0$ to $S_1 S_1$ to $S_2 S_2$ in Figure 17.2 as the economy grows along trend. The problem now is to find the path of the demand-side variables, especially the money supply M and the government budget deficit $d = g - t(y)$, that will shift the demand curve $D_0 D_0$ of Figure 17.2 out just fast enough to pass through points 1 and 2 , so that the economy remains in equilibrium as y and P grow according to equations (3) and (4).

TREND GROWTH OF THE MONEY SUPPLY

We will begin on the demand side by finding the trend rate of growth of the money supply that will hold interest rates constant along trend as y and P grow according to equations (3) and (4). Then we can determine the movements of the government's fiscal policy variables that will maintain the product market in equilibrium. These results can then be modified by assuming that interest rates are not constant along trend. This will change the M path and the movement of investment along trend, changing the fiscal policy path that will maintain product market equilibrium.

The equilibrium condition in the money market from Part III is

$$\frac{M}{P} = m(r, y).$$ [9]

In Chapter 12, we suggested that the long-run elasticity for real balances with respect to changes in real income is about 1. Thus, if the rate of change in real balances is equal to the rate of change in real income, the money market equilibrium condition expressed in equation (9) will remain satisfied with no change in interest rates. Thus to hold interest rates constant, we have

$$\frac{\dot{M}}{P} = \dot{y}.$$ [10]

Since the term on the left can be rewritten as

$$\frac{\dot{M}}{P} = \dot{M} - \dot{P},$$ [11]

then (10) implies that growth of the nominal-money stock given by

$$\dot{M} = \dot{y} + \dot{P}$$ [12]

will hold interest rates constant along the trend growth path of y and P. If nominal income grows at 8 percent or so along trend, the money supply also must grow at about 8 percent with a unitary income elasticity of demand for money to keep the money market in equilibrium with constant r. This money supply behavior will also hold velocity $v = Y/M$ constant as the economy grows along trend.

Equation (12) gives the growth in the money supply that will shift the LM curve of Figure 17.3 out fast enough to maintain money market equilibrium as y grows according to equation (3) with r constant. As y

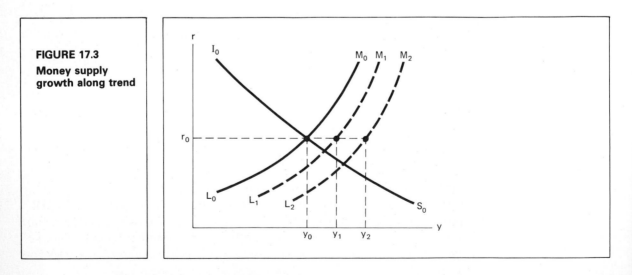

FIGURE 17.3
Money supply growth along trend

grows at rate $\dot{y}$, the *LM* curve must shift out at the same rate to maintain money market equilibrium at the initial interest rate r_0. To shift the *LM* curve out at that rate, the money supply must grow at the rate $\dot{Y} = \dot{y} + \dot{P}$, given by equation (12), to supply the increased transactions demands stemming from both the p and y increase.

This section has given us the rule for trend growth in the money supply. *To keep the money market in equilibrium at constant—or, more precisely, trendless—interest rates with y and P growing along the trends given by equations (3) and (4), the trend growth rate of the money supply should be about the same as that of nominal GNP.* If the price level grows at about 8 percent per year, this indicates a trend money supply growth rate of about 10 percent. If prices are constant, the money supply should show a trend growth rate of about 1.0 to 1.5 percent to hold interest rates constant. Again, we should note that this is the rule for the long-run average, or trend, growth in the money supply to keep the economy near its potential growth path. As private demand fluctuates about its long-run trend, policy variables will also have to fluctuate to maintain total demand at the full-employment level, as we saw in Parts II and III. Here we are developing the long-run average outcome for the policy variables given the trend growth in private demand. Now we can turn to the fiscal policy prescription that shifts the *IS* curve out just fast enough to maintain demand-side equilibrium as y grows from y_0 to y_1 in Figure 17.3.

PRODUCT MARKET EQUILIBRIUM AND THE BUDGET

The equilibrium condition in the product market can be written as

$$c + i + g = c + s + t, \tag{13a}$$

or

$$i + g = s + t. \tag{13b}$$

Here each variable is set at its *ex ante*, or planned level; product market equilibrium is maintained when planned $i + g =$ planned $s + t$. Equation (13b) can be divided through by y to obtain the product market equilibrium condition with all items stated as fractions of real output,

$$\frac{i}{y} + \frac{g}{y} = \frac{s}{y} + \frac{t}{y} . \tag{14}$$

Rearranging the terms in equation (14), we obtain the necessary equality between net private-sector saving $s - i$, and net public-sector expenditure, the deficit $d = g - t$, to maintain the product market in equilibrium:

$$\frac{g - t}{y} = \frac{d}{y} = \frac{s - i}{y} . \tag{15}$$

This just restates the fact that in equilibrium the government deficit d must equal the excess of private saving over investment in the economy. If the saving fraction s/y and the investment fraction i/y have fairly stable trend values, equation (15) will give us the trend ratio of the deficit to output that will be needed to keep the product market in equilibrium as the economy grows along trend.

The saving-income ratio

In Chapter 10 we saw that the long-run data on consumption and income and the three main theories of the consumption function all say that the ratio of real consumption to real income is roughly constant over the long run. If c/y is roughly constant along trend and the tax structure is proportional so that $t(y) = ty$, then the ratio of planned saving to income must also be constant along trend.

One way to write the product market equilibrium condition is

$$y = c + s + t, \tag{16}$$

so that the ratios of c, s, and t to income must add to unity,

$$1 = \frac{c}{y} + \frac{s}{y} + \frac{t}{y} . \tag{17}$$

If c/y and t/y are constant, then s/y must also be constant. A permanent increase in tax rates, raising t/y, will reduce both c/y and s/y, presumably in the same proportions that consumption and saving come out of disposable income. Thus, in the fiscal policy equation (15) s/y will be roughly constant with any given tax structure which determines t/y. An increase in t/y will yield a smaller decrease in s/y, as perhaps 10 percent of the t increase comes out of saving.

The investment-income ratio

In Chapter 11 we found that empirical estimates show a long-run elasticity of investment demand with respect to changes in output of unity. This implies a constant ratio of investment to real output along trend, as increases in output call forth equal percentage increases in investment.

This result can also be obtained by assuming that the capital-output ratio, K/y, is constant, as shown in assumption 3 above. If K/y is equal to a constant v (here v is the capital-output ratio), then we have

$$\text{Net investment} = i_n = \Delta K = v \cdot \Delta y,$$

as an expression for net investment, which is just the rate of increase of the capital stock. Dividing the net-investment expression by y yields

$$\frac{i_n}{y} = v \cdot \frac{\Delta y}{y} = v \cdot \dot{y}. \tag{18}$$

If both v and $\dot{y}$, the trend growth rate of output, are constant along trend, then the ratio of net investment to output will also be constant along trend.

Replacement investment is generally assumed to be a fraction δ of the capital stock K, so that replacement investment is given by

$$i_r = \delta K = \delta v \cdot y, \tag{19}$$

and the ratio of replacement investment to output, along trend, will just be the constant δv. If both net and replacement investment are roughly constant fractions of output, then total investment i will also be a constant fraction of y along trend.

Both net and replacement investment, in equations (18) and (19), depend on the capital-output ratio v. This gives the desired capital stock at any given level of y. The *level* of this stock then determines replacement investment through δ and *the rate of growth* of this stock is net investment. Thus, equations (18) and (19) show that for any given v there is a constant long-run average ratio of investment to output.

As we saw in Chapter 11, the desired capital-output ratio should, in turn, depend on the interest rate through the cost of capital. The higher the interest rate, the lower the desired capital-output ratio v. Thus if the economy moves from one roughly constant level of the interest rate r_0 to another lower level r_1, there will be a corresponding increase in the capital-output ratio v from v_0 to v_1 and an increase in the investment-output ratio from $(i/y)_0$ to $(i/y)_1$. This says that for any given level of interest rates there will be given equilibrium capital-output and investment-output ratios. A change in rates will change the ratios to new equilibrium levels.

The government budget along trend

We can now return to the equilibrium rule for the government budget given earlier by equation (15):

$$\frac{g - t}{y} = \frac{d}{y} = \frac{s - i}{y} .$$

If s/y and i/y are constant along trend, equation (15) gives the long-run trend in the budget position that is needed to maintain product market equilibrium. The saving ratio is determined by trend real income and the tax rate; the investment ratio is at least partially determined by the level of interest rates.

If private-sector full-employment saving tends to exceed investment demands, $s > i$ and a government deficit equal to the difference will be needed on average over the long run to maintain equilibrium full-employment growth. Conversely, if $s < i$, a surplus will be needed. This is the rule that will keep the *IS* curve of Figure 17.4(a) and the demand curve of Figure 17.4(b) shifting out just fast enough to maintain static equilibrium in the economy as potential output grows from y_0 to y_1 to y_2 with the interest rate constant at r_0 and the price level rising steadily from P_0 to P_1 to P_2.

The long-run equilibrium deficit or surplus, then, depends on the long-run tendencies of the s/y and i/y ratios. The s/y ratio can be affected by tax rate changes, and the i/y ratio can be changed somewhat by interest rate changes, but there is no particular reason to expect the two ratios to be the same so that the government budget can be just balanced over the long run.

THE MONETARY-FISCAL POLICY MIX ALONG TREND

Equation (15), giving the full-employment budget surplus or deficit needed to maintain equilibrium along trend, is a useful point of departure for a final discussion of the long-run allocation implications of the monetary-fiscal policy mix. Assume that stabilization policy is maintain-

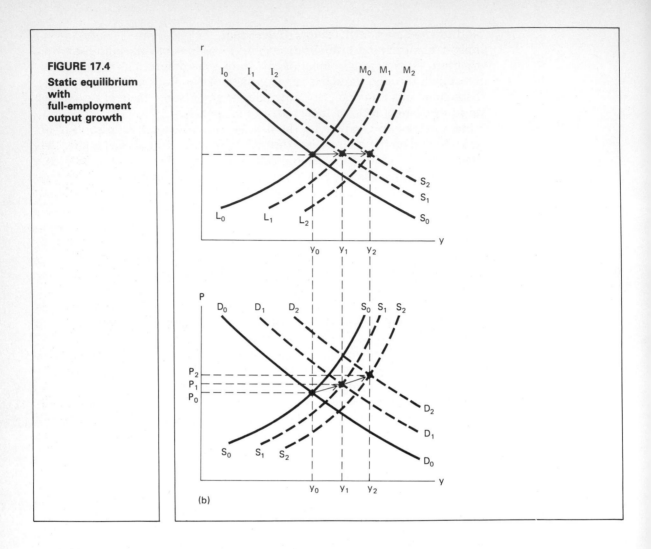

FIGURE 17.4
Static equilibrium with full-employment output growth

ing the economy near its potential growth path by balancing exogenous deviations from long-run trend behavior in s/y and i/y by short-run changes in government purchases, tax rates, or the money supply. In other words, the government counters exogenous short-run shifts in private demand components by changing its own demand, changing consumer demand through tax rate changes, or changing investment demand through deviations from trend money supply growth. These policy actions keep the economy close to the potential growth path so that the remaining monetary-fiscal policy question concerns the mix of output along trend.

The trend mix of output

Presumably the long-run desired output mix—the c, i, and g combination as y grows along its potential path—should be determined by balancing the marginal social gain of additional units of real consumer, investment, and government expenditures within the constraint that they can add up to no more than potential output. This decision concerning the long-run mix is a political decision to be taken with the understanding that current investment may affect the future potential growth rate.

Once the mix decision is reached by weighing the marginal social benefits of increases in each kind of expenditure, equation (15) shows how to implement that decision. First, the interest rate *level* should be set to obtain the desired i/y ratio. This will involve an initial period of higher-than-trend M growth to reduce rates, or lower-than-trend growth to raise them. This sets the trend i/y ratio.

Next, given the desired g/y ratio, tax rates must be set to yield the ratios of tax revenue and saving to income that just balance supply and demand in the economy. The determination of this equilibrium tax rate is shown in Figure 17.5. The $[\bar{g} - t(y)]/y$ line in Figure 17.5 shows the relationship between the tax rate and the ratio of the government deficit at potential output to potential y itself as tax rates rise. With g fixed at $\bar{g}$ by the balancing of marginal social benefits of expenditures, as tax rates rise to increase $t(y)$, $[\bar{g} - t(y)]/y$ falls fairly sharply.

The $(s - i)/y$ line in Figure 17.5 shows the relationship between the tax rate and the ratio of net private saving at potential output, $s - i$, to potential output. Here i is the desired investment level at potential output. An increase in the tax rate reduces saving, reducing $s - i$, but by less than it increases $t(y)$, since most of the $t(y)$ increase comes out of consumption.

With i/y and $\bar{g}/y$ set by policy along trend, Figure 17.5 shows the tax rate t_0 that will equate net private saving and the deficit at potential output. In Figure 17.5, the tax rate t_0, yields a negative deficit—a surplus— along trend, measured by $-(d/y)_0$. In that example, the desired investment level i is large enough that the $s - i$ line is low enough to intersect the $\bar{g} - t(y)$ line below the horizontal axis, giving a required surplus as the economy grows along trend.

There is no way to determine *a priori* whether the potential output equilibrium intersection of Figure 17.5 will be above or below the horizon-

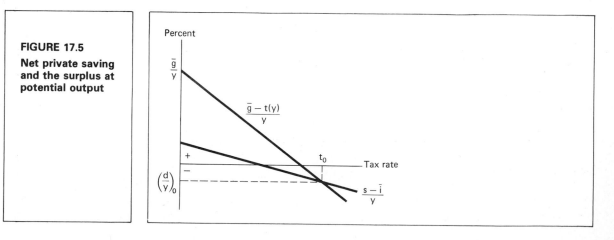

FIGURE 17.5

Net private saving and the surplus at potential output

tal axis; that is, whether a deficit or surplus will be required to maintain the economy near its potential output path. Monetary policy can shift the $s - i$ curve by adjusting the level of interest rates. The government budget can shift the $g - t(y)$ line by changing g. In the end, the equilibrium deficit will be to a large extent determined by these policy decisions concerning the output mix.

Two interpretations of the product-market equilibrium condition

Thus we see that equation (15) giving the necessary budget position along trend can be viewed two ways. First, if we take the level of interest rates and the tax rate as given, we can use it to determine the possible level of government purchases and the deficit. If, in the equation

$$\frac{g - t}{y} = \frac{s - i}{y}, \qquad [20]$$

we take interest rate as given, then i/y is fixed. Potential output and the tax structure determine both s and t. This leaves only g/y to be determined as

$$\frac{g}{y} = \frac{s}{y} + \frac{t}{y} - \frac{i}{y}. \qquad [21]$$

If $s > i$, g will be greater than t and there will be a deficit; if $s < i$, then there will be a surplus with $g < t$.

Second, if we determine the level of the interest rate needed to achieve some target investment level, fixing i/y by policy, and then fix g/y to equate the marginal social benefits of public versus private spending, equation (20) can be used to determine the tax rate needed to maintain static equilibrium as the economy grows along its potential output path.

Summary on equilibrium growth in the static model

This completes our exposition of the behavior of the static model as the economy grows along its potential path. The rates of growth of productivity and the labor force determine the rate of growth of potential output,

$$\dot{y} = y/L + \dot{L}. \qquad [22]$$

The Phillips curve gives us the rate of growth of wages $\dot{W}$, and this, combined with the assumption of constant relative-income shares, gives us the growth rate of the price level,

$$\dot{P} = \dot{W} - y/L. \qquad [23]$$

To maintain money market equilibrium at any given level of the interest rate, along trend we have M growing at the same rate as nominal GNP,

$$\dot{M} = \dot{Y} = \dot{y} + \dot{P}. \qquad [24]$$

To raise interest rates, $\dot{M}$ should be temporarily lower than $\dot{Y}$ and vice versa to lower interest rates.

The level of interest rates determines the investment ratio i/y, and the tax structure determines the tax and saving ratios t/y and s/y, leaving the product market equilibrium condition,

$$\frac{g - t}{y} = \frac{s - i}{y},$$

to determine the necessary values of g and the deficit $(g - t)$ that keep the economy near its potential growth path. If s, t, and i are all roughly constant fractions of y, then g/y will also have to be roughly constant, that is, g must grow as fast as y to maintain product market equilibrium along this balanced growth path.

We can now move on to a brief review of the facts of economic growth in the United States and then to the development of models that explain the trend growth path of the economy. Here we have seen how the economy can be kept in static equilibrium along its trend growth path, assuming such a path exists. Later we look at explanations of why such a growth path does exist and what determines its level and slope, or rate of growth. Before moving on, it is convenient to discuss very briefly two questions of interest raised by this exposition of equilibrium growth—the notion of *fiscal drag* and the relationships between the deficit, the national debt, and potential output.

FISCAL DRAG AND THE FULL-EMPLOYMENT SURPLUS

The product market equilibrium condition with the economy growing along its potential output path is

$$\frac{g - t(y)}{y} = \frac{s - i}{y} = \frac{d}{y} = \text{a constant,} \qquad [25]$$

on average, over time.

For that to hold true with a given tax structure, the level of government purchases g must grow at the same rate as output y. If g does not grow as fast as y, the tax rate must be continually reduced to keep $g - t(y)$ growing at the same rate as y. If both g and the tax rate were to stay constant, then as potential y grows the deficit would shrink, and the economy would begin to slow down, falling off the full-employment path. This phenomenon is known as "fiscal drag" and is illustrated in Figure 17.6. Let us assume in Figure 17.6 that the deficit, given by equation (25), needed to maintain product market equilibrium at potential output is zero, with the initial *level* of government purchases fixed at g_0 and the proportional tax structure given by $t_0 y$. Under these assumptions, the economy initially is in equilibrium at the full-employment level of output y_F^0.

As potential output grows with g_0 and t_0 fixed, the full-employment surplus increases with $t_0 y$ rising and g_0 constant, violating the equilibrium condition for full-employment trend fiscal policy, putting increasing downward pressure on the economy, and increasing unemployment.

To avoid fiscal drag, one of two things must occur. Either the tax rates must be reduced as income grows, shifting the ty line from $t_0 y$ to $t_1 y$, in Figure 17.6, or the level of government expenditure must be increased from g_0 to g_1 in Figure 17.6 as full-employment output rises from y_F^0 to y_F^1.

The point here is that budget procedures fix the *level* of govern-

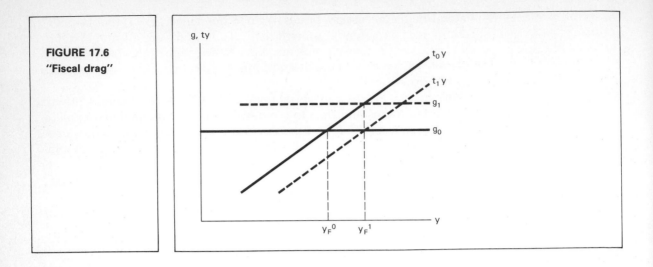

FIGURE 17.6
"Fiscal drag"

ment purchases and tax *rates*. Thus as y grows, revenues grow automatically but government purchases increases have to be legislated. This means that a neutral budget position, over time, must involve steady increases in g or steady cuts in tax rates to maintain the product market equilibrium condition (25) as the economy grows along trend.

PUBLIC DEBT WITH TREND GROWTH

One final question is raised by the product market equilibrium condition given in equation (25). Suppose along trend private saving exceeds investment, so that the fiscal rule says that $g > t$ and the deficit-income ratio d/y must be positive. If the government must persistently run a deficit as the economy grows along trend, what happens to the ratio of debt to income? Will the public debt—the accumulated deficit—grow relative to income, or will it tend to some stable ratio to income? The answer is that the debt-income ratio will tend toward a constant given by $(d/y)/\dot{y}$. The problem is the same as that of the investment-output ratio implied by a constant capital-output ratio; in that case investment was the rate of change of the capital stock. Here the deficit is the rate of change of the debt. In the capital stock case we went from a constant capital-output ratio to a constant investment-output ratio, here we will go from a constant deficit-output ratio to a constant debt-output ratio.

Suppose the deficit-income ratio is given by δ, so that the deficit in time t is given by

$$d_t = \delta y_t. \tag{26}$$

At time t, we have a particular ratio of accumulated debt to income, D_t/y_t. We will add to the debt $d_t = \delta y_t$ or the deficit in time t. Thus, in time $t + 1$ the debt-income ratio will be

$$\frac{D_{t+1}}{y_{t+1}} = \frac{D_t + d_t}{y_{t+1}} = \frac{D_t + \delta y_t}{y_{t+1}}.$$ [27]

The change in the debt-income ratio will be

$$\frac{D_{t+1}}{y_{t+1}} - \frac{D_t}{y_t} = \frac{D_t + \delta y_t}{y_{t+1}} - \frac{D_t}{y_t} = \frac{D_t y_t + \delta y_t^2 - D_t y_{t+1}}{y_{t+1} \cdot y_t}.$$

If we combine the terms in D_t in the numerator, and recognize that y_t^2 is approximately equal to $y_{t+1} \cdot y_t$ (for small changes in y), the final expression for the change in debt-income ratio can be written as

$$\frac{D_{t+1}}{y_{t+1}} - \frac{D_t}{y_t} = \delta - \frac{D_t \cdot \Delta y_t}{y_{t+1} \cdot y_t} = \delta - D_t \cdot \frac{\dot{y}}{y_t}.$$ [28]

Here we assume, again, y_t and y_{t+1} are approximately the same for small changes in y. Whenever $D_t/y_t > \delta/\dot{y}$, this change will be negative and D_t/y_t will fall; whenever the debt-income ratio is below $\delta/\dot{y}$, it will rise. Consequently, the debt-income ratio D/y will approach the ratio of δ (the deficit-income ratio) to the growth rate of income as time passes:

$$\frac{D_t}{y_t} \to \frac{\delta}{\dot{y}} \quad \text{as} \quad T \to \infty.$$ [29]

Thus, if the deficit is about 1 percent of GNP along trend, so that $\delta = 0.01$, and the growth rate of real output is about 2 percent, so that $\dot{y} = 0.02$, the debt-income ratio will tend toward 50 percent as time passes.

With the U.S. GNP running about $2.5 trillion, a 1 percent deficit would be about $25 billion. The arithmetic of deficits and debts in a growing economy thus says that if the United States continually ran deficits of this magnitude relative to GNP, in the long run the public debt would stabilize at about one-half of GNP, hardly any cause for alarm, no matter what one's theory is concerning the burden of the public debt.

The last two sections digressed from our introduction to growth in order to pick up two points that are frequently raised by the discussion of trend growth in the static model, especially on the rule for fiscal policy. We can now move back to the basic theme of the chapter—determination of the economy's equilibrium growth path.

THE STYLIZED FACTS OF GROWTH

The stylized facts of growth introduced by Nicholas Kaldor in 1958, refer to the long-term regularities in the relationships that seem to appear in most industrial countries—between growth rates of output and capital and labor inputs, and between factor prices and relative-income shares. These are the facts that a growth model must explain. This section summarizes these stylized facts and gives some rough numerical estimates for their values in the United States since World War II.

The growth rate of available man-hours in the labor force is fairly steady over time; that is, $\dot{L}$ is roughly constant. Through the 1950s and the first half of the 1960s the labor force grew at a rate of about 1.2 percent per year. Subtracting 0.2 percent for a shrinking work week gave a growth rate of available man-hours of about 1 percent per year during that period. During the late 1960s, as the people born during the post-World War II "baby boom" began to enter the labor force, the rate of labor force growth picked up. In addition, the participation rate of women in the labor force also began to rise in the late 1960s. These effects have raised the growth rate of the labor force by about half a percentage point, so that in the early 1970s the labor force is growing by about 1.7 percent per year. With the work week still shrinking by about 0.2 percent per year, this gives a trend $\dot{L}$ growth rate of about 1.5 percent.

The rate of growth of labor productivity in the private sector of the economy fluctuates with the business cycle, but along trend in the United States it had been fairly steady at about 2.9–3.2 percent per year. The growth rate was at the upper end of this range from 1960–1965 as the unemployment rate fell and resource utilization rose. From 1966 to 1970 the rate of growth of productivity was lower as the economy reached full employment and then went through a period of excess-demand pressure followed by a recession. For the 1970s, private-sector labor productivity at full employment was expected to grow along trend at about 3 percent per year. Since the output of the government sector of the economy is measured essentially as labor input, the rate of growth of labor productivity in the government sector is zero by definition. With the private sector producing about 90 percent of total real output, this would have yielded a growth rate of economy-wide average labor productivity of about 2.7 percent per year.

Since 1973, however, the growth in average labor productivity has been significantly below the postwar trend and this fact may account for much of the difficulty in dealing with the unusually high rates of inflation in the last half of the 1970s. We will return to a description and tentative explanation of the decline in productivity later in this chapter.

Total potential output in the economy can be defined as the product of average labor productivity, Q/L, and total labor force,

$$Q_t = \left(\frac{Q}{L}\right)_t \cdot L_t. \tag{30}$$

The growth rate of output, $\dot{Q}$, is then the sum of the growth rates of labor input and productivity:

$$\dot{Q} = (Q\dot{/}L) + \dot{L}. \tag{31}$$

Thus the trend growth rates of productivity and available man-hours give us the trend growth rate of potential output, $\dot{Q}$.

In the 1950s and early 1960s, with labor productivity growing at a rate of about 2.7 percent annually and available hours growing at about 1 percent, the growth rate of potential output was about 3.7 percent per year—somewhat lower in the early part of the period and rising in the later part of the period. As the growth rate of the labor force, in terms of available hours, has risen from about 1 percent to the rate of about 1.5 percent in the 1970s, the growth rate of potential output, $\dot{Q}$, might have risen from 3.7 percent to 4.2 percent. In the 1970s, with labor supply growth $\dot{L}$ of about 1.5 percent per year and potential output growth $\dot{Q}$ well below 4.2 percent per year, the growth of output per man-hour input, $\dot{q}$, was below the 2.7 percent per year of earlier decades.

Captial stock growth

The second set of stylized facts concerns the rate of growth of the capital stock and the capital-labor ratio $k = K/L$. In general, the rate of growth of the capital stock seems to be fairly steady and greater than the rate of growth of the labor force. Thus the capital-labor ratio k is rising through time. The following table gives the compound rate of growth of the net capital stock for all U.S. industries for the period 1950–1978.

	1950– 1955	1955– 1960	1960– 1965	1965– 1970	1970– 1975	1975– 1978
$\dot{K}$ (%)	4.2	3.1	3.5	4.9	3.3	2.6

Source: *Survey of Current Business,* March 1974, April 1976, and August 1979; straight-line net stocks

The sluggish performance of the economy in the late 1950s pulled the rate of growth of the capital stock down to 3.1 percent during 1955–1960. This reflects the effects of a high level of unemployment on profit prospects and investment. As the economy slowly picked up after 1961, the rate of growth of the capital stock, $\dot{K}$, rose to 3.5 percent in the period 1960–1965, and as an excess-demand boom developed in the late 1960s, $\dot{K}$ rose to 4.9 percent. The economic slowdown that started in 1969 and carried over to the early 1970s leveled off investment demand and reduced $\dot{K}$ to its mid-1960s level. This reduction continued in the latter half of the 1970s, and $\dot{K}$ fell to its lowest level in the post-World War II period.

The long-term rate of growth of the capital stock from 1950 to 1978 was a little under 4 percent, roughly equal to the growth rate of potential output, and greater than the growth rate of the labor force. If the capital stock grows at the long-run rate in the 1980s, the rate of growth of capital per man-hour, $\dot{k}$, will be about 2.5 percent per year. If, however, the sharply reduced rates of growth of the capital stock witnessed in the 1970s continue into the 1980s, $\dot{k}$ may be closer to 1 percent per year.

The capital-output ratio

The ratio of capital K to output Q has been, historically, a central variable in growth theory. In the first part of this section we saw that the rate of growth of potential output has risen from about 3.7 percent in the 1950s and early 1960s to about 4.2 percent in the 1970s. With the capital stock growing at about 4.0 percent annually, this would give a roughly constant, or slightly declining, capital-output ratio, K/Q.

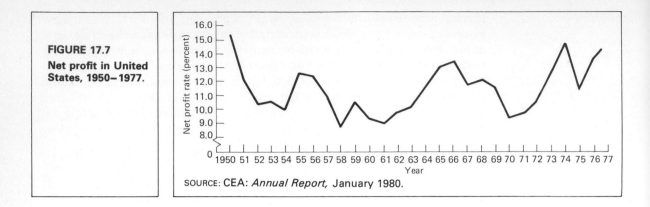

FIGURE 17.7

Net profit in United States, 1950–1977.

SOURCE: CEA: *Annual Report,* January 1980.

The last important stylized fact is that the profit rate ρ, defined as the ratio of profits P to the value of the capital stock K, shows no perceptible long-run trend. In other words, $\rho \equiv (P/K)$ is roughly constant in the long run, although it shows substantial variation over the business cycle.

If both the profit rate ρ and the capital-output ratio are constant, then the relative share of profits in output must be roughly constant in the long run. Since the profit share in income P/Q can be written as

$$\frac{P}{Q} = \frac{P}{K} \cdot \frac{K}{Q}, \qquad\qquad [32]$$

if ρ and K/Q are constant, so is the profit share P/Q. Furthermore, if the wage share W/Q is simply $1 - P/Q$, then a constant profit share implies a constant wage share, and a constant long-run relative distribution of output. It should be clear that this follows from the two stylized facts of (a) a constant K/Q ratio and (b) a constant profit rate in the long run.

Figure 17.7 shows the net profit rate—measured by the ratio of net profits to total stockholder's equity value of capital—in the U.S. corporate manufacturing sector since 1950. There is no apparent trend in the profit rate, although it does show a clear pattern of cyclical fluctuation. Thus this last stylized fact stands up fairly well in the U.S. data.

Here we can provide a brief summary of the stylized facts, or rough empirical observations, that growth models must explain.

1. The growth rates of potential output and labor input are fairly steady, with $\dot{Q} > \dot{L}$, so that $\dot{q} > 0$.
2. The growth rate of the capital stock is also fairly steady, with $\dot{K} > \dot{L}$ so that k is also positive.
3. The growth rate of the capital stock is about the same as the growth rate of output, so that $\dot{K} = \dot{Q}$, and the K/Q ratio is fairly constant.
4. The profit rate, $\rho = P/K$, is fairly constant in the long run. Combined with a constant capital-output ratio, this implies a constant long-run relative distribution of output between wages W and profits P.

Having established the "stylized facts" of growth, we now turn to a more systematic analysis, which will allow us to interpret them. In addition, a more systematic approach to the sources of growth may provide some insight into how policy can alter the rate of growth.

We begin with a general production function that relates inputs at time t of labor, L_t, and capital, K_t, to output, Q_t:

$$Q_t = F(K_t, L_t). \tag{33}$$

We assume that labor and capital are substitutable and that the production function is homogeneous of first degree, that is, exhibits constant returns to scale. This means that if all inputs are changed proportionately, then output will change by the same proportion. In other words,

$$aQ_t = aF(K_t, L_t) = F(aK_t, aL_t). \tag{34}$$

If K_t and L_t are doubled ($a = 2$), then output will also double. The change in output, ΔQ_t, that will result from a change in inputs can be approximated by

$$\Delta Q_t = f_K \, \Delta K_t + f_L \, \Delta L_t, \tag{35}$$

where f_K stands for the marginal product of capital, that is, the amount of additional output resulting from an incremental change in capital. Likewise, f_L represents the marginal product of labor. Multiplying the terms on the right-hand side of equation (35) by K_t/K_t and L_t/L_t yields

$$\Delta Q_t = f_K \cdot K_t \cdot \frac{\Delta K_t}{K_t} + f_L \cdot L_t \cdot \frac{\Delta L_t}{L_t} \tag{36}$$

and dividing both sides by Q_t:

$$\frac{\Delta Q_t}{Q_t} = f_K \cdot \frac{K_t}{Q_t} \cdot \frac{\Delta K_t}{K_t} + f_L \cdot \frac{L_t}{Q_t} \cdot \frac{\Delta L_t}{L_t}. \tag{37}$$

Recognizing that $\Delta Q_t/Q_t = \dot{Q}_t$ and similarly for K and L, and defining $\eta_K \equiv f_K \cdot K_t/Q_t$ and $\eta_L \equiv f_L \cdot L_t/Q_t$, we have a relationship between the growth rate of output and the growth rates of the inputs:

$$\dot{Q}_t = \eta_K \dot{K}_t + \eta_L \dot{L}_t. \tag{38}$$

If the growth rate of capital rises, the growth rate of output will increase by η_K times the $\dot{K}$ increase, and similarly for $\dot{L}$ changes.

**Output elasticities and
relative shares**

The coefficients η_K and η_L have two interesting interpretations. Rewriting η_K, we have

$$\eta_K = f_K \cdot \frac{K_t}{Q_t} = \frac{\Delta Q}{\Delta K} \cdot \frac{K_t}{Q_t}.$$

We see that η_K is the elasticity of output with respect to the input of capital. Thus equation (38) says that the growth rate of output equals the sum of the growth rates of inputs, each multiplied by its elasticity.

A second interpretation follows if we assume competitive pricing of factor inputs; that is, each input is paid its marginal product. If the real wage, $W/P = w$, is equal to the marginal product of labor, then

$$\eta_L = f_L \cdot \frac{L_t}{Q_t} = w \cdot \frac{L_t}{Q_t} = \frac{W_t \cdot L_t}{P_t \cdot Q_t} = \text{labor share of output.}$$

In the same way, η_K is equal to capital's share of output.

We have stated that constant returns to scale means that an equi-proportionate increase in the inputs will lead to the same proportional increase in output. If the proportion is a, then

$$a = \eta_K \cdot a + \eta_L \cdot a$$

or

$$1 = \eta_K + \eta_L.$$

The elasticity-share coefficients must sum to one under the constant re-turns to scale assumption.

A "measure of our ignorance"

We can now use the production function expression for $\dot{Q}$ to interpret the "stylized facts" of U.S. growth. We saw that in the U.S. economy, up to 1970, the capital stock and output were growing at about 4.2 percent per year, and the labor force was growing at about 1.5 percent. Thus, along trend, $\dot{Q} = \dot{K} = 0.042$, and $\dot{L} = 0.015$. We also know from Chapter 2 that, depending on how proprietors' income is split between capital and labor income, the labor share of national income is about 75 percent, while the capital share is about 25 percent. Thus, $\eta_L = 0.75$ and $\eta_K = 0.25$.

Inserting the values for factor input growth rates and relative shares into the growth equation gives us, on the assumption that the economy's production function exhibits constant returns, an explained output growth of

$$\eta_K \dot{K} + \eta_L \dot{L} = 0.25(0.042) + 0.75(0.015) = 0.023.$$

But in fact output grew along trend at about 0.042, or 4.2 percent per year! Thus only a little more than half the growth in output is explained by input growth. The unexplained growth in output is the *residual:*

$$\dot{Q} - \eta_K \dot{K} - \eta_L \dot{L} \approx 0.02 = \text{residual.}$$

This residual factor in economic growth is the growth of output that can-not simply be explained by input growth with a constant-returns produc-tion function. It is what Edward Denison has called "the measure of our ignorance."

A large, and sometimes controversial, literature centered on the works of Denison, Kendrick, Solow, and Jorgenson and Griliches, developed after the late 1950s over the explanation of the residual factor in economic growth. In general, if inputs are being correctly mea-sured and the production function at any given moment is homogeneous to degree one, then the residual would come from the existence of technical progress. In other words, the production function would be shifting up through time as a result of (a) improvements in organization, (b) improvements in capital goods, or (c) improvements in the labor force. Whether this technical progress factor *augments* specific inputs or simply shifts the production function in a neutral way, and whether it must be *embodied* in new inputs, as opposed to augmenting both old and new inputs alike, will affect both the rate of technical progress that is compatible with a residual factor of a given size and the sensitivity of output growth to changes in input growth rates.

A given rate of technical progress, if it simply shifts the production function up, will generate a larger residual than if it augments just the labor force, in which case it affects $\dot{Q}$ only through the labor input elasticity η_L. It will give a residual that is smaller yet if it has to work through the capital elasticity η_K. To put the point another way, to explain a residual factor of 2 percent per year, the rate of technical progress must be larger if it works through the labor elasticity η_L than if it shifts the entire production function up, and larger yet if it works through η_K. In addition, if technical progress must be embodied in one or another of the factors, the sensitivity of output growth to investment in these factors will be increased. Again, if technical progress must be embodied in new machines, an increase in saving and investment will raise output growth not only by producing *more* machines, but also *newer* and *better* machines.

Neutral disembodied technical change The simplest technical progress assumption, introduced by Solow in 1957, is that it comes as manna from heaven. It simply shifts the production function up over time. Capital and labor inputs which yield Q_t at time t will yield Q_{t+1} in the next time period where $Q_{t+1} = (1 + a)Q_t$ and $a > 0$.

Under this assumption, we write the production function as

$$Q_t = A_t \cdot F(K_t, L_t), \tag{39}$$

and changes in Q are given by

$$\Delta Q_t = \Delta A_t \cdot F(K_t, L_t) + A_t[f_K \Delta K_t + f_L \Delta L_t]. \tag{40}$$

Dividing through by $Q_t = A_t F(K_t, L_t)$ gives us a growth rate expression:

$$\dot{Q}_t = \frac{\Delta Q_t}{Q_t} = \frac{\Delta A_t}{A_t} + \eta_K \cdot \dot{K}_t + \eta_L \cdot \dot{L}_t. \tag{41}$$

If we assume there is a steady rate of technical progress, then $\Delta A_t / A_t$ can be written as a constant, a, and our growth rate equation becomes

$$\dot{Q}_t = a + \eta_K \cdot \dot{K}_t + \eta_L \cdot \dot{L}_t. \tag{42}$$

The residual has been defined as the growth rate of A, the technical progress shift factor. Using our "stylized facts" from the 1960s to estimate a,

$$a = \dot{Q}_t - \eta_K \cdot \dot{K}_t - \eta_L \cdot \dot{L}_t$$
$$= 0.042 - 0.25(0.042) - 0.75(0.015),$$

and

$$a \approx 0.02.$$

Substitution of 0.02 for a back into our expression for $\dot{Q}_t$ yields

$$\dot{Q}_t = 0.02 + 0.25\,\dot{K}_t + 0.75\dot{L}_t. \tag{43}$$

Almost half of our expected growth of 4.2 percent is accounted for by disembodied technical progress: it just happens!

Under this assumption, significant change in the growth rate is unlikely to be achieved by an alteration in the rate of capital formation. To increase growth from 4.2 to 5 percent would require $\dot{K}_t$ to increase by 3.2 percent. Annual investment which is now 10 to 12 percent of GNP would have to rise to 18 to 21 percent of GNP.

Under different technical progress assumptions, we shall see that the returns to different growth policies vary markedly.

CAPITAL-EMBODIED TECHNICAL PROGRESS

Both Solow and Nelson have developed simple models that embody technical progress in the capital stock through the assumption that new machines are more efficient than old ones. In this case, an increase in investment will reduce the average age of the capital stock, giving an increase in the rate of technical progress. This increase in the rate of technical progress associated with a drop in the average age of the capital stock will, in turn, increase the rate of growth of output beyond the increase associated with a simple increase in the number of machines available. Thus, as long as investment is sufficient to reduce the average age of the capital stock, the growth rate of output will rise both because there is more capital and because the average machine is becoming younger. Once the capital stock reaches its equilibrium average age for a given ratio of investment to output, this additional "kick" to output growth from capital stock growth will disappear, and the growth rate of output will settle down to its long-run value.

Here we will develop the model with capital-embodied technical progress following Nelson. The capital-embodied production function can be written as

$$Q_t = F(J_t, L_t), \tag{44}$$

with F homogeneous to degree one in labor and *capital jelly, J,* inputs. The growth rate of output is now determined by the growth rates of technologically enriched capital—capital jelly, J—and the labor force:

$$\dot{Q} = \eta_J \dot{J} + \eta_L \dot{L}. \tag{45}$$

Capital jelly is defined as the aggregate capital stock with each machine weighted by a technical progress factor reflecting its newness. Thus, we can write J as

$$J_t = \sum_{v=0}^{t} K_{vt}(1 + \lambda_K)^v. \tag{46}$$

Here K_{vt} is the capital stock of vintage v, built v years *after* the oldest machine in use, which has $v = 0$, that is in operation at time t. λ_K is the technical progress factor, a constant growth rate per year, so that $(1 + \lambda_K)^v$ gives the technical progress adjustment that converts each vintage K_{vt} into equivalent current units of capital jelly.

From equation (46) we can see that if the capital stock is constant, so that net investment is zero and each year's gross investment just replaces dying machines with new ones, then the growth rate of J would be λ_K. Each year the technologically enriched capital stock would be more efficient by a factor of λ_K due to replacement. If the capital stock itself is growing at a constant rate, as it would in long-run growth equilibrium, then the expression for the growth rate of capital jelly is

$$\dot{J} = \dot{K} + \lambda_K. \tag{47}$$

This gives the growth rate of J in the long-run steady state with a given ratio of investment to output.

Now a constant growth rate of the capital stock also implies a constant average age of the capital stock. What would happen if the investment ratio were increased so that the average age would fall? If suddenly each machine in the capital stock became one year younger, so that $\Delta\bar{a}$, the change in the average age $\bar{a}$, were -1, then the growth rate of J would go up by λ_K, since suddenly each machine would be one year more efficient. This tells us that to introduce the effect of changing $\bar{a}$ into equation (47) for $\dot{J}$ we should add $(-\lambda_K \Delta\bar{a})$ to it. Then if $(-\Delta\bar{a}$ is, say, one-half year, $\dot{J}$ will rise by half of a year's increase in productivity. This yields as an expression for $\dot{J}$ with an average age changing,

$$\dot{J} = \dot{K} + \lambda_K \Delta\bar{a}. \tag{48}$$

For the growth rate of output, this gives us

$$\dot{Q} = \eta_J(\dot{K} + \lambda_K - \lambda_K \Delta\bar{a}) + \eta_L \dot{L}. \tag{49}$$

Next we should examine the relation between the rate of growth of the capital stock, which is the policy variable in this analysis, and the change in the average age. This relationship will give us the effect of increasing investment on Q *through* increasing the rate of technical progress.

Nelson shows that we can approximately express $\Delta\bar{a}$ as

$$\Delta\bar{a} = 1 - (\dot{K} + \delta)\bar{a}, \tag{50}$$

where δ is the percentage depreciation rate of the capital stock. If gross investment I_g is the sum of net investment I_n plus depreciation δK,

$$I_g = I_n + \delta K,$$

then the expression in parentheses in equation (50) is

$$\dot{K} + \delta = \frac{I_n}{K} + \delta = \frac{I_g}{K}$$

the ratio of gross investment to the capital stock. Thus, equation (50) says that if gross investment is zero, that is, $\dot{K} + \delta = 0$, then the average age of the capital stock will increase by one year, since no old capital is being replaced. If *net* investment equals zero so that only the dying capital is being replaced, then

$$\Delta \bar{a} = 1 - \delta \bar{a} = 0,$$

since the average age of the capital stock is approximately the inverse of the depreciation rate so that $\delta \bar{a}$ equals one. Finally, the greater $\bar{a}$, the more a given increase in gross investment will reduce the average age. For example, if the existing capital stock consisted entirely of 100 machines, all 10 years old, so that $\bar{a}$ were equal to 10, then gross investment of 100 new machines would reduce $\bar{a}$ to 5, so that $\Delta \bar{a}$ would be 5. If the existing stock had been 20 years old, the same amount of gross investment would have reduced $\bar{a}$ to 10, so that $\Delta \bar{a}$ would be 10.

Substituting equation (50) for $\Delta \bar{a}$ into the expression for $\dot{Q}$ gives us

$$\dot{Q} = \eta_J\{\dot{K} + \lambda_K - \lambda_K[1 - (\dot{K} + \delta)\bar{a}]\} + \eta_L\dot{L}.$$

Combining terms with in the braces yields

$$\dot{Q} = \eta_J[\dot{K} + \lambda_K(\dot{K} + \delta)\bar{a}] + \eta_L\dot{L} \qquad [51]$$

as the expression for $\dot{Q}$ in the case of capital-embodied technical progress. We can now use the representative U.S. data from the 1960s to estimate λ_J—the rate of technical progress in the capital-embodied model that explains a residual of 2 percent per year. We already have estimated that $\dot{Q} = \dot{K} = 0.042$, $\dot{L} = 0.015$, $\eta_J = 0.25$, and $\eta_L = 0.75$. We can estimate δ at about 0.10; that is, depreciation is about 10 percent of the capital stock, and $\bar{a}$ at about 10 years. Inserting these values into equation (51) gives us

$$0.042 = 0.25[0.042 + \lambda_K(0.142)10] + 0.75(0.015).$$

Solution of this equation for λ_K yields a value of 0.058, or 5.8 percent. Thus with capital-embodied technical progress, the residual to be explained is still 0.02, but since λ_K works on $\dot{Q}$ only through the small capital elasticity η_J, it must take on a larger value than λ to explain the same residual.

We can rewrite the expression for $\dot{Q}$ with capital-embodied technical progress at the rate of 5.8 percent per year to find the sensitivity of $\dot{Q}$ with respect to $\dot{K}$ in this model:

$$\dot{Q} = 0.25[\dot{K} + 0.058(\dot{K} + 0.10)10] + 0.75\dot{L},$$

so that

$$\dot{Q} = 0.014 + 0.39\dot{K} + 0.75\dot{L}. \qquad [52]$$

Assuming that technical progress is embodied in new machinery increases the intermediate-run sensitivity of $\dot{Q}$ with respect to $\dot{K}$ from 0.25 in the disembodied models to about 0.40 here. This increase is a measure of the effect of investment, giving the economy not just *more* capital, as in the first model, but also *newer* capital.

Thus, assuming all technical progress is embodied in new capital raises the estimate of the sensitivity of $\dot{Q}$ to changes in $\dot{K}$ to at most 0.4, a fairly small return on a program of, for example, subsidy of capital investment. A similar model embodying progress in the labor force would probably increase the η_L coefficient to perhaps 0.8 or 0.85, making human capital programs much more attractive in terms of growth policy.

Denison's sources of growth

Another explanation of U.S. growth was attempted by Edward Denison. He analyzed what occurred between 1929 and 1957, two years he considered reasonably similar, in that output was reasonably near its potential level in both. Although conventional in many of his assumptions, such as the use of income shares to measure factor productivity, his analysis differs from that of Solow and Nelson in a number of important and interesting respects. His categorization of factor inputs is sufficiently broad to associate some sources of growth with particular inputs rather than assign them to the residual. This is particularly true with respect to changes in the quality of the labor force. Further, he disaggregates the inputs, labor and capital, to allow separate estimates of the effect of the changing age and sex composition of the labor force and of various forms of capital. Finally, he attempts to disaggregate even his reduced residual so that it is not all attributed to technical change. Of particular importance, he abandons the assumption of constant returns to scale and replaces it with the assumption of increasing returns to scale.

Denison's accounting of growth between 1929 and 1957 is shown in Table 17.1. There we see that real national income grew by an average annual rate of 2.93 percent over this period. Of this growth, Denison attributes 2 percent per year to growth of inputs and 0.34 percent per year to economies of scale. In Denison's accounting, the residual is reduced to 0.67 percent out of a growth rate of output of 2.93 percent.

Denison's growth figures differ from the stylized facts due to differences in the time periods used and method of analysis. It is interesting, however, to note the differences in the relative importance of different sources of growth, since they imply different policies to encourage growth (Table 17.2). Growth in the capital stock is most important if we assume that technical change has its impact through new capital stock. Capital growth is less important in Denison's analysis where improvement in the quality of labor is stressed. In the neutral, disembodied technical progress

TABLE 17.1

Allocation of growth of total output, 1929–1957 (annual growth rates)

Real national income			2.93
Increase in inputs			2.00
Labor		1.57	
Employment		1.00	
Impact of shorter hours		−0.20	
Annual hours	−0.53		
Quality impact	0.33		
Education		0.17	
Increased experience		0.11	
Change in age-sex composition		−0.01	
Land		0.00	
Capital		0.43	
Nonfarm residential structures		0.05	
Other structures and equipment		0.28	
Other		0.10	
Increase in output per unit of input			0.93
Advance of knowledge		0.58	
Growth of national market		0.27	
Growth of local market		0.07	
Other		0.09	

Source: *The Sources of Economic Growth in the United States,* Committee for Economic Development, New York, 1962, p. 266.

TABLE 17.2

Relative importance for growth

	Labor	Capital	Technical Change
		(percentages)	
Neutral disembodied model	26	25	49
Capital embodied model	26	39	35
Denison	54	15	20

model with which we began, neither factor is as important as the fact of technical change and less can be expected of policies that alter the growth rate of labor or capital. Whether growth policies should be oriented toward capital investment or toward improvement of the labor force through education, for example, will depend on important assumptions regarding embodiment of technical progress in capital or labor. In addition, the Solow-Nelson results are pessimistic about the ability of policy to change the growth path, while Denison's are more optimistic. But none are very certain; this remains a major area for research in macroeconomics.

Decline in the 1970s rate of productivity increase

As noted earlier in this chapter, growth in the United States in the 1970s was well below the rates we had come to expect. From 1948 to 1973, real national income grew at 3.7 percent a year, but from 1973 to 1978 the increase slumped to 2.1 percent a year. The wage-price arithmetic of Chapter 15 has indicated how important productivity growth is if inflation is to be avoided. Economic growth is similarly important if we are to bring substantial improvement in standards of living to those citizens at or below the poverty level without lowering the standard of living for others. It thus becomes an important question whether the slowdown in productivity growth in the 1970s represents a temporary departure from the long-term trend or indicates a fundamental change to which policy makers will have to adjust in the 1980s.

Edward Denison has applied his accounting of growth technique to the postwar period, in *Accounting for Slower Economic Growth*, in an effort to identify the source of the decline. Table 17.3 contrasts 1948–1973 to 1974–1976 and indicates how much of the aggregate growth in the economy can be attributed to changes in the factors leading to growth.

The most striking fact to emerge is the sharp change in the residual component which is grandly titled "Advances in knowledge." The average growth rate fell almost 3 percent, and over two-thirds of this change was in the residual. Change in the rate of investment contributed 0.04 to the decline, further reductions in hours worked contributed 0.30 to the decline and increased attention to the health of workers and the protection of the environment caused 0.38 of the decline. Yet none of these often cited explanations serves to reduce greatly the amount of the change that remains unexplained.

Denison offers a number of possible explanations including a curtailment of research and development expenditures, an increased lag in the application of knowledge as capital ages, increased government regulation excluding those for safety and to prevent pollution, impairment of efficiency due to inflation, and so on. Possibly each includes some germ of truth, and they certainly indicate future avenues of research. Alterna-

TABLE 17.3

Allocation of growth in national income per person employed in nonresidential business

	1948–1973	1973–1976
Growth rate	2.43	−0.54
Factor input:		
Labor		
Hours	−0.24	−0.54
Age-sex composition	−0.17	−0.25
Education	0.52	0.88
Land/labor	−0.04	−0.03
Capital/labor		
Inventories	0.10	0.02
Structures and equipment	0.29	0.25
Output per unit of input		
Improved allocation of resources	0.37	−0.01
Changes in legal and human environment	−0.04	
Economics of scale	0.41	0.24
Irregular factors	−0.18	0.09
Advances in knowledge	1.41	−0.75

Source: *Survey of Current Business Part II,* August 1979

tively, the large "unexplained" change in productivity may indicate a basic fault in the technique used.

What is distressing is that as one considers the possible sources of the unexplained portion of the decline in growth rates, none appears to be of a nature likely to be reversed in the 1980s. At the very least, this means the tasks of policy makers, particularly in dealing with inflation, will be extremely difficult.

QUESTIONS FOR DISCUSSION AND REVIEW

1. If the long-term growth rate in output per unit of labor is 2.5%, and the rate of growth of the labor force is 1.5%, and the nominal stock of money balances grows at 7%, what would you estimate as the rate of growth in real money balances? On what key elasticity assumption does your answer depend? How would your answer vary if this elasticity varies between .7 and 1.3?

2. It is often claimed output would grow faster if only we would invest more. Is this true in the short run? Is it true in a steady state long run in which capital and labor grow at the same rate?

3. Will a long-run increase in capital per unit of labor lead to an increase in consumption per unit of labor? What about output per unit of worker?

4. Examining Denison's allocation of U.S. growth, what specific policies would you expect to have the greatest impact on future growth?

5. What combination of tightness and ease in monetary and fiscal policy will have the greatest impact on growth? How might this combination adversely affect other legitimate policy goals?

SELECTED READINGS

M. Abramovitz, "Review of Denison," *American Economic Review*, September 1962.

E. F. Denison, *Accounting for Slower Economic Growth*, Brookings Institution, 1979.

E. F. Denison, "The Importance of the Embodied Question," *American Economic Review*, March 1964.

E. F. Denison, *The Sources of Economic Growth in the United States and the Alternatives Before Us* (New York: Committee for Economic Development, 1962).

E. F. Denison, "Sources of Postwar Growth in Nine Western Countries," *American Economic Review*, May 1967.

D. W. Jorgenson and F. Griliches, "The Explanation of Productivity Change," *Review of Economic Studies*, July 1967.

J. W. Kendrick and R. Sato, "Factor Prices, Productivity, and Growth," *American Economic Review*, December 1963.

R. R. Nelson, "Aggregate Production Functions," *American Economic Review*, September 1964.

R. M. Solow, "Investment and Technical Progress," in K. J. Arrow, S. Karlin, and P. Suppes, eds., *Mathematical Methods in the Social Sciences* (Stanford University Press, 1960).

R. M. Solow, "Technical Change and the Aggregate Production Function," *Review of Economics and Statistics,* August 1957.

J. Tobin, "Economic Growth as an Objective of Government Policy," *American Economic Review,* May 1964.

INDEX